The Politics of Antagonism

CONFLICT AND CHANGE IN BRITAIN SERIES
– A NEW AUDIT

Series Editors Paul Rock and David Downes (London School of Economics)

The series provides reports on areas of British life conventionally conceived to be conflict-laden. It assesses the scale and character of the conflict in those areas, considering new or little heeded evidence, balancing the claims of different commentators and placing such conflict in its historical and social context, allowing intelligent judgements to be made. It provides prognoses about the likely development of that conflict; and ascertains what measures have been taken to manage it and what success they have met with; drawing on international experience where helpful.

Already published volumes include
Vol. 1   John Davis **Youth and the Condition of Britain: Images of Adolescent Conflict** (1990)
Vol. 2   Nigel Fielding **The Police and Social Conflict: Rhetoric and Reality** (1991)

Later volumes will include
John Carrier & Ian Kendall **Health and the National Health Service**
Rod Morgan **Rethinking Prisons**
Christopher Husbands **Race in Britain**

CONFLICT AND CHANGE IN BRITAIN SERIES
– A NEW AUDIT

3

The Politics of Antagonism

Understanding Northern Ireland

BRENDAN O'LEARY & JOHN MCGARRY

THE ATHLONE PRESS
London and Atlantic Highlands, NJ

First published 1993 by The Athlone Press Ltd
1 Park Drive, London NW11 7SG and
165 First Avenue, Atlantic Highlands, NJ 07716

© Brendan O'Leary and John McGarry 1993
Reprinted 1994

British Library Cataloguing in Publication Data
A catalogue record for this book is available
from the British Library

ISBN 0-485-80003-9
ISBN 0-485-80103-5 pbk

Library of Congress Cataloging in Publication Data

O'Leary, Brendan.
  The politics of antagonism: understanding Northern
    Ireland / Brendan O'Leary & John McGarry.
  p. cm. -- (Conflict and change in Britain series ; 3)
  ISBN 0-485-80003-9. -- ISBN 0-485-80103-5 (pbk.)
  1. Northern Ireland--Politics and government--1969-
  I. McGarry, John. II. Title. III. Series.
DA990.U46052 1992
941.60824--dc20   92-26103

Typeset by Bibloset

*Printed and bound in Great Britain by the University
Press, Cambridge*

To the memory of John Whyte,
who would have found every remaining error.

Contents

Series Editors' Preface

The works in this series are intended to offer a grand tour of the social and political landscape of Britain, looking most closely at areas conventionally thought to be troubled by conflict. No area has had a more obvious, dramatic, bloody and sustained history of conflict than Northern Ireland, and the history has been distinguished by a mischievous power to feed, transform and confuse itself. Myths and half-truths have folded into one another, creating a kind of political miasma. About no area has it seemed more difficult to obtain a clear, informed and disinterested analysis. One of us can recall a seminar at the London School of Economics at which a student from one side of the communal divide presented a strongly partisan account of the province's politics and structure. When asked how someone from the other side would have talked about the same matters, he replied that he did not know and did not care to know. He refused to take the role of this adversary. It is that deep, excluding hostility that marks so much of the argument about the province.

Northern Ireland's conflicts are in urgent need of an examination that would be at once part-sociology, part-history and part-political science. In *The Politics of Antagonism*, O'Leary and McGarry have transcended faction and muddle by providing just such a detached and penetrating audit of the province's adversities. They have grounded their interpretation in political and social history, tracing the roots of the present discontents; given the first authoritative inventory of the deaths and injuries inflicted by the Troubles; told us what politicians have done to manage (or augment) Northern Ireland's difficulties; and have surveyed competing proposals for constitutional reform. Perhaps for the very first time, readers will be able to unravel some of the special, bitter and complicated problems that beset what remains of John Bull's other island.

David Downes
Paul Rock
London School of Economics

List of figures

List of tables

Acknowledgements

We have incurred multiple debts in the construction of this book. Our intellectual and marriage partners, Lorelei Watson and Margaret Moore, have been constructive critics. Paul Rock and David Downes, the editors of this series, and Brian Southam of The Athlone Press deserve a vote of thanks for their advice and patience, as do the research staff of the Irish Information Partnership, particularly Helen Dady, Marian Larragy, Tom Lyne, and Michael McKeown. Jane Pugh of the LSE drew the maps and Figures 1.4, 1.5, and 1.6. We extend our thanks to Paul Arthur, Arthur Aughey, Paul Bew, Steve Greer, Adrian Guelke, John Hutchinson, Ian Lustick, Chris McCrudden, David McKittrick, David Smith, Paul Teague, Brian Thompson, and Robin Wilson for commentary and insight.

Brendan O'Leary thanks the LSE staff research fund (for funding research-assistance carried out by John Peterson and Brendan O'Duffy), and the Nuffield Foundation (for grants to conduct interviews in 1988–9 and 1990–1). The hospitality of Hans Blomkvist and Li Bennich-Björkman meant that the Department of Government at Uppsala provided a congenial environment in which to complete some writing in the spring of 1991. The Nuffield grants enabled O'Leary to interview Irish politicians, and civil servants in the Department of Foreign Affairs and the Department of the Taoiseach who were constructive, helpful and discreet. Most British ministers and spokespersons with past and present responsibilities for Northern Ireland agreed to be interviewed in London in 1990–1. Past and present civil servants in the Northern Ireland Office and the Foreign Office were informative, generous and cautious, as were the staff in the Irish Embassy in London. Political advisers to Harold Wilson, James Callaghan, and Charles Haughey agreed to be interviewed, while other political advisers were interviewed on a non-attributable basis, including advisers to Northern Irish political parties. The

Joseph Rowntree Reform Trust kindly made available the full data-sets of polls throughout the British Isles which are referred to in Chapter 8 and the Epilogue. O'Leary expresses warm appreciation to Brian Barry, Alan Beattie, Percy Cohen, Patrick Dunleavy, Amanda Francis, George Jones, Christopher Hood, Howard Machin, James Mayall, Desmond King, Michael McGrath, Tom Nossiter, Brendan O'Duffy, George Schöpflin, Anthony Smith, Gordon Smith, and the students who took MSc courses in Nationalism and the Government and Politics of Ireland at LSE between 1985 and 1990.

John McGarry thanks the Social Sciences and Humanities Research Council of Canada for a grant which enabled him to travel to Great Britain, Northern Ireland, and the Republic of Ireland. He expresses special gratitude to Sid Noel for many stimulating discussions of ethnic conflict, some of the fruits of which can be found in this book; and to Jim Crimmins and Michael Keating for their helpful reactions to the drafts of material published here.

Our secretaries, Sharon Batkins and Jane Borecky, deserve our mutual admiration for their assistance with copying, faxing, mailing, phoning, printing, scanning, word-processing, and for dealing cheerfully and efficiently with all the fire-fighting tasks that preceded the publication of this book. We are accountable for its content.

Brendan O'Leary
  Reader in Political Science and Public Administration at the London School of Economics, England
John McGarry
  Assistant Professor in the Department of History and Political Science, King's College, London, Ontario

Introduction

The nationalist not only does not disapprove of atrocities committed by his own side, but he has a remarkable capacity for not even hearing about them.

(George Orwell, *Notes on Nationalism*, 1945)

In 1968, the Dutch political scientist Arend Lijphart wrote a book entitled *The Politics of Accommodation*. It was not about housing in The Netherlands. Rather it attempted to explain why the Dutch had evolved a stable democratic political order despite their deep ethno-religious divisions. This book echoes Lijphart's endeavour, but with a different title and purpose. We attempt to understand why Northern Ireland has failed to develop a stable democratic political order, or a politics of accommodation, and why it is instead characterized by a politics of antagonism.

Every viewer of contemporary television is aware of the fact that the politics of Northern Ireland are profoundly antagonistic. No state structures have emerged in the region which have possessed sustained and widespread support amongst *both* the unionist, and mainly Protestant, and the nationalist, and mainly Catholic, ethnic communities who live on its narrow ground with apparently even narrower minds. After street disturbances which accompanied civil rights demonstrations in 1968 there have been over twenty years of political violence in Northern Ireland. At the time of writing, there are few reasons to believe that hostilities are likely to be terminated, let alone resolved, in the immediate future. Expectations of progress rose when inter-party talks began on 30 April 1991. The talks stuttered to a halt on 3 July 1991, only to resume once more on 30 April 1992. Hopes were tempered by pessimism: false dawns are as common as political murders in Northern Ireland. The construction of stable and legitimate institutions in the region is a daunting task of political architecture, the unenviable lot of British and Irish ministers assigned the relevant portfolios and of those local politicians who genuinely seek peace.

The fundamental antagonism in Northern Ireland is easily stated: Ulster unionists insist that Northern Ireland must remain part of the United Kingdom; Irish nationalists that it must immediately or eventually become part of an all-Ireland Irish nation-state. The political aspirations of nationalists and unionists are therefore not only conflicting but apparently mutually exclusive. Political scientists view the conflict as a 'zero-sum' game in which the antagonists cannot co-operate to their mutual advantage and what one antagonist gains the other must lose. This structure of exclusive, dualistic, and intensely felt aspirations that generate internal war marks Northern Ireland off as an 'exception', 'a place apart' within the internally peaceable polities of western Europe. However, events east and south of the River Elbe since 1987 have made more British and Irish people aware that Northern Ireland is not exceptional in the wider world.

The overriding purpose of this book is to outline the historical evolution and entrenchment of the politics of ethnic antagonism in Northern Ireland by using simple explanatory concepts developed in political science. *The Politics of Antagonism* presents an audit of the scale and nature of the present conflict, an analytical history of ethnic conflict in Northern Ireland, and prognoses about the likely development of the conflict and conflict-management. We provide analytical rather than chronological history. Our evidence is drawn from the existing historical literature, our own research materials (interviews, data-sources and data-evaluation) and multiple primary sources (the press, broadcasting transcripts, and parliamentary and official governmental publications). Sound political science is often parasitic upon sound history; and we acknowledge our debts to historians throughout. Nevertheless we believe it is imperative, and distinctive, to provide an analytical rather than a chrono-logical history of Northern Ireland: first, to counterbalance the partisan doctrinal histories in the public domain which are usu-ally nationalist, unionist, or Marxist; and second, to demonstrate how simple concepts developed in political science elucidate key elements in the origins and evolution of the conflict – especially the concepts of settler colonialism, hegemonic control, arbitration, and consociationalism. *The Politics of Antagonism* is designed to serve as an introduction to understanding Northern Ireland for students of government, political science, history, and political sociology.

Nationalist mobilization occurs when a political movement seeks autonomy or independence for a nation; and nationalists with sufficient opportunities almost invariably seek to build their preferred 'nation-state'. National conflict occurs when different nations (and/or nation-states) compete over the composition of their nation(s), and their national territories. That the conflict over Northern Ireland is fundamentally national does not mean that there are no other antagonisms in the region, including deep divisions within each national community. But our premise is that the internal conflict is between two (internally divided) national communities rather than between two religious communities. More distinctively, however, we maintain that conflict has been sustained by conflictual external relations between the British and Irish nations and the specific patterns of political development of the British and Irish states in the twentieth century.

Ethnic communities are culturally bounded and self consciously differentiated from other such communities. They are mostly endogamous descent-groups. They are not to be confused with races or religious communities, even though they may be based upon the latter categories. Ethnic communities share with races and religious communities the fact that they are obvious materials for nationalist mobilization and national conflict. But the conflict in Northern Ireland should not be seen just as an endogenous ethnic conflict; it has equally important exogenous dimensions. Northern Ireland is where Irish and British nationalism remain locked in a stand-off, often to the embarrassment of British nationals in Great Britain and Irish nationals in the Republic of Ireland. The endogenous and exogenous dimensions are linked because the two ethnic communities in Northern Ireland have been partially mobilized into the Irish and British 'nations'. One community, the Irish nationalists of Northern Ireland, is a sub-set of a wider ethnic community, the 'native' Irish of Ireland, whose ancestors once spoke Gaelic. Irish nationalists are usually but not invariably Roman Catholic in religion; but not all Roman Catholics in Northern Ireland are Irish nationalists in their politics and those who are vary considerably in the intensity of their nationalist convictions. The other community, that of Ulster Protestants, is usually religiously labelled even though by no means all of its members are religious. This community mostly consists of the descendants of Scottish and English settlers in Ireland. Ulster Protestants see themselves as a sub-set of the multi-ethnic UK polity, even if their membership of that polity is not invariably recognized by the other members. Extremely few Ulster Protestants are Irish nationalists. They now regard themselves as British but they remain divided over the precise nature of their ethnic identity.

Religious institutions, especially endogamous marriage and denominational education, provide the most obvious mechanisms through which ethnic differentiation is sustained in Northern Ireland. However, that is not to say that the secularization of the region or ecumenism would guarantee the withering-away of ethnic conflict. Religious beliefs and religiosity are not irrelevant or epiphenomenal in accounting for the politics of antagonism: in any thorough analysis their role must be carefully specified rather than dismissed, and we have attempted this task elsewhere (McGarry and O'Leary, forthcoming: ch. 5). However, the assumption of this book is that the national conflict, which derived from ethnic and religious differentiation, is primary and has an autonomous dynamic of its own.

Plan of the book

Our analytical history starts with the present. Any objective understanding requires an appreciation of the scale and nature of violent conflict in Northern Ireland. Chapter 1 'Auditing the antagonism' fulfils this goal. It demonstrates that Northern Ireland is the site of an ethnic war. The subsequent Chapters (2–7) are devoted to explaining the roots and dynamics of the present conflict. Chapter 2 situates the historical antecedents of the politics of antagonism in the patterns of English and Scots settler colonialism in Ulster in the three centuries following 1609 and in the imperfect partition of the island of Ireland in 1920–5. Chapter 3 explains how the British constitutional system permitted ethnic majoritarianism in Northern Ireland between 1920 and 1972. This system, which we describe as one of hegemonic control, regulated ethnic conflict through the subordination of the Irish nationalist minority. The Northern Ireland conflict thus has roots which are generally neglected by British observers: it is partly an outcome of English political institutions. However, it is also partly an outcome of the development of the Irish state. Chapter 4 provides

an account of why the system of hegemonic control eventually collapsed in the late 1960s. Chapters 3 and 4 demonstrate the interplay
between endogenous and exogenous factors in sustaining the politics
of antagonism. In Chapters 5–7 we examine and explain the failure of
successive British efforts to engage in conflict-resolution. Chapter 5
shows why solitary British arbitration between 1972 and 1985 ended
in failure, and why attempts to promote voluntary power-sharing, or
consociation, proved unsuccessful. Chapters 6 and 7 bring the reader
up to the present, and evaluate the British and Irish governments'
reasons for signing the Anglo-Irish Agreement and its impact on
conflict-management. We explain why this experiment in 'coercive
consociationalism' has so far proved unsuccessful. Finally, Chapter
8 evaluates the prospects for conflict-resolution in the 1990s.

Terminology and how to read this book

The glossary lists all the abbreviations used in this book and a
glossary entry is indicated by the superscript G. We make our own
analytical and normative preferences as clear as possible throughout
the book, leaving readers to judge their merits. However, terminol
ogy raises more complex question about objectivity. Since charges
of sectarianism accompany any writing on Northern Ireland we have
been explicit, if not neutral, in our conventions. The following norms
should enable acute decoders to decide in advance where we stand on
all the important issues. First, we refer to 'Northern Ireland' as the
formal political unit, not the 'Six Counties' or 'Ulster' as nationalists
and unionists respectively prefer. When we use the latter expressions
it is because we are citing or discussing nationalist or unionist views,
although we do use Ulster to refer to 'historic Ulster', i.e. the
province which encompassed nine counties of pre-1920 Ireland.
We also avoid the use of the expression the 'North of Ireland'
which is employed by nationalists. Second, we normally refer to
Northern Ireland as a 'region', not as a 'province' or 'Province'.
When we use the latter expressions it is because we are citing or
discussing nationalist or unionist views, or the historic province of
Ulster. Third, we use the expression 'Great Britain', not 'the British
mainland' to refer to England, Scotland, and Wales. 'The British
mainland', preferred by unionists, is ideologically charged, and both
geographically and politically inaccurate, and when we use the term

it is because we are citing or discussing unionist views. Fourth, we refer to 'the Republic of Ireland', rather than 'Eire', 'Ireland' or 'the twenty-six counties'. When we use the latter expressions it is because we are citing or discussing unionist, nationalist, or republican views. We employ 'Ireland' to refer to the geographical entity, or the unit of administration before 1920. Fifth, we use capital-letter designations to refer to formal political membership of an organization, and lower-case designations to refer to political disposition or doctrine. Thus 'Nationalist' refers to the Nationalist party, whereas 'nationalist' refers to somebody of that persuasion who may or may not have been a member of the Nationalist party. Similarly, 'Unionist' refers to one of the parties which bears this name, whereas 'unionist' refers to anybody who believes in preserving the Union between Great Britain and Northern Ireland, whether or not they are supporters of political parties like the Ulster Unionist Party or the Democratic Unionist Party. Sixth, we do not use Catholic and Protestant as synonyms for nationalist and unionist. Seventh, we use Derry/Londonderry for the disputed second city of the region. The ordering of the term was dictated by the alphabet rather than political bias. We wanted to designate it Stroke city to reflect its contested name, our hyphenated compromise, its high rate of heart disease, and the fact that the local cooking is nearly as lethal as its politics (as consumers of 'Ulster fries' will testify). However, this re-baptism would have detracted from serious analysis. Finally, throughout we deliberately use the term 'paramilitaries' rather than 'terrorists', because the former expression is more precise and less emotive. Terrorism can be practised by both the state and insurgents, but presently the term is used almost exclusively to refer to insurgent paramilitaries. When we use the terms 'terrorist' or 'terrorism' we are generally reporting the views of the authorities or members of constitutional political parties. Our preference for the term 'paramilitaries' does not indicate, and should not be construed to mean, that either of us supports, critically or otherwise, any of the relevant paramilitary organizations. Readers should also note that since this book went to press the largest loyalist paramilitary organization, the UDA, has been proscribed.

This book is a stand-alone introduction to understanding Northern Ireland and should be read and reviewed as such. It also serves as an introduction to a simultaneously written book, *Explaining Northern Ireland: Broken Images* (McGarry and O'Leary, forthcoming), which evaluates in more technical detail the multiple and rival explanations of the conflict, of violence, and of the apparent intractability of the stalemate put forward by political actors within Northern Ireland, Ireland, and Great Britain, as well as historians and social scientists. These explanations are treated more summarily here but have framed the way in which we have composed *The Politics of Antagonism*.

1
Auditing the antagonism

*The struggle to govern Ireland may fairly be regarded as
Britain's longest counterinsurgency campaign.*
(Charles Townshend, 1986: 45)

The politics and societies of Northern Ireland are antagonistic. Over
twenty years of continuous political violence since 1969 have made
the region a byword for intractable ethnic conflict, and the idea
is regularly aired that British and Irish ministers must manage
a problem which has no solution. The manifest cause of the
antagonisms is simple to state: whereas Ulster unionists insist that
Northern Ireland must remain part of the United Kingdom, Irish
nationalists maintain that it must immediately or eventually become
part of a sovereign Irish nation-state. This conflict of aspirations has
produced 'republican' paramilitaries dedicated to the triumph of Irish
nationalism, and 'loyalist' paramilitaries committed to maintaining
Northern Ireland within the UK. It has also generated ethnic
political parties representing different strands of the rival aspirations.
Mutually exclusive aspirations have ruled out the 'normal' politics of
accommodation characteristic of other western liberal democracies.

The small population of Northern Ireland consists of approximately 900,000 people who are Protestants, or are descended
from Protestants, and almost invariably unionists in their political persuasion; the remaining 600,000 people are mostly Roman
Catholics, or descended from Roman Catholics, and are usually,
but not invariably, nationalist in their politics. This small but
deeply divided population has generated the most intense political violence of any part of the contemporary UK, the highest
levels of *internal* political violence of any member-state of the
European Community, and the highest levels of internal political
violence in the continuously liberal democratic states of the post-
1948 world.

Since 1969 nearly 3,000 people have died because of political violence in Northern Ireland (IIP, 1990; RUC, 1990). Political murders, sectarian assassinations, tit-for-tat shootings, car-bombings, petrol-bombings, and 'human bombs' have made Northern Ireland infamous, as have armed robberies, 'tarring-and-feathering', knee-cappings, and other forms of communal intimidation associated with the actions of local paramilitaries. The security forces have often added to the region's notoriety, cataloguing developments which have done little for the UK's reputation amongst civil libertarians: internment and detention without trial between 1971 and 1975; the torture of civilians suspected of being nationalist paramilitaries in the 1970s; the killing in January 1972 of thirteen unarmed civilians on 'Bloody Sunday' by troops from the Parachute regiment; 'dirty-tricks' by army and intelligence personnel conducting 'low-intensity war' operations in the 1970s and 1980s; the use of 'supergrasses' (paid informants) to generate 'assembly-line' justice; and allegations about 'shoot-to-kill' policies throughout the 1980s and early 1990s.

The conflict has often spilled outside the borders of the region, leading to the deaths of approximately 200 people in Great Britain, the Republic of Ireland, and sites elsewhere in Europe, ranging from Gibraltar to western Germany. Arms have been supplied to Northern Ireland's paramilitaries from political actors and arms-merchants operating in North Africa, North America, and eastern Europe. However, the bulk of the violence has occurred within the region, and even then much of it has been spatially concentrated within sub-districts of Northern Ireland, notably in greater Belfast. Thus over 50 per cent of killings by the security forces, over 68 per cent of killings by loyalist paramilitaries, and over 36 per cent of killings by nationalist paramilitaries have occurred within Belfast.[1] The maps in Figure 1.1 confirm what everybody in Northern Ireland knows: violence does not occur with equal intensity in every area, and there are areas where years go by without the occurrence of a single death.

The comparative scale of the conflict: 'troubles' or 'war'?

Nearly three thousand dead may seem a relatively small toll in a conflict which in its present phase has lasted for over two decades and has attracted immense international publicity. However, scale matters. The population of Northern Ireland in the 1981 census, itself

Figure 1.1 (a) Northern Ireland and Belfast

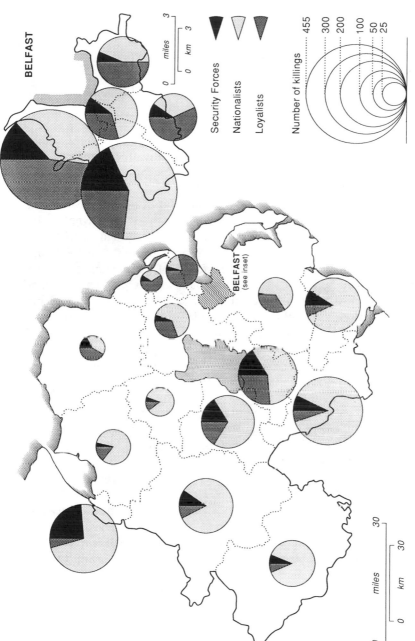

Figure 1.1 (b) The spatial distribution of killings in Northern Ireland, 1969–89
Source: McKeown (1985) and IIP (1989)[2]

BELFAST

Security Forces
Nationalists
Loyalists

Number of killings

455
300
200
100
50
25

0   miles   3
0   km   3

BELFAST
(see inset)

0   miles   30
0   km   30

disrupted by violence and abstention, was estimated as 1,488,077. If the equivalent ratio of victims to population had been produced in Great Britain in the same period some 100,000 people would have died, and if a similar level of political violence had taken place the number of fatalities in the USA would have been over 500,000, or about ten times the number of Americans killed in the Vietnam war.

When gauging the scale of the conflict observers must beware of distortions created by the media, the British government, the security forces, paramilitaries, and tourist agencies. The external media report in depth only on selective atrocities, and can mislead people into thinking that in the intervals all is calm. The government and the security forces have obvious incentives to downplay the scale of the conflict and to stress 'normality'; and tourist and economic development agencies are keenly aware that the external perception of violence affects the success of their endeavours. The police force, the Royal Ulster Constabulary (RUC), emphasizes that the number of civilians killed annually as a result of road-accidents in the period 1969–89 usually exceeded the total number of those who died annually because of political violence, or, 'as a result of the security situation' as they prefer to put it (e.g. CCAR, 1989, 1990: 24). Others note that the numbers killed in political violence in Northern Ireland are much less than the homicide-tolls in large US cities (e.g. Zimring, 1987: 3 ff.),[3] or emphasize that the risk of death in being a resident of Northern Ireland is considerably less than that of being a denizen of many urban centres in advanced industrial states. Such 'realistic' comparisons persuade the uncritical consumer of official press briefings that the conflict merits classification as a small-scale and parochial quarrel, or, more technically, as a 'low-intensity' conflict (Kitson, 1971).

Yet such comparisons are misleading. The contrast between deaths from political violence and deaths from road-accidents is grotesquely inappropriate. Deaths because of political violence are an addition to other socially caused deaths, and in functioning and stable liberal democracies deaths caused by road-accidents should be, and usually are, higher than deaths caused by political violence.[4] There is nothing exceptional about Northern Ireland's road-accident/political violence ratio, except that it is used as a distracting indicator by a police force anxious for a good press. Citizens of liberal democracies and their governments support private and public transport policies which have known and built-in risks of death. There is no comparable way in which they explicitly accept built-in risks of deaths from political violence when they make and enforce public policy.[5] Rather, any self-respecting modern state and its citizenry seek to establish a monopoly of legitimate force to prevent political violence: but nearly 2 per cent of the population of Northern Ireland have been killed or injured through political violence in the last two decades.

The comparison of the death-rate in the Northern Ireland conflict with the homicide-rate in US or other major cities is equally misleading. The people who died in the USA between 1948 and 1977 as a result of *political* violence (434) were fewer than those killed in Northern Ireland in 1972 alone, and much less than those killed in the entire period (1,835),[6] and the per capita death-toll from political violence was radically less in the USA. 'Ordinary' violent criminality is dramatically less in Northern Ireland: it is politically – not criminally – violent, whereas the converse applies to the USA.[7] Moreover, US homicide-rates owe something to constitutional provisions, which protect the citizen's right to bear arms, and widespread drug-related criminality, factors irrelevant in accounting for deaths in Northern Ireland.

To evaluate the nature and intensity of the Northern Ireland conflict it is better to compare the total deaths and the per capita death-tolls from internal political violence in liberal democracies (see Figures 1.2 (a) and (b)). The *World Handbook of Political and Social Indicators* provides us with the latest available data on these matters for the three decades 1948–77 (Taylor and Jodice, 1983). Figures 1.2 (a) and (b) are drawn from a slightly modified version of this data-set, and bring home the astonishing scale of the conflict in Northern Ireland when seen in a comparative perspective.[8] Northern Ireland was by far the most internally politically violent of the recognizably continuous liberal democracies during the period 1948–77, both in absolute numbers killed and relatively, as indicated by the per capita death-toll.[9]

Sceptics might suggest that Figure 1.2 misconstrues the comparative evidence because Northern Ireland is a sub-unit of one liberal democracy, namely the UK, and therefore we are not comparing 'like with like', and because states are excluded which have some claim to being regarded as liberal democracies during the years 1948–77, notably India, Sri Lanka, and Israel. Yet, as Figure 1.2 (a) shows,

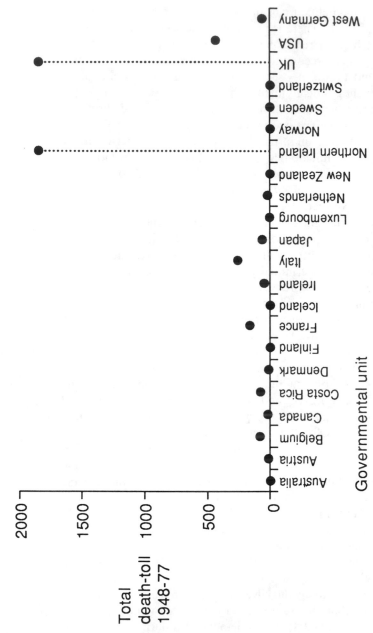

Figure 1.2 (a) The death-toll in liberal democracies from internal political violence, 1948–77
Sources: Taylor and Jodice (1983: Table 2.7) and IIP (1990)

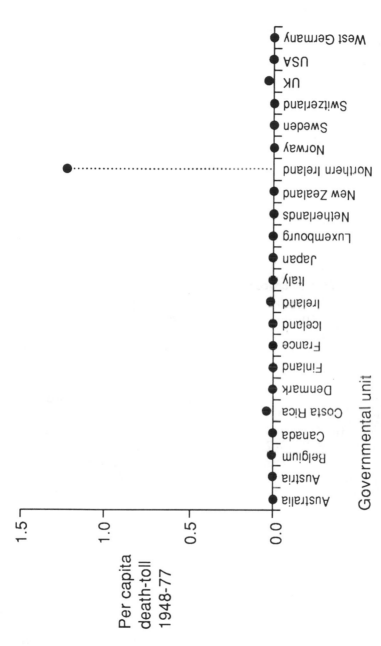

Figure 1.2 (b) The per capita death-toll from internal political violence in liberal democracies, 1948–77.
Sources: Taylor and Jodice (1983: Table 2.7) and IIP (1990)

the death-toll in Northern Ireland alone made the UK absolutely the most violent liberal democracy during the same time-span, and, as Figure 1.2 (b) reveals, just marginally less violent than Costa Rica relatively, with a per capita death-toll of 0.032 compared to 0.038. Furthermore, even though the continuously liberal democratic character of India, Israel, and Sri Lanka throughout the years 1948–77 is questionable[10] their inclusion would not significantly alter the picture. The absolute death-toll in India far surpassed that of the UK, but according to the *World Handbook of Political and Social Indicators* the per capita death-toll in independent India between 1948 and 1977 (0.012)[11] is less than our estimate for Northern Ireland (1.222) and the same is true for Sri Lanka (0.399) and Israel (0.025).[12] If the UK rather than Northern Ireland is considered the appropriate unit of analysis then Sri Lanka surpasses the UK in its per capita death-toll during these years, but the UK remains ahead of both India and Israel. The Lebanon is the one country excluded from Figure 1.2 which might be regarded as continuously liberal democratic between 1948 and 1975, and which would make a significant difference to the comparative ranking of the Northern Ireland conflict, on both the absolute and the per capita dimensions. Being 'second to the Lebanon' is an unenviable classification.

Figure 1.3 is a scattergram of the natural logs of the absolute and per capita death-tolls in the thirty most internally politically violent regions in the world during the years 1948–77, based upon our transformation of the data-set in the *World Handbook of Political Indicators*.[13] It includes for comparison the equivalent data for Northern Ireland and Cyprus.[14] Although the minutiae of the data collected in the *World Handbook of Political and Social Indicators* may be open to criticism, the comparative evidence in Figure 1.3 is surprising. The per capita death-tolls in Northern Ireland and Cyprus during this period exceeded those in fifteen of the thirty most internally politically violent states (including Ethiopia, the Philippines, Argentina, Greece, Columbia, India, Iraq, Sri Lanka, and Mozambique).

Sceptics might challenge the validity of the comparison in Figure 1.3 because Northern Ireland is a sub-unit of the UK whereas the other thirty cases (and Cyprus) refer to entire states in which conflicts were or are localized. However, in the bulk of the thirty cases violent conflict occurred throughout most of the area encompassed by the relevant state. The obvious exceptions – China, India, Madagascar,

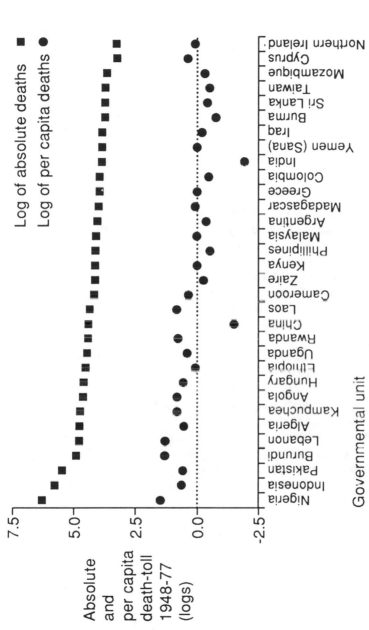

Figure 1.3 The (logs of the) absolute and per capita death-tolls in the thirty most violent governmental units in the world, 1948–77, compared with Cyprus and Northern Ireland

Sources: Taylor and Jodice (1983: Table 2.7) and IP (1990)

Zaire, and Kenya – do not detract from the general picture. We might argue that given its geographical, administrative, and political isolation from the rest of the UK it is reasonable to compare violence in Northern Ireland with that of other states. But even if we take the UK to be the relevant unit of comparison then on our estimates the absolute death-toll from internal political violence in Northern Ireland alone places the UK as the 41st most violent state in the list of 150 states covered in the *World Handbook of Political and Social Indicators*, and as the most violent continuously liberal democratic state in the world in the thirty years 1948–77.

Yet Northern Ireland is not a Third World country in the throes of radical economic and political underdevelopment, rather it is part of an advanced industrial state, the United Kingdom of Great Britain and Northern Ireland, widely regarded as having an enviable tradition of civic peace and stable liberal democratic institutions. Northern Ireland is the most politically violent region in the peaceable European Community, far more violent than the Basque region of post-authoritarian Spain. The numbers of people killed between 1969 and 1990 in Northern Ireland exceeded the numbers killed as a result of terrorist incidents or political violence in *all* other EC countries put together over the same time-frame. In the decade 1973–82 violence in Northern Ireland alone placed the UK at the top of a league table of nineteen western European societies in three categories: deaths from political violence, numbers of armed attacks, and successful political assassinations (Zimmermann, 1989). Unhappily a replication of this exercise for the decade 1983–92 will produce the same ranking for the UK.

These comparisons suggest it is legitimate to classify the Northern Ireland conflict as similar to those which have riven Lebanon, Sri Lanka, and Cyprus. It is an ethnic war, a communal war, or an *inter-national* war. The Irish euphemism for the conflict, 'the Troubles', is just that: a euphemism.

The absolute death-toll in Northern Ireland naturally pales by contrast with the major civil, colonial, and ethnic wars of the post-war world. Massacres, the systematic killing of dozens of people on one occasion because they 'represent' an enemy-group, have not occurred. The British authorities have not ruthlessly and brutally suppressed the population which explicitly or tacitly supports insurrection in the manner experienced by Algerian Muslims, Afghan peasants, Iraqi Kurds, Kashmiri Muslims, Palestinian

Muslims and Christians, South African blacks, Sri Lankan Tamils, and Vietnamese peasants. The incarcerated insurrectionaries have been treated relatively mildly by the British authorities by contrast with the treatment meted out to their counterparts in Latin American, African, or South Asian jails and concentration camps. Yet these observations, which might push us back towards classifying the Northern Ireland conflict as relatively small-scale, can mislead the unwary. After all, superpower involvement and rivalry characterized most of the major wars waged between 1945 and 1990, and nearly all other wars and civil wars between 1945 and 1990 were exacerbated by the interests of regional powers or neighbouring states. But these factors have not operated in Northern Ireland (Guelke, 1988). The US government officially deplores violence in Northern Ireland and has sought to prevent unofficial support from Irish-Americans, in the form of guns and money for nationalist paramilitaries, from reaching the region. Professions of sympathy for a united Ireland flow regularly from Irish-American politicians, or politicians in Irish-American constituencies, but are overwhelmingly constitutional in character; and before the signing of the Anglo-Irish Agreement in November 1985 officials in the executive branch of American government usually considered Northern Ireland 'an internal matter' for the government of the UK (see Ch. 5: 220–41). The Atlantic Alliance, the special relationship with the UK, has consistently proved more important for American geopolitical interests than the ethnic sentiments of Irish-Americans. The Soviet Union, by contrast, used to bring up the Northern Ireland experience to embarrass the UK: when British complaints about human rights in the USSR exceeded permitted diplomatic niceties Soviet officials raised questions about British repression in Northern Ireland and the jailing of innocent Irish people in Great Britain, like the Guildford Four, the Birmingham Six, and the Maguire Seven. Nevertheless the Soviets played no role in fomenting conflict in Northern Ireland. And after *perestroika* the Soviet Union became enmeshed in multiple 'Ulsters' within its own disintegrating borders and ceased to raise Northern Ireland with British officialdom.

Regional or neighbouring states have not sought militarily to embroil themselves in Northern Ireland with the intention of exacerbating the conflict for their own strategic ends – although the unionists often accuse the Irish government of such behaviour. In this respect the Northern Ireland conflict differs radically from the civil wars in Cyprus, Lebanon, Israel/Palestine, Ethiopia/Eritrea, Nicaragua, Sri Lanka, and southern Africa. The two states with most at stake, the UK and the Republic of Ireland, despite multiple disagreements, have generally sought to co-operate to contain the conflict, officially so since the Anglo-Irish Agreement of 1985. The Provisional IRA do not champion and are not championed by the Republic of Ireland, and loyalist paramilitaries embarrass British politicians. The two sets of paramilitaries in Northern Ireland are regarded and treated as subversive within their own potential 'patron-states'. Although politicians from the governments and parliaments of the European Community have offered to mediate and to assist in ameliorating social conditions in Northern Ireland, these have been offers of genuine goodwill rather than efforts to advance the strategic interests of their states. The sole external state which has sought to inflame the conflict, Libya, is neither a regional power nor a neighbouring state. Its small-scale interventions mostly have been retaliatory responses to American and British actions against the regime of Colonel Gadaffi.

The scale of the Northern Ireland conflict should therefore be seen as very intense given that it has been taking place in the presence of moderately amicable relations between the relevant neighbouring states and regional powers, and in the absence of superpower rivalries.[15]

There are less global but equally arresting comparisons we can make in evaluating the scale of the conflict. The most obvious comparison is with the historic experience of political violence in Ireland since the late nineteenth century. Table 1.1 lists some estimates of the relevant death-tolls. The number killed in Northern Ireland in the last two decades is proportionately greater than the number killed in the whole of Ireland in each episode of extended political violence in the first six decades of this century (see Table 1.1 column 4). The number killed in the last two decades is absolutely and proportionately higher than the death-tolls in the Irish war of independence (1919–21) and the fighting which accompanied the formation of Northern Ireland (1920–2). The present death-toll exceeds the combined toll during the Irish war of independence and the formation of Northern Ireland. On one extreme estimate the present death-toll in Northern Ireland is absolutely and proportionately higher than the numbers killed in the Irish civil war of 1922–3 (Hickey and Doherty, 1980: 73); while on the other

Table 1.1 Numbers killed in political violence in Ireland (1886–1990)

(1) Years (location)	(2) Numbers killed: estimates	(3) Population of location (census year)	(4) Ratio of (2)/(3) expressed as per cent
(a) 1813–1907 Communal riots (Belfast)	60	121,602 (1861)	0.05
(b) 1886 Home rule riots ('six counties')	86	1,304,816 (1881)	0.006
(c) 1916 Easter rising (Ireland)	(i) 514 (ii) 450	4,390,219 (1911)	0.01 0.01
(d) 1919–21 National war of independence or Anglo-Irish war (Ireland)	1,468	4,390,219 (1911)	0.03
(e) 1922–3 Irish Civil War (Irish Free State)	(i) 600–700 (ii) 4,000	2,971,992 (1926)	0.021 0.13
(f) 1920–2 Formation of Northern Ireland (Northern Ireland)	(i) 544 (ii) 428 (iii) 232	1,256,561 (1926)	0.04 0.03 0.02
(g) 1939–40 IRA bombings (Great Britain)	7	47,559,300 (1951)	0.00001
(h) 1956–62 IRA campaign (Northern Ireland)	(i) 18 (ii) 19	1,425,042 (1961)	0.001 0.001
(i) 1969–90 The present war (Northern Ireland)	2,849	1,488,077 (1981)	0.19

Sources: (a) Budge and O'Leary (1973: 143); (b) Townshend (1984: 342); (c) (i) Fitzpatrick, (1989: 514) (ii) Lyons (1973: 375); (d) Fitzpatrick (1989: 249); (e) (i) Hickey and Doherty (1980: 73) (ii) Lyons (1973: 467–8); (f) (i) Budge and O'Leary (1973: 143), Aunger (1981: 157) (ii) Townshend (1984: 342) (iii) Rose (1971: 89); (g) Hickey and Doherty (1980: 256); (h) (i) Bowyer Bell (1979: 334) (ii) Aunger (1981: 157); (i) RUC (1990).

extreme estimate the present death-toll is proportionately but not absolutely higher than the death-toll in the Irish civil war (Lyons, 1973: 467–8).[16] In duration, twenty-three years, the present conflict easily outranks all other episodes in twentieth-century Ireland, and only the Irish civil war fought out in 1922–3 exceeds it in intensity. The worst five years of the present crisis in Northern Ireland (1971–6) led to more deaths (1,651) than any other episode of political violence in twentieth-century Ireland apart from the Irish civil war; and proportionally the death-toll in these five years was very close (0.10) to the higher estimate of the per capita death-toll in the Irish civil war (0.13).

These comparisons confirm that Northern Ireland deserves its designation as 'a place apart' in both the British Isles and Europe, although national and ethnic conflicts in some of the newly democratized post-communist regimes have removed its European 'exceptionality'.

The militant agents and their civilian victims

Who are the agents of this ethnic war, and what is their nature? The conflict is best understood as two wars: one between three sets of armed or militant agents, and a second between the three sets of militant agents and civilians.[17] The three sets of agents involved in the first war can be represented in a triangle (Figure 1.4), and each of the three agencies' responsibilities for civilian deaths are shown in Figure 1.5. An overall picture of the two wars can be found in Figure 1.6.[18] The arrows in Figures 1.4–1.6 represent the line of attack by each agency and their widths are proportionate to the numbers killed in each line of attack during the twenty years 1969–89. The number killed in the formal 'war-theatre' represented in Figure 1.4 was 1,229 or 44.1 per cent of the total killed in this time-period. By contrast, as Figure 1.5 shows, the number of civilians killed by militant agents amounted to 1,409 people (including 25 prison officers), or 50.6 per cent of the total killed.[19] Of the two wars, that waged on civilians has been more intense. The paramilitary 'defenders' of the relevant communities have had dramatically fewer casualties than those they claim to be defending.

The three sets of militant agents are nationalist paramilitaries, loyalist paramilitaries, and the security forces of the UK. Nationalist

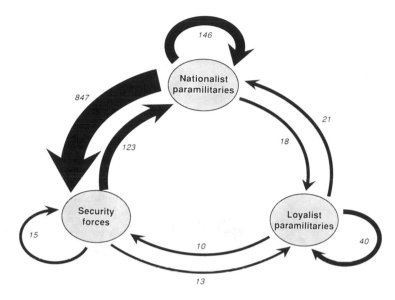

Figure 1.4 The triangle of ethnic war: the war between the paramilitaries and the security forces, 1969–89
Source: IIP (1990)

paramilitaries are revolutionaries dedicated to the overthrow of British rule in Ireland and the establishment of an independent Irish nation-state throughout the island. They see themselves conducting a 'long war' of attrition against the British state, and regard members of British security forces as 'legitimate targets' in a war of national liberation (Bishop and Mallie, 1987; Coogan, 1970, 1980, 1987; Kelley, 1982, 1988; Smith, 1991). The largest and most important of the nationalist paramilitary organizations is the Provisional IRA or (P)IRA. It was formed in 1969 when the older paramilitary organization of the IRA split into two factions. The Provisionals were more militarist and traditionally nationalist than the remaining Marxist and largely dormant 'Official' IRA faction. The Provisionals declared themselves at war with the British Army which had come to Northern Ireland in 1969 in a peace-keeping role, and argued that only a British withdrawal from Ireland would solve the conflicts on the island. They portrayed themselves as 'defenders' of the nationalist or Catholic population, against the incursions of loyalist paramilitaries and repression by the security forces. In 1970–1 the Provisionals rapidly surpassed the Official IRA in militancy and

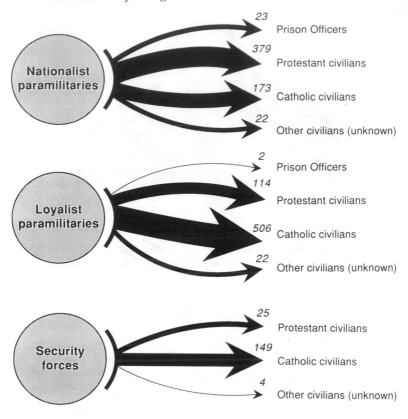

Figure 1.5 The second war: the war on civilians, 1969–89
Source: IIP (1990)

recruitment amongst Catholic youths and ever since have been the major 'players' in nationalist paramilitary actions. They have killed and injured more people than any other agency in the conflict, tied down tens of thousands of British soldiers for two decades, imposed immense economic damage on the region, launched bombing campaigns regularly in Great Britain and the European continent, assassinated key members of the British political élite, including Lord Louis Mountbatten, a member of the royal family, and twice come within a whisker of blowing up the British Prime Minister and Cabinet.[20] Their power persuaded the British authorities to negotiate with them in 1972 and 1975, and as long as it persists observers are agreed that violent conflict will continue. The active membership of the Provisionals is variously estimated at anywhere between 500

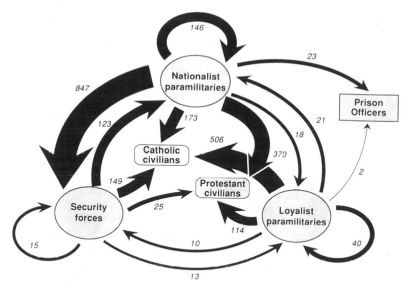

Figure 1.6 The two wars, 1969–89
Source: Figures 1.5 and 1.6

and 2,000 but they enjoy wider if passive and minority support within the nationalist community. In the 1980s Provisional Sinn Féin, the political party which supported the Provisionals, decided to participate in Northern Irish elections and in successive contests averaged 10 per cent of the regional vote and over 30 per cent of the nationalist vote.

The Official IRA, in competition with the Provisionals, also waged 'armed struggle' against the British state between 1969 and 1972, but, they argued, in a purely defensive capacity. They then declared a unilateral cease-fire, maintaining that paramilitancy was dividing the working class. Since then the Officials have gradually ceased to be of any importance, although rumours persist that the organization still exists and has supplies of arms. Since the demise of the Officials it has become standard practice to refer to the Provisionals as the IRA, and vice versa, and we follow this convention.

From 1975 until 1987 the Provisionals faced one minor rival within the nationalist camp: the Irish National Liberation Army or INLA, another break-away from the Official IRA. Styling themselves as a Marxist national liberation army the INLA displayed none of the inhibitions of the Officials about causing working-class disunity: they maintained that class unity could come only after the national struggle had been won. In 1979 the INLA assassinated Airey Neave, the Conservative MP and Shadow Secretary of State for Northern Ireland, who was a close confidant of Margaret Thatcher. However, the INLA remained very small and faction-ridden, and in 1987 destroyed itself in an internal feud from which the Irish People's Liberation Organization (IPLO) emerged 'triumphant' but miniscule in size and resources.[21] Nationalist paramilitaries combined have been responsible for over 57 per cent of all deaths in the present crisis.

Loyalist paramilitary organizations, which recruit from Ulster Protestants, are counter-revolutionaries, dedicated to maintaining Northern Ireland's status as part of the UK. They regularly break the law or take it into their own hands to save the Union. They are highly fissiparous: 'a glossary of loyalist paramilitary organizations compiled in the mid-70s listed no fewer than 35 groups. Many were tiny and some were entirely fictional, but up to a dozen were real – that is, with at least a rudimentary command structure and access to weapons' (McKittrick, 1989a: 152). By contrast with nationalist paramilitary organizations, which are all outlawed, there is one large and legal loyalist paramilitary organization: the Ulster Defence Association or the UDA. At its peak in the early 1970s the UDA had nearly 40,000 members, mostly working-class Protestants, mobilized with military training to resist the actions of the IRA and defend the loyalist community. However, in recent years its membership has dwindled to below 10,000. Formally the UDA does not carry out assassinations and attacks on nationalist paramilitaries and civilians suspected of supporting nationalist paramilitaries, but it is universally recognized that the killings and actions carried out in the name of such bodies as the Ulster Freedom Fighters, the Ulster Protestant Action Group, and the Protestant Action Group are in fact those of the UDA (albeit in some instances dissident factions within the UDA), and in jail incarcerated loyalists behave as members of the UDA, not the UFF. The UDA has occasionally sponsored political parties to compete against the mainstream unionist parties but with little success. The other main loyalist paramilitary organization is the Ulster Volunteer Force, the UVF. It is illegal. Founded in 1966 as a sectarian organization,[22] and then led by Gusty Spence, a working-class Protestant, it was soon outlawed. The UVF peaked in 1972, when it had some 1,500 members. It has been responsible for many sectarian assassinations of Catholic civilians, sometimes under the pseudonym of the Red Hand Commandos. In 1990–1 the UVF and the UDA began to sponsor joint operations, and in the summer of 1991 renewed the scale of their operations on a scale not witnessed since the mid-1970s. Loyalist paramilitary organizations combined have been responsible for over 25 per cent of all deaths in the present crisis.

The security forces that are now the primary targets of nationalist paramilitaries are the British Army, including that section recruited and deployed in Northern Ireland (the Ulster Defence Regiment or UDR[23]), and the armed police force, the Royal Ulster Constabulary (the RUC). In 1989 there were 9,658 members of the British Army in Northern Ireland,[24] 6,343 members of the UDR, and 12,889 members of the RUC, making a total security force membership of approximately 29,000.[25] The overwhelming majority of British soldiers are recruited from Great Britain, whereas the RUC and the UDR are almost entirely recruited from Northern Ireland. The RUC, despite efforts to professionalize its image in the 1970s, and its formal commitment to impartial policing, recruits overwhelmingly from the Protestant population (over 90 per cent). The percentage of Catholics in the UDR, by contrast, is so low that the government has ceased to provide data on the subject. The role of the security forces, according to the British government, is to keep the peace within the rule of law, to act impartially against both nationalist and loyalist terrorists, to arrest terrorists where possible, and to use only 'reasonable' force in the pursuit of these goals. The security forces are regularly accused of not being impartial, and there is evidence of collusion between some members of the security forces and loyalist paramilitary organizations (Ch. 7: 268-70). However, the security forces are responsible for less than 12 per cent of all deaths suffered in the present crisis.

Nationalist and loyalist paramilitaries combined have suffered radically fewer casualties (13.2 per cent of all deaths) than either religious category of civilian. They have also sustained fewer casualties than the security forces (31.4 per cent of all deaths). The paramilitaries' low share of the overall death-toll explains why their activities are relatively easily sustained. But nationalist paramilitaries have died more than four times as frequently as loyalist paramilitaries, and all paramilitants face a high likelihood of incarceration.

Forms of killing

The types of incident in which victims died between the summer of 1969 and the summer of 1989 are displayed in Table 1.2. In this period 978 people died in assassinations (37.5 per cent of all deaths); 761 died in gun-battles, in crossfire, through snipers' bullets and in ambushes (29.2 per cent of all deaths); 635 died as a result of explosions or anti-personnel devices (24.3 per cent of all deaths); and 146 died in riots or affrays (5.6 per cent of all deaths). Over 65 per cent of loyalist killings were assassinations of people (at home, work or at leisure, or in transit between work and home). By contrast over 56 per cent of nationalist killings took place during gun-battles/crossfire, sniping incidents, ambushes, or as a result of the use of explosives and anti-personnel devices. However, over 32 per cent of deaths caused by nationalist paramilitaries were assassinations, and they executed a higher absolute total (513) of persons than loyalist paramilitaries (451). Over 43.7 per cent of those killed by the security forces died in gun-battles, crossfire, ambushes or sniping incidents, while 27 per cent of their victims died during riots or affrays. The data in Table 1.2 confirm that there are two wars: a war of ethnic assassination and a guerrilla war.

In quantitative order there were four main fields of death between 1969 and 1989:

*   paramilitary killing of civilians (44.2 per cent of all deaths);
*   war between nationalist paramilitaries and the security forces (34.8 per cent of all deaths);
*   internecine conflict and self-killings within paramilitary organizations (6.7 per cent of all deaths); and
*   killings of Catholic civilians by the security forces (5.3 per cent of all deaths).

Trends in deaths 1969–90

The annual death-toll between 1969 and 1990 is presented in Table 1.3 (column 2). The cumulative annual death-tolls and percentages show that nearly one quarter of all deaths occurred in the first four years of the current crisis. Nearly 58 per cent of all deaths up to 1990 occurred in the five years 1971–6. Since 1977 the annual average rate of death from political violence has been just less than 83 persons per

Table 1.2 The types of incidents in which victims died, July 1969–June 1989

Source: adapted from IIP (1989)

Type of incident in which victim died	Agent responsible			
	Loyalist paramilitaries	Nationalist paramilitaries	Security forces	Paramilitaries + security forces
accident	4	0	31	35
assassination at home	128	128	5	261
assassination at work	78	124	1	203
assassination at leisure/in transit	245	261	8	514
gun-battle/crossfire	6	45	62	113
sniping/ambush	63	351	81	495
specific explosion	5	147	1	153
anti-personnel device	117	365	0	482
riot/affray	19	38	89	146
self-inflicted: deliberately	5	13	0	18
self-inflicted: accidentally	20	98	0	118
unclassified	0	23	49	72
total	690	1593	327	2610

Table 1.3 Political deaths in Northern Ireland, 1969–90
Source: RUC (1990)

Year	Deaths	Total (per cent)	Cumulative	Total (per cent)	5 year total
1969	13	0.46			
1970	25	0.88	38	1.33	
1971	174	6.10	212	7.44	
1972	467	16.40	679	23.83	
1973	250	8.78	929	32.61	929 (32.61%)
1974	216	7.58	1145	40.19	
1975	247	8.67	1392	48.86	
1976	297	10.42	1689	59.28	
1977	112	3.93	1801	63.22	
1978	81	2.84	1882	66.06	1882 (33.45%)
1979	113	3.97	1995	70.02	
1980	76	2.67	2071	72.69	
1981	101	3.55	2172	76.24	
1982	97	3.40	2269	79.64	
1983	77	2.70	2346	82.34	2346 (16.28%)
1984	64	2.25	2410	84.59	
1985	54	1.90	2464	86.49	
1986	61	2.14	2525	88.63	
1987	93	3.26	2618	91.89	
1988	93	3.26	2711	95.16	2711 (12.82%)
1989	62	2.18	2773	97.33	
1990	76	2.67	2849	100.00	

annum, and the numbers killed in the last five years of the data-set (1986–90) make up 13.51 per cent of the total killed since 1969. This evidence suggests a dramatic fall-off in annual deaths since 1976. Figure 1.7 confirms this impression.

The high death-toll in the early years is explained by three factors. The first is the decision by the Provisional IRA to launch an unrestrained war against what they called the British occupation of Ireland in 1971: in the next five years they employed the classical techniques of urban and rural guerrilla warfare against army and police personnel, but they also engaged in large-scale bombings of commercial targets such as factories and shopping centres. Guerrilla warfare produced large numbers of casualties amongst inexperienced police and army personnel, whereas commercial bombings led to large numbers of civilian deaths. The second factor is the 'loyalist backlash' against civil rights demonstrations

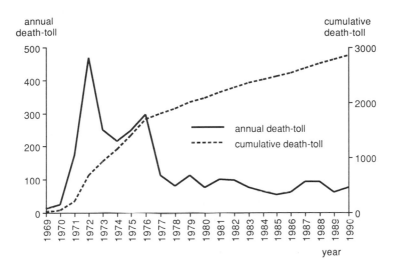

Figure 1.7 The annual and cumulative death-toll from political violence, 1969–90
Source: Table 1.3

N.B. This graph has a double 'y' axis: the left-hand side measures the annual death-toll, whereas the right-hand side measures the cumulative death-toll.

by Catholics in the late 1960s and increasing nationalist militancy in the early 1970s. The British government's decision to abolish the Northern Ireland parliament in 1972, and its efforts between 1973 and 1976 to establish a power-sharing^G government with institutional affiliations to the Republic of Ireland, exacerbated loyalist fears. Loyalist paramilitaries feared that the British government was about to abandon Northern Ireland and wanted to show that this path would result in a blood bath, so they created one. Very high numbers of Catholic civilians were victims of sectarian assassinations by loyalist paramilitaries between 1971 and 1975. One other purpose of loyalist killings of Catholic civilians was to deter Catholics from supporting nationalist paramilitary organizations, but because loyalists did not have reliable information on who were the members of the IRA 'representative' violence against randomly selected Catholic civilians was carried out instead. The third factor which explains the high death-toll in the early years was the repressive and counter-productive policy of internment of suspected terrorists without trial which lasted between 1971 and

1975. Initially targeted (but inaccurately so) exclusively at the nationalist community this policy produced widespread resentment throughout the Catholic population of Northern Ireland and acted as a recruiting agency for the IRA. Rather than dampening down conflict it added fuel to the fire.

The explanations for the fall-off in deaths since 1976 are logically connected to the previous analysis. First, nationalist paramilitaries changed their strategies and organizations in ways which reduced the annual death-toll. Many of them have been arrested and jailed; and in response their organizations have become smaller and structured in cells or 'active service units' (Bishop and Mallie, 1987). The 'cell structure' was partly adopted in response to their declining popularity in nationalist areas in the mid-1970s but also for strategic reasons – to avoid penetration by the security forces. Since 1976 the Provisionals have aimed primarily to attack 'military targets' (i.e. members of the security forces), and consequently reduced their use of bombs in urban areas – a tactic which killed many civilians, both Catholic and Protestant, in the early 1970s and threatened to undermine their support within the wider nationalist community. However, nationalist paramilitaries were responsible for over 70 per cent of political deaths in the twelve and a half years 1977–June 1989, compared with 50 per cent of political deaths during the first seven and a half years of conflict from June 1969 until 1976 (calculated from IIP data-base). Second, loyalist paramilitaries ceased to engage in killings of Catholics on the same scale as they did in the years 1971–6, in part because their fears of a British withdrawal had diminished, and were not revived until the Anglo-Irish Agreement was signed in 1985. Moreover, many loyalists were arrested and jailed, and their organizations became more factionalized, corrupt, and directionless (McKittrick, 1989a: 159–61). In the twelve and a half years from 1977 until June 1989 loyalist paramilitaries were responsible for only 16 per cent of all political deaths, compared with their responsibility for 31 per cent of all killings between June 1969 and 1976 (calculated from IIP Agenda data-base).[26] Third, more effective surveillance and knowledge on the part of the security forces dampened down the levels of violence. This explanation has to be qualified in the light of firm evidence that the other actions of the security forces have frequently, if sometimes unintentionally, raised the levels of violence. The authorities did abandon the provocative policy of internment in 1975–6 and since then have supported policies which have not been so counter-productive. A battery of techniques has been employed to contain the conflict. Up to 30,000 personnel regularly patrol the countryside and city-streets of the region, establishing armed 'check-points' at will. 'Forts' and observation posts with the latest surveillance technologies have been established in the heart of nationalist districts. House-searching (Hillyard, 1988: 199) and civilian-screening take place on a massive scale, backed up by computerized data-bases on over one quarter of the civilian population. Newly constructed urban housing has been designed to be less friendly to the urban paramilitant – Victorian terraces and 1960s' tower-blocks might have been built for urban guerrillas. Armoured vehicles, bomb-disposal robots, and 'jelly-sniffers' are used to protect security force personnel. From time to time entire 'town-centres' are cordoned off and everybody entering such areas is subjected to rigorous searching. Emergency legislation in the 1970s, renewed in the 1980s, removed certain standard civil rights and made the apprehension and sentencing of suspected paramilitaries much less problematic for the authorities.

Finally, all militant agents and their potential victims have experienced 'learning curves'. In 1970 the IRA had to make an average of 191 attacks to kill a single member of the security forces; by 1984 18 attacks were sufficient (Flackes and Elliott, 1989: 394). The persistence of republican violence, albeit at a reduced level, explains Secretary of State Peter Brooke's controversial declaration in 1989 that the IRA could not be *militarily* defeated. In consequence the security forces have had to become more vigilant to defend themselves. They have also, formally, become more politically restrained: in the early 1970s they were permitted to shoot at identified petrol-bombers but now they are supposed to use 'minimum force' weaponry, like plastic bullets. Moreover, the return to 'police primacy' in 1977, a deliberate policy of the authorities, has been associated with reduced levels of deaths caused by the security forces. Armed police are more restrained in their use of weaponry than soldiers who are trained to kill. Personal and collective surveillance by ordinary citizens have also increased. Both civilians and security force personnel travel warily in certain 'shatter-zones' or avoid them altogether; and migration from 'mixed areas' to areas of ethnic residential segregation in the 1970s reduced the opportunities for 'easy' killings.

Time-series on deaths are available in a crude form in RUC data, but do not enable us to follow victims by religious category over time. They confirm the downward trend in non-security force deaths since 1976, and show a dramatic falling-off in the number of deaths sustained by the British Army (excluding the UDR). Since the early 1980s the local security forces (the RUC/RUC reserves and the UDR) have suffered an increasing proportion of the deaths sustained by all the security forces. These trends reflect 'Ulsterization', the Northern Ireland Office's policy-preference for using local as opposed to British security forces (see Ch. 5: 202-5), but also confirm a switch in the targets chosen by nationalist paramilitaries. It is easier to kill members of the local security forces, at their homes or off-duty, than to kill soldiers in fortified barracks or police in armoured vehicles.

The status of victims and responsibility for their deaths, 1969–89

A detailed breakdown of the status of victims, as well as the agents responsible for their deaths is provided in Table 1.4.[27] Figures 1.8 and 1.9 clarify the data in Table 1.4. Figure 1.8 (a) shows the agencies responsible for all deaths between 1969 and 1989, whereas Figure 1.8 (b) shows the status of all victims over the two decades. The largest single category of victims has been Catholic civilians (32.4 per cent) who just shade members of the security forces (31.4 per cent). Since Protestant civilians outnumber Catholic civilians in the Northern Ireland population by approximately 3 to 2, Catholic civilians (902 deaths) have evidently suffered both *absolutely* and *relatively* more than Protestant civilians (575 deaths).

There are four explanations for this variance. First, Catholic civilians are the primary targets of loyalist paramilitaries (506), whereas the security forces – including the British Army – are the primary targets of nationalist paramilitaries. Second, since the local security forces (the RUC and the UDR) are recruited primarily from Protestant civilians the simple comparison of Catholic and Protestant civilian death-rates obscures the number of victims suffered by the Protestant community as a whole. Third, a rather high number of Catholic civilians (173) have been killed by nationalist paramilitaries, whether mistakenly, as 'collateral by-products' of other actions, or deliberately in the 'disciplining' of their own community. Finally, Catholic civilians are far more likely to be killed, mistakenly or otherwise, by members of the security forces (149) or by nationalist paramilitaries (173), because armed combat between the latter two groupings is more likely to take place in predominantly Catholic areas.

It is evident from Table 1.4 that nationalist paramilitary violence has been primarily strategic rather than simply ethno-sectarian. Nationalist paramilitaries have killed far more members of the security forces (847) than Protestant civilians (379), so they partially fulfil their objective of fighting 'a war of national liberation', as opposed to a mere sectarian war. However, Protestants understandably *interpret* killings of Protestant members of the local security forces as sectarian. It is equally evident, and contrary to what Irish-American nationalist propagandists imply, that the security forces have been responsible for only 11.8 per cent of the overall death-toll. Even if they were (wrongly) held responsible for all the deaths by 'other and unidentified' agents, their overall responsibility for deaths would still be considerably less than either of the two categories of paramilitants. Between 1969 and 1989 the security forces killed less than half as many people as loyalist paramilitaries; loyalist paramilitaries less than half as many people as nationalist paramilitaries; and nationalist paramilitaries were responsible for more than half of all deaths.

Figure 1.9 shows our estimates of each militant agency's success in hitting its intended targets, and of civilian deaths as a proportion of all deaths caused by each militant agency. These estimates rely upon three crude assumptions: that the intended targets of the security forces are nationalist and loyalist paramilitaries; that the intended targets of loyalist paramilitaries are nationalist paramilitaries, prison officers and Catholic civilians; and that the intended targets of nationalist paramilitaries are the security forces, prison officers, and Protestant civilians. These assumptions would be challenged by supporters of the paramilitants and by officials of the security forces. Loyalists deny that they intend to kill Catholic civilians, claiming that they intend to kill only supporters or members of nationalist paramilitary organizations; republicans deny that nationalist paramilitaries intentionally kill Protestant civilians; and members of the security forces claim that they have no intended targets, they simply use the force necessary to prevent violent actions. We believe the evidence supports our crude assumptions

Table 1.4 Political deaths in Northern Ireland, 1969–89
Source: adapted from IIP (1990: 295)

status of victim	agency responsible for deaths				Total	As % of Total
	Security forces	Nationalist paras	Loyalist paras	Others/ Unknown		
Security forces	15	847	10	4	876	31.44
Nationalist paramilitaries	123	146	21	6	296	10.2
Loyalist paramilitaries	13	18	40	2	73	2.62
Catholic civilians	149	173	506	74	902	32.38
Protestant civilians	25	379	114	57	575	20.64
Civilian religion unknown	4	22	12	1	39	1.4
Civilian total	178	574	632	132	1,516	54.41
Prison officers	0	23	2	0	25	0.90
Total	329	1,608	705	144	2,786	100
responsibility-share						
per cent of all deaths	11.81	57.72	25.31	5.17	100	
per cent of civilian deaths	11.7	37.9	41.7	8.7	100	
civilian deaths as per cent of killings	54.1	35.7	89.7	91.7	54.4	

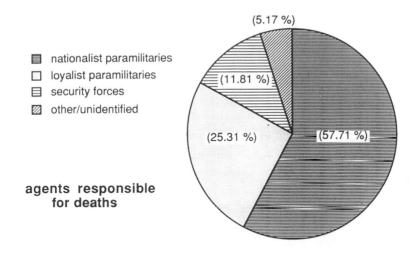

Figure 1.8 (a) Militant agents responsible for all deaths, 1969–89
Source: Table 1.4

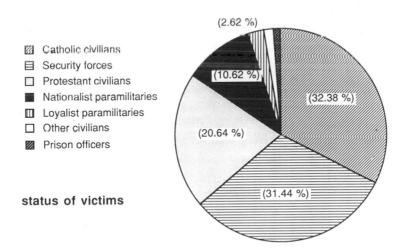

Figure 1.8 (b) Status of victims, 1969–89
Source: Table 1.4

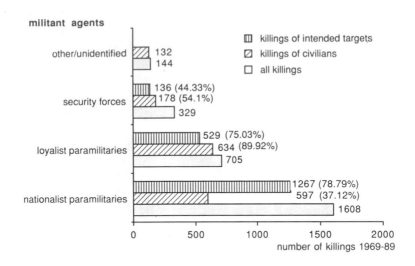

Figure 1.9 Estimates of the success of militant agents in killing their intended targets, and their responsibilities for civilian deaths
Source: Table 1.4

better than the apologias made on behalf of the three sets of militant agents.

Our estimates suggest that the security forces hit their intended targets on less than 45 per cent of all occasions in which they cause deaths, whereas both sets of paramilitaries hit their intended targets on over 75 per cent of all occasions in which they cause deaths. The security forces kill a civilian more than one time in two, i.e. they kill paramilitaries, legally or otherwise less than one time in two. This evidence of incompetence, error, or malevolence (depending upon one's point of view) is made somewhat more palatable by the low overall share of the death-toll attributable to the security forces. However, the low ratio of 'appropriate' to 'wrongful' killings, especially the disproportionate wrongful killings of Catholics (149 deaths), helps to explain why the security forces are poorly regarded by nationalists.[28] By contrast nationalist paramilitaries kill non-civilians just over three times in five, a 'kill-ratio' which indicates a high degree of incompetence, error, or malevolence concerning civilians. Although they are more likely to kill their declared targets than the security forces, the absolute number of civilian deaths which they have caused (574) is very close to the number killed by loyalist paramilitaries (632), and nationalist paramilitaries kill a very high number of Protestant civilians. The final striking feature of Figure 1.9 is that loyalist paramilitaries almost exclusively kill civilians. This facet of their activities has been consistent since the 1970s (Boulton, 1973; Dillon and Lehane, 1973), and is easy to explain.[29] Catholic civilians are easier to identify – for example by their first names, surnames, or residence – than nationalist paramilitaries. They are thus more accessible and softer targets. Although loyalist killing is often portrayed as more random and less instrumental than nationalist killing it too is generally 'rational', i.e. goal-governed behaviour. Nearly 75 per cent of loyalist victims are made up of Catholic civilians or nationalist paramilitaries (506 + 21 deaths out of a total of 705). Loyalists have engaged in systematically 'retributive' rather than purely random killing, but there have been a notable number of psychopathic killings by supposedly politically motivated loyalists, the most barbarous of which were carried out by the 'Shankill butchers' (Dillon, 1989).

The data reveal surprises. Thus nationalist paramilitaries kill almost as many nationalist paramilitaries (146) as all other agencies combined (150). Like all guerrilla or paramilitary organizations they engage in a high degree of 'internal disciplinary' killing, i.e. the execution of (often merely alleged) informants and wayward (or unreliable) members. There has also been a high degree of faction-fighting between and within nationalist organizations. The Provisional IRA and the Official IRA fought one another in the early 1970s. The Official IRA and the INLA killed each other's members in 1975, and in the spring of 1987 the INLA imploded in an internal feud which accompanied the formation of the IPLO. Additionally, many of the deaths of nationalist paramilitaries are put down by English soldiers to 'Paddy factors' or 'own goals', i.e. bungled actions, such as nationalist militants blowing themselves up by mistake. Another remarkable feature of the data is the fact that over half of all deaths (40 out of 73) suffered by loyalist paramilitaries have been caused by other loyalist paramilitaries – mirroring the picture of nationalist paramilitary internal feuding and self-inflicted deaths. A final interesting feature is that Catholic and Protestant civilians have been killed by a diverse group of agents. Loyalist paramilitaries have killed over half of the Catholic civilians who have died in the war. However, nationalist paramilitaries have killed almost one in five Catholic civilian casualties *and* have killed more of them than members of the security forces. Nationalist paramilitaries by contrast have killed two-thirds of the Protestant civilians who have died, but loyalist paramilitaries have nevertheless been responsible for one in five of the civilian deaths within their own community. This figure includes those killed in error or as part of 'internal disciplining' of their community.

Injuries, explosions, shootings, robberies, intimidation and incarcerations, 1969–90

Ethnic violence has extended far beyond killings. Data are available on injuries sustained because of the war, as well as the annual number of explosions (and defusions of explosive devices), the number of bombs neutralized, the scale of findings of explosives and firearms, the number of shooting incidents, the use of rubber and plastic bullets, the number of armed robberies, and the money taken in armed robberies. Figure 1.10 smooths the data on numbers of injuries, explosions, armed robberies, shootings, and the firing of plastic and rubber bullets to present the main trends in the time-series. They show the same patterns as the annual death-toll data presented in Figure 1.7 (very high levels of violent activity in the years 1971–6 with 'normalization' thereafter) and suggest that our explanations for the falling death-rates after 1976 apply to all the other indicators of violence (see also Ch. 5: 202-5).

Over 33,000 people have suffered serious injuries since 1968, a figure close to one in fifty of the population. The social impact of such violence is easily imagined. Although the data include knee-capping injuries they do not include the mental injuries suffered by those who have been kidnapped, those held hostage in their homes during 'stake-outs', those arrested when guilty of no crime, or those maltreated by the authorities; nor do they measure the distress caused by being the friend or relative of a victim of the conflict or being a witness to violent deaths, injuries, and other intimidating episodes. The data confirm that civilians have borne the brunt of the conflict over time. However, overall injuries have declined since the early 1970s, although the hunger strikes of 1980–1, and the aftermath of the Anglo-Irish Agreement of 1985, saw deviations from this downward trend.

The numbers of explosions (and devices defused), armed rob-

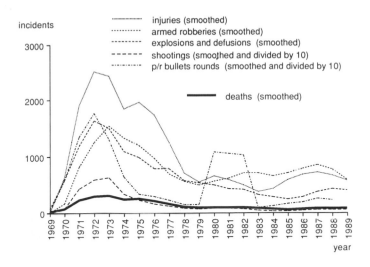

Figure 1.10 Smoothed data on injuries, explosions (and defusions), armed robberies, shooting incidents, and the firing of plastic and rubber bullets
Source: RUC (1990)

beries, and explosive finds over time reveal a similar pattern to the other indicators, i.e. peaks between 1971 and 1976 followed by secular declines thereafter. The use of rounds of rubber bullets (and subsequently plastic bullets) fired by the security forces to control and repel street-demonstrators peaked in the early 1970s and again during the hunger strikes of 1980–1: high use of these devices coincides with peaks of (nationalist) civilian mobilization in demonstrations. Their deterrence effect, but not their legitimacy, is easy to document. Fifteen civilian fatalities were caused by these devices between 1970 and 1989, including Sean Downes whose death in 1984 was recorded by television cameras. In the 1980s 191 cases of plastic-bullet use resulting in death or injury were referred to the Director of Public Prosecutions. In total 4 prosecutions had been made by the end of 1989. The RUC received 123 complaints about their use of plastic bullets in the 1980s; but by the end of 1989 none of these complaints had been upheld and disciplinary action had been taken against only one officer (IIP, 1990: Tables B21 and B21 i).

The RUC provide data on the numbers and value of armed robberies. Since Northern Ireland had extraordinarily low rates of 'ordinary, decent' crime before the late 1960s almost all of

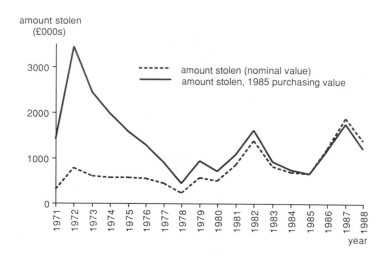

Figure 1.11 The nominal and actual value of armed robberies, 1969–88
Source: O'Duffy and O'Leary (1990)

the subsequent rise in armed robberies is attributable to the political crisis. Armed robberies are an important source of finance for paramilitary organizations: others sources include voluntary donations from the relevant community, protection rackets, 'legitimate' front-enterprises, and, in the case of the IRA, funds from Irish-American organizations (Holland, 1987). In Figure 1.12 we adjust the RUC data to show the annual real value of armed robberies, after transforming the nominal values into 1985 prices. The evidence suggests that paramilitaries 'geared up' for conflict in the early 1970s, during the 'hunger strikes' of 1980–1, and after the Anglo-Irish Agreement: in other words, 'armed robberies' are rationally related to paramilitants' strategic perceptions of when 'Armageddon' is likely to occur.[30]

Intimidation, both collective and individual, has been persistent and widespread throughout the last twenty years, and perpetrated by all militant agents in various forms. It is less amenable to straight quantification but no one denies its dramatic increase since the late 1960s. New types of intimidation have been added to the repertoire of 'cultural' practices already engaged in by loyalists before the 1960s: large-scale marching through rival ethnic space, and 'marking' out territories with paint, flags, threatening slogans, and bunting. In the early 1970s thousands of people in the Belfast region were frightened into leaving their houses or council-flats by death-threats, fire-bombings of their homes, and gentler forms of 'persuasion' (Darby and Morris, 1974). Within and outside work-places sectarian intimidation remains evident today: the aggressive display of the Union Jack, the Red Hand of Ulster, royal regalia, bunting, and loyalist posters in predominantly Protestant work-places discourage Catholics from considering them as 'welcoming', let alone as 'equal-opportunity employers'.

Nationalist paramilitaries have 'tarred-and-feathered' young women involved in alleged or actual relations with male members of the security forces. They march in hoods or masks, bedecked with dark sun-glasses, and proceed in military formation during funeral processions and on the occasions of key political anniversaries, firing volleys of bullets if they can avoid arrest by the security forces. Nationalist paramilitaries regularly take hostages or take over people's homes to enable them to carry out attacks on the security forces; in the worst cases they have sent people to carry out 'human-bombings' while holding their families hostage. Since 1986 they have classified as 'legitimate targets' all those who work for organizations which supply the security forces, dramatically extending their potential targets in both communities.

Suspected informers and alleged juvenile delinquents may first be 'warned to leave' and are routinely 'knee-capped' by paramilitaries in acts of 'communal justice', leaving them crippled for life. Knee-capping usually involves firing bullets at point-blank range through the back of a person's knees; 'crucifixions' involve the shattering of both elbows and knee-caps. Since 1973 nationalist paramilitaries have carried out 1,023 'punishment-shootings' compared to a loyalist paramilitary total of 558 (RUC source), although every year since 1986 loyalist punishment-shootings have exceeded nationalists' ones. These measures of 'justice without juries or prisons' put extreme pressure on the social services to remove and resettle the potential targets.

Both sets of paramilitaries intimidate government officials, representatives of nationalized industries, teachers, social workers, and medical staff; and preside over protection and extortion rackets[31] which put a large number of employees in fear of their lives and livelihoods. They place 'death-notices' in newspapers for people whom they wish to 'counsel', and 'inform' people who need to know what is good for them that they know where their children go to school, where they work, and where they live. The security forces are not above acts of routine oral or physical intimidation, harassment, and threatening behaviour. Especially in Catholic areas mutual hostilities between the policed population and the security forces lead to multiple unreported incidents of generalized intimidation: death-threats, rape-threats, sexist innuendoes, 'warnings' and the same kind of dissemination of knowledge of addresses, friends, and relatives. The security forces also seek to exploit divisions within the communities which support paramilitaries, using and creating 'touts', 'informers', 'supergrasses', and 'double-agents', and engaging in 'black propaganda'.

Over twenty years of ethnic war have led to a large rise in the numbers of persons incarcerated and 'charged with terrorist offences' (see Figure 1.12). From existing sources it is not possible to tell easily how many prisoners have been incarcerated for offences related to political violence.[32] However, data for the years 1982–3 and 1985–6 indicate that two-thirds of prisoners serving sentences in these years were convicted of 'scheduled offences' (IIP, 1990: Table B13 col. 11). The number of persons charged with terrorist offences is not the same as the number convicted of such offences but the two are usually systematically related. The two curves in Figure 1.12 tell the same story. A dramatic rise in the number of persons charged and convicted of terrorist offences occurred in the early 1970s, leading to a tripling of the total prison population by 1978. The numbers imprisoned and charged then level off until the mid-1980s, and the late 1980s have seen a fall in both figures. However, the prison population in 1988 was double the level of 1970, and was likely to rise again after the government revised the regulations on remission of sentences in late 1988.

The other costs of the war

The war has not simply cost lives and limbs, and exposed people to intimidation, shootings, bombings, armed robberies, and imprisonment. The impact of organized violence upon constitutional politics in Northern Ireland frames our concluding chapters; it is sufficient here to make the obvious point that violence reinforces ethnic antagonism, suspicion and distrust, and inhibits conflict-resolution.

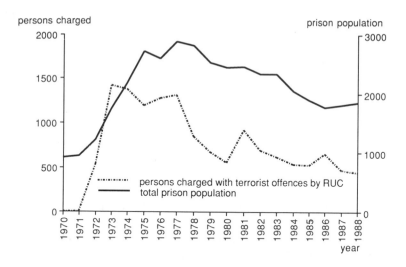

Figure 1.12 Persons charged with terrorist offences and total prison population, 1970–88
Sources: RUC (1990) and IIP (1990: Table B13, 1987 figure is the average of 1986 and 1988)
N.B. This graph has a double 'y' axis. The left-hand side measures persons charged with terrorist offences since the summer of 1972, and the right-hand side measures the total prison population (males and females, inmates of prisons, borstal and young offender centres)

Violence in Northern Ireland has resulted in heavy financial burdens being placed upon both the British and the Irish exchequers. For the Republic of Ireland the extra security costs ensuing from the crisis between the years 1969 and 1982 were estimated at over £ (IR) 1,050 million (IIP, 1986b: Table D14, in 1982 prices): for the same period the additional expenditure on security incurred by the British government owing to the crisis in Northern Ireland was estimated at £ (UK) 4,150 million (ibid.: Table D12). One audit carried out in 1985 estimated that the annual direct costs of violence connected with the Northern Ireland conflict incurred by the UK government ran at £ (UK) 1,194 million per annum (IIP, 1986b: Table D17, in 1985 prices) – an estimate which excluded the indirect economic costs of lost output and employment arising from the political crisis. The cost of providing security in Northern Ireland in the fiscal year 1990–1 was just under £ (UK) 1 billion –

per capita more than three times the UK average.[33] Moreover certain costs are not apparently calculated by the authorities: such as those entailed in tightening security at military bases in Great Britain and Germany, intelligence-gathering and surveillance in Great Britain, and protecting members of the political and civil establishments.

Other economic costs, besides those directly incurred in extra military and police expenditure, include the stress placed upon the public services: health and welfare services, housing administration, public utilities, and the penal services (Darby and Williamson, 1978). Prison officers have been shot and injured. Social workers are often suspected of being informers and are therefore intimidated. Public utilities like telephone exchanges, post offices, railway networks, bus garages, gas depots, power stations and reservoirs have been bombed or robbed and their staffs intimidated. Civil disobedience campaigns against internment between 1971 and 1975 included non-payment of bills to utilities and public services, leading to large deficits within the relevant organizations (White, 1978: 23). Frauds perpetrated by paramilitaries against public-sector organizations have run into millions of pounds. Compensation payments to victims of violence or owners of properties destroyed through paramilitary violence run much higher. Claims for compensation exceed 13,000 cases per annum. Between 1968 and 1985 the UK authorities paid over £ (UK) 570 million in compensation for criminal injuries, criminal damage, and other compensations directly related to the conflict – including over £500,000 in compensation to private-property owners in border areas of the Republic of Ireland in the year 1982–3 (IIP, 1986b: calculated from Table D10). In the years 1968 to 1984 over £ (IR) 37 million was paid by the Irish authorities in compensation payments for criminal injuries and damage to property sustained as a result of the Northern Ireland conflict (ibid.: calculated from Table D11).

In addition paramilitary protection rackets have affected the profitability of many private-sector organizations; as have the requirements imposed by insurance companies upon shops and offices to pay for private-security services. Violence has also affected business confidence and behaviour. Entrepreneurs have emigrated, as have their customers. Organizations work for the security forces at considerable risk. The insurance costs of private transport have risen dramatically to reflect the high numbers of vehicle thefts, hijackings, and car-bombings. The incredibly high proportion of the population now involved in security has led two commentators to describe the Northern Ireland economy as a 'workhouse' in which most people are employed in controlling or servicing one another (Rowthorn and Wayne, 1988: 98). Paramilitary violence has also severely inhibited economically rational all-Ireland cross-border co-operation in infrastructural services, especially in roads, energy production and distribution, transportation, and other communication networks. Finally, the most obvious economic costs are the least measurable: the economic 'opportunity-costs' of two decades of war, in lost investment, output, and productive employment.

The human-rights costs and the costs to liberal democratic institutions are in some respects easier to measure, but they have had incalculable negative effects on public trust in political institutions in the British Isles and upon the legitimacy of the Westminster model of government. The legal authorities of Northern Ireland, Great Britain, and the Republic of Ireland have been granted formidable emergency powers. The Emergency Provisions Act (EPA) in Northern Ireland and the Prevention of Terrorism Act (PTA) in Northern Ireland and Great Britain have been regularly renewed and have become permanent features of the UK statute book. The powers granted have been abused to arrest 'ordinary decent criminals'. Between 1978 and 1989 nearly 25,000 people were arrested in Northern Ireland under the EPA, and over 18,000 people were arrested in the UK under the PTA on suspicion of involvement in Northern Irish terrorism (IIP, 1990: Table A3i (a)). Moreover between June 1972 and 1989 over 27,000 people were arrested under §30 of the Offences Against the State Act (OASA) in the Republic of Ireland (ibid.). The ratios of arrests to charges, and of charges to convictions, have been relatively low in all three jurisdictions, suggesting the systematic and large-scale deprivation of many innocent citizens of their liberty throughout the British Isles.

The UK government has been found guilty of violations of the European Convention on Human Rights and its officials' treatment of suspects has led to consistent and empirically supported criticisms of infringements of basic civil rights (Jennings, 1988; Walsh, 1983). The European Commission and Court of Human Rights have ruled that certain interrogation practices employed by the UK authorities infringed the right not to be subjected to torture or cruel or inhumane treatment; and that the time under which suspects can be held without judicial supervision under the Prevention of Terrorism Act is against the European Convention. Indeed since the UK became a signatory it has derogated from some of the rights and freedoms protected under the European Convention for a far longer period of time than it has not; and that is entirely because of its arrangements for governing Northern Ireland.

Departures from traditional English legal procedures have become normal as a result of the conflict in Northern Ireland. Since 1973 no-jury single-judge courts have presided over cases arising from 'scheduled offences', i.e. 'terrorist offences', on the grounds that jury-trials are not safe from perverse verdicts or the intimidation of jurors and witnesses. Confessions are admissible as the sole basis for conviction on charges of having committed scheduled offences – as they are in the Republic of Ireland – including confessions which are subsequently retracted by defendants. Until 1983 confessions were obtained from 85 per cent of people tried for terrorist offences in Northern Ireland (Walsh, 1983) which may be taken as a rough indicator of the roughness of interrogation. Police experiments with 'supergrass evidence' as the basis for prosecutions began in the early 1980s before being quashed by the judges in 1986. (In supergrass trials, informers guilty of other offences were used to implicate very large numbers of other people suspected of being paramilitaries). In 1988 the British government announced that it was taking the unprecedented step of abandoning the traditional common law 'right of silence', henceforth courts and prosecutors were entitled to draw inferences from the silence of those suspected of having committed offences. Additionally, according to Amnesty International, delays of several years are routine in holding inquests on persons killed by the security forces.

The belief in the impartiality of British justice has been severely damaged in the last two decades; in Ireland, internationally (Helsinki Watch, 1991), and finally in Great Britain. The most notorious cases to date of wrongful imprisonment are the arrests, interrogations, trials, and the long sentences imposed in the mid-1970s on the Guildford Four, the Maguire Seven, and the Birmingham Six, either for bombings or for alleged running of 'bomb-factories'. These cases demonstrated police-fabrication of evidence against entirely innocent people; incompetent or malevolent forensic practices; judicial wishful thinking and professional partisanship; and ethnic bias in the printed and broadcasting media. They have generated the greatest twentieth-century crisis of confidence in the administration of justice in Great Britain and prompted the establishment of a Royal Commission in 1991.

The war in Northern Ireland has impaired other key institutions of pluralist democracy. Certain sections of the British intelligence services appear to have run amok in the 1970s. They believed that the authorities were 'giving in to terrorism', plotted directly against the elected Labour government, and spread false rumours about people of whom they politically disapproved. They also ran 'black propaganda' and 'media-management' strategies which falsely represented the actions of the security forces (Wright, 1987 and Foot, 1989). The broadcasting authorities in both islands have been subjected to vigorous internal and external censorship, including censorship of Sinn Féin, a legal political party in both Northern Ireland and the Republic of Ireland. Censorship has gone to perverse lengths even for those who accept the case for some modification of broadcasting freedoms in the light of armed paramilitary violence. Some of the more curious examples of censorship include the exclusion from the air-waves of pop songs, like Paul McCartney's 'Give Ireland back to the Irish!' and 'Streets of Sorrow/Birmingham Six', sung by The Pogues, and the banning of live telephone surveys on whether British troops should leave Northern Ireland (IIP, 1990: 340–59). Journalism on Northern Ireland, whether in the print or broadcasting media, is now subject to much greater editorial and political interference. The furore caused by *This Week*'s programme *Death on the Rock* in April 1988 is typical of the strained relations between the British government and the media ensuing from the Northern Ireland crisis. News of *Death on the Rock*, which investigated the killing of three IRA personnel in Gibraltar and challenged the accounts of the British and Gibraltar authorities, led the Foreign Secretary Sir Geoffrey Howe to ask for its transmission to be postponed, and forced Thames TV to set up an independent inquiry into the making of the programme (which exonerated the broadcasters). Thames's prospects of keeping its TV franchise were widely agreed to have been damaged by its display of political independence.

There is vigorous debate about how one should apportion the blame for the costs of the Northern Ireland conflict. Are nationalist paramilitaries responsible through the politics of the 'self-fulfilling prophecy'? Similar questions are posed to loyalist paramilitaries. Have their actions deliberately engineered authoritarian responses from democratic governments? Tough questions are targeted at the British state: are the governing authorities responsible for failing to generate legitimate political institutions, or for placing security considerations above those of liberal democratic institutions? Some also ask: why have the British authorities not fought the war more vigorously, or even recognized that it is a war? They address the same questions to the conduct of the Irish authorities. However these questions are answered, our audit of the scale and consequences of the present antagonism should convince readers that Northern Ireland is the most serious source of political conflict and instability in the British Isles. Understanding why that is so is the task of the next six chapters.

Notes

1. These calculations are based on the Irish Information Partnership (IIP) briefing of 11 August 1989. Declaration of interest: O'Leary was on the editorial advisory board of the IIP.

2. We thank Michael McKeown for the original map which is based upon political constituencies rather than administrative boundaries. There are four in-depth studies of the geographical location of political deaths within Northern Ireland (Schellenberg, 1977; Mitchell, 1979; Murray, 1982; and Poole, 1983).

3. The Northern Ireland Office in 1990 made much of the statistical comparison of the overall homicide-rate in Northern Ireland (6 per 100,000) with that in Washington DC (31 per 100,000).

4. If the RUC is looking for the single most persistent cause of premature death to compare with the death-rate from political violence it would do better to cite the death-rate from heart disease: 'Ulster fries' are more lethal than Northern Ireland's drivers or paramilitaries.

5. Reginald Maudling, British Home Secretary (1970–2), notoriously declared his ambition to produce 'an acceptable level of violence'.

6. See Note 8 below for data-sources.

7. The 'ordinary' homicide and violent crime-rates for Northern Ireland, both before and after 1969, are consistently less than those reported for the rest of the UK (Heskin, 1985). In a recent international survey (Van Dijk, Mayhew, and Killias, 1990) Northern Ireland had the lowest percentage of respondents who had been victims of crimes (15 per cent): lower than Switzerland, Finland, Norway, Belgium, Scotland, France, England and Wales (20 per

cent), West Germany, Spain, The Netherlands, Australia, Canada and the USA (30 per cent).

8. The data in Figure 3 are not entirely taken from the *World Handbook of Political and Social Indicators*. The Northern Ireland death-estimates for 1948–1977 are based upon (a) the IIP's submission to the New Ireland Forum which estimates 1,814 deaths for the years 1969–77 and (b) our estimate of 21 killed during the IRA campaign of 1956–62 and UVF actions in 1966, producing a total of 1,835 between 1948 and 1977. For emphasis we have taken the UK death-toll during the same years to be identical to that for Northern Ireland. The datum provided by Taylor and Jodice for the UK is suspect: their figure of 1,463 for deaths because of political violence in the years 1948–77 is an error as it is nearly 400 short of the death-toll in Northern Ireland alone.

9. The per capita death-toll is the total number of persons killed because of internal political violence during the years 1948–77 divided by the estimated population of the relevant political unit in 1975 (in 000s).

10. These states departed significantly from liberal democratic norms during the relevant period: after 1948 and 1967 Israel incorporated large numbers of people denied full citizenship, while Sri Lanka (between 1971 and 1976) and India (during 1975–6) had their constitutions suspended.

11. The Indian figures exclude the holocaust that accompanied the partition of the Indian sub-continent in 1947 8.

12. The Israeli figures exclude all victims of the Arab–Israeli inter-state wars since 1948 because the *World Handbook of Political and Social Indicators* confines itself to 'internal' political violence.

13. Using natural logs is a standard mode of presenting data when the actual figures cause too many extreme data-points to be bunched together in a way which prevents visual inspection of differences. In this case the sheer scale of political violence in the Nigerian, Pakistani, Burundian, Indonesian, and Lebanese civil wars swamps that in other countries, which is why we transformed the data into logs.

14. Cyprus is an appropriate comparator because like Northern Ireland it has a small population (just over 650,000 in 1975), is a zone of high ethnic conflict between two communities (Greek and Turkish Cypriots), and has its sovereignty disputed by two states.

15. In nationalist eyes there has been an 'external' army operating in Northern Ireland since 1969, the British Army; and the operations of this army have been consistently criticized by the Irish government and Irish nationalists; but generally speaking the Irish government have accepted that the role of the British Army in Northern Ireland has been that of an 'arbiter' if not a 'peacemaker', and it has not been universally assumed that the role of the army is to pursue some British strategic interest in the island of Ireland.

16. Lyons's figure is the more credible of the two.

17. Official and independent data on violence in Northern Ireland are generally

reliable even though different methodologies are employed by the two principal monitors: the RUC, and the voluntary organization, the Irish Information Partnership. Analysis in this chapter is based on these two data-bases. The RUC's and IIP's aggregate figures differ marginally: in their annual death-tolls the difference is generally less than 1 per cent (McKeown, 1985: 4). But the IIP is more exhaustive in categorizing the status of victims and the agents responsible for violent acts.

18. Figure 1.6 excludes deaths suffered by 'other/unidentified civilians' and deaths caused by 'other/unknown' agents.

19. The agents responsible for 5.1 per cent of all deaths remain unidentified.

20. In October 1984 five people were killed and many more injured (including the UK Industry Secretary Norman Tebbit and his wife) when an IRA bomb exploded in the Grand Hotel at Brighton during the Conservative party conference. Margaret Thatcher and most of her Cabinet were present in the hotel. In February 1991 an IRA unit operating in Westminster launched rockets from a van. They aimed directly at the Cabinet Office and just missed hitting John Major and his colleagues.

21. Paramilitary actions have been claimed by the INLA since 1987, but it is sometimes suggested that the IRA uses INLA's name to cover for events it does not wish to claim as its responsibility.

22. Its name deliberately echoed that of the Ulster Volunteer Force established by unionists before World War I (see Ch. 2: 91 ff.).

23. See Ch. 9, p. 324.

24. These figures exclude the Territorial Army.

25. The UDR figures are for 1986. The RUC figure includes reservists who make up 35 per cent of the total, and the UDR figure includes approximately 57 per cent part-timers.

26. However, the available data for 1991 show that in the first part of the year loyalist paramilitary killings exceeded those executed by nationalists for the first time since the 1970s.

27. The RUC simply record whether or not victims were members of the security forces so the IIP data-base is indispensable in clarifying the status and distribution of victims and responsibility for their deaths.

28. The 'lay' assumption that bombings as opposed to shootings result in more indiscriminate killing is questioned by those with security experience. The placement of bombs in certain locations predictably kills people from a particular community (i.e. deaths from bombings are often neither indiscriminate nor unintended), whereas shoot-outs, especially in urban districts, may over time cause a higher toll of unintended civilian deaths than bombings.

29. See Ch. 9, p. 324.

30. Loyalist paramilitaries are known to prepare for 'Armageddon' (the biblical site of apocalyptic battle) i.e. for the aftermath of a British withdrawal from Northern Ireland.

31. According to British government figures £500,000 of the IRA's estimated annual income of £5,300,000 comes from protection and extortion – i.e. less than 10 per cent (calculated from *The Independent*, 6 Nov. 1990).

32. While many persons are arrested under emergency legislation, and charged with scheduled offences, there are significant numbers of persons who are charged under 'ordinary' laws for offences related to paramilitary activities.

33. The amount spent annually on law and order in Northern Ireland is £440 per person, compared to an overall UK figure of £145 (McKittrick, 1991).

2

The colonial roots of antagonism: fateful triangles in Ulster, Ireland, and Britain, 1609–1920

Ireland, like Dracula's Transylvania, is much troubled by the undead.

(A. T. Q. Stewart, 1986: 15)

Are we forever to walk like beasts of prey over the fields which our ancestors stained with blood?

(Internal document of the United Irishmen, 15 December 1791)

Many analyses of Northern Ireland explain all aspects of the conflict by reference to 'history', as if this solitary noun suffices for comprehension. This reification of 'history' is understandable because the antiquarian knowledge, beliefs, and references displayed in the region seem so extensive to outside observers, especially those on brief journalistic forays. Karl Marx's expression that 'the traditions of dead generations weigh like nightmares on the minds of the living' might have been invented for Northern Ireland. Historical narratives and myths are used by the principal parties both to explain their situation and to justify their cause. Thus nationalists begin their histories of Ireland in 1169 with the first Norman invasions, and seek to persuade their audiences of uninterrupted English brutality in Ireland; while unionists begin their histories with the plantation of Ulster in 1609, and regale their listeners with tales of the survival of Protestants of British stock steadfastly withstanding barbaric sieges ever since. The typical English reaction to this Irish 'obsession' with history is bemused boredom: 'The passions which are shared by

Mass-going Gael and Calvinist planter, which sustain them indeed in the fashion of two drunks tilted out of the horizontal into a triumphal arch, are nothing to us' (Pearce, 1991).

The salience of 'historical causes' can be grossly exaggerated. The present conflict is not an exotic rave from the grave of Europe's past, a 'replay' of twelfth-century feudal wars of conquest, or a 'repeat' for modern television audiences of seventeenth-century wars of religion. The key ideas of nationalism and unionism, the central political doctrines which polarize the communities in contemporary Northern Ireland, were not present, and made no sense, in the twelfth or seventeenth centuries. There are 'historical' dimensions to the conflict, but many of its key characteristics and causes are modern rather than archaic, and can be seen as part of the processes of 'modernization' which have not stopped in the wider world – despite fashionable assertions to the contrary.

The plantation of Ulster

There is one indisputable historic cause of the current conflict. Without the colonial plantation of Ulster in the seventeenth century, and its legacy, Northern Ireland would not exist. The roots of the present antagonisms lie in the conquest of Ireland by the Tudor monarchs of England in the sixteenth century, and the subsequent consolidation of English rule through the colonization of Ulster by Scots and English settlers. Since the Irish refused to become loyalist Protestants the Tudors decided that loyalist Protestants should be brought to Ireland. The plantation of Ulster was executed under the authority and patronage of the Tudors' successors, the Anglo-Scottish Stuarts, James I and Charles I, who sponsored Crown and mercantile settlements and undertakings.[1]

The Ulster colony was initially strategically and ethnically precarious. The native Irish were not, as had been intended, completely driven off the lands earmarked for colonization; and, contrary to the original grand plan, the Scots settlers eventually far outnumbered the English (Beckett, 1966: 40–81; and Foster, 1988: 59–78). Far from guaranteeing English rule the plantation took much investment of blood and money to be secured. Both Ulster and Ireland had to be reconquered twice more in the seventeenth century to make the island firmly subject to English authority: by Oliver Cromwell at the head of his model army of Protestants, and by King William of Orange. Tudor, Stuart, Cromwellian, and Williamite state-building conquests and settlements established patterns of ethnic and religious differentiation which have persisted to the present day, and understanding their consequences is indispensable for understanding Northern Ireland.

Ulster, the most northerly of the four historic provinces of Ireland, was the least Anglicized and most Gaelic region of the island in the sixteenth century, affected least by the successive Norman, Anglo-Norman, and English incursions and conquests which had dominated Irish history since the twelfth century. Its colonization at the beginning of the seventeenth century, after the defeat and exile of its last semi-independent Gaelic lords, the O'Neills and the O'Donnells, was to be a prototype for English imperial plantations elsewhere. Unlike its predecessors in Ireland the plantation of Ulster 'worked': the settlers were neither rapidly outnumbered, nor culturally absorbed by the natives, and a large-scale building programme led to the construction of over twenty new towns, which became both garrisons and centres for the diffusion of the settler culture. The ordered towns and villages of colonial Ulster were visible outposts of Scots and English culture: the province had become an 'ethnic frontier' (F. Wright, 1987: 1–27) between the communities of Great Britain and the communities of the island of Ireland, and a unique region within the British archipelago. The newly created and surveyed counties of Armagh, Cavan, Coleraine (later Londonderry), Donegal, Fermanagh, and Tyrone were declared Crown lands in 1608, and settled the following year (see Figure 2.1). Parts of two of the remaining counties of Ulster, Antrim (south) and Down (north), had already been colonized privately, mostly by three planters: Arthur Chichester, James Hamilton, and Hugh Montgomery.

The territory of Northern Ireland encompasses the sites of the most enduring of these plantation settlements. Since the seventeenth century Protestants have been more densely concentrated in Ulster than any other region of Ireland, especially in Antrim, Down, Armagh, and Londonderry, but they have also been present in very significant numbers in Fermanagh and Tyrone. Their presence in Ulster is most easily measured by the lower concentration of Catholics in the six counties of Northern Ireland by comparison with the concentration of Catholics in the Republic of Ireland (see Figure 2.2). The patterns of plantation-settlement have persisted through three centuries, perturbed relatively little outside the areas of nineteenth-century urban growth, with the better valleys and lowland, taken by the settlers, staying in Protestant hands, and the inferior hilly land and poorly drained lowland which was left to the natives still predominantly settled by Catholics (Robinson, 1982: 19–49).

The Ulster plantations were formally organized on segregationist principles, the intention of some of the architects being to drive out the 'mere Irish'[2] natives, and replace them with reliable planters.[3] These principles were never fully implemented. The grand strategy of the Crown gradually became more pragmatic. As Wentworth, Charles I's deputy in Ireland, put the English governing imperative in 1633: 'The truth is, we must . . . govern the native by the planter, and the planter by the native' (Beckett, 1966: 65). This triangle of intergovernmental relations – planters, natives, and the Crown (the English equivalent of the state) – became an enduring motif in Ulster history. Three ethnic communities confronted one another over the classical and interrelated questions of agrarian society: political power, the distribution of land, and the definition and worship of God. The interplay of 'sword, plough and book' form the structure of much of human history (Gellner, 1989) and Irish history is no exception.

The three communities were originally subjects of the three kingdoms of the seventeenth-century British Isles: Ireland, Scotland, and England. The first, at least in geographical precedence, was the native Gaelic Irish who claimed descent from the Celts who had conquered Ireland nearly two millennia previously. They were pastoral people, with a small number of nomads, ruled by an increasingly feudalized aristocracy, and were Roman Catholic by religious persuasion. The lands of their aristocrats were expropriated after the military defeat of Hugh O'Neill prompted the Gaelic earls to flee to the European continent in 1607, where they and their heirs fought in the armies of Catholic monarchs. The natives were divested of their traditional access to the land, especially the best land, by the colonizers, and a century later, after the Cromwellian and Williamite settlements, were almost entirely landless.

The second community was made up of the lowland Scots settlers. Many Scots had settled before the plantations of the early seventeenth century: the narrow North Channel separating Ireland from Scotland had been a conduit for migrations in both directions

Figure 2.1 The Stuart plantation of Ulster

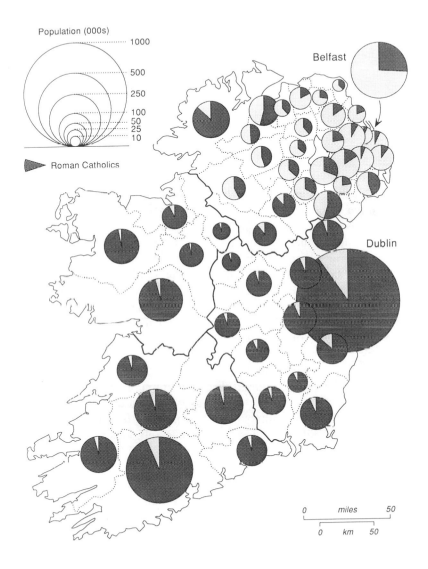

Figure 2.2 The distribution and concentration of Catholics in Ireland, 1981
Source: NI census (1981), RoI Statistical Abstract (1981)

for centuries. However, the plantations differed both in scale and imposition from previous Scots settlements. The Scots were to be small tenant farmers, agricultural labourers, and artisans. They cut down the forests and began extensive arable farming. They were mostly Presbyterians or 'dissenters' in their religious convictions.[4]

The third community was composed of the garrison stock: the Anglo-Irish or the new-English planters. There had been some English settlers in Ulster for centuries – indeed some claimed descent from the Norman incursions of the twelfth century[5] – but the plantations marked a decisive discontinuity in their power and status. Nominally Anglican in religion, in practice they behaved like exclusivist Calvinists. They were the nobles, the owners and controllers of the land, although they included considerable numbers of humbler tenants and artisans amongst their ranks.

The three communities were divided by their languages, dialects, religion, and political status. Although some of these cleavages cross-cut one another, for most of the succeeding centuries they marked and maintained ethnic boundaries. The native Irish of west Ulster spoke Gaelic, as did a minority of the Scots settlers (and their predecessors); but over the next three centuries the Gaelic language would practically die out in Ulster, except in the remoter parts of Donegal. The new inhabitants of Ulster mostly spoke English, as it seems did some of the native Irish of east Ulster, although the 'Ulster-Scots' spoke English with a different dialect and accent. Each ethnic community had its own distinctive material culture and customary norms.[6] Although all three communities were Christian, they were post-Reformation Christians who regarded one another as heretics or devil-worshippers. In the post-Reformation regimes of early modern Europe political status and religious identity were indivisible; and religion would soon supersede language as the sharpest ethnic marker between the communities.

The Anglicans were the established religious believers after Henry VIII's seizure of the monasteries. The Church of Ireland was the Anglican 'national' church, that is the English 'state-church' in Ireland. The organization and personnel of the Church of Ireland were paid for by tithes and taxes collected from all non-Anglicans as well as Anglicans. The early Anglicans of Ireland were not, it is widely agreed, genuine Anglicans in their theology: rather Calvinism, the deterministic and exclusivist Protestant salvationist belief-system, held sway with them, and made them uninterested in converting the natives or the 'old English'. This exclusivism cemented ethnic boundaries.

The Roman Catholics, as Papists, became both religious and political outcasts in the centuries after the Reformation. Until the eighteenth century there were two types of Catholic in Ireland, the Gaelic Irish, and the 'old English' of Anglo-Norman descent. The latter were not common in Ulster but elsewhere in Ireland they were a political force to be reckoned with. Under the newly fashionable doctrines of sovereignty the political beliefs of the old English were anachronistic because they claimed to be loyal both to the king and to Rome. For Anglican monarchs dualistic loyalties were increasingly unacceptable: the subjects of the monarch had to share his or her religion on pain of being branded disloyal. The Act of Uniformity, passed under Elizabeth I in 1560, and on the statute book until 1793, made attendance at the state-church on Sundays compulsory for all, subject to a fine of one shilling. Although this act was not rigorously implemented and 'recusancy fines' were not collected, the political position of old-English Catholics became increasingly precarious as new-English Protestants sought to displace and dispossess them.

In Ulster the large population of Presbyterians, mostly of Scottish stock, was also subject to the Act of Uniformity, and obliged to pay tithes to the Church of Ireland. Their numbers were replenished in the century after the original plantation by new waves of Calvinist immigrants who found Ulster more congenial than Scotland. Although one must be wary of generalization, given their propensity to split, the dissenters are usually portrayed as theologically and intellectually independent, self-righteous, critical of civil government, and suspicious of religious toleration (e.g. Stewart, 1986: 88). They too were intermittently persecuted by Anglicans in the seventeenth and eighteenth centuries, and were excluded from the religious and political establishments.

To change one's religion in early modern Ireland was to change one's ethnicity and one's political status. In the three centuries following the Ulster plantation some did convert, mostly from Catholicism to Protestantism, or from Presbyterianism to Anglicanism. Motivations for conversion varied. Marriage, economic opportunism, fear, famine, and, no doubt, cognitive conviction all played their parts. However, people from the three religious communities never simultaneously converted in such numbers that the rival cultures were assimilated. Marriage-patterns remained highly endogamous. Although the boundaries between Presbyterians and Anglicans did lessen over time it was not until the nineteenth century that they gradually – but not universally – came to think of themselves as Irish Protestants of British stock. Only in speech, dialect, the use of the English language, and material culture can we speak of gradual acculturation in Ulster.

The ethnic frontier of pre-industrial Ulster, with its discriminatory institutions and rival religious sects can be compared with many other regions in Europe's agrarian empires or principalities. Religious persecutions and wars were prevalent elsewhere in early modern Europe: in Holland, Germany, France, and Spain. However, Ulster differed in three major respects from many analogous European conflict-zones: it was a colony; the policy of religious persecution was aimed at the majority of the governed population not the minority (Wall, 1989a: 8–9);[7] and the region was to play a pivotal role in the successive efforts of English and British rulers to govern Ireland. Once a site for the attempted diffusion of the dominant culture in the British Isles, English-speaking Anglicanism, the Ulster colony became a major obstacle to the successful incorporation of Ireland into the emerging British nation, but before we explain why this was so we must warn readers against certain treatments of Irish and Ulster history in conventional textbooks.

The political development of the British archipelago

The history of political development in the British Isles is no longer told as a Whig fairy tale. The benign evolutionary fiction of English cultural advancement and diffusion, ethnic acculturation, and gradualist political evolution towards liberal representative government, is now widely discredited amongst historians and political sociologists (see Hechter, 1975: 22–30).[8] Political development in the British Isles was profoundly affected by the conquest and incorporation of the Celtic periphery, by religious antagonisms, ethnic conflict, and revolutionary and counter-revolutionary religio-ethnic war.

However, myths about political development in the British Isles continue to infect political science texts. Consider one well-known theory of nation-state formation in western Europe which postulates a four-stage trajectory (Rokkan, 1975): in the first a state apparatus is created, i.e. a centralized coercive authority with the ability to generate tax-revenues ('state-penetration'); in the second a national, cultural, and linguistic identity is forged by political élites ('standardization'); in the third the masses are modernized and educated, and the suffrage is extended as they are gradually changed from subjects into citizens ('participation'); and finally the democratization of the state leads to a welfare system characterized by universal social and economic citizenship ('redistribution'). This abstract description of nation-state formation in western Europe is not a caricature of the story of *English* political development as still told in many textbooks of British government and politics. In 'England', such textbooks imply, the transition between each of Rokkan's four stages was evolutionary, constitutional, and peaceable and thus deviant from continental Europe (leaving aside the 'un-English' civil war). The better texts do have passages labelled 'except for Ireland!', but this recognition of Irish deviation from English norms is generally begrudging and misleading. Ireland's political development is not treated as an integral component of the state history of the British Isles.

The politics of antagonism in contemporary Northern Ireland are not some strange and inexplicable deviation from English normality. To understand the political development of the British archipelago the correct unit of analysis is neither 'England', nor 'Ireland', but rather the British Isles as a whole, as the best modern historians appreciate (Foster, 1988; Frame, 1990; Kearney, 1989). With the correct unit of analysis Rokkan's model of stages in the development of modern European states can be used to present a very different account of the history of Ireland in the British archipelago. The English (subsequently the British) state's penetration of Ireland was very slow, extending over four hundred years before the colonization of Ulster. Moreover, state-penetration was not fully accomplished before the onset of the nineteenth-century crises attending 'standardization' and 'participation'. Indeed full British state-penetration, i.e. the state's monopoly of legitimate force within Ireland, was never accomplished. Second, Anglican and British standardization failed, in religion, laws, property systems, and other social customs. This differential level of standardization arrested the rooting of British political institutions in the neighbouring island, inhibiting 'nation-building' throughout the British Isles. Finally, the crises of 'participation', especially the extension of the parliamentary suffrage, occurred in Ireland before 'state-penetration' and 'standardization' had been achieved on the same scale as in Great Britain. In consequence modernization produced political disintegration within the British Isles. Nationalist Ireland mobilized for independence, while counter-revolutionary unionism brought the political system to the verge of a civil war, averted only by the outbreak of World War I.

The incomplete penetration of Ireland by the English Crown and the British state

The entire island of Ireland, contrary to legend, was not conquered by Norman (French-speaking) and Anglo-Norman (old-English-speaking) lords in the twelfth and thirteenth centuries (Beckett, 1976: 16; and 1986: 17). Indeed the power of the English state in Ireland, measured by the capacity of its administrators to raise taxes and enforce laws, remained much less than absolute before 1603, when Hugh O'Neill, the Gaelic lord of Ulster, surrendered to Lord Mountjoy days after the death of Elizabeth I. The English feudal lordship, first claimed by Henry II, failed to establish its universal authority in Ireland in the four centuries after the invasions launched by Norman marcher lords (Simms, 1989). It was constantly challenged, both by native Gaelic chiefs and by gaelicized Norman feudal lords, known as the 'old English'. Resistance to Norman and subsequently English rule had a strong ethnic component although it was not nationalist in a doctrinal sense: rather it took the form of particularist hostility to Crown authority. Until the sixteenth century the grip of the English monarchy over the neighbouring island remained confined to the colonial heartlands of 'the Pale', an area in Leinster centred on Dublin, and the major towns and ports of the sea coasts and the inland rivers outside Ulster. The native Irish lived 'beyond the Pale', where, as the phrase suggested, the writ of the English civilization often failed to be heard let alone run.

Tudor diplomacy under Henry VIII, and the development of programmes of intermittent plantation and conquest under his children Edward VI, Mary, and Elizabeth I, led to Ireland being more thoroughly subjected to the Crown. Henry was the first English monarch crowned King of Ireland, a step that marked his 'new departure' of the 1520s. He planned to subordinate the Anglo-Irish lords and co-opt the Gaelic Irish chiefs into the recently centralized monarchy. This policy was obstructed by the nobility of the Pale, and not revived until the 1540s, when Henry's Irish deputy St Leger, attempted to co-opt the Gaelic chiefs through encouraging them to surrender their lands in return for having them 'regranted' under Crown authority. Despite some signs of success, this strategy was reversed under Edward VI, and for the same reason: resistance by the nobility of the Pale, recently buttressed by the 'new English' Protestant settlers who had been the major beneficiaries of Henry's monastic confiscations in Ireland (Bradshaw, 1979).

Thus began the fateful triangle of the modern history of Ireland, that of the English state, Irish Catholics, and Protestant settlers (Lustick, 1985). To maintain control over Ireland the English Crown, and subsequently British ministers, faced a strategic *trilemma*. They generally ruled out three 'final solutions': that of mass genocide (which Cromwell contemplated and partially practised); forced movements of population (partially undertaken by Cromwell, who 'transplanted' large numbers of the native Irish to Connaught after having offered them 'hell' as an alternative residence); and rigorously imposed acculturation (which was fitfully tried by Protestant evangelicals and state officials with even more fitful success). As and when these three 'final solutions' were ruled out, English control-strategies were confined to three fundamental choices, each of which had predictable costs and benefits. First, they could choose to integrate and co-opt the native Irish, or their élites, into the English or British political system, as they were to succeed in doing with most of the Welsh and Scots. The costs of this strategy were obvious: the alienation of the Protestant interest in Ireland, as well as provoking the anti-Catholic sentiment which was extremely vigorous in Great Britain until World War I. It was not feasible without partially repealing the Ulster plantation and other colonial land-confiscations. The second strategy, attempted from the 1690s until 1800, was to rule Ireland indirectly, through reliance upon the 'new English' Protestant settlers who opposed any integration or co-option strategies which might benefit the natives. The downside of this strategy was the estrangement of the native Irish, leaving Great Britain's western flank under permanent threat of insurrection from an ethnic community with potential allies in Catholic Europe and the enemies of the English Crown. 'England's danger is Ireland's opportunity' soon became the watchword of the native Irish. Spanish rulers in the sixteenth and seventeenth centuries, French rulers in the seventeenth and eighteenth centuries, and German rulers in the twentieth century sought to exploit religio-ethnic division within the British isles by subsidizing native Irish insurrections, with money, *matériel*, and sometimes invading armadas and armies. The final English control-strategy, chosen after 1801, was to rule Ireland directly from Westminster and Whitehall, through parliamentary union, but with the Crown and its ministers arbitrating conflicts between settlers and natives in Ireland. The difficulties of this strategy were to become apparent after the processes of modernization were well under way.

In the early 1600s James I could not see matters with the benefit of hindsight. He supported the plantation of Ulster to secure the Crown's control over Ireland and to integrate it with his other two kingdoms, Scotland and England. He thought he could transcend the dilemma of choosing between integrating natives and relying upon settlers by pursuing a mixed strategy. In theory the plantations were to divide Ulster equally between the Gaelic Irish and new-English and Scots settlers. In practice they were characterized by drastic land-expropriation of the natives, with the new settlers deliberately pursuing aggressive attacks on native property and institutions, and on occasions pursuing forms of 'frontier genocide', which met resistance from native 'woodkern'. Indeed because some of the plantations were privately sponsored and some settlers operated as 'privatized' agents, enduring features of Ulster's political culture were established. The Crown, whatever its formal declarations, lacked the capacity to pursue 'the rule of law', and left the definition and implementation of 'order' and protection of property rights to the settlers. Since the natives were not exterminated but lived beside the settlers, albeit segregated on the higher and inferior land, class status, religion, and ethnicity were fused, and Ulster developed all the traits of a colonial caste society (Brady and Gillespie, 1986). Moreover, since the settlers built their domains themselves, rather than under the direct supervision and assistance of the armies and bureaucracies of the modern rule-governed state, they became firm exponents of military self-reliance and 'defence'. There was a reciprocal corollary, in as far as there was a state officialdom it was a settler officialdom: thus not surprisingly the natives relied on 'private' violence rather than (impotent or biased) legal institutions to redress their grievances.

Although the Crown intended the plantations of Ulster to confirm its control of Ireland, its power and authority were rapidly delegated to and at times usurped by the settlers. The colonization produced an unsurprising if delayed response: the Ulster uprising of native Irish clans resulted in the deaths of some 2,000 settlers and large-scale expulsions in 1641.[9] The uprising began the war of three kingdoms, known in more parochial circles as the 'English' civil war. The bewildering complexity of these years need not detain us (Fitzpatrick, 1988) because the consequences are the important matters. The Anglo-Irish Catholic nobility (the old-English) was pushed, against its will, into an alliance with the native Irish as fellow Catholics and royalists in opposition to the Protestant/Puritan parliamentary forces who were to prove dominant in England and Scotland. Henceforth the old English were usually treated as indistinguishable from the 'mere Irish'. In the war of the three kingdoms Catholics were royalists while Protestants were republicans.[10] The price paid by the native Irish and the old English for the insolence of the Ulster uprising and their support for the royalist cause was a very high one: 'the wrath of Cromwell'.

After the execution of Charles I Cromwell's armies triumphed rapidly if bloodily in Ireland, between 1649 and 1652. Sir William Petty estimated the population of Ireland at 1,448,000 in 1641, and thought that 616,000 people perished between then and 1652 (504,000 natives and 112,000 colonists and English troops). This estimate suggests a veritable holocaust from the war, and the deliberately induced famines which featured in the Cromwellian campaign. Petty estimated later that some 40,000 Irish men left to serve European armies and that 100,000 Irish people were transported to the American colonies (Beresford Ellis, 1988: 25). Even if these figures are considered gross exaggerations the impact of the Cromwellian 'settlement' was historically decisive and devastating for the natives/Catholics (see Figure 2.3). Within a decade Protestants had quadrupled their share of the population of Ireland (from 5 to 20 per cent), and through large-scale confiscations their share of land-ownership doubled between 1641 and 1685 (from 40 to 80 per cent). Full-scale genocidal programmes (entailing executions, transportation, and transplantation of the native Irish to the colonies) were initiated but halted by pragmatic considerations. The new-English settlers wanted the native Irish to be their labourers (Barnard, 1973, 1975; Corish, 1976). However, the Cromwellian settlement did not lead to the 'Ulsterization' of the rest of Ireland.

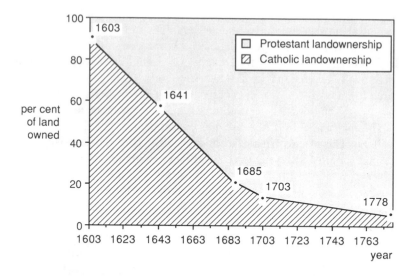

Figure 2.3 Two centuries of colonial land-confiscation: the impact of the Ulster plantation, the Cromwellian confiscation (as modified at the restoration), the Williamite confiscation, and the Penal Laws on Catholic land-ownership in Ireland
Source: data in Dudley Edwards (1981: 177–8)

No long-run widespread establishment of Protestant communities occurred, except in some towns. The fundamental impact of the Cromwellian settlement was to transfer nearly all landed wealth from Catholics to Protestants (see Figure 2.3) and to create a new-English Protestant aristocracy which ruled over Catholics (both natives and the submerging old English).

The restoration of Charles II in 1660 led the surviving old English and the native Irish to entertain hopes that the Cromwellian land-confiscations would be repealed, and that there would be political and administrative 'relief' for Catholics. However, although he died a Catholic, Charles II made no major alteration to the Cromwellian settlement. Matters changed when his brother, James II, came to the throne in 1685. He appointed Catholics as key officials in Ireland, including the Viceroy, and an Act was passed which overturned the land settlement. But a full-blown 'Catholic restoration' in the British Isles was prevented in 1688 by 'the Glorious revolution', during which the Dutch Prince William of Orange and his wife Mary, the daughter of James II, were jointly offered the English

Crown by the English parliament. A second conquest of the three kingdoms was then undertaken. England fell almost without a blow, while Jacobite forces in Scotland were rapidly defeated, leaving only Catholic Ireland loyal to King James. In Ulster Irish Catholic royalists had captured most of the province, again overrunning the plantation towns, but they failed to win the siege of Derry/Londonderry in 1689. This epic saga became a central event in Ulster Protestant mythology, providing Ulster loyalists with their most enduring slogan: 'No surrender!' In the summer of 1690 William landed at Carrickfergus and made his way to the River Boyne, where he defeated James's forces on 12 July. James fled to France after the battle of the Boyne, and in the following year the remaining Catholic royalists surrendered. Under the Treaty of Limerick, signed in October 1691, the soldiers of the Irish Catholic armies were allowed to leave for France after promises had been made that Catholics would enjoy religious toleration.

However, the so-called Williamite settlement[11] led to further land-confiscations in the settler interest. During the 1690s through until the 1720s Catholics were subjected to batches of formidably repressive 'penal laws' which remained in force until the late eighteenth century, and were not repealed until the nineteenth century.[12] These laws anticipated the twentieth-century system of apartheid. Catholics were excluded from the religious, political, and social establishments, i.e. from the ownership of property, membership of the professions, and representation in parliament and government. Catholic ecclesiastics were made outlaws; inter-marriage with Catholics was banned; Catholic schools and Catholic burials were made illegal; a Catholic patriarch could not dispose of his estate by will, instead his land was divided amongst all his sons unless the eldest son converted to the Church of Ireland;[13] Protestant guardians were imposed on Catholic minors due to inherit land; and a host of other statutes were passed 'which had they been enforced or enforceable would have extirpated Catholicism in Ireland in a generation' (Wall, 1989: 8).[14] The penal laws succeeded in the more limited but still drastic objective of almost eradicating the Catholic landed élite: 'driving the more enterprising Catholics into the towns, where only the bye-laws of the various councils and corporations could be invoked in an attempt to keep them from developing into a prosperous middle-class' (ibid.: 65). By the time of the Relief Act of 1778, under which Catholics could acquire leases of land for indefinite tenure if they took the oath of allegiance, Catholic ownership was reduced to 5 per cent of all land in Ireland. As pariah people Catholics were to become small farmers and landless labourers, and in most of Ireland predominant in trade and urban commerce apart from banking, but not in Ulster where the settlers flourished in the urban trades. Agrarian class, ethnic origins, and religious denominations became mutually reinforcing demarcations in colonial Ireland. Ulster, however, was more complex in its demarcations than the rest of the island. The greater density of the plantation settlements meant that there was a considerable proportion of the settler population which was neither part of the landlord class nor Anglican, and the dissenters experienced some of the same religious and class oppression at the hands of the Anglican oligarchy as the native Irish.

The seventeenth century had seen fierce civil wars throughout the British isles, and the Cromwellian and Williamite reconquests and 'settlements' of Ireland were integral parts of these wars. However, Ireland appeared at last to have been conquered, and its native Catholics were quiescent during the Jacobite uprisings of 1715 and 1745 in Great Britain. Indeed the long eighteenth century (1691–1801) was the heyday of 'the Protestant ascendancy' in Ireland. The island was owned and administered by an Anglo-Irish (new-English) Protestant oligarchy with their own parliament in Dublin, although effective power remained vested in an executive officialdom appointed by the English Crown. Though the Irish parliament was subordinate to Westminster the form of government nevertheless remained indirect. The contrast with Scotland was striking: the latter kingdom entered a full parliamentary Union, creating Great Britain with England in 1707.

If native Ireland remained politically quiescent during most of the eighteenth century it was not socially quiet. Agrarian violence, in which communal customary norms were enforced against the predations of landlords and the law, remained commonplace and continued to have an ethno-religious character. In parts of Ulster, especially in Armagh, armed conflict between rival secret societies of Protestant and Catholic peasants was rife: the Protestant 'Peep O' Day' boys, forerunners of the Orange Order, clashing with Catholic Defenders. However, the native Irish/Catholics were sufficiently repressed that the self-confidence of the Protestant oligarchy grew over the course of the eighteenth century, to the extent that 'colonial nationalism' manifested itself amongst what became known as the Patriot faction of the Anglo-Irish. Confident that the native/Catholic issue had been resolved they began to question Ireland's subordination to the Crown, especially in trade relations. They sought greater autonomy for Ireland's parliament after the American Revolution, and in 1782, at the nadir of Britain's fortunes in the American war of independence, wrested formal legislative independence for the Irish kingdom (although it remained curtailed by the power of Crown patronage and control over the executive). Within the Patriot faction of the oligarchy many were prepared to contemplate 'relief' for both Catholics and dissenters from the worst excesses of the penal laws. This willingness was partly because of the efforts from the 1760s of the middle-class Catholic Committee to secure some legal rights for Catholics: they lobbied with the argument that it was possible to be Catholic and loyal to the Crown and parliament.

The prospect of slow evolution towards repeal of the penal laws, land reform, and religious toleration was dramatically foreclosed by the French Revolution. After the outbreak of war with revolutionary France the British government, eager to secure its western flank, pushed a Catholic Relief Act through the Irish parliament in 1793, giving Catholics the right to vote for MPs (on a very restricted property-franchise) but not the right to sit in parliament. As with the American Revolution the ideas of the French Revolution, particularly republican nationalism and a non-denominational state, proved especially attractive to Presbyterian radicals in Antrim, Down, and Dublin, who in 1791 formed an organization called the United Irishmen, centred in Belfast and Dublin. The United Irishmen embraced Catholic emancipation (because the French Revolution had demonstrated that Catholics could be liberals), and their organization gradually found wider support amongst Catholics and dissenters in English-speaking areas, and forged linkages with peasant secret societies. The leadership cadre of the United Irishmen remained mostly Presbyterian, with the bulk of the politically conscious Catholic middle class holding to a form of constitutional liberalism which was to flourish under O'Connell in the nineteenth century. The programme of the United Irishmen was articulated by their most celebrated leader, Wolfe Tone: 'To subvert the tyranny of our execrable government, to break the connection with England, the never-failing source of all our political evils, and to assert the independence of my country – these were my objects. To unite the whole people of Ireland, to abolish the memory of all past dissension, and to substitute the common name of Irishman in place of the denominations Catholic, Protestant and Dissenter, these were my means' (cited in Cronin and Roche, 1973: 78).[15] The means also included a military alliance with the French revolutionary leadership (Elliott, 1982). A co-ordinated insurrection was planned for 1796 but cancelled when a French fleet failed to land at Bantry Bay. This stroke of luck provided the Irish executive with time to organize the coercion of Ulster and to penetrate the United Irishmen's organization. Thus when the rebellion eventually came in 1798 it was crushed within the year (Pakenham, 1969). The epicentres of insurrection in the summer of 1798 were in Wexford and eastern Ulster where both Catholics and descendants of settlers were present in large numbers (Cullen, 1981: 210–33), and the West did not rise until a small-scale French force arrived. The high ideals of the United Irishmen were not wholly accomplished in practice. The actions of many Catholic peasants in the Defender organizations which joined the rebellion were difficult to distinguish from ethnic sectarianism, and Catholic killings of Protestants undoubtedly had the long-term effect of deradicalizing the more liberal Presbyterians, weening them off their interest in republican and non-denominational Irish nationalism.

The insurrection of the United Irishmen indicated that native Irish and some dissenter sensibilities were latently revolutionary rather than merely motivated by communal grievances. To address this problem and secure the geopolitical security of the British Isles William Pitt proposed that Ireland join the Union and that Catholic emancipation be passed simultaneously. Under the Act of Union of 1801 the Irish parliament was formally integrated into the imperial parliament of Great Britain and Ireland: 100 (later 105) Irish MPs, 28 Irish peers and 4 Church of Ireland bishops were to hold seats in Westminster. But Pitt failed to muster a winning coalition for Catholic emancipation, being opposed by King George III, the Lords, the Anglo-Irish nobility, and others in Great Britain, and was obliged to resign. Had the Union and Catholic emancipation been passed together it is conceivable that the history of Ireland within the British state would have been different. However, the Protestant ascendancy was to continue unabated, and a small-scale United Irish rebellion in Dublin in 1803, organized by Robert Emmett, provided a harbinger of future republican insurrections.

British state-penetration of Ireland was therefore, at best, formally accomplished no earlier than 1801. Yet it remained incomplete and persistently illegitimate. Ireland was never treated as if it were just like England or the rest of Britain. In the long centuries between the Norman invasions and the conquests of the Tudors and Stuarts Ireland was only nominally under the control of English monarchs who were 'overlords' rather than kings of the second island. The failure of the Reformation in Ireland meant that the second island was a permanent threat to English and British security, and the programme of plantations meant that the ethnic politics of the island could not develop on the model of the English, Welsh, or Scots: cultural autonomy within a wider political union. In the aftermath of the Cromwellian and Williamite conquests and confiscations Ireland was not integrated with England and Scotland. Rather the British Isles were nominally a dual monarchy from 1707 until 1801. Although both parliaments were staffed by the same kind of landed oligarch the Irish parliament was radically differentiated from its subjects in ethnic origin, language, and religion, and enjoyed none of the tacit legitimacy accorded to Westminster. Moreover, the Irish legislature was much more firmly in the grip of the Crown than its Westminster counterpart. Finally, when Ireland was at last formally integrated into the significantly named United Kingdom of Great Britain and Ireland it was still governed differently from the rest of the kingdom, and marked off as a semi-colonial dependency. The lord-lieutenant was a recognizable descendant of the viceroy, and Ireland's legal and religious institutions were to remain organized against the interests of its majority ethnic community.

The Union was continually challenged by small-scale nationalist/republican rebellions in Ireland, in 1803, 1848, and 1867, each of which was organized by underground insurrectionaries. The United Irishmen, Young Ireland, and the Irish Republican Brotherhood (or the Fenians) established a tradition of revolutionary nationalism that might have proved a potent military threat but for a record of romanticism and incompetence by their leaders which would not be transformed until Michael Collins took the IRB in hand after World War I. Until then Irish nationalists fought more ferociously and effectively in the armies of other states than they did against the English Crown. However, the British state's authority was constantly confronted in a less directly political way, by anarchic peasant violence or local agrarian class warfare, which frequently had an ethnic and religious colouration. Whiteboy, Defender and Ribbon societies were constant perpetrators of 'agrarian outrages' in the decades after the Union; and sectarian violence was especially common on the south Ulster/north Leinster frontier (Hoppen, 1989: 45). The countryside remained in a state of 'diffuse insurgency' throughout the nineteenth century, prompting the British authorities to create a centralized and militarized police force and to pass innumerable measures granting extraordinary powers of arrest and detention by English standards (Townshend, 1986: 45–50). While not all violence took the form of native–settler/Catholic–Protestant conflicts, and 'the night sky was not constantly lit up by burning hayricks nor rent with the shrieks of victims being mutilated or put to death' (Hoppen, 1989: 44), none the less the comparative scale of agrarian violence in Ireland dramatically outranked that in Great Britain. The writ of the state was limited: ample testimony is provided by the scale of the coercion which accompanied whatever reform or reconciliation proposals the British élite considered necessary to redress agrarian or religious grievances.

The failure of Anglican and British standardization

Britain's eventual state-building defeat in Ireland owed most to the failure to create standardized and stable foundations for a durable sense of common citizenship throughout the United Kingdom. Instead of becoming a mechanism for ethnic and religious toleration, as intended by Pitt, the Union became the bulwark of the colonial settlers and their descendants: the Anglo-Irish nobility throughout Ireland and the Protestants of Ulster. Colonial legacies produced an imbalanced Union and no equality of opportunity for Catholics as the UK modernized, and led modernizing Irish nationalists to seek political protection for the native Irish and expression of their identity through the establishment of a separate Irish parliament, to be nominally under the British Crown, or completely independent of it. The former idea was central to the 'Repeal of the Union' organized by Daniel O'Connell in the 1830s and 1840s, while the 'Home Rule' movements organized by Isaac Butt and Charles Stewart Parnell after the 1870s left ambiguous the scale of independence they sought for an Irish parliament. These 'repeal' and 'home-rule' projects were blocked by successive British governments, and by the Protestant settler population, fearful of loss of power and of being dominated in the new arrangements. The blockage of these autonomous and parliamentary nationalist movements in turn fertilized a more broad-based militant Irish republicanism which sought to create an independent Irish nation-state, if necessary through violence.

These factors were not the sole obstacles preventing British nation-building in Ireland. In early modern Europe 'the nation' became defined as a community of institutions which bound citizens together in solidaristic ties within a common culture. Historical sociologists emphasize the reinforcing developments which bound European ethnic communities into nation-states: the economic and industrial integration of territories through the expansion of market relations; the diffusion of common normative and linguistic codes; the administrative integration of territories through the imposition of uniform standards and laws; the development of a meritocratic division of labour without ascriptive blockages to social mobility; the communicative integration of territories through print and national media; and the rationalization of bureaucracies, in which loyalty was no longer attached to traditionally legitimated persons but rather to impersonal abstractions (such as the 'state' or 'nation'). But the processes which encouraged ethnic integration and nation-building elsewhere in early modern Europe were mostly absent from the relationships between the two largest islands of the nineteenth-century UK.

The economies of the two islands, although partially interdependent, increasingly diverged. Great Britain industrialized, whereas Ireland largely did not. Great Britain ran a global economic empire, exporting its industrial goods and services throughout the world, whereas Ireland mostly exported agricultural produce to Great Britain. Ireland's growth-rate over the course of 1848–1914 was about 0.5 per cent per annum, the lowest rate of growth of national income in western Europe (Lee, 1973: 35). Ireland's population, which was 25 per cent of the population of the UK in 1845 (and on some estimates higher than England's in the early nineteenth century), was reduced to a tenth of the UK's by 1914, as decades of famine, underdevelopment, and emigration took a colossal toll. Modern commercial agriculture, both for export and the domestic market, developed in Ireland, especially after the Great Famine of 1846–51, but large-scale industrialization did not. The exceptions were in Ulster, or rather around Belfast and the Lagan valley, where ship-building, engineering, and textile production boomed. Urbanization, heavy industry, and textile production grew in Great Britain at absolute and per capita rates which far exceeded the equivalent rates in Ireland, again with the exception of the Belfast region. All of Ireland lagged behind Great Britain in urban infra-structure – in sanitation, housing, and town-planning. The British political élite did not believe in government-directed or regulated economic development on the German model, and thus the state, 'the most powerful potential agent of economic development in Irish circumstances, simply opted out in obeisance to dogmas originally promulgated on the basis of English and Scottish conditions' (Lee, 1973: 35).

The uneven spatial development of industrial capitalism in the British Isles, and within Ireland itself, reinforced the most important colonial, ethnic, and religious cleavages. Ireland as a whole was an agrarian periphery in contrast to urban and industrial Great Britain. Belfast and the north-east of Ireland, by contrast, looked like Glasgow and Liverpool: industrial enclaves of the British economy within agrarian Ireland. The modern urban factory-based working class rapidly became more numerous in Belfast than Dublin. Ominously, discriminatory labour markets, in which Protestants had a superior position, developed with the growth of Belfast – working-class sectarianism manifesting itself as early as the 1830s (Budge and O'Leary, 1973). Discrimination in employment had become entrenched in adamantine forms by 1901 (Hepburn, 1983; Hepburn and Collins, 1983). The Belfast working class promoted their interests through 'factional conflict rather than trades unionism' (Fitzpatrick, 1989: 229); and the Protestant working class successfully excluded Catholics from the better-paid and more highly skilled employment, sometimes through the device of driving their fellow Christians from the work-place, as occurred many times in the Belfast shipyards from the 1860s to 1920. These economic and material differences between Ireland and Great Britain, and within Ireland, help account for the subsequent protectionist and agrarian thrust of Irish nationalism, and the free-trading and industrial thrust of Ulster unionism.

The Great Famine (1846–51) was the socio-economic water-shed of nineteenth-century Ireland (Goldstrom, 1981; Green, 1966; Mokyr, 1985; Woodham-Smith, 1962). Its devastating impact on the Irish population and class-structure is well known: over one million deaths in excess of what otherwise would have occurred; over one million people forced to emigrate within four years, and three million within three decades; over one million deaths in the decade after the first wave of potato-blight in the mass migrations in 'coffin ships' to America, Canada, and Australia; the fall in the total population of Ireland from 8.3–8.5 million in 1841 to 6.5 million in 1851; and the dramatic shrinkage of the landless labourers and small-farmer class whose lack of property-entitlements explain their extremely high share of the death-toll. The Famine transformed the Irish landed economy as well as its population. Agriculture based on pasture and livestock production rapidly surpassed that based on tillage. It also accentuated and transformed emerging marriage, inheritance, and demographic patterns. The Irish 'stem-family' became dominant: economic marriages were contracted between the eldest son – frequently aged – who inherited the land as a tenant-farmer or small-owner and a much younger doweried-woman, while their respective siblings were usually obliged to emigrate. The Famine also laid the final blow to Gaelic culture, obliterating many of the extant Irish-language-speaking in west Ulster and Ireland west of the River Shannon.

The Famine caused the most brutal feasible 'modernization' of Ireland's economy, population, class-structure, and culture. It made Ireland more like England and Great Britain in significant socio-structural and linguistic if not demographic respects, but it did not erase Irish socio-economic differences from the rest of Great Britain. The Famine scarcely promoted ethnic integration or nation-building 'To the majority of Irishmen the Union was now identified with hopes disappointed, grievances unremedied, liberties denied, with poverty, backwardness, and above all with the catastrophe of the great famine' (Moody, 1966: 276). The folk-memory of the Famine, cultivated by Irish nationalists, attributed it to the English landlord class, the English agrarian system, and the *laissez-faire* doctrines of English governments hidebound by the dogmas of liberal political economy. This folk-memory had a very high degree of truth-content. Food continued to be exported from Ireland during the Famine, both before and after Sir Robert Peel's decision to repeal the Corn Laws (which removed the tariffs imposed on imported grain in the interest of English farmers). Whereas Peel's Tory government engaged in paternalistic relief-measures – and to some effect in 1845–6 – the Whig doctrinaires who came to power under Lord John Russell decided that the government should not purchase food if the potato-crop failed again. Private enterprise and market-mechanisms should be left to supply food. When they awoke from their dogmatic slumbers it was too late. Although much of the contemporary Irish population is held to have believed that the potato-blight was sent by God, its surviving descendants held the English government culpable for the Famine. The folk-memory of the catastrophe was most vigorously sustained by the migrant Irish and their descendants, and their 'diaspora nationalism', especially in North America, proved a significant force in the eventual triumph of Irish nationalism.

The Famine did not have the same dramatic demographic, cultural, or economic impact upon east Ulster as on the rest of Ireland. Agriculture in Ulster was more diversified and stable, landlord–tenant relations were less economically exploitative, and industrialization had provided an alternative locus for employment and economic security.

The economic and demographic differentiation of Ireland and Great Britain, and parts of Ulster from the rest of Ireland, came on top of the already evident religious differentiation of the same geographical units. In England and Scotland there were two different established churches, the Anglican and the Presbyterian, both pro-tected by the Union and the churches of the relevant ethnic majority – even if they made the British monarch a theological schizophrenic. The Church of Ireland (like the Church of Wales) by contrast was the church of the relevant minority, and it was not disestablished and partially disendowed until 1869. After 1829 and Daniel O'Connell's successful constitutional campaigning, Catholics were politically emancipated and free to stand for the Westminster parliament and political office (O'Ferrall, 1981, 1985; Whyte, 1966).[16] Thereafter the British administration in Ireland made successive efforts to incorporate the Catholic church. Having failed in their efforts to pacify agrarian Ireland through centralized policing, Protestant education, and subsidized emigration, the British administration sought to use the Catholic church as a more effective instrument of social control (Inglis, 1987: 97–109), but the *rapprochement* between the Irish Catholic church and the British state, which began before the Famine, came too late to build a decisive bloc of British Catholics. While careful to tap the state to gain control of schools which were intended to be non-denominational, and vigorous in condemning militant republicanism, the Irish Catholic church could not become enthusiastically pro-Union without endangering its ethnic base. It resisted the state's offer to subsidize its clergy. Under the leadership of Paul Cullen, Catholics consistently rejected the idea of 'concurrent endowment' which proposed to establish both the Catholic church and the Church of Ireland. Cullen, Ireland's first Cardinal, built modern Catholicism in Ireland. Politically he worked for no established church in Ireland rather than two, despite the Vatican's declaration that the separation of church and state was an evil. Between 1849 and 1878 he 'transformed the Irish Church . . . into one of the most efficiently marshalled Churches in Europe' (Lee, 1973: 44). No liberal in theological matters, nor a 'castle Catholic',[17] he followed an ultramontane line tempered by Irish circumstances, one which placed the Catholic church outside the temptation of blandishments from the British state. Cullen's construction of an autonomous, centralized, and reinvigorated Catholic church put a major road-block in the path of British nation-building. It also served to exacerbate traditional Protestant and Presbyterian anxieties about Catholic expansionism and authoritarianism, which were reinforced as the international Roman Catholic Church became both more Papal and anti-Protestant in the late nineteenth century.

Reformed, politically freer, and newly confident Catholicism posed a political and religious threat to Irish Protestants. The non-denominational school system established in the 1830s, under which religious instruction was to take place outside school hours, rapidly became denominational in practice: the Catholic parish priest became the school manager in most parts of Ireland. This national school system, once established, meant that the Church of Ireland could never become the church of a majority in Ireland, even if it had wanted to do so. However, it should not be imagined that the Catholic Irish were the only or the most clerical of the three ethno-religious communities: 'Protestant Ireland was a highly clericalised society, and as late as 1914 Protestant soul-saving techniques were about twice as labour-intensive, and probably three times as capital-intensive, as Catholic techniques' (Lee, 1973: 18–19). Nineteenth-century Irish Presbyterianism had undergone decisive and dramatic change. In the 1830s, especially in Ulster, the 'new light' Presbyterian forces which embraced the Enlightenment, were crushed by theological fundamentalists, gathered around the preacher Henry Cooke, widely regarded as one of the nineteenth-century's versions of the Reverend Ian Paisley. Cooke argued in favour of maintaining the Church of Ireland as the established church: it being better to have the *wrong* Protestant state-church than either none at all or a Catholic one. Whatever residues of liberalism and radicalism remained within the dissenter tradition were largely displaced by support for Toryism, and often for the rabidly sectarian Orange Order. Irish Protestantism, like Irish Catholicism, underwent a religious revival after the Famine, notably in a wave of hysterical conversions of the 'born-again' in Ulster in 1857. Religious revivals were not unknown in nineteenth-century Great Britain but in Ireland they were taking place within a milieu of deeply rooted ethnic divisions: vigorous Christianity reinforced antagonisms rather than bringing 'peace and light to all nations'.

British nation-building under the Union was further hindered by the fact that Ireland was not administratively integrated into the kingdom (McDowell, 1964). A separate Irish legal system and statute book were preserved. Ireland was centrally administered by a lord-lieutenant who was always a peer, a chief secretary, and an under-secretary, who were commoners. In the nineteenth century there was no Catholic lord-lieutenant or chief secretary, and merely two Catholic under-secretaries (Hoppen, 1989: 31–2).[18] Until the 1890s they presided over boards and governmental agencies which were not accountable to parliament, let alone Irish MPs. The lord-lieutenant resided in Phoenix Park Dublin, whereas the chief secretary as the minister for Ireland in the Commons spent the parliamentary year in London. The attempt to govern Ireland through centralized bureaucracy marked it off from the rest of the UK where 'a dual polity' had evolved in which local politics were left in the hands of local élites and high politics were reserved for Westminster (Bulpitt, 1982). In Ireland the police, poor-law administration, and education were under more central control for much of the Union than the respective services in Great Britain. The police were the most dramatic illustration: Robert Peel, the under-secretary for Ireland, established the beginnings of a paid force in Ireland in 1814 ('Peelers'), and Ireland was the first and only part of the UK to have a paramilitary, uniformed, and armed police. 'Two entirely different police systems . . . developed for a supposedly "united" kingdom. Britain got an unarmed policeman, answerable not to central government but to a watch committee and depending in the last analysis on the moral support of the community to enforce the law. Ireland, by contrast, got an armed garrison, rigidly disciplined and directly controlled by Dublin Castle, operating with the backing of the Martini-Carbine, the bayonet and the sword rather than the support of the community' (Brady, 1974: 3).

Successful nation-building requires meritocratic social mobility. In the 1780s and 1790s Catholics had acquired the right to maintain schools, join the professions, and vote at parliamentary elections, which liberated them from previous caste-restrictions, but until emancipation in 1829 they remained debarred from all the important offices of state. They could not be ministers, MPs, judges, army-colonels, naval captains, or senior civil servants. After 1829 the only offices of state which remained barred to Catholics were the lord-lieutenancy of Ireland, the lord chancellorships of England and Ireland, and the monarchy. The lower-middle-class and middle-class Catholic/native Irish experienced educational advancement and meritocratic career-advancement in the nineteenth century, but their prospects for social mobility, both objectively and subjectively, were blocked by extensive ethno-religious discrimination. The numbers of Catholics attending superior schools and colleges tripled between 1871 and 1911, and over the same time-frame the ratio of Catholics attending secondary schools rose from 50 to 73 per cent, almost exactly the share of Catholics in the Irish population in 1911 (Hutchinson, 1987: Table 8.1). The number and percentage share of Catholics employed in the secular professions rose steadily between 1861 and 1911 within a *declining* population (ibid.). However, large numbers of Catholics had to emigrate to Great Britain and elsewhere to pursue professional careers, and the position of Catholics was not improving especially fast or consistently across all professions. If by 1911 Catholics had been employed in the higher professions in proportion to their share of the total population (more than a century after the repeal of the most serious penal laws and more than eighty years after Catholic emancipation), then the lines measuring the representativeness of the professions in Figure 2.4 should all have been near zero on the 'x' axis. In fact the lower status professions, schoolteachers, civil service officers, and clerks, were the only ones approaching representativeness by 1911; and in the case of schoolteachers there was evidence of an oversupply of qualified personnel for available vacancies (ibid.: 275). Over the same half-century the

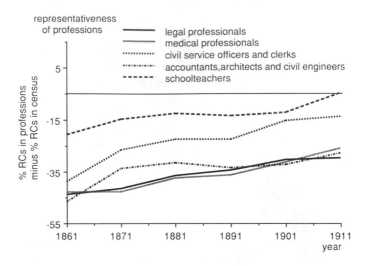

Figure 2.4 The under-representation of Catholics in the secular professions in
Ireland, 1861–1911
Source: calculated from Hutchinson (1987: Table 8.1)
N.B. The 'y' axis measures under-representation by taking the percentage of
Catholics in the relevant professional category and subtracting the percentage
of Catholics in the Irish population

relative position of Catholics remained much more static in the
old, superior status professions of law and medicine, and the
newer, prestigious professions of accountancy, architecture, and civil
engineering. The high professions were bastions of the Protestant
ascendancy; as were 1,600 top-posts in the civil service until as
late as 1906 (where political appointment rather than merit was
justified on the grounds of 'trustworthiness'). The predominantly
Protestant ownership of private-sector enterprises in banking and
commerce led to dramatic and static Catholic under-representation
amongst white-collar employees (ibid.: Table 8.4). The participation
of large numbers of the Catholic intelligentsia, schoolteachers, law
graduates, and civil servants in the Gaelic revival from the 1890s to
the 1930s cannot therefore be regarded as surprising. The 'United'
Kingdom was not a land of equal opportunity.

   The Gaelic revival of the late nineteenth century was both a
'revival and invention' of ancient sports and pastimes and a literary
renaissance. Its organizations were rapidly penetrated by old Fenians

and the IRB. The revival produced a renewed interest in and recovery of the Irish language and history, and the saving and reinvention of lost Gaelic civilization. Elaborated by poets, historians, and other cultural intellectuals, and much later by politicians, the revival left the Ulster Protestant population cold. The English language, the Protestant religions, and the British state were responsible for the destruction of Gaelic civilization. It followed that 'de-Anglicizing Ireland' could not be warmly embraced by Ulster Protestants, something which the Anglo-Irish Protestant President of the Gaelic League, Douglas Hyde, failed to appreciate.

Anglican or British 'standardization' succeeded only in one important respect: English became the modern language of the British Isles. Although British national identification made some headway in Protestant Ulster, Ireland as a whole did not become 'West Britain'. The British identity never became more than a minority taste, in striking contrast to Scotland and Wales (Robbins, 1988). Scotland was not a conquered *and* colonized nation, unlike Ireland, and had possessed the institutions of statehood, many of which were preserved in the Union. After 1885 it had a Scottish department headed by a Secretary of State who represented a Scottish constituency. Wales had been conquered, like Ireland, but its native élites were co-opted; it had not possessed many of the institutions of statehood, nor was it planted with colonial settlers. Central Scotland and south Wales, where most of the population was concentrated, were integral parts of the British industrial economy, sharing the prosperity enjoyed by north-east Ulster and avoiding the disadvantages suffered by the rest of Ireland.

Thus even without a colonial settlement in Ulster British nation-building in Ireland might still have failed because of the major cultural and economic differences between Ireland and Great Britain, but given the existence and the evolution of the colony British nation-building throughout Ireland was a labour of Sisyphus.

The crises of 'participation': nationalism and unionism

Crises of participation focus on who is to be included within the domain of political power, and mark the entry of the masses into political decision-making (Binder *et al.*, 1971; Huntington, 1971). Given its proximity to England, then the most dynamic modernizing state in the world, Ireland displayed mass-pressures for 'participation' earlier than most European territories, well before commercialization, urbanization, and industrialization had performed their alleged democratizing functions.

The United Irishmen included universal adult male suffrage in their political programme in the 1790s, a programme as radically democratic as the Irish-influenced Chartist movement which campaigned in Great Britain in the 1830s and 1840s. O'Connell's mobilization of Irish peasants and townsmen to win Catholic emancipation in the 1820s was one of the earliest examples of mass democratic pressure constitutionally exerted on the British state (O'Ferrall, 1985). The British authorities responded to O'Connell's campaign by eventually conceding Catholic emancipation but by further restricting the property-franchise under which Irish MPs were elected, thereby reducing the potential pool of Catholic voters from 216,000 to 37,000 (Foster, 1988: 302). Nevertheless O'Connell managed by the 1830s and 1840s to construct the first prototype of the modern political party in the British Isles in his campaign for the 'Repeal of the Union'. The demand of the 'Repealers' was tantamount to demanding legislative independence for an Ireland in which Catholics would form the majority of the electors, an extraordinary majority if the franchise were ever to be widened. When O'Connell introduced a motion in 1834 to allow Repeal to be considered by a committee of the House of Commons it was defeated by 523 votes to 38: with one solitary British MP supporting O'Connell. 'Repeal' was then simply an 'unthinkable' proposition for the British establishment (Lustick, 1990); as it was in 1843 when they called O'Connell's bluff by outlawing his 'monster-meetings' and imprisoning him the following year. O'Connell's prophetic address to the establishment was not heard: if the people of Ireland were well governed then they 'are ready to become a kind of West Britons, if made so in benefits and justice; but if not we are Irishmen again' (cited in MacDonagh, 1989). He died at the height of the Famine in 1847, having failed to win Repeal, and in constant controversy with the cultural and militarist romanticism of the recently formed Young Irelanders. He had pioneered universalist liberalism and (more ambiguously) the separation of church and state in Ireland, and was the first European Catholic layman to do so.

In post-Famine Ireland the 'participatory' crises of modernization revolved around the issues of the plough, book, and sword in their modern forms: land-law and landownership, church and state relations, and national independence. Irish farmers, small-holders, tenants, and labourers, although locked in internecine local and intra-class conflicts, were able to mobilize and transform the patterns of land-law and landholdings. Bodies like the Tenant League of the 1850s and the Land League of the late 1870s and early 1880s provided the muscle which persuaded British administrations to engage in land reform: 'conflict and conciliation' became the ruling themes in agrarian politics (Bew, 1987). Gladstone's Land Act of 1870 which granted legal recognition to the 'Ulster Custom'[19] was the first in a series of steps which over thirty-five years would culminate in the British government buying out the Anglo-Irish landlords and establishing Irish peasants as land-proprietors. Ulster was again exceptional: east Ulster remained the only part of Ireland in which the Anglo-Irish nobility remained prosperous and maintained their social and political power.[20] However, the persistence of land-questions throughout all of Ireland enabled Irish nationalists, both constitutionalists and militant republicans, to build materially motivated bases of political support.

The post-Famine growth in religiosity, religious revivalism, and church-organizations has been noted. Ireland's religious organs spent the latter half of the nineteenth century in interdenominational battles for control of schools and universities, and competing to outbid one another in illiberal puritanism. Gladstone's disestablishment of the Church of Ireland in 1869 decisively weakened a pillar of the Anglo-Irish nobility, but it could not assuage the competitive hostilities of Irish Catholics and Ulster Protestants. The churches were given effective control over state-subsidized education, and the universities were not left 'godless' as prelates and ministers had feared. Religion and ethnic identity remained fused given the British state's strategic responses to educational development. To be Protestant ensured a British education, to be Catholic guaranteed a more Irish one. The absence of a major secular bloc in the educational modernization of Ireland reinforced the fusion of ethnic and religious identity.

After the Famine Irish nationalist politics veered onto two paths which were continually to fuse and split for the next century. Militant Irish nationalism was organized by the Irish Republican Brotherhood, known as the Fenian Brotherhood in America (and later as *Clan na Gael*). Although the Fenian 'uprisings' of 1865 and 1867 proved ineffective, the organization remained an important subterranean influence in Irish politics on both sides of the Atlantic.[21] The Fenians' half-cocked dynamiting campaign in England was crucial in converting Gladstone to the need to reform Ireland from 1868 onwards. Two major Fenians, John Devoy and Michael Davitt, pioneered a 'new departure' in the 1870s, combining revolutionary conspiracy, agrarian agitation, and co-operation with parliamentary forces. The Land League founded by Davitt in 1878–9, and subsidized by Irish America, proved a far more effective vehicle for agrarian change than the old secret societies, organizing tenants to intimidate landlords, and giving the word 'boycott' to the English language. The Fenians hoped that this social mobilization, 'the Land War', would precede a revolutionary nationalist political mobilization. However, they were prepared to use parliamentary representation, and envisaged building a bloc of MPs which would withdraw from Westminster and establish Irish independence, much as Sinn Féin were to do after the 1918 election.

Parliamentary nationalism by the late 1870s had come under the sway of Charles Stewart Parnell, a Protestant landlord of Irish-American roots, and chairman of the Home Rule Confederation of Great Britain. He attracted popular attention when he championed the Land League and became its President in 1879. In 1874 the Home Rule League, under the leadership of Isaac Butt, had won 59 of Ireland's 105 seats in the Westminster elections, on a very restricted franchise, although in a portent of things to come the League won a mere two seats in historic Ulster, both in Cavan. The 1880 general elections led to many seats being won by radical Land Leaguers and to Parnell's election as the leader of the Irish parliamentary party. In response Gladstone's government passed a Land Act in 1881 which conceded the three 'Fs': 'fair rent' to be decided by arbitration; 'fixity' of tenure while the rent was paid; and 'freedom' for the tenant to sell his right of occupancy to the highest bidder.

In the 1880s Parnell ably exploited the organizational panache of the neo-Fenians and the resources sent to the Irish parliamentary party by Irish America. He turned the Irish party into the first modern, disciplined political party at Westminster, one in which candidates pledged, if elected, 'to sit, act and vote with the Irish Parliamentary Party' and to resign if the party decided they had not fulfilled their pledge. The introduction of the secret ballot in 1872, the ending of the ban on party-demonstrations and the tripling of the franchise under the electoral reform act of 1884 not only dramatically extended popular participation but also made plain the nationalist empathies of the vast majority of the Irish population. In 1885 and 1886 the Irish party, campaigning to win home rule for Ireland, did spectacularly well in the Westminster elections. It won 85 of the 105 Irish seats, including 17 of the 33 Ulster seats (see Table 2.1). Just as importantly Parnell's party held the balance of power at Westminster and could negotiate from advantage with the Liberals and the Conservatives. After complex manœuvres Gladstone's conversion to 'Irish home rule' was announced and a Liberal government formed with Parnell's support.

Gladstone's support for home rule led the Conservatives to accuse him of treason. The Conservatives under Lord Salisbury and Randolph Churchill chose to fight vigorously. Mobilizing English ethnic pride, imperialist ideology, and religious sentiment to resist home rule, Churchill played the 'Orange card', declaring that 'Ulster will fight and Ulster will be right'. Ulster Protestants needed little encouragement. They were already Orange and already fighting. They had backed Conservative candidates in 1885, and thought that home rule would mean the end of their local ascendancy, Rome rule, and economic immiseration. The summer of 1886 saw an upsurge of fierce rioting in Belfast; 86 people died in various affrays between supporters and opponents of home rule.[22] Ulster Protestants had been encouraged 'to press their claims to the uttermost, even if it meant involving the whole of Ireland, and the whole United Kingdom, in a civil war' (Beckett, 1966: 400).

The threat of civil war was averted. Gladstone's conversion to the cause of Irish home rule had split his own party; and a break-away faction of Liberal Unionists helped defeat the first home-rule bill by 343 votes to 313 in the House of Commons. The 1886 bill would have created an Irish executive responsible to an Irish parliament, and abolished Irish representation at Westminster. Parliamentary sovereignty would have remained with Westminster, as would all matters affecting defence, foreign affairs, and the Crown; and the Irish parliament's economic powers would have been rather limited. This modest measure of autonomy, together with a bill to buy out the Anglo-Irish landlords, was accepted by Parnell on pragmatic grounds.

Gladstone's initiative and his government fell with the home-rule bill, and in the ensuing elections the Conservatives, renamed the

Unionists, came back to office, pledged to coerce Ireland through the good offices of Arthur Balfour, thereafter immortalized as 'Bloody Balfour'. Despite the set-back of 1886 the alliance between Irish nationalists and Gladstonian Liberals held, and would continue until World War I; in consequence Irish nationalist resentment refocused upon 'the Tories' rather than 'the English',[23] and home-rulers looked forward to their MPs again holding the balance of power in Westminster. Ulster Protestants by contrast had become embedded components of the Conservative and Unionist movement, delighted to be defended by the Tories as the British loyalists in Ireland.

Although the Irish party had broken the solidity of English resistance to any measure of Irish autonomy, one partially unexpected cost had become starkly visible. Ulster was sharply divided on predictable ethnic and religious lines, and available for party-political competitive football in Great Britain and Ireland. In the three provinces of Leinster, Connaught, and Munster the Irish party would enjoy an almost complete monopoly of parliamentary representation for the next thirty years, the exception being the Trinity College Dublin members elected by Anglo-Irish Protestant graduates. But the results of parliamentary contests in Ulster between 1885 and 1910, all fought on the same restricted male franchise, would show that the home-rule controversy had set the province into segments of nationalist and unionist concrete (see Table 2.1). Antrim, north and mid-Down, north and mid-Armagh, and most of Belfast were solidly Unionist, whereas Cavan, Donegal, south Fermanagh, south Armagh, south Down, and Monaghan were solidly nationalist. Londonderry city, and the county-seats of Londonderry, Fermanagh North, and Tyrone were more evenly balanced constituencies and occasionally swung. There were precious few 'floating voters' in Ulster, just two fundamentally antagonistic ethnic communities advertising their rival colours of orange and green.

The Irish nationalist–Liberal alliance survived the scandal and controversies which accompanied the fall of Parnell,[24] and in 1892 the Irish party once more held the balance of power at Westminster. A second home-rule bill was introduced by Gladstone in February 1893, and provided for continuing but reduced Irish representation at Westminster, a measure designed to placate Unionists. The bitterly contested bill passed through the House of Commons only to be immediately overturned by the House of Lords. Gladstone resigned soon afterwards, and the Unionists returned to executive power in

Table 2.1 Seats won by parties in parliamentary constituencies in Ulster, 1885–1910

Source: calculated from Walker ed. (1978: 130–81).

safe unionist seats	1885	1886	1892	1895	1900	1906	1910i	1910ii
Antrim (n)	C	U	U	U	U	Ind U	U	U
Antrim (m)	C	U	U	U	U	U	U	U
Antrim (e)	C	U	U	U	U	U	U	U
Antrim (s)	C	U	U	U	U	U	U	U
Armagh (n)	C	U	U	U	U	U	U	U
Armagh (m)	C	U	U	U	U	U	U	U
Belfast (e)	Ind C	U	U	U	U	U	U	U
Belfast (s)	Ind C	U	U	U	U	Ind U	U	U
Belfast (n)	C	U	U	U	U	U	U	U
Down (n)	C	U	U	U	U	U	U	U
Down (e)	C	U	U	U	U	U	U	U
Down (w)	C	U	U	U	U	U	U	U
Londonderry County (n)	C	U	U	U	U	U	U	U
safe nationalist seats								
Armagh (s)	N	N	N*	N*	Ind N	N	N	N
Cavan (w)	N	N	N*	N*	N	N	N	N
Cavan (e)	N	N	N*	N*	N	N	N	N
Donegal (n)	N	N	N*	N*	N	N	N	N
Donegal (w)	N	N	N*	N*	N	N	N	N
Donegal (s)	N	N	N*	N*	N	N	N	N
Donegal (e)	N	N	N*	N*	N	N	N	N
Down (s)	N	N	N*	N*	N	N	N	N
Fermanagh (s)	N	N	N*	N*	N	N	N	N
Monaghan (n)	N	N	N*	N*	N	N	N	N
Monaghan (s)	N	N	N*	N*	N	N	N	Ind N
Newry	N	N	N*	N*	N	N	N	N
Tyrone (e)	N	N	N*	N*	N	N	N	N
'swing seats'								
Belfast (w)	C	N	LU	LU	LU	N	N	N
Fermanagh (n)	N	N	U	U	U	U	U	U
Londonderry City	C	N	U	N*	U	U	U	U
Londonderry County (s)	N	LU	LU	LU	LU	LU	U	U
Tyrone (n)	C	U	U	L	L	L	L	L
Tyrone (m)	N	N	N*	N*	N	N	U	N
Tyrone (s)	N	LU	LU	LU	LU	U	U	U

Key. C = Conservative; Ind C = Independent Conservative; L = Liberal; LU = Liberal Unionist; N =Nationalist; N* = anti-Parnell Nationalist; and Ind N = Independent Nationalist. Unionists were Conservatives, Unionists and Liberal Unionists who opposed home rule; and Nationalists were Nationalists, anti-Parnellite Nationalists and Liberals who supported 'home rule'. There were two elections in 1910.

1895, and were to remain in government for a decade. Resistance to home rule in Ulster in 1886 had been ill-disciplined; in 1892–3 it took a more menacingly organized form. Edward Saunderson, the leader of the Irish Unionists, set up an Ulster Defence Union in 1893 and was in the preliminary stages of organizing an Ulster Protestant army when the second home-rule bill was vetoed by the Lords. 'Ulster' meaning 'Protestant Ulster' was evidently serious about fighting to prevent home rule; at this stage for all of Ireland, but most of all for Ulster.

The defeat of the second home-rule bill temporarily dissuaded Orangemen and Ulster unionists from militant activity, but it had the effect of persuading large numbers of young Irish nationalists that constitutionalism stood little chance of success. The cultural nationalism of the Gaelic League and the GAA spawned personnel and organizations outside the grip of the Irish party. The IRB/Fenians reorganized, Arthur Griffith established Sinn Féin ('Ourselves') as a political party which recommended parliamentary abstentionism, and small revolutionary syndicalist, socialist and feminist movements developed in Dublin in the 1890s and at the turn of the century. The Irish party, while still dominating the Irish electoral arena, no longer commanded the same enthusiasm or generated the same conviction. The Conservative government of 1895–1905 sought to exploit what they saw as an opportunity 'to kill home rule by kindness', and embarked upon a series of administrative and legal changes which aimed to ameliorate and redress economic grievances. The culmination of these efforts was the Wyndham Act of 1903 which enabled most Irish tenants to buy the land they farmed; and bought out the Anglo-Irish aristocracy at generous rates to be paid for by annuities collected from the peasants. The Act eventually made the Irish peasants conservatives, as intended, but it did not make them into British or English conservatives. They remained nationalists.

The Unionist government which sought to kill home rule through constructive kindness eventually imploded over the issue of protectionism, and was crushed in the Liberal landslide of 1906. But the landslide was so extensive that the Liberals did not need the Irish alliance or to put home rule before the Westminster parliament. Instead Campbell-Bannerman introduced very modest devolution proposals for Ireland. However, when the Liberals, under the leadership of Asquith (who replaced Campbell-Bannerman after the latter's death in 1908) and Lloyd George, ran into conflict with the House of Lords, they needed to revive the Irish alliance; and before the first 1910 election John Redmond, the leader of the Irish party, extracted a promise that home rule would be in the Liberals' election manifesto. The Liberals defeated the Unionists but lost their overall majority in the two elections of 1910. For the last time the Irish party held the balance of power in UK politics, and a home rule bill looked legislatively feasible. The power of the Lords was broken by the Liberals, supported by the Irish party, during 1911. The Lords' veto (which had destroyed the 1893 bill) could last no more than two years after the second reading of the home rule bill in the Commons, if it passed through the Commons three times.

Asquith formed a new government in January 1911, and his Cabinet began to draft the third home-rule bill. In September the Ulster Unionist Council, formed as early as 1905 to resist home rule, announced it was preparing to establish a provisional government.[25] The leader of the UUC, Sir Edward Carson, maintained that if home-rule were to reach the statute book, unionists should ignore it, and set up a provincial government loyal to the Crown. Carson wished to use 'Ulster's' resistance to home rule to prevent home rule for all of Ireland. The UUC, unlike Carson, were not bluffing, and established a constitutional commission to develop contingency plans. In November 1911 the hands of the UUC were strengthened when Bonar Law, a Scots-Canadian of Ulster Presbyterian stock, replaced Balfour as the leader of the Conservative and Unionist Party at Westminster. In April 1912 Bonar Law told a semi-military demonstration in Belfast that the cause of Ulster was 'the cause of the empire'. By the summer he had declared 'I can imagine *no* length of resistance to which Ulster will go which I shall not be ready to support', and that the Tories regarded 'the Liberal Government as a revolutionary committee which has seized by fraud upon despotic power. In our opposition . . . we shall not be restrained by the bonds which would influence us in an ordinary political struggle. We shall use any means – whatever means seem to us likely to be the most effective.'

In January 1912 Ulster unionists openly raised and trained a military force of thousands of Protestants, soon to be named the Ulster Volunteer Force (UVF), although they stayed within the letter of the law by obtaining the permission of sympathetic magistrates. With the developing threat of a counter-revolutionary coup the home-rule bill was introduced into the Commons in April. It proposed a heavily circumscribed autonomy for an all-Ireland parliament. The supreme sovereignty of Westminster 'over all persons, matters and things in Ireland' would be retained, and control of the police force would not go overnight to the Irish executive. The bill nevertheless had a stormy passage. In June 1912 a proposal, made by Agar Robartes MP, to exclude Antrim, Down, Londonderry, and Armagh from the bill was opposed by the government. However, the amendment suggested that leading Liberals were looking to draw the teeth of Conservative resistance by considering separate treatment for Ulster.[26] In September the UUC published 'Ulster's Solemn League and Covenant'[27] which on 'Ulster Day' (28 September 1912) received 218,206 male signatures.[28] In December the UUC demanded the exclusion of all of Ulster from the home-rule bill, and Carson proposed an amendment to that effect in January 1913. For Carson it was a wrecking amendment; but for James Craig, the leading Ulster unionist, it was a serious but problematic proposal. In all of Ulster, unionists at best were in a precarious majority. The rhetoric of 'Protestant Ulster' could not disguise that Catholics formed nearly half of the population of the province, the overwhelming majority in the three counties of Cavan, Donegal, and Monaghan, and small but clear majorities in Fermanagh and Tyrone (see Figure 2.5). If the UUC bargained for the exclusion of Ulster's nine counties then they were unlikely to be able to keep it out of Nationalist control, but if they surrendered parts of Ulster to control the rest, they would betray their covenant with their brethren.

The home-rule bill completed its route through the Commons in January 1913, only to be rejected by the Lords two weeks later. The bill was then carried through the Commons again, to be vetoed yet again by the Lords in July 1913. If maintained in its original form, it would become law in the summer of 1914. Political antagonisms were rising to fever pitch. In July 1913 Lieutenant-General Richardson was appointed GOC of the UVF; and in September the UUC turned itself into a provisional government ready to take over the administration of the province after the passage of the home-rule bill. The example of the UVF prompted the IRB to consider how they could match it with an Irish force, and by the end of the year they were part of a broad front of the Ancient Order of Hibernians,[30] and GAA and Gaelic League activists, establishing the Irish Volunteers. The Volunteer

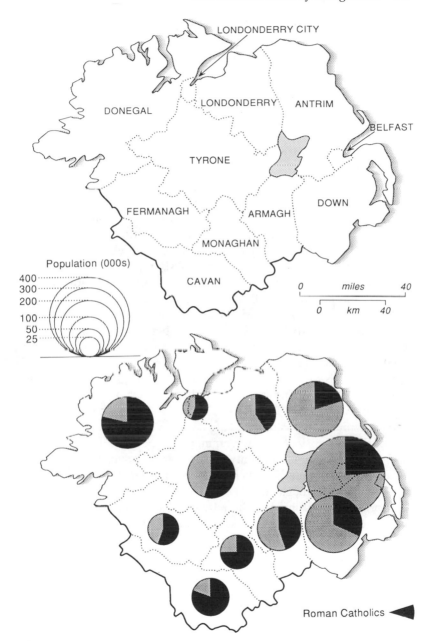

Figure 2.5 Catholics in Ulster, 1911   Source: 1911 Census of Ireland

movement was so successful in enrolling young nationalist men that Redmond was forced to put the Irish party in nominal control of them in the spring of 1914; although the IRB leadership remained within the Volunteers' governing body, and well organized.[31]

In October 1913 Asquith invited 'an interchange of views' between the parties to establish an agreement. Redmond welcomed any settlement consistent with national self-government for all of Ireland which was accomplished by consent. In February 1914 Lloyd George suggested that a 'county-option' clause be added to the bill – any Ulster county could vote itself out of home rule for five years. Redmond agreed to a three-year county-option, winning the agreement of Ulster's nationalist MPs in March 1914, but earning himself the undying suspicion of more militant nationalists. Asquith suggested six years, to permit a general election in the interval. Carson damned the 'county-option' amendment when it was raised in the House of Commons, contemptuously rejecting a 'sentence of death with a stay of execution for six years'. The Liberal government pressed ahead with the bill, Asquith apparently believing he could call the Tories' bluff. In March orders were given to strengthen the position of Crown forces in Ulster, but the 'Curragh mutiny' by officers unwilling to coerce Ulster damaged the government's confidence. In April the UVF landed 25,000 German rifles and 3 million rounds of ammunition at Larne and Donaghadee; in July the Irish Volunteers reciprocated by landing a much smaller supply of German arms at Howth, although Crown troops tried to intervene and killed civilian demonstrators.

On 23 June 1914 the government's amending bill to permit temporary exclusion by county-option was introduced in the Lords. Five days later Franz Ferdinand was assassinated at Sarajevo and the European powers began the descent into the Great War.[32] The House of Lords, with its in-built Unionist majority, altered the amending bill, and demanded the exclusion of all of Ulster. On 12 July the UUC declared itself the provisional government of Ulster, prompting King George V to summon a 'Buckingham Palace Conference'. The conference was preceded by secret negotiations in which Unionist leaders indicated willingness to hive off many, but not all, of the areas of Ulster with nationalist majorities; with Carson at one stage appearing to contemplate a five-county unit (Antrim, Armagh, Down, Derry/Londonderry, and Tyrone) to be excluded from the home-rule parliament (Gwynn, 1950: 102–31). Redmond and his colleagues, by contrast, indicated willingness to see four counties (including Belfast borough) temporarily excluded. They refused to consider exclusion for Tyrone, which had three home-rule MPs as opposed to one Unionist MP. The minimum price for a compromise for Carson, Bonar Law, and Craig became the exclusion of the six so-called 'plantation counties' from home rule, the ones which eventually became Northern Ireland. They wanted these six counties to vote as a bloc on exclusion, and to be administered through 'ordinary' local government under the imperial parliament. The Conference was deadlocked.

The onset of war between the UK and the Central Powers in August 1914 prevented the Ulster crisis from immediate resolution through negotiation or civil war.[33] The party political élites agreed to postpone the crisis: the home-rule bill passed into law in September, but was made subject to a new suspensory act, delaying its operation until after the war (the amending bill with the county-exclusion bill was dropped). Both Irish nationalists and Ulster Unionists voted to support the UK's war effort, each side 'establishing a claim on the gratitude of Great Britain' (Beckett, 1966: 435), and the respective volunteers went off to die in droves on the battlefields of France: the UVF men butchering and being butchered for 'the empire', while the Irish National Volunteers slaughtered and were slaughtered for the 'rights of small nations'. At the outset of the war the UVF received much the better deal for their 'loyalty', being able to nominate their own officers, an offer refused to Redmond's Volunteers. In disgust with Redmond, over 10,000 Irish Volunteers under Eoin MacNeill split from the renamed National Volunteers whose 150,000 men remained loyal to Redmond. However, hostility to the traditional enemy, the belief that 'England's danger was Ireland's opportunity', and fear of conscription as the war dragged on combined to swell the ranks of the anti-war movement and slowly turn Irish nationalist public opinion in favour of militant separatism.

The extension of the parliamentary suffrage and democratization had crystallized the linked and twin obstacles to successful British state-penetration and standardization in Ireland: the Anglo-Irish oligarchy and the consequences of the long-established Ulster colony. The former obstacle proved manageable: the oligarchy's political power, established church and its lands were taken from them by both Liberal and Conservative administrations, albeit under the threat of mass-mobilizations. Ulster proved much less tractable.

Nationalist and unionist electoral mobilization had merely been the historical prelude to a thoroughgoing paramilitary mobilization of the rival ethnic communities. The Ulster question had provoked a hornet's nest, bringing the UK to the verge of civil war and a Tory-backed military *coup d'état*, averted only by the Great War.

The Great War and partition

Northern Ireland materialized because of the partition of Ireland after the Great War. The partition of Ireland had been foreshadowed in the three home-rule crises. However, the supposition of nearly all pre-war partition schemes had been that partition would either be temporary, pending all-Ireland unity (the nationalist assumption), or would prevent home rule altogether, by making an Irish parliament unviable (the unionist hope). It was also supposed that the sections of Ulster which remained outside the jurisdiction of the Irish parliament would come under the direct government of Westminster and Whitehall. The post-war 'settlement' of Ireland differed from pre-war expectations in three key ways: a new independent Irish Free State was created which had dominion status, i.e. far more extensive autonomy than had been envisaged for Ireland in the third home-rule bill; the partition-arrangements proved more permanent than anyone envisaged; and finally the British government created a home-rule parliament in Belfast which became the capital of a devolved government in 'Northern Ireland'.

The reason home rule for all of Ireland was not enough to satisfy Irish nationalists after the Great War is explicable through the oft-told tales of the Easter Rising, the rise of Sinn Féin, and the triumph of separatist nationalism (see *inter alia* Beckett 1966: 435–61; Dudley Edwards 1977; Foster 1988: 461–515; Garvin 1981; Laffan 1983; Lee 1989: 1–55; Lyons 1973: 315–470; and Williams 1966). The bare bones are all we can relate. The UVF's unparliamentary resistance to home rule, and the postponement of home rule with the onset of the European war, prompted the IRB to organize an insurrection in Ireland. The Easter Rising of 1916 was bloodier and more wide-ranging than any nineteenth-century rebellion, but was nevertheless rapidly crushed because the entirety of the Volunteers and the Irish Citizens Army failed to be mobilized, the rising was mainly confined to Dublin, and the underground conspiratorial élite, unsurprisingly, had not prepared public opinion. The execution of the leaders of the Rising, together with the threat of war-time conscription, nevertheless decisively shifted nationalist opinion. Sinn Féin merged with the IRB as a broad-front separatist party in 1917 and began to make headway in by-elections against the Irish parliamentary party. Sinn Féin's advance was aided by a major negotiating blunder by Redmond. After the Easter Rising Asquith directed Lloyd George to arbitrate between unionists and nationalists. Redmond agreed with Lloyd George that in return for immediate home rule for the rest of Ireland, then at least for the duration of the war Fermanagh and Tyrone should be added to 'statutory Ulster', and a post-war imperial conference would then settle the province's future. This potential compromise was wrecked by Conservatives in the wartime coalition Cabinet. Home rule was not implemented in any form; a democratic reformist route to Irish autonomy was blocked; and the prestige of Redmond and the Irish party stood in tatters. The Irish party had offered to sacrifice Fermanagh and Tyrone but had failed to win home rule. The failure of cross-party talks at an Irish Convention, which sat between July 1917 and April 1918, further destroyed the Irish party's standing, and it went down to a crushing defeat at the hands of Sinn Féin in the December 1918 Westminster election, the first conducted under universal male franchise.

Sinn Féin won 25 seats unopposed, and a total of 73 of Ireland's 105 seats (see Table 2.2). It won 47.6 per cent of the popular vote in all the contested seats (its share of the total vote artificially reduced by the large number of uncontested seats); and 65.5 per cent of the popular vote in the twenty-six counties which eventually became the Irish Free State. The Irish parliamentary party won a mere 6 seats, although it polled a respectable 21.6 per cent of the vote in contested seats. Unionists won 23 seats (1 in Dublin county, 3 in the Universities, and the rest in the six counties of the north-east), while Labour Unionists took 3 seats in Belfast. All nationalist candidates won over 69.2 per cent of the popular vote in contested seats in Ireland, but in the six counties of the north-east unionists won almost the same percentage of the popular vote (69 per cent) as nationalists did throughout Ireland (although the nationalist share of the vote was deflated by the high number of uncontested seats won by Sinn Féin). The new Sinn Féin MPs refused to take their seats at Westminster, set up an Irish parliament, Dáil Éireann, and began to construct a parallel independent republican administration to that of Dublin Castle. The British authorities decided to coerce Ireland, prompting republican militants to organize a guerrilla war.

The 1918 election returned Lloyd George to the British premiership, but at the head of a coalition in which the Conservatives and Unionists were dominant. The election considerably strengthened the parliamentary bargaining position of the Ulster Unionists by comparison with the years preceding 1914, especially because Sinn Féin MPs boycotted Westminster. The new constituency boundaries in 1918, which were fairer to industrialized areas, also meant that the Unionists (and Labour Unionists) regained the majority of seats in Ulster, which they had lost in 1913. They found it easier to negotiate for the permanent exclusion of the six counties of north-east Ulster from any pending independence for Ireland, even though Sinn Féin or nationalist candidates had won the Londonderry city seat, two of the three seats in Tyrone, and the seats in Fermanagh South, Down South, Armagh South and the Falls constituency of Belfast. In the six counties which became Northern Ireland the nationalist minority took the same share of the vote as the unionist minority in all of Ireland, but this fact did not figure in unionist arguments.

From October 1919 until late 1920 a British Cabinet committee, chaired by an Irish Unionist, Walter Long, drafted a fourth home-rule bill, which eventually became the Government of Ireland Act of 1920 (known by Irish nationalists as the 'Partition Act'). The committee ruled out county-plebiscites, which would have undermined the Unionists' case for the exclusion of all of Ulster or all the six counties of the north-east. However, no plebiscites meant that any settlement of Ireland would violate the doctrine of self-determination which was officially being supported by President Wilson, the Versailles conference, and the victors over the Central Powers. The solution the Cabinet committee invented was certainly imaginative, even if it became the source of 'a factory of grievances' (Buckland, 1979). It decided to create two home-rule parliaments, one to be established in Belfast, as the capital of a six-county Northern Ireland, and the other in Dublin, as the capital of a twenty-six county Southern Ireland. All the Irish were to receive self-government and the two parliaments were to be free to achieve Irish unity on an agreed basis.

Ulster Unionists, now increasingly led by Craig rather than Carson, had not sought home rule for any part of Ireland, but they

Table 2.2 The Westminster election in Ireland, 1918

(a) all of Ireland
(includes four university seats)

Party	Seats won	(%)	Seats won unopposed	Votes won (%) in contested seats*
Sinn Féin	73	(69.5)	25	47.6
Irish Parliam'ary Party ¶	6	(5.7)	0	21.6
All Nationalists	79	(75.2)	25	69.2
Unionists #	23	(21.9)	0	25.7
Labour Unionists	3	(2.9)	0	2.9
LRC	0	(0.0)	0	1.2
All Unionists	26	(24.8)	0	29.8

(b) the twenty-six counties which became the Irish Free State
(includes three university members)

Party	Seats won	(%)	Seats won unopposed	Votes won (%) in contested seats*
Sinn Féin	70	(93.3)	25	65.5
Irish Parliam'ary Party ¶	2	(2.66)	0	29.0
All Nationalists	72	(95)	25	94.5
Unionists #	3	(2.85)	0	5.5

(c) the nine counties of historic Ulster
(includes Queen's University seat)

Party	Seats won	(%)	Seats won unopposed	Votes won (%) in contested seats*
Sinn Féin	10	(26.3)	2	23.5
Irish Parliam'ary Party ¶	5	(13.2)	0	15.7
All Nationalists	15	(39.5)	2	39.2
Unionists #	20	(52.6)	0	51.6
Labour Unionists	3	(7.9)	0	6.5
LRC	0	(0.0)	0	2.6
All Unionists	23	(60.5)	0	60.7

(d) the six counties which became Northern Ireland
(includes Queen's University seat)

Party	Seats won	(%)	Seats won unopposed	Votes won (%) in contested seats*
Sinn Féin	3	(10)	0	19.1
Irish Parliam'ary Party ¶	4	(13.3)	0	11.8
All Nationalists	7	(23.3)	0	30.9
Unionists #	20	(66.6)	0	58.3
Labour Unionists	3	(10)	0	7.6
LRC	0	(0)	0	3.1
All Unionists	23	(76.6)	0	69

Source: calculated from Walker (1978: 185–91).

* The votes for the four university seats, three of which were won by Unionists and one by Sinn Féin, have not been counted in calculating votes won in contested seats.

¶ Nationalists include Independent Nationalists.

Unionists include Independent Unionists.

Notes.

(i) Walker's text has Sinn Féin winning Limerick city unopposed with 17,121 votes polled, but shows the electorate of Limerick city as 17,121. Clearly this entry is erroneous. Our tables treat Limerick as an unopposed return. (ii) The high number of uncontested seats won by Sinn Féin underrepresents voting support for nationalist candidates throughout all of Ireland. (iii) All seats in what became Northern Ireland were contested, showing a 69:31 division between all unionists and all nationalists. (iv) In historic Ulster Sinn Féin won two uncontested seats in Cavan. Thus support for nationalists in all of Ulster is underrepresented in the column showing per cent of votes won in contested seats.

quickly saw the advantages of a Belfast parliament.[34] They were prepared to accept the 'supreme sacrifice' of home rule, especially because it was being sold by the British government as the first part of a package of home rule throughout the British Isles, a package which never materialized (Murphy, 1986). Home rule in Northern Ireland would provide Unionists with an effective bulwark against the untrustworthy intentions of London governments and the claims of Irish republicans. Unionists lobbied hard to ensure that the Belfast parliament would govern the six counties of the north-east rather than the nine of historic Ulster; and to appear reasonable Craig proposed a boundary commission to consider minor modifications at the edges of the six counties. The Cabinet eventually backed Craig and Westminster enacted the Government of Ireland Act. The Unionists had succeeded in winning as much territory as possible without endangering their long-term security. In the nine counties of historic Ulster Protestants precariously outnumbered Catholics (56 : 44), but without Cavan, Donegal and Monaghan the religious ratio altered dramatically in favour of Protestants (65.5 : 34.5). The Unionists got what they wanted: 'those districts which they could control' (Miller, 1978: 122 ff). Sir James Craig, the first Prime Minister of Northern Ireland after elections were held there in 1921, envisaged the six counties as a new 'impregnable Pale', a rampart behind which the descendants of British settlers in Ireland could defend civilization. Despite his earlier willingness to consider a boundary commission he declared the six counties (almost) non-negotiable: 'I will never give in to any rearrangement of the boundary that leaves our Ulster area less than it is under the Government of Ireland Act' (McArdle, 1951: 658).[35]

The territorial definition of Northern Ireland guaranteed an in-built Protestant/unionist majority, providing Catholic/nationalist population-growth did not dramatically exceed that of Protestants. The partition was dramatically imperfect on national, ethnic, or religious grounds. The Catholic, and largely Irish nationalist, population not only composed over a third of the entire population, but was also a local majority in two of the six counties (Fermanagh and Tyrone), the second city of the territory (Derry/Londonderry), and in almost all of the local government jurisdictions contiguous with the new border.

The designers of the Government of Ireland Act, especially Lloyd George, were aware of the imperfections of the partition they imposed, especially the injustice of incorporating all of Fermanagh and Tyrone into Northern Ireland. None the less they sought to obtain recognition for the Government of Ireland Act with nationalist Ireland. They failed. The Irish fought for more autonomy. The war of independence, fought bitterly between 1919 and 1921 by IRB/IRA volunteers against Crown forces, eventually brought the British government and Sinn Féin representatives to the negotiating table. In the Anglo-Irish Treaty of December 1921 the British conceded Irish independence for the twenty-six counties, granting Ireland dominion status under the Crown, but maintained almost the entirety of the settlement already implemented in Northern Ireland under the Government of Ireland Act. Lloyd George's team of negotiators reassured the Sinn Féin negotiators in four ways: by emphasizing that the Treaty would allow Northern Ireland to join the Irish Free State, if it wished; by permitting an all-Ireland Council of Ireland which would enable the two parliaments to co-operate even if there was to be no immediate Irish unity; by promising a boundary commission to adjust the border between Northern Ireland and the Irish Free State; and with the thought that the presence of a large minority would make Northern Ireland both unworkable and illegitimate. The British negotiators, especially Lloyd George, were less than sincere, and the Irish negotiators were not fully awake, especially to the weakness of the clauses governing the proposed boundary commission.[36] Northern Ireland had been established.

Conclusion

This résumé of the historic roots of antagonism in Northern Ireland has emphasized settler colonialism and the crises of political development which accompanied the democratic modernization of the British Isles. The failure of British state-building in Ireland owed most to the failure to build a British national identity which would have enabled the descendants of Catholic natives and Protestant settlers to transcend their differences, either under a home-rule parliament or under the Westminster parliament. Democratization prompted profound crises of participation in the late nineteenth and early twentieth century, and the descendants of the Ulster settlers were the biggest obstacles to the resolution of these crises in the British Isles. Northern Ireland was and is a legacy of settler colonialism. When the Ulster colony was secured in the seventeenth century, Ireland itself was thoroughly conquered: its native élites were displaced, many of its natives transplanted, and its lands subjected to alien landlords. The exclusivist religions of landlords and settlers preserved colonial caste structures long after the initial colonization. State-sponsored religious persecution, ensuing for two centuries after the conquest, reinforced ethnic segmentation despite other homogenizing pressures which might have promoted assimilation.

In emphasizing the colonial roots of the present antagonism we have not embraced crude nationalist myths. The inhabitants of Ireland, *pace* Irish nationalists, have not shared one singular ethnic or national identity for over a millennium. Ireland, *pace* Irish nationalists, had no modern or medieval history of political unity. The *peoples* of Ireland have only been unified under one state as part of another state, i.e. under the Act of Union. But other nationalist myths have a very high quotient of truth. Ireland was a colony (McCaffrey, 1979); and so was Ulster. Before the Great War there had never been an era of Irish history in which a legitimate regime prevailed throughout the island. The natives formally remained inferior subjects until 1829. It was not until the 1880s (or 1903) that the land-conquest was reversed, and the Irish agrarian economy managed for the benefit of those who worked it. The 'centuries of foreign oppression' thesis advanced by Irish nationalists and socialists, for all its emotive colouration, is not without validity.

Notes

1. There had been an earlier plantation in Ulster. The Norman baron John de Courcy conquered the principality of East Ulster in the last quarter of the twelfth century, establishing Carrickfergus Castle on the south Antrim coast, and his successor, Hugh de Lacey, exercised hegemony in the area of Strangford Lough. The power of the old Anglo-Norman colony was destroyed in the invasions of Edward Bruce (1314–18), the brother of Robert, the king of Scotland. In the 1570s another precursor of the plantation of Ulster failed when it proved impossible to attract sufficient Scots and English settlers (Beckett, 1966: 21).

2. The Latin word *merus* means 'pure, unmixed, undiluted'. The native Irish were known by the English as the 'mere Irish'.

3. Crown officials differed over how the Gaelic Irish should be treated: Sir

Arthur Chichester favoured some recognition of their position whereas Sir John Davies advocated their eradication.

4. The first Presbyterian ministers in Ulster held posts within the established Church of Ireland even though they were opponents of 'episcopacy', i.e. church-government by bishops. They consequently became victims of Anglican persecution, and some responded by emigrating again, to America. They were the ancestors of the 'Scotch-Irish' of North America.

5. See Note 1.

6. The differences in material culture between Planters and Gaels were not as great as is frequently suggested; cultural (non-material) markers sustained ethnic boundaries (Buchanan, 1982: 49–74).

7. Wall's comparison is legitimate because Ireland remained a separate kingdom with a separate parliament until the Act of Union of 1801. Thereafter Catholics were a minority within the UK.

8. The myth of Britain's (especially England's) peaceful and evolutionary political development runs deep. On the bicentenery of the French Revolution Margaret Thatcher preached in Paris on the theme of peaceful English evolution (compared to violent French revolution). Better-educated people contrasted England's muted tercentenery celebrations of the 'peaceful' Glorious Revolution with the plans of Orangemen and women in Northern Ireland to celebrate the tercentenery of the far from peaceful Battle of the Boyne.

9. Historians debate the question of whether the 1641 uprising was planned by native clans, provoked by the new English to discredit the native Irish, or planned by clan leaders in collusion with Charles I (intent on subordinating the Scots to Anglicanism), or a permutation of all three intrigues (Fitzpatrick, 1988).

10. Jonathan Swift noted 'The Catholics of Ireland . . . lost their estates for fighting in defence of their king. Those who cut off the father's head, forced the son to fly for his life, and overturned the whole ancient frame of government . . . obtained grants of those very estates the Catholics lost in defence of the ancient constitution and thus they gained by their rebellion what the Catholics lost by their loyalty' (cited in Simms, 1966: 205–6).

11. The settlement imposed by the new English in the Irish parliament was not that negotiated at Limerick by William.

12. The last Catholic Relief Act went through the Westminster parliament in 1926, five years after the formation of the Irish Free State! (Machin, 1987: 330). At least one penal law remains: a British monarch cannot be a Roman Catholic.

13. If the son converted to the Church of Ireland during his father's lifetime, his father became a life-tenant and could not dispose of his property.

14. In 1719 the Irish parliament passed an ordinance requiring Catholic priests to be branded with a red-hot iron if they failed to register. The Irish Privy Council proposed castration as a suitable punishment: 'the most effectual

remedy . . . to clear this nation of the disturbers of the peace and quiet of the kingdom'. Their proposal was rejected by the British House of Lords (Burke, 1969: 200–1). The Irish Privy Council evidently did not believe that celibacy-vows inhibited the breeding-propensities of Papist priests.

15. Tone memorably refuted the thesis that Catholics were ignorant and therefore incapable of liberty: 'I have heard men . . . make a flourishing declamation on the danger of blinding them, by suddenly pouring a flood of light on their eyes, which, for a century, have been buried in darkness. To the poetry of this I make no objection, but what is the common sense or justice of the argument? We plunge them by law, and continue them by statute, in gross ignorance, and then we make the incapacity we have created an argument for their exclusion from the common rights of man! We plead our crime in justification of itself.' (*An Argument on Behalf of the Catholics of Ireland*, in Cronin and Roche, 1973: 113–4).

16. O'Connell's success owed more to his organizational ability to 'manage' the violent activities of proto-nationalist secret societies than is usually acknowledged (B. O'Duffy, Violence in Ireland and Northern Ireland: ch. 3, PhD in progress, University of London).

17. 'Castle Catholic' was the derogatory epithet applied by Irish nationalists to collaborators who worked with Dublin Castle, the centre of British administration in Ireland.

18. Between 1801 and 1902 there were 35 lord-lieutenants, and between 1801 and 1900 there were 51 chief secretaries (calculated from Pickrill, 1981: 127–8).

19. Though found elsewhere in Ireland this custom was mainly Ulster-based. It recognized the tenant's saleable interest in his landholdings (making investment in improvements worthwhile). The more feudal pattern of land-relations in the rest of Ireland inhibited peasant productivity.

20. The 'solvency of Ulster's large landlords and the strength of the sectarian context in which they operated provide some explanations as to why Unionism proved an irresistible force in Ulster' (Curtis, 1980: 367).

21. The Fenians revised their constitution in 1873, limiting themselves 'in time of peace' to moral support for 'every movement calculated to advance the cause of Irish independence'. War was to be declared only through 'the decision of the Irish nation, as expressed by a majority of the Irish people'.

22. The riots were sparked when 'one Patrick Murphy, a Catholic dock labourer, revealed to a Protestant colleague a vision of home rule culminating in a one hundred per cent Orange unemployment rate' (Lee, 1973: 133).

23. Opposition to Irish home rule in 1886 was distinctively English. Three-fifths of the Scottish members and five-sixths of the Welsh supported Gladstone (Beckett, 1966: 398).

24. Parnell's affair with Kitty O'Shea became public when her husband sued for divorce and named Parnell as co-respondent. The Irish parliamentary

party initially remained loyal to Parnell. However, non-conformist Liberals demanded that Gladstone end the alliance with the Irish party if Parnell remained its leader. Gladstone then requested Parnell's head as the price of the alliance. The Irish party split, but the majority sensibly put the Liberal alliance and the prospect of home rule before their leader's pride. Parnell's vanity knew no bounds, and he divided his party before his death in 1891, a split which lasted until the early twentieth century.

25. The UUC co-operated with the all-Ireland Irish Unionist Alliance, centred in Dublin, but it presaged the emerging separation of interests between Ulster and Irish unionists, masked by the appointment of Sir Edward Carson, a Dublin lawyer and MP for Trinity College, as the leader of the UUC in 1910.

26. In August 1912 Churchill privately warned Redmond that he would propose 'a moratorium of several years for the characteristically Protestant and Orange counties' (Gwynn, 1950: 238).

27. The key passages in the Covenant can be found in Stewart (1967: 62).

28. A total of 228,991 women signed a similar 'Declaration'; and 19,162 men and 5,055 women elsewhere in Great Britain and Ireland signed the Covenant or the Declaration (Stewart, 1967: 66). The 'Covenant' was a deliberate echo of the Scottish Presbyterian covenant of 1580 (Beckett, 1966: 428). 'Banding' and 'covenanting' against home rule self-consciously drew upon the settlers' descendants ethnic heritage (D. Miller, 1978).

29. In January 1913 the Nationalists won a by-election in Londonderry city. Thus as the third home-rule bill progressed 17 of Ulster's 33 constituencies were held by supporters of home rule.

30. The Ancient Order of Hibernians (AOH[G]) was the Irish Catholic equivalent of the Orange Order.

31. The Volunteers drew on another example of paramilitarization. In response to a syndicalist strike, organized by the Irish Transport Workers' Union in Dublin in 1913, the employers organized a lock-out and relied on the police to break the strike. Some of the strikers retaliated by setting up the Irish Citizen Army as their defence force, although it was plainly a revolutionary socialist cadre. The strike had been defeated by early 1914 but the small Irish Citizen Army remained in being.

32. It is easy to imagine how the Continental powers regarded the preparedness of the UK for war in the summer of 1914. Sir Henry Wilson, director of military operations at the War Office, *and* the chief liaison officer between the army and the UUC, had some explaining to do with his French allies.

33. Laffan (1983: 48) maintains that the war saved Carson and the Tories from having their bluff called: 'if Carson had led a rebellion in August or September 1914 his aim would not have been to exclude Antrim, Down, Derry and Armagh, for their exclusion had already been conceded. It would have been to impose exclusion on Fermanagh, Tyrone and Derry City where home rule was desired by small but clear majorities.'

34. Carson pointed out that 'you cannot knock Parliaments up and down as you do a ball, and once you have planted them there, you cannot get rid of them' (Laffan, 1983: 64).
35. Craig chose 'Not an inch!' as his election slogan for the Northern Ireland parliamentary elections of 1925 (Younger, 1972: 212), an expression which still epitomizes the philosophy of unionist die-hards.
36. Michael Collins, unlike Arthur Griffith, thought that a plebiscite was preferable to a boundary commission (Laffan, 1983: 83).

3
Exercising control: the second Protestant ascendancy, 1920–62

In the twentieth century as in the seventeenth God was a protestant.

(Michael Laffan, 1983: 123)

I am an Orangeman first and a politician . . . afterwards . . . In the South they boasted of a Catholic State. They still boast of Southern Ireland being a Catholic State. All I boast of is that we are a Protestant Parliament and a Protestant State. It would be rather interesting for historians of the future to compare a Catholic State launched in the South with a Protestant State launched in the North and see which one gets on the better and prospers the more.

(Lord Craigavon, Prime Minister of Northern Ireland, 1934)

Northern Ireland is the paradigm case of state- and nation-building failure in western Europe. Neither a nation nor a full state, its creation in 1920 was the joint by-product of British and Irish state- and nation-building failures. It marked the territorial line of retreat of the British state in Ireland, and was testament to the failure to build a British identity which would have enabled the descendants of Catholic natives and Protestant settlers to transcend their differences. It was also proof of an Irish failure: nationalists lacked the coercive and ideological resources to achieve a popularly supported revolution throughout the whole island between 1916 and 1925. Their inability to coerce or persuade Protestant Ulster owed something to the military weakness of guerrillas and the power of the British empire, more to the resistance of Protestants, but had its most profound roots in the ideological development of Irish nationalism which seemed to spell the blunt message that the English language, the Protestant religions, and the British state were its antitheses.

Northern Ireland was also the product of differential political power. A 30 per cent minority in the island (in the 1918 voting returns) was able to prevent one area from seceding, but this area in turn contained a 30 per cent minority (in the same voting returns) in favour of the secession of the whole island. One minority had greater political resources than the other.

The subsequent development of 'the Northern Ireland problem' is not simply the product of this historical matrix, or 'unfinished business' in Anglo-Irish relations. This chapter emphasizes the external environment of Northern Ireland in explaining develop-ments since 1920, but in so doing does *not* restate traditional Irish nationalist or Ulster unionist accounts of the external sources of the conflict. British imperialism and Irish irredentism, while important in explaining the historic roots of conflict, became less important in the later twentieth century.

Hegemonic control and particularist regimes

'Who should rule the state?' is *the* political question. Aristotle pro-vides three answers: the one (a monarch), the few (an aristocracy), and the many (a democracy). That 'the people' should rule, however indirectly, is the only permissible answer in modern states. Yet *the* question is 'who are the people?', or, alternatively, 'who should be citizens?' There are four obvious answers. Three are egalitarian, but one is not. The *statist* asserts that the people are all adults permanently resident within the state's boundaries; the *nationalist* claims they are all adults who belong to the nation; whereas the *universalist* answers that they are the entire human species. These three answers prescribe the multi-cultural state, the nation-state, and the global-state respectively. Of these three options the nation-state has proven the most potent modern ideal (Anderson, 1983; Gellner, 1983; Kedourie, 1960; and A. Smith, 1986).

There are, however, more states which are not homogeneous nation-states than otherwise. One set of such states are *particularist*, because they provide an inegalitarian answer to the question: 'who are the people?' They define the people by reference to an Other, who are not part of the people, but are to be subjected to the rule of *the* people. Particularists oppose the ethnic egalitarianism implicit in liberal nationalism; and often fear that they will be a subordinated minority within an Other's regime. They can develop an exclusive nationalism in which *the* nation consists merely of a fraction of the state's population. Particularist regimes are not rare, especially in conditions of settler colonialism: think of South Africa before de Klerk's political initiative; of Israeli rule in Palestine; or of settler rule in Liberia. Northern Ireland between 1920 and 1972 was also a particularist polity; the disloyal Catholic population were not regarded as part of *the* people by Ulster Protestants.

Modern thinkers assume that particularist regimes are archaic survivals, or transitional deviations on the road towards universalist nation-states or balanced multi-ethnic states, but they are feasible reactions to a world in which the construction of nation-states is the dominant paradigm. They can exist and thrive in 'modern' parts of the world, and we may see several new ones formed in the debris of the Soviet Union and Yugoslavia. Particularist governmental units can also be found at the sub-state level within many multi-ethnic states, like those which dominated the American south before the mid-1960s. Once formed, they can be very stable, enduring because they are based upon hegemonic control[G] the most common mode through which multi-ethnic societies have been stabilized in world-history. Control is 'hegemonic' if it makes an overtly violent ethnic contest for state power either 'unthinkable' or 'unworkable'.[1]

Hegemonic control is coercive and co-optive rule which successfully manages to make unworkable an ethnic or nationalist challenge to the state order.[2] In liberal democracies hegemonic control appears less feasible than in empires or authoritarian regimes. Liberal democracies with statist conceptions of citizenship permit, indeed facilitate, ethnic organization and mobilization; and ethnic contests for state power become eminently 'thinkable' and 'workable' in liberal democratic institutions. The mobilization of 'the Irish nation' in favour of home rule in the late nineteenth century coincided with the extension of male suffrage in the UK. But hegemonic control *is* feasible in nominal liberal democracies, even if it is ideologically difficult to maintain. Hegemonic control can be created and persist in a liberal democracy where one ethnic community, or perhaps coalition of communities, effectively dominates another community (or communities) through its political, economic, and ideological resources; and where this superordinate community, or coalition of communities, can extract what it requires from the subordinated, or prevent redistributive demands being made by them. Northern Ireland between 1920 and 1968 was an example of a society in which hegemonic control was exercised by the Ulster Unionist Party. The prospects for effective dissent and disobedience were minimal, and nationalist insurrection by the minority, if not unthinkable, was made unworkable before the late 1960s. The genesis, structure, and maintenance of hegemonic control in Northern Ireland after 1920 is surveyed below; in the next chapter we explain why this system broke down after 1963.

Hegemonic control in Northern Ireland

From 1920 until 1969 Northern Ireland's constitutional status was stamped by four distinctive features. First, sovereignty over its territory was formally contested by the British and the Irish states. Second, it was not fully integrated into either of those states. The Irish Free State was excluded from Northern Ireland, and the British deliberately withdrew from exercising coercive state power within the territory, leaving the devolved government with complete autonomy over law and order, and considerable independence in domestic public policy. Third, from its inception Northern Ireland's institutions lacked bi-communal legitimacy. Externally the Irish contested their existence, whereas the British regarded them as temporary, and they have never acquired international legitimacy (Guelke, 1988). The internal legitimacy of the new political institutions was to be entirely one-sided: the Unionists made almost no efforts to win full legitimacy through seeking Catholic or nationalist support; Catholic compliance rather than support was the most that was sought (Rose, 1971: 92–3). Finally, the political unit created by the Government of Ireland Act was a semi-state, a regime rather than a state. It had, *de facto*, some of the key Weberian features of a state: an effective monopoly over the means of coercion and law-enforcement, law-making authority, and clearly demarcated territorial boundaries. However, it lacked and did not seek sovereignty in foreign affairs, and its fiscal autonomy was sharply circumscribed by its dependence upon the British Treasury (Lawrence, 1965). None the less this 'semi-state' was sufficient to build a system of hegemonic control. The Stormont[3] parliamentary regime (1920–72) became a textbook illustration of Mill and Tocqueville's prediction that democratic rule was compatible with 'tyranny of the majority'. Territorial, constitutional, electoral, economic, legal, and cultural domination and control became pervasive in what its critics were to dub 'the Orange state' (Farrell, 1976).

Territorial Control

The demarcation of Northern Ireland as six counties of the historic province of Ulster laid the foundations of control. It guaranteed an in-built Protestant majority, providing Catholic population-growth did not dramatically exceed that of Protestants. Since Protestants remained unionists and Catholics remained largely nationalist the territorial partition established the conditions under which the Ulster Unionist Party (UUP) would win all the elections for the Northern Ireland parliament between 1920 and 1969, drawing almost all of its support from the Protestant population, irrespective of class or income. The partition was imperfect on national, ethnic or religious grounds: whereas the Irish Free State had arguably been backed by almost 95 per cent of its future population, Northern Ireland had been supported by just less than 70 per cent of its population (see Table 2.2). The British negotiators of the Anglo-Irish Treaty had consequently assured the Irish negotiators with the promise of a boundary commission to consider areas in which nationalists were local majorities.

The implication of this promise for the territorial integrity of the fledgling regime was taken very seriously by the UUP leadership. Many nationalist councils were situated on the border and had declared their allegiance to Dáil Éireann. They were advertisements for the merits of revising the border. Unionists immediately decided to change the election system and to gerrymander local government jurisdictions. They sought to reduce radically the number of local councils held by nationalists (25 out of nearly 80 in 1920). Consequently they abolished proportional representation (STV) in local elections in 1922, replacing it with the conventional British plurality rule, and simultaneously passed a law requiring all councillors to take an oath of allegiance to the Crown. They then postponed the local elections due in 1923, and appointed Sir John Leech to head a one-person judicial commission to reorganize electoral districts. He speedily executed extensive gerrymandering, and after the 1924 local elections nationalists were reduced to holding two councils. The results of the changed election system and 'Leeching' were compounded by nationalist boycotts and abstentionism. (When boycotting was abandoned nationalists normally won 10 or 11 councils out of 73.)

These measures helped Unionists to ensure that the boundary commission would not cause immense damage: had the minor changes recommended by the boundary commission (which sat between 1924 and 1925, but whose conclusions were not implemented) been put into effect Northern Ireland would have gained a considerable slice of East Donegal. In any case the boundary commission's terms of reference and composition were loaded against the interests of nationalists and contributed to its failure (for a fuller discussion *see* Laffan, 1983).

Constitutional control

Northern Ireland was governed under the Government of Ireland Act. As we have seen two parliaments, rather than one, were created in Ireland in an attempt at compromise: home rule for both parts of Ireland would meet the Irish demand for self-government, whereas home rule for Ulster unionists would enable them to avoid domination by Dublin. Clauses in the Act suggested that the political reunification of the island could take place, albeit under the jurisdiction and sovereignty of the British empire, provided both parliaments consented. However, the Northern Ireland parliament was given the right to opt out of rule by Dublin, and the same right was extended in the Anglo-Irish Treaty of 1921, and it was exercised promptly.

Under the Government of Ireland Act (§1) a devolved parliament was established in Belfast modelled on the Westminster system. The Act, as with other 'exports' of the British system attempted to codify key features of the Westminster model[G].[4] These features are: representative majoritarian government under parliamentary sovereignty unconstrained by a codified constitution; a unitary rather than a federal state form; concentration of executive power in (usually) one-party and bare-majority Cabinets; the fusion of executive and legislative powers under Cabinet dominance; and the existence of a bicameral legislature in which the first chamber is far more powerful than the second. Westminster parliamentary sovereignty, including the right to suspend or abolish the Government of Ireland Act, remained unaffected by the creation of the Northern Ireland parliament (§75), although the existence of what might generously be described as a written constitution did mark a formal differentiation of the region from the rest of the UK. The Northern Ireland parliament had the power to make laws for the 'peace, order and good government of Northern Ireland' (§4), but its powers were circumscribed: it was unable to repeal or alter the Government of Ireland Act or any act of the Westminster parliament passed after the Act came into force; and 'imperial matters', such as the Crown, control of the armed forces, and the conduct of foreign policy were retained by London.

Northern Ireland's government consisted of the Crown, represented by the Lord-Lieutenant (replaced by a Governor in 1922), and a bicameral legislature: a 52-member House of Commons, and a 26-member Senate. Although the Governor formally appointed members of the Northern Ireland Cabinet, he did so at the behest of the leader of the party with a majority of seats in the House of Commons. The Northern Ireland Cabinet was expected to develop power over the legislature similar to that enjoyed by its counterpart at Westminster.

The framers of the Government of Ireland Act apparently presumed that politics in Northern Ireland would evolve as they had in the rest of the UK: i.e. there would be regular alternation in the holding of executive power. However, from 1920 all Cabinets and Prime Ministers were drawn exclusively from the Ulster Unionist Party (UUP), which won convincing parliamentary majorities in all the elections held before the suspension of the Stormont parliament in March 1972. The lack of alternation is starkly demonstrated by the durability of Northern Ireland's ministers. There were a mere four Prime Ministers between 1920 and 1969: James Craig, later Lord Craigavon (1920–40); John Miller Andrews (1940–3); Basil Stanlake Brooke, later Lord Brookeborough (1943–63), and Terence O'Neill, later Lord O'Neill of the Maine (1963–9). The Cabinet was equally stable, a veritable gerontocracy in which death was the basis for transitions in the leadership. Under Craig's premiership, terminated by his death in office, there was no major change in Cabinet personnel (1921–40). Upon becoming prime minister in 1943 Brooke felt obliged to declare that 'The office of a cabinet minister is not, and should not be, a life appointment' (Lawrence, 1965: 70–1), but his Cabinets proved almost as stable as his predecessors.

The existence of a permanent majoritarian bloc in a constitutional system designed to establish Cabinet predominance facilitated the abuse of power. In 1968 all members of the Cabinet were members of the Orange Order; and between 1921 and 1969, 138 of the 149 UUP MPs elected to the Northern Ireland parliament were members of the Order at the time of their election (Aunger, 1981: 123, citing Harbinson, 1973). Unionist ministers were able either actively to support political discrimination, through framing appropriate legislation and sanctioning biased forms of administration, or tacitly to endorse discriminatory practices by not using their offices to prevent abuses at lower levels of government and administration. Since their power was dependent upon maintaining the cohesion of the unionist bloc, they had no clear incentive to make concessions to the minority and every incentive to help their own supporters. Abuses of power could be practised without fear of retribution when the opposition had no feasible prospect of forming the government and providing that Westminster and Whitehall did not seek to regulate the region's internal affairs. The permanent Cabinet-monopoly of one political party weakened the essential check and balance in the Westminster model. The necessary conditions required to make the model compatible with an authentic pluralist democracy were not present: the temporary exclusion of large political parties from governmental power and a fundamental consensus on the definition of the state.[5]

The nationalist minority, permanently deprived of government office and its benefits, had little stake in maintaining the system. For the first forty-five years of the regime their representatives refused to accept the role of official opposition in the legislature, and thereby accept its constitutional legitimacy. Nationalist moderates like Joseph Devlin were frustrated, and abandoned parliamentary politics for long periods, playing into the hands of those who considered extra-parliamentary activity, including violent revolution, more likely to produce substantive change. The Northern Ireland 'constitution' did little to persuade them that ballots were more efficacious than bullets.

Majoritarian control also affected the workings of the legislature.

It was modelled on the adversarial pattern: government supporters sat on one side of the Speaker and opposition members on the other. The architecture illustrated the impotence of the opposition, who never numbered more than 18 out of 52 members (Arthur, 1977: 100). The minority's sole legislative achievement was a Wild Birds Act, and the government rarely accepted opposition amendments on issues of substance. Parliamentary appointments went to Unionist backbenchers rather than to members of the opposition - even the chairmanship of the Public Accounts Committee, a post traditionally held by an opposition member at Westminster, was always held by a member of the UUP. The parliament's task was simply to express unionist domination.[6]

Of the twenty six senators, two were *ex officio*: the mayors of Belfast and Londonderry. The rest were elected by the members of the Lower House on a proportional basis, a provision designed to ensure that its role in the legislative process would be minimal, as it meant the Upper House would be a political replica of the lower one. An ineffective attempt was made to avoid exact duplication of the Commons and the Senate by staggering elections to the Upper House: senators were to have eight-year terms, with half of them replaced every four years. In the event of a disagreement between the two Houses, the Governor was empowered to convoke a joint meeting at which a majority vote would apply. No such joint meeting was ever necessary.[7] The Senate did nothing to protect the nationalist minority; indeed the sole minority it protected was a hypothetical Unionist minority. Since senators were elected for eight-year terms, with one half of them retiring at the end of every fourth year, a nationalist majority in the House of Commons would not have been enough to ensure the passage of parliamentary consent for a united Ireland. It would have taken another four years and similar voting patterns to ensure a nationalist majority in both houses.

The Government of Ireland Act deviated from the Westminster model in two respects, both of which were formally aimed at protecting the minority. First, it provided that the legislation of the subordinate parliament and its executive's acts could be declared unconstitutional if they infringed sections of the act outlawing religious discrimination (§5 and §8), or if they transgressed upon the powers retained by the United Kingdom parliament. Second, it provided for an electoral system, proportional representation, for the Northern and 'Southern Irish' parliaments, and local governments

(§14). It was intended to protect minorities in both parts of Ireland – especially Protestants in the still-born 'Southern Ireland' – and we discuss its effectiveness below.

The Northern Irish and the UK courts, proved to be ineffective guardians of minority rights or regulators of the division of powers. The cult of parliamentary sovereignty discouraged litigation against parliaments, even subordinate ones, and did not offer reasonable prospects of success to litigants.[8] The incentives to pursue judicial review were further weakened by the absence of legal aid before 1965 (New Ireland Forum, 1984b: 41; Palley, 1972: 390). In any case nationalists believed that the courts would be unlikely to find in their favour since they were a unionist and British establishment, a viewpoint reinforced by Protestant over-representation on the bench (see p. 128).[9]

Just as importantly the clauses of the Government of Ireland Act outlawing discrimination were awkwardly and narrowly worded: §5 (1) read 'the Parliament of Northern Ireland shall not make a law so as either directly or indirectly to establish or endow any religion, or prohibit or restrict the exercise thereof, or give a preference, privilege or advantage, or impose any disability or disadvantage, on account of religious belief or ecclesiastical status', whereas §8 (6) read 'In the exercise of power delegated to the Governor of Northern Ireland in pursuance of this section no preference, privilege or advantage shall be given to, nor shall any disability or disadvantage be imposed on, any person on account of religious belief.' On one interpretation, §5 (1) made public funding of Catholic education unconstitutional because it was a form of religious discrimination (Calvert, 1968: 257). Rather than protecting the minority against discrimination the possibility of such an interpretation being upheld by the courts inhibited Catholics from bringing test cases under this clause. Moreover, the protection given by §5 (1) did not extend to political opinion and therefore did not prevent discrimination against nationalists, as opposed to Catholics.[10] It did not prohibit discrimination in the private sector, or protect fundamental civil liberties crucial for minorities – such as freedom of speech and press, of assembly, of association, and trial by jury and freedom from arrest without warrant. It therefore afforded no protection against the repressive Special Powers Act which the government was allowed to enforce with impunity (see p. 127). Nor did it protect cultural or communal rights: thus the Flags and Emblems Act of 1954 which outlawed the flying of the Irish flag was legal. Finally §5 (1) did not extend explicitly to sub-parliamentary organs, such as local councils, which were the most visible promoters of discriminatory practices. Neither §5 nor §8 were therefore ever invoked to deal with charges of discrimination against the Catholic minority.

The courts also proved unwilling to strike down Northern Ireland legislation because it infringed the division of powers between Westminster and Stormont, despite their policing powers under §49–51 of the Government of Ireland Act. This passivity weakened the possibility that the minority could deploy the argument that Northern Ireland legislation, unacceptable to them and not covered by §5 or §8, contravened the constitutional division of powers.[11] When the courts did adjudicate on cases involving the division of powers they applied the 'pith and substance' doctrine, declaring acts to be *intra vires* providing that the pith and substance of the law was within their jurisdiction, any transgression being incidental.[12] The minority's natural perception was that their complaints could not even be formally judicially investigated, let alone redressed: in 1964 the Campaign for Social Justice, one of the organizations which initiated the civil rights movement, complained to the British Prime Minister, Sir Alec Douglas-Home, that they were informed by an eminent legal authority that 'the discrimination practised by local authorities is not capable of review by the courts under the terms of the Government of Ireland Act 1920 or any other statutory provisions' (McCloskey, 1989, Appendix II).[13]

The Government of Ireland Act contained provisions which allowed Westminster and Whitehall to supervise closely the actions of the subordinate legislature if they so chose. Matters of concern to the UK as a whole were 'excepted' from the authority of the Belfast parliament: the armed forces, foreign affairs, and the Crown. Other matters (including the Supreme Court) were 'reserved' to the imperial parliament pending the reunification of Ireland which was envisaged in the Act. However, since the Act never operated in 'Southern Ireland' and Northern Ireland opted out of the provisions enabling it to unite with the Irish Free State, the difference between 'excepted' and 'reserved' matters lapsed, although the retention of UK jurisdiction over 'excepted' and 'reserved' matters provided a rationale for Northern Ireland continuing to have parliamentary representation at Westminster. The Government of Ireland Act allowed the British government to veto Northern Ireland legislation (§12);

Westminster to legislate for Northern Ireland, even on transferred matters (§6); and retained Westminster's sovereignty: '. . . the supreme authority of the Parliament of the United Kingdom shall remain unaffected and undiminished over all persons, matters and things in Northern Ireland and every part thereof' (§75).

Formally the relationship between the Northern Ireland government and parliament and those of Westminster was that of a local government unit within a decentralized unitary state. Northern Ireland was not a dominion, a status which would have formally conferred a considerable and increasing degree of autonomy from Westminster. However, in practice Northern Ireland had a degree of independence more akin to that of a state in a federation or that of a dominion than to that of a strictly subordinate level of local government in a decentralized unitary state.[14] The generous grant of powers in the Government of Ireland Act and the connected desire on the part of the British that the devolution experiment 'work', in the sense that Irish affairs should be kept away from Westminster and Whitehall, made Northern Ireland a 'quasi-dominion', or even a 'quasi-state' in domestic affairs. Westminster and Whitehall made no attempt to detract from the grant of powers between 1920 and 1968; clarified or extended the competence of the Northern Ireland parliament by enabling it to enact legislation which did or might involve an excepted or reserved matter; and sought to settle questions which might otherwise have led to litigation (Birrell and Murie, 1980: 7).[15]

Originally it was envisaged that the British government would use its powers under §12 to veto unacceptable legislation. However, this power was employed only once, and then temporarily, in 1922. The offending bill, which abolished proportional representation (STV) for local government elections and replaced it with the first-past-the-post system, lay within the legislative powers of the Northern Ireland parliament but the lord-lieutenant's assent was delayed for two months. However, faced with a threat of resignation from Craig's government if the bill was not allowed, the British government lifted its veto. The consequences of the decision as we have seen were wide-ranging (pp. 111-2). Westminster's pusillanimity convinced the minority that it was an ineffective court of appeal; and it encouraged the UUP to extend the abolition of PR to Northern Ireland parliamentary elections in 1929.

The UK government chose not to use its leverage to affect public policy impinging on the antagonisms between the two ethnic communities. The official channels of communications between the two governments through the Home Office were not designed for the task of political leverage: 'The province was not one of the Home Secretary's major concerns; it was the responsibility of the General Department . . . which was concerned with such matters as liquor licensing and British Summer Time, and one of its divisions dealt with the Channel Islands, the Isle of Man, the Charity Commission and Northern Ireland. This group of subjects was under the control of a staff of seven, of whom only one was a member of the administrative class' (Birrell and Murie, 1980: 11). When the 'Troubles' erupted in 1967-8, the Home Office had no full-time civil servants monitoring Northern Ireland. If administrative structures reflect political will then no more dramatic confirmation could be found of Westminster's desire to quarantine Northern Ireland from its concerns.

Administrative separatism was reinforced by a political convention, stemming from the Speaker's ruling in 1923, that questions could not be asked in Westminster on matters for which responsibility had been transferred to Northern Ireland. Had substantial discussion of Northern Ireland matters been allowed, the British executive might have been put under pressure to employ the powers provided under the Government of Ireland Act. In the 1960s attempts by Westminster Labour backbenchers, notably Paul Rose and Kevin McNamara, to debate religious discrimination in housing and the local government franchise in Northern Ireland, were prevented by the deputy Speaker because these were matters for Stormont and because there was no responsible minister at Westminster. Indeed the Speaker accepted the Home Secretary's false contention in 1964 that matters concerned with religious discrimination could not be discussed at Westminster since the transferred matters in which the discrimination allegedly took place were within the 'sole' competence of the Belfast parliament (Bogdanor, 1979: 54).[16] The UUP were left in full constitutional control of Northern Ireland.

Electoral control

Plurality-rule and gerrymandering of constituency boundaries remained constant features of Northern Ireland local government for fifty

years, especially west of the River Bann. The extent of electoral
domination throughout Northern Ireland's local government system
is evident from one striking statistic: whereas unionists represented
at most 66 per cent of the population in the late 1920s they
controlled 85 per cent of all local authorities (Buckland, 1981:
60; Gallagher, 1957: 225–65). Measures guaranteeing electoral
domination were reinforced by the restriction of the local franchise – which was confined to rate-payers and their spouses –
and by the retention of company votes (which gave company
directors up to six votes, depending upon the rateable valuation
of their company). Since Catholics were disproportionately poorer
than Protestants this pattern of franchise was seen as religiously
biased as well as class-based. When the 1945 Labour government
introduced universal suffrage for local government the Stormont
parliament passed its own Representation of the People Act (1946)
which retained most of the old system, but restricted it further by
removing the franchise from lodgers who were not rate-payers.
The UUP Chief Whip, Major Curran, declared that the entire
measure was necessary to prevent 'Nationalists getting control
of the three border counties and Derry City'. He added that
'the best way to prevent the overthrow of the government by
people who had no stake in the country and had not the welfare
of *the people of Ulster* at heart was to disenfranchise them'
(*Northern Whig*, 11 January 1946, cited in Farrell, 1976: 85–6,
our italics). The Stormont *Hansard* was incompetently edited in an
attempt to hide this frank remark: it curiously records opposition
outrage at a statement mysteriously absent from the proceedings.

   The most spectacular example of the combined impact of the
combination of plurality-rule, gerrymandering, and the restricted
franchise occurred in the second city, Derry/Londonderry. In the
1960s there was a decisive Catholic majority amongst the adult population. The restricted local government franchise reduced Catholic predominance, but still left them with a substantial majority. However, the electoral division of the city into three districts, South, North and Waterside wards, produced the dramatic
results shown in Table 3.1. Gerrymandering created a UUP majority of councillors by the simple expedient of concentrating the
Catholic (and therefore) anti-UUP vote in one ward, and creating
two smaller wards which could be guaranteed to produce UUP
councillors.

Table 3.1 Wards and local government election results Londonderry, 1967

Source: Cameron (1969: para. 134)

Ward	Non-Unionists		Unionists	
	votes	councillors	votes	councillors
South	10,047	8	1,138	0
North	2,530	0	3,946	8
Waterside	1,852	0	3,697	4
Total	14,429	8	7,781	12
votes/councillors	1,804:1		732:1	

The Government of Ireland Act had instituted a proportional rep-resentation (PR) electoral system, the single transferable vote (STV) for the Northern Ireland parliament (§14). However, subclause §14(5) made provision for the alteration of the electoral system after three years (provided that the number of MPs remained the same and that population was considered in any redistribution of seats). This provision was difficult to justify given the ostensible purposes of PR, and that the Unionists had made it clear that they opposed PR and planned to abolish it if they could (Mansergh, 1936: 133). They took the opportunity to abolish it before the 1929 Stormont parliamentary elections, and would have done so earlier but for their fear that the British government might have responded to such behaviour by taking a repartitionist line in the boundary commission (ibid.).

The abolition of PR (STV) and its replacement with the plurality or 'first-past-the-post' electoral system was defended in the orthodox nostrums of the Westminster model. Unionists argued that PR was not British, was undemocratic, prevented strong government, and contributed to indecisiveness and inefficiencies by enhancing the prospect of 'hung parliaments'. Craig maintained that PR(STV) was costly, caused confusion, created constituencies which were too large and as a result 'Members . . . are not able to give to the whole of those wide constituencies that meticulous care and attention that the electors are really entitled to receive' (Mansergh, 1936: 135). One unionist academic later reiterated this 'argument': 'proportional representation requires multiple-member constituencies, and the sparse population in rural areas of Northern Ireland meant that such constituencies were fantastically large' (Newark, 1955: 32).

These criticisms of PR(STV) were threadbare and self-serving.

The democratic credentials of STV are more impressive than the first-past-the-post system, which treats some votes as more important than others and exaggerates the strength of majorities. The preference for strong majority governments was a rhetorical shibboleth masking party-interest. There was no compelling evidence, then or now, that coalitions are any more inefficient or any less democratic than one-party governments. Whatever the merits of strong majority government in homogeneous societies, these advantages are reduced in ethnically divided societies with sizeable permanent minorities. The alleged problem of over-large constituencies could have been resolved by reducing the size of the largest constituencies, which is what the Irish Free State did in 1934 (Mansergh, 1936: 130). Finally, the patronizing allegation that STV confused voters is refuted by the fact that less than 2 per cent of the votes cast in 1925 were invalid. The experience of elections in independent Ireland since 1922, and in Northern Ireland after 1973, has shown that familiarity with STV(PR) breeds knowledge not confusion.

Moreover the UUP never proved reluctant to digress from Westminster electoral practice when it suited it. In 1928, Unionists legislated that no one could be registered to vote in a Northern Ireland parliamentary or local election unless born there or resident there for three years (extended to seven in 1962). They aimed to exclude from the franchise relatively recent immigrants from the Irish Free State who continued to be eligible for the Westminster franchise after three months' residence (Palley, 1972: 394). They refused to follow British practice, as we have seen, when the Westminster parliament assimilated the parliamentary and local franchise in 1948, maintaining a property-based local franchise. Finally, whereas university constituencies were abolished for Westminster elections in 1948, this vestige of class privilege remained in Northern Ireland until 1968, with the Queen's University of Belfast returning four members to Stormont.[17]

No analyst disputes that the change to plurality rule for parliamentary elections in 1929 was designed to cement the hegemony of the UUP, although there is debate over whether its primary purpose was to weaken labourist political movements which threatened unionist solidarity, to reduce all types of fragmentation within the unionist camp, or to weaken further the position of nationalists (Bew, Gibbon, and Patterson, 1979; Buckland, 1979; Farrell, 1976; Osborne, 1979; and Pringle, 1980). Resolution of the debate is not vital since the abolition of PR and the redrawing of electoral boundaries achieved all functions equally effectively. Plurality-rule weakened labourist movements and ultra- loyalist populists (the latter being the major threat to unionist unity in the 1930s) and thereby inhibited unionist fragmentation. This entrenchment of the UUP weakened the strategic position of nationalists, even though their numerical representation in parliament was not significantly affected. The UUP were able to ensure that all future Stormont elections were referenda, or 'sectarian headcounts', on the legitimacy of Northern Ireland and the border, just what the Prime Minister had ordered: 'What I want to get in this house and what I believe we will get very much better in this house under the old-fashioned plain and simple system, are men who are for the Union on the one hand, or who are against it and want to go into a Dublin parliament on the other.'[18] The electoral institutionalization of ethnic divisions meant that many Westminster, Stormont, and local government seats were not even contested as the results were foregone conclusions. UUP hegemony was established.

The impact of the change from proportional representation to plurality rule on political competitiveness can be measured in various ways.[19] Figure 3.1 displays the total vote in Stormont elections between 1920 and 1969 and the percentage of the 52 seats which went uncontested. The total vote fell dramatically in 1929 and 1933, the first two elections after the change in voting-system, and remained more or less static (despite a slightly rising population and electorate) until 1969, when the political crisis surrounding the civil-rights movement and O'Neill's premiership generated a much higher turn-out. Similarly the percentage of seats which went uncontested rose steeply in 1929, peaked in 1933 at the incredibly high level of nearly two-thirds of all seats (Elliott, 1973: Tables 1.02–1.04), and then hovered at between 40 and 50 per cent until the crisis election of 1969. The change in electoral system in 1929 drastically impaired the degree of electoral competition in Northern Ireland.

Figure 3.2. displays another way of visualizing the impact of the abolition of PR on political competitiveness. We have taken each party's percentage share of seats won in parliament and subtracted from this figure its percentage share of votes (first-preference votes in 1921 and 1925). These indices, graphed in Figure 3.2., measure the benefits (if the figure is above zero) and costs (if the figure is below zero) to each party of (STV) proportional representation

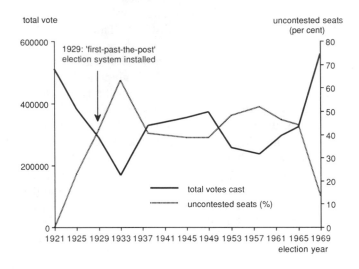

Figure 3.1 The impact of plurality-rule on political competition in Northern Ireland
Source of data: Elliott (1973)
N.B. This graph has a double 'y' axis. The left-hand side measures the total vote, whereas the right hand side measures the percentage of parliamentary seats which went uncontested.

in 1921 and 1925 and of plurality rule between 1929 and 1969. They cannot properly take account of uncontested seats (which were a direct product of the change to plurality-rule in the 1929 election) but they do demonstrate how plurality-rule cemented the UUP's electoral hegemony. The UUP's excess of seats over votes was consistently high - in nine out of ten elections after 1929 its excess was over 10 per cent - an effect achieved without any evident gerrymandering. The Nationalist party did moderately well under plurality-rule before World War II. The principal losers under plurality-rule were the UUP's unionist opponents (the right-wing Protestant/Independent Unionists in the 1930s and the Northern Ireland Labour Party (NILP) between 1945 and 1965), although it provided little incentive for republican or socialist nationalists to participate in constitutional politics.

The most sophisticated way to estimate the impact of Craig's decision to change the voting-system for parliamentary elections is to

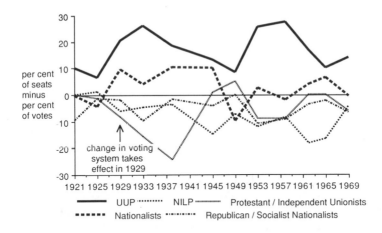

Figure 3.2 How plurality-rule cemented the electoral hegemony of the UUP
Source of data: Elliott (1973)

calculate how the two different voting-systems reduced the effective number of parties, using the method developed by Taagepera and Shugart (1989: 77–91, 273 ff.). The relative reduction index **r**, calculated in Appendix 3.1 for the 1925 and 1929 elections, measures the reduction in the effective number of parties from percentage of votes won to percentage of seats won, and has an upper limit of 100 per cent. Whereas under PR(STV) in 1925 the relative reduction in the effective number of parties from votes to seats in 1925 was 13 per cent, in 1929 under plurality-rule it rose dramatically to 45 per cent (see Appendix 3.1).[20] The UUP obtained exactly what it wanted: a British voting-system which focused elections on a straight fight between nationalists and unionists, cemented its status as the hegemonic party, and disadvantaged all smaller electoral groupings which might have fragmented the unionist vote.[21]

Coercive control

Territorial, constitutional, and electoral control were key elements in cementing the political security of the UUP, but hegemonic control ultimately had to be sanctioned by coercive resources. Revolt had to be made unworkable. Unionists' minds were concentrated by the presence of an irredentist neighbour which had eventually won its political autonomy through guerrilla war, the existence of traditional practices and legitimations of violence within Irish political culture, and by an ethnic minority prepared to offer both overt and covert support to armed insurrection against the regime. The monopolization of force in reliable hands seemed imperative.

Even before the formal creation of Northern Ireland, key Unionist leaders had built a 'state-in-waiting', an administration backed by a body of armed men. A provisional government, with a paramilitary organization supplied through illegal gun-running, had been envisaged before World War I to oppose home rule. A second 'arming of the Protestants' in the Ulster Special Constabulary (USC) took place in 1920, under Dawson Bates, who was to become the Minister of Home Affairs in the new Northern Ireland government (Farrell, 1983). The core membership, 5,500 full-time A-specials, was recruited from the UVF which had been mobilized before 1914, and had fought as a unit in that war. They were backed by 19,000 part-time B-specials, and an uncertain number of C-specials. All told one in five Protestant males are estimated to have been 'specials', and together with the armed police, the Royal Ulster Constabulary, they were able effectively to repress IRA incursions into Northern Ireland in the early 1920s. Thereafter the A- and C-specials were disbanded and approximately 10,000 B-specials were maintained as a part-time paramilitary police force. Together with the RUC they were subsequently able to control and defeat IRA offensives against the regime during World War II, and between 1956 and 1962.

The specials were nakedly sectarian, Protestant to a man. The police force, by contrast, was not nakedly sectarian. In the beginning it was envisaged that it would be representative of the whole popu-lation. However, less than a sixth of the new force was Catholic, and this proportion declined to about a tenth in the late 1960s. Catholics did not join the police because they did not regard it as legitimate, and because they faced potential ostracism or worse from their own community. Ethnically imbalanced policing was reinforced by the development of institutional affiliations between police units and Orange lodges, which confirmed Catholic perceptions of the RUC as Protestants with guns (unlike their British or Irish counterparts the RUC were armed). However, since the police were the primary agents in controlling the threat of insurrection from the Catholic minority, ethnic perceptions did not need much encouragement. In 1969, after the first wave of disturbances induced by the civil rights movement, a committee headed by Lord Hunt indicted prejudicial attitudes and practices within the RUC, suggested that it be disarmed, and recommended the disbandment of the controversial USC (Hunt Report, 1969). The fact that the report sparked rioting in Protestant areas of Belfast could leave nobody in any doubt as to how Protestants saw 'their' police force. The extent to which the police before 1972 were politically subordinated to the ruling party 'stunned' the first Labour politicians to intervene in Northern Ireland during 1969–70.[22]

Legal control

The constitutional structure of Northern Ireland was fully exploited by the UUP to counter the threat of insurrection by the minority. The Civil Authorities (Special Powers) Act of 1922 – renewed annually until 1928, renewed for five years until 1933, and then made permanent – was one of the most Draconian pieces of legislation ever passed in a liberal democracy. Two of its sentences have achieved deserved notoriety in jurisdictions based on English law: 'The Civil Authority shall have power, in respect of persons, matters and things within the jurisdiction of the Government of Northern Ireland to take all such steps and issue all such orders as may be necessary for preserving the peace and maintaining order' (§1(1)); and 'If any person does any act of such a nature as to be calculated to be prejudicial to the preservation of the peace or the maintenance of order in Northern Ireland and not specifically provided for in the regulations, he shall be deemed to be guilty of an offence against the regulations' (§1 (3)). The Special Powers Act (and subsequent regulations developed under it) provided for other extraordinary powers, even though they were hardly necessary given the above two clauses. The government had the right to intern people without trial (which it did between 1922 and 1925, between 1938 and 1946, and between 1956 and 1961), to arrest people without warrant, to issue curfews, and to prohibit inquests - a power which tacitly prevented the investigation of illegal killings by the security forces. The security forces also had the right to compel people to answer questions on pain of being guilty of an offence. Other laws, notably the Public Order Act (1951) and the Flags and Emblems Act (1954), enabled the government to control non-violent forms of political opposition, and effectively outlawed symbolic displays of nationalist allegiance amongst the minority population.

These extraordinary powers were used to repress nationalist rather than loyalist paramilitary violence - which 'rarely elicited any response' (Hogan and Walker, 1989: 14). They were also frequently used for symbolic or political purposes rather than for any evident security-requirement: the continuation of the Special Powers Act in 1928, and the decision to make it permanent in 1933, were not justified by the present existence of nationalist paramilitary violence. Northern Ireland continued to be governed, like Ireland before 1914, under a panoply of coercive legislative instruments which marked it off from the rest of the UK.

A system of order and of law is held together by rule-interpreters as well as enforcers. Supervising and interpreting the maintenance of order and the administration of justice was an overwhelmingly Protestant judiciary, integrated into the UUP, and sometimes into the Orange Order. These arrangements further reduced the prospects that the law might protect the civil liberties of the minority. The first Chief Justice of Northern Ireland was a Catholic, but after his death in 1925 no other Catholic was appointed to the Supreme Court until 1949; and as late as 1969 Catholics held a mere 6 out of 68 senior judicial appointments (Corrigan, 1969: 28, cited in Whyte, 1983; and see Table 3.2).

Table 3.2 Senior judicial posts in Northern Ireland in 1969

Source: CSJ (1969)

Status	Protestant	Catholic	Total
High court judges	6	1	7
County court judges	4	1	5
Resident magistrates	9	3	12
Crown solicitors	8	0	8
Under sheriffs	6	0	6
Clerks of the peace	6	0	6
Total(s)	39	5	44

Economic control

The UUP's control over Northern Ireland was consolidated by direct and indirect economic discrimination in employment, both in the public and private sectors, and in the distribution of public consumption benefits, especially public housing. In an infamous declaration during the depression of the 1930s a future Prime Minister of Northern Ireland, Basil Brooke, exhorted members of the UUP in Derry/Londonderry: 'I recommend those people who are Loyalists not to employ Roman Catholics, 99 per cent of whom are disloyal; I want you to remember one point in regard to the employment of people who are disloyal . . . You are disfranchising yourselves in that way.'[23] Not all discrimination was the product of public policy: the UUP could rely upon ingrained ethnic prejudices to sustain discrimination as well as informal or indirect discrimination through recruitment on the basis of school or familial networks. 'Unintended' historically established structural inequalities were also important in sustaining persistent inequalities, and remain so up to the present day (Smith and Chambers, 1987a, 1987c, 1991). The efforts of some unionist analysts to explain away the differential economic status of Protestants and Catholics are unconvincing (see ch 7: 262-5), and historians of different political dispositions have had no difficulty in documenting explicit exhortations by Unionist politicians during the Stormont era which encouraged discrimination in employment (Bew, Gibbon, and Patterson, 1979; Buckland, 1981: 55 81; Farrell, 1976: 121–49).

The structural pattern of male-occupations[24] within each ethnic community in the 1971 census, fifty years after the formation of Northern Ireland, is shown in Table 3.3.[25] The first detailed comparison of the 1961 and 1971 censuses demonstrated that three principal forms of stratification existed between Protestants and Catholics (Aunger, 1975: 16–17). First, there was horizontal, or inter-class stratification: Protestants dominated the upper occupational classes while Catholics were found predominantly in the lower classes. Second, there was horizontal intra-class stratification: Protestants predominated in superior positions within occupations within the same class. Finally, there was vertical stratification: Protestants were concentrated in the higher status industries and locations, while Catholics were disproportionately represented in the lower status industries and locations.[26] On the basis of modal averages the

Table 3.3 Religion and occupational class in Northern Ireland, 1971:
economically active men

Source: adapted from Aunger (1975: 10)

occupational class	Catholics (%)	Protestants (%)	Total (%)	Protestants (%) minus Catholics (%)
professional/managerial	9	16	14	+7
lower-grade non-manual	12	17	16	+5
skilled manual	23	27	26	+4
semi-skilled manual	25	24	24	−1
unskilled/unemployed	31	16	20	−15

'typical' Protestant male was a skilled worker, whereas the 'typical' Catholic male was unskilled; most occupations which were strongly Protestant were 'male', whereas those which were disproportionately Catholic were 'female'; Protestants were over-represented in positions of authority and influence; the Catholic middle class were largely a 'service-class', servicing their 'own' community; and Catholics constituted a majority of the unemployed even though they were less than a third of the economically active population. The last dramatic finding has remained a constant feature of Northern Ireland, and the most revealing indicator of its political economy. In 1971 Catholic males were 2.6 times as likely to be unemployed as

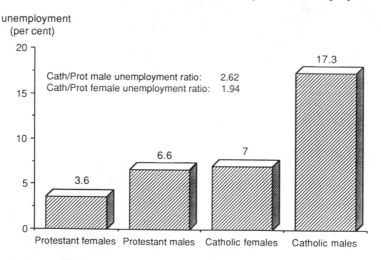

Figure 3.3 Religion, sex, and unemployment in Northern Ireland, 1971
Source: Smith, D. (1987a: Table 2.1)

Table 3.4 Estimated impact of emigration on Northern Ireland's religious balance, 1926–81

Source: adapted from Rowthorn and Wayne (1988: 209)

		Catholics	**non-Catholics**
1.	population in 1926	420,000	836,000
		(33.4% of total)	66.6% of total)
2.	natural increase 1926–81	431,000	289,000
		(102.6%)	(34.6%)
3.	hypothetical population 1981	851,000	1,125,000
		(43.1% of total)	(56.9% of total)
4.	actual population in 1981	588,000	947,000
		(38.3% of total)	(61.7% of total)
5.	effect of emigration (4 – 3)	–263,000	–178,000

Protestant males, whereas Catholic females were 1.94 times as likely to be unemployed as Protestant females (see Figure 3.3).

Discrimination and the preservation of existing clientelist/ethnic labour markets invigorated the UUP's position at the core of a system of patronage. Vested interests across all Protestant classes in the maintenance of hegemonic control were underlined and mightily encouraged Catholic emigration, which remained disproportionately higher than Protestant migration during the Stormont regime (Barritt and Carter, 1972: 107–8; Rowthorn and Wayne, 1988: Appendix 7). In Table 3.4. (adapted from Rowthorn and Wayne, 1988: 209) the influence of emigration in sustaining Protestants' numerical predominance is crudely calculated. Catholics emigrated in significantly disproportionate numbers; constituting approximately 35 per cent of Northern Ireland's population they composed approximately 60 per cent of its emigrants. This pattern sustained hegemonic control.

Administrative control

Unionist hegemonic control can be illustrated by two aspects of public administration: housing-management and public employment. The allocation of housing and the organization of electoral districts of Northern Ireland were connected in straightforward ways (Cameron, 1969: para. 140). Housing-segregation maintained predictable electoral outcomes and prevented the development of mixed communities. Local authorities under UUP control west of the River Bann, where Catholics were far more likely to be the local majority of the electorate, were most zealous in using planning controls and allocation systems to maintain their political domination. East of the Bann, where Protestants were far more likely to constitute a local electoral majority, housing allocation patterns were less influenced by sectarian electoral considerations.[27] Aside from electoral-districting manipulation the political control of housing allocation procedures maintained clientelism within the Protestant community and ensured that the UUP could function as an effective cross-class party.

Public-employment patterns in policing, in both the normal and 'paramilitary' domains, have already been discussed. Police employees were mostly self-selecting: intentional discrimination was not required here. The same case could not be made for the employment patterns in the civil service, local authorities, and quasi-governmental agencies. In the higher grades of the civil service Catholics made up a total of 5.8 percent of those employed in 1943. This figure is quoted by Buckland (1979: 20) from the official records of an inquiry conducted by the Northern Ireland Ministry of Finance. It had been set up to answer the accusation that Catholics were taking over the service (sic!). Another estimate suggested that the percentage of Catholics in senior civil-service positions stood at 6.5 in 1929 and had risen to 6.6 by 1959 (adapted from Barritt and Carter, 1972: 96). In 1969 the Campaign for Social Justice researched the number of Catholics in the higher grades of the civil service. Their estimates are displayed in Table 3.5, and suggest that the Catholic share was as low as 7 per cent.[28] These figures were not accidents. The amazingly petty case of the dismissal of a Catholic gardener from Stormont, because of pressure from the Orange Order, demonstrates the pervasiveness of Orange surveillance of the civil service (Bew, Gibbon, and Patterson, 1979: 97, n. 12). The man in question had a worthy army record *and* a reference from the Prince of Wales, but all to no avail. In local authorities a government commission of inquiry in 1969 found that unionist-controlled councils had systematically discriminated in favour of Protestants especially in key administrative posts (Cameron, 1969: para. 138). In nationalized industries and public utilities Catholics were also grossly under-represented at all levels (Aunger, 1975); and in other statutory bodies, such as the judiciary, we have already noted a similar picture.

Table 3.5 Catholic representation in the Northern Ireland civil service, 1969

Sources: Aunger (1981: 126–7) and CSJ (1969)

Occupational grade	% Protestants (N=492)	% Catholics (N=36)	% Total (N=528)
senior administrative	94	6	100
professional, technical	93	7	100

Senior administrative positions	% Protestants	% Catholics	Total (N)
administrative secretaries	98.1	1.9	53
principal officers	89.2	10.8	102
deputy principal officers	93.3	6.7	164
total	92.8	7.2	319

Why 'hegemonic control' describes the Stormont system

This picture, derived from government commissions and secondary sources, suggests systematically organized domination rather than the 'not particularly inequitable' system identified by critics of the claims of the civil-rights movement of the late 1960s (Hewitt, 1981: 377).[29] It is also at odds with the curious thesis that Northern Ireland between 1920 and 1972 was simply a case of 'normal British misconduct' – based on one-party dominance in local government (Squires and Cowling, 1991). Northern Ireland's government after 1920 had powers more extensive than those of British local government, including coercive powers, and was based upon ethnic domination and control, not simply upon political party-patronage.

Our interpretation of the system as one of hegemonic control is worth contrasting with unionist apologias. Consider one historian's complaint against the 'cant phrase' that the Stormont period was characterized by 'fifty years of misrule': 'Certain obdurate facts cannot be swept aside, though it may be argued that much is concealed by them . . . Northern Ireland remained a parliamentary democracy, in which government was conducted on the same lines as in the rest of the United Kingdom. It was never a police state, because the police, like every other branch of the executive was subject to the scrutiny of parliament. There was no question which could not be aired in parliament. The press was not censored. With one important exception, there were no official curbs on free speech or the free expression of political opinion . . .[30] Moreover the period of Unionist rule was, with the exception of some ugly riots in the early 1930s, almost free of sectarian violence' (Stewart, 1986: 177).

These 'obdurate facts' conceal that hegemonic control is entirely compatible with the Westminster model of representative government. Hegemonic control can effectively prevent riots and revolution. However, the claim that there were no curbs on free speech is not convincing: parliamentary freedom of speech was restricted by the convention which prevented the raising of Northern Ireland issues in Westminster; and broadcasting freedom of expression was also materially restricted as demonstrated in a reputable academic and television producer's analysis of the BBC archives (Cathcart, 1984). Before 1969 there were two phases in the history of the BBC in Northern Ireland, then the most important medium in the region. From 1924 until 1948, its directors were openly absorbed into the unionist establishment, and sought to suppress the fact that Northern Ireland contained two opposed communities. One director, George Marshall (1932–48), stopped the inclusion of GAA sports-results in Sunday news broadcasts after receiving loyalist protests; backed the Northern Ireland government's attempt to prevent a programme called *Irish Half Hour*, targetted at Irishmen in the British armed forces, on the grounds that it denied the distinction between the two parts of Ireland; and simply banned any discussion of the constitutional question, or reporting of events south of the border (ibid.: 67, 116–21, 148). In the second phase, which lasted until 1969, the BBC became more pluralist. Catholic, nationalist, and labour voices were heard. However, partition could not be raised, and discrimination was seldom even discussed (ibid.: 171–2). Stewart cites as 'the exception' to freedom of speech the ban placed on the publication and distribution of republican and IRA literature. However, he misleads his readers. Aside from the self-censorship imposed by the BBC there were at least the following restrictions on free speech and free expression: the Flag and Emblems Act of 1954, and the 1967 Special Powers Order which proscribed the 'Republican Clubs' *and* 'any like organisation howsoever described'. A House of Lords verdict on the meaning of the latter provision held that it included 'any organisation which had the characteristic or object of a republican club, namely to introduce republican government into

Northern Ireland', a ruling which implicitly proscribed all nationalist organizations (McCormick, 1970).

That Northern Ireland is accurately characterized after 1920 as a particularist regime exercising hegemonic control does not imply that it was the most oppressive regime in the world for a minority to live within. However, the appraisal of Whyte (1983) which maintained that *direct* discrimination in Northern Ireland was not as extensive as ultra-nationalists implied fails to recognize the political functions of discrimination, both direct and *indirect*, namely the establishment of control. Our characterization does not imply that the degree of Unionist domination explains, let alone justifies, in some simplistic way the level of republican violence from 1971 onwards. But there was 'a consistent and irrefutable pattern of deliberate discrimination against Catholics' (Darby, 1976: 77–8); a hermetic system which seemed incapable of change or reform; and there was apparently little effective political, or military, action which Catholics or nationalists could take to remedy their lot before the mid 1960s.[31]

What motivated hegemonic control?

An explanation of this system requires an account of the motivations of the actors who created and sustained it, and of the environment which made it possible. The motivations of Ulster unionists are easy to establish, although ranking their salience is more controversial. They feared incorporation into a Gaelic, Catholic Irish nation-state, betrayal by Britain, insurrection and expropriation by the Catholic minority, and disunity and fragmentation within their community.

Irish unionism had been mobilized against Irish home rule. The Irish Free State and the Irish Republic, as it became in 1949, seemed to develop in ways which confirmed Ulster Protestants' predictions as to what would happen in an independent Irish parliamentary regime. The speeches and statements of UUP leaders demonstrate an obsessive fear of Irish nationalism in the years between 1920 and the formation of the Irish Republic in 1949 (Kennedy, 1988: 6). The major theme of the unionist press was the constitutional evolution of the Irish Free State away from the dominion status negotiated in the Anglo-Irish Treaty of 1921 (ibid.: 21). This evolution towards an autonomous republic, achieved *de facto* in 1937, and *de jure* in

1949, not only meant the end of Ireland's participation within the UK, but also within the British empire, and eventually the British Commonwealth. For most unionists this evolution was calculated treason, disloyalty, and a dishonest breaking of the Treaty. The neutrality of Ireland in World War II 'proved' they had been right to reject incorporation within the Irish Free State.

The second unionist fear focused on Irish irredentism. The early years of Northern Ireland were profoundly uncertain, as civil war and the prospective Boundary Commission threatened the regime's territorial integrity. The defeat of the republican side in the Irish civil war of 1922–3, and the absence of major boundary revisions in 1925, briefly lessened unionist fears, but not for long. The electoral mobilization of the bulk of the defeated republicans under de Valera's Fianna Fáil changed matters. Fianna Fáil were openly 'semi-constitutional' in the late 1920s and early 1930s, not only hostile to the Treaty, but also ambiguous in their relationships with the IRA. They were unambiguous about their desire to obtain a republic and the territorial unification of the island. De Valera's electoral victory in 1932, and the entrenchment of Fianna Fáil as the dominant party in the Irish party system amply confirmed unionists' worries. The rewriting of the Irish Constitution in 1937, under de Valera's personal supervision, carved their anxieties in stone. It claimed the whole island of Ireland: 'Article 2. The national territory consists of the whole island of Ireland, its islands and the territorial seas. Article 3. Pending the re-integration of the national territory and without prejudice to the right of Parliament and Government established by this Constitution to exercise jurisdiction of the whole of that territory, the laws enacted by that Parliament shall have the like area and extent of application as the laws of Saorstát Éireann and the like extra-territorial effect' (*Bunreacht Na hÉireann* (Constitution of Ireland) 1937). These articles repudiated the Government of Ireland Act, the Treaty, and the 1925 boundary settlement between the Irish Free State and Northern Ireland.

The Irish Free State also seemed to confirm unionist prophecies that Vaticanism, Gaelicisation, and economic retardation would prevail under a Dublin parliament. The rapid fall in the Protestant population between 1911 and 1926, mostly due to voluntary out-migration to England, reinforced stereotypical attitudes (see Figure 3.4., which shows the rise or fall in the percentage of Catholics in each county and county borough of Ireland between 1911 and

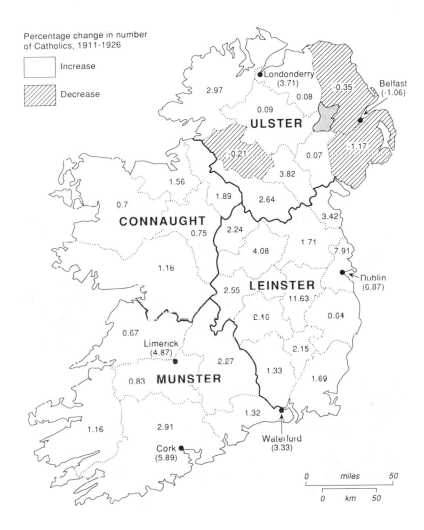

Figure 3.4 The percentage rise and fall of Catholics in Ireland between 1911 and 1926 (by counties)
Sources: Censuses of Ireland 1911, Saorstát Éireann 1926, Northern Ireland 1926

1926). The fall of the Protestant population by 32.5 per cent while the Catholic population fell by 2.2 per cent (Buckland, 1972: 285) is only partly attributable to the emigration of those whose families held 'garrison posts' – they accounted for just a quarter of émigrés (Bowen, 1983: 20–5). Although outsiders have generally argued that the independent Irish state treated its Protestant minority well, both by international and (especially) by Northern Irish standards (Bowen, 1983: 324–37), this judgment has never been shared by Ulster Protestants. Catholic social morality, especially in family law, divorce, contraception, and abortion, determined the majority's attitudes in the Irish Free State, and eventually the law and the constitution. Unionist leaders were able to argue that the Irish state was a Catholic state for a Catholic people, and that 'home rule' had meant 'Rome rule': inferring, as Craig did, that having a Protestant state for a Protestant people was a legitimate response. Compulsory bilingualism (English and Gaelic) in schools was regarded as cultural ethnocide by most Ulster Protestants. Finally, the merits of their decision to exclude themselves from the Irish Free State were shown by the even greater scale of the economic depression in the South in the 1920s and 1930s, its lack of economic growth between the 1920s and 1958, and the baneful repercussions of de Valera's pursuit of economic autarky and 'economic war' with Britain in the 1930s.

Fear of the Irish state, and of incorporation within it, provided some of the essential motivations for the establishment and main-tenance of hegemonic control by Ulster Protestants, but they were not sufficient. Their criticisms of the Irish state, after all, might suggest that they were, or would be, more sincere advocates of equal citizenship, and more tolerant of their minority's religious, cultural, and economic liberties. Self-evidently they were not. One reason they were not was an external fear: the threat that the British state would abandon them, or hand them over to the Dublin parliament, whenever it seemed expedient. This fear was well-grounded. The home-rule bills of the 1880s, 1890s, and the Home Rule Act of 1914 envisaged a Dublin parliament with authority over Ulster. During the planning of the Government of Ireland Act some British policy-makers considered subordinating the prospective Belfast parliament to the Dublin parliament. The Council of Ireland proposed in the Act was intended to mollify the implications of partition and to be a means through which partition might one day be reversed. Moreover, British policy-makers reraised the idea of subordinating the Belfast to the Dublin parliament during the Anglo-Irish Treaty negotiations (Laffan, 183: 82).[32] The Boundary Commission conceded by Lloyd George in the same Treaty threatened the security of Northern Ireland during its formative years, and firmly wed Unionists to the merits of having their own parliament.

Although unionist anxiety about British commitment to the Union briefly receded after 1925, it was soon increased by the willingness, as they saw it, of successive British governments to appease de Valera's strident nationalism in the 1930s. It was raised to coronary-level by a famous episode in World War II that occurred following the fall of France. In 1940 Winston Churchill secretly offered to support Irish unification in return for Eire's entry into the war on the side of the British empire and its allies (Fisk, 1983: 186–219). The offer was turned down by de Valera primarily because of his Cabinet colleagues' estimation that Nazi Germany would defeat Britain; and he therefore held out consistently, but wishfully, for both unification and neutrality. The offer could not be kept 'secret' from Unionist leaders who were outraged.[33] Although Britain's eventual victory and Eire's neutrality created support amongst the British post-war élite for Northern Ireland's status as part of the UK the episode was not forgotten. The unionists' strategic dilemma had been confirmed: full integration with Britain would make them more British, but by depriving them of the instruments of hegemonic control would make them correspondingly more vulnerable to abandonment in future Anglo-Irish negotiations. 'Loyal Ulster', despite its record of support for Britain in two world wars, was an expendable, negotiable territory, and its people inessential to the British definition of their nation or their state. Eternal vigilance and hegemonic control seemed appropriate responses.

The third motivation for the genesis and maintenance of hegemonic control was straightforward. Protestants feared the attitudes and capabilities of the 'enemy within'. Catholic Ireland, whether in revolutionary or parliamentary guise, had always threatened Protestant 'ascendancy'. Northern Ireland would inevitably face the threat of rebellion from its Catholic/nationalist minority who would regard the regime as illegitimate. In the interlude between the Government of Ireland Act of 1920 and the Irish civil war of 1922–3, which followed the Anglo-Irish Treaty, the IRA engaged in active combat in Northern Ireland. Moreover, although distracted by and defeated in the Irish civil war, it continued to oppose the existence of Northern Ireland. It remained an underground organization and launched military offensives between 1938 and 1941 and between 1956 and 1962 (Bowyer Bell, 1979: 73–336; Coogan, 1987: 173–418). The reality of this threat made the case for repressive security self-evident to Protestants. Catholics were disloyal so there was no case for equal treatment, or authentic equal citizenship. The equally self-evident fact that Catholics' unequal treatment would reinforce their disloyalty did not matter as long as they could be controlled.

Thus the colonial legacy was preserved into the liberal democratic era. Protestant settlers were loyal and under siege from native Catholics; and being besieged they were justified in crushing rebellion with whatever means lay to hand. The messages of control were spelled out in the formal practices of electoral, coercive, legal, and economic domination, but were also culturally and psychologically expressed in sectarian organizations, like the Orange Order, in triumphalist marches through Catholic areas, in regular acts of 'representative violence' (Wright, 1987: 11–20) against the minority, and a vitriolic rhetoric which spelled out the insecurities of those who articulated it. The meaning of the desire of Orange marchers to parade through 'their' territory is very simple: 'communal deterrence'. Continuous reminders and expressions of the Protestant ascendancy, hammered out in the rhythms of Lambeg drums, deter nationalist/Catholic rebellion. Orange marches have recently been defined as integral components of Protestant culture, but if this is culture, it is like diplomacy, war by other means.

Successful control of the minority necessitated majority unity. Fear of disunity within the ranks is pervasive within settler colonial communities and their descendants. Vulnerable to native insurrection and abandonment by the metropolis they cannot afford internal dissent. Since hegemonic control required a conception of politics as a zero-sum game, it was essential to inhibit heretical or dissident Protestant voices, whether socialist or otherwise. Fear of disunity and betrayal from within their own ranks is one of the most constant elements in the history of Protestant Ulster (Nelson, 1984; Stewart, 1986). It explains the Lundy fixation. 'The most hated character in Orange history is not some fiendish rebel, or devil-worshipping communist agitator, but one Robert Lundy, the Protestant Governor of Londonderry, who in 1689 attempted to surrender the city to the Catholic King James II, rather than wait for the arrival of the glorious Protestant King William III. For the Ulster Protestants the name Lundy has become synonymous with traitors and turncoats. To be a 'Lundy' is the capital crime of Ulster loyalism . . .' (Bell, 1976: 65; and see Stewart, 1986: 48). After 1920 'Lundyism' came in two forms. Lundyism 'from below' was manifest in socialist and labourist movements which threatened to transcend sectarianism in the 1930s, and in the late 1950s and early 1960s. The threat posed by such movements was relatively easily handled by the UUP. Explicit accusations of disloyalty, reminders of the dangers inherent in splitting the unionist vote, and overt renewals of ethnic appeals usually elicited the required responses. However, 'Lundyism from above' was another matter: 'modernizing' Unionist élites eventually endangered the regime.

There is no need to elaborate further: unionist fears were clear, and in their eyes, well-founded. Coerced incorporation into a Gaelic, Catholic Irish nation-state, betrayal by perfidious Britain, insurrection by the Catholic minority, and internal disunity and fragmentation remained enduring possibilities within their political milieu, and persuaded most of them that the relaxation of any of the elements of control spelled destruction. These accumulated and intermeshed anxieties are sufficient to explain Protestant motivations.[34]

However, our argument is contestable. The key challenge, which would be supported by many nationalists, is that Ulster Protestant motivations were determined by an identity which actually required hegemonic control for its preservation; i.e. Ulster Protestantism just is an ideology of hegemonic control, typical of settler colonial minorities threatened by democratization and modernization (MacDonald, 1986; Weitzer, 1990). However there is not just one homogeneous Ulster Protestant identity based on colonial domination of Catholics. There are at least two traditions in Unionist political culture (Todd, 1987). One of these, Ulster loyalist ideology, is a settler-ideology, but the other, Ulster British ideology, professes liberal political values which *prima facie* refute it. A purely colonial reading of unionist political culture requires us to discount Ulster Protestants' expressed fears in favour of external, reductionist, and imputed conceptions of their core identity. The environment in which hegemonic control was maintained shows that the development and sustenance of the fears of Ulster Protestants is comprehensible without recourse to a historicist and essentialist conception of their identity.

The external environment of hegemonic control

Unionists' fears about the Catholic minority and disunity within their own ranks were based on sound appreciations of their internal political environment. Furthermore, their anxieties about the independent Irish state and of betrayal by Britain were not paranoid. However, there were two further elements in their environment which unintendedly encouraged the building of hegemonic control by Ulster Unionists, British state-development, and Irish nation-building failure.

The British state, as we have seen, was ill-equipped to deal with Northern Ireland because of its constitutional tradition. The framers of the Government of Ireland Act assumed that Northern Ireland was different, therefore it needed special treatment, but on the other hand they assumed its devolved government would develop as a miniature version of the British political system. Contemporary liberal unionists regret that Northern Ireland was not fully incorporated into the British state (Aughey, 1989; Roberts, 1991): a devolved parliament left unionists in limbo, both outside and within the British political system, without the Union they had mobilized to defend. They believe that the presence of Great British political parties, competing over non-ethnic ideological principles and interests, would have eroded sectarianism within Northern Ireland. This regret was shared by a very small minority of Unionists in 1920, but today is conventional wisdom amongst revisionist unionists (Aughey, 1989; Roberts, 1987; Wilson, 1989). However, their regrets ignore the very detailed affiliations between the UUP and the Conservative *and Unionist* party (our emphasis) between 1920 and 1972, and beg the question: why did British policy-makers not integrate Northern Ireland into the British political system after 1920 or 1925?

Having decided to partition Ireland in 1920, and having conceded dominion status to the Irish Free State in 1921, British policy-makers were faced with a strategic choice. On the one hand, in the external interests of the British state, they could have chosen to improve relations with the new Irish Free State. There were two dramatic ways to meet this objective: either by cajoling Ulster unionists into accepting some mode of Irish unification, or by reducing the size of Northern Ireland to homogenize it. These options would have facilitated the retrenchment of the over-burdened British imperial state, and enabled it to preserve its geo-political and defence interests in Ireland (even if the Irish state eventually became a republic rather than a dominion).

On the other hand, in the internal interests of British nation-building, British policy-makers could have chosen the equally dramatic objective of assimilating the Northern Irish into the British nation. There were two principal ways to achieve this objective: either the full integration of Northern Ireland (including its Catholic minority) into Britain, or the full integration of a territorially reduced (and more homogeneously Protestant) Northern Ireland into Britain.[35] The vigorous pursuit of either strategy, (external interests of state, or of nation-building), might have resolved Britain's 'Irish Question' before World War II, but the question is still begged: why were the strategic choice rarely explicitly posed, let alone resolved?

First, it was widely believed that Lloyd George had solved the major Irish questions through partition and the Treaty. The bloody wars and difficult negotiations which produced the Government of Ireland Act and the Anglo-Irish Treaty were regarded as final settlements. The spectacular achievement of Lloyd George was to have reorganized the British archipelago so that Irishmen would fight with Irishmen rather than against Englishmen. Reopening Irish questions promised Pandora's box. Ireland was best managed with a barge pole. A parliament at Stormont was an excellent device for 'screening out' Irish questions from entering British politics. The creation of two Irish governments and the reduction of the number of (Northern) Irish MPs at Westminster removed Irish questions from the centre of the political agenda. The convention that Northern Irish questions were matters for the Northern Ireland parliament which should not be discussed meant that the mother of parliaments spent an average of two hours per year on Northern Ireland between partition and the emergence of renewed troubles in the late 1960s (Lyons, 1973: 700).

In the 1920s and 1930s Great British party-competition increasingly focused on economic and class cleavages, partly as a by-product of the 'solution' of Irish questions between 1920 and 1921. Territorial and religious issues receded in importance. The focus of political competition on the more bargainable issues of economic welfare took the heat out of the British political system, facilitating its stability. British national development would proceed more smoothly without further interventions in Ireland. It was no longer in the interests of ambitious politicians to raise Irish questions in British politics. Northern Ireland commanded a mere 12 seats in the House of Commons, by comparison with the 105 seats to which Ireland was entitled in the 1918 election. The abolition of Stormont would have required increased representation for the region, and whose interests would that have served? Labour had no interest in the revival of internal party-debate over the territorial definition of the British state, especially given its electoral heartlands in Scotland and Wales. Northern Ireland was best left alone as a place apart. Contributions from Northern Irish trade unionists were welcomed by the Labour party, but the party deliberately refused to organize in the region. The Conservatives had been and remained the Conservative and Unionist party, and felt no need fully to incorporate the UUP within its ranks: nor would the UUP have embraced such an offer automatically because it wished to maintain its cross-class appeal amongst Protestants. Labour avoided organizing in Northern Ireland to prevent creating possible divisions within its own ranks; whereas the Conservatives felt no need to do so given that nearly all of Northern Ireland's Westminster MPs habitually took their whip. The UUP were left to control 'Ulster' like junior prefects.

These reasons explain why no moves were made by British policy-makers to integrate Northern Ireland into the British nation. Knowledge of their force encouraged the establishment of local domination by the UUP. Hegemonic control, provided its uglier manifestations were not too visible, was preferable for British policy-makers to the known historical costs of direct intervention and management of Irish affairs. Westminster and Whitehall shut their eyes. For example, Sir Henry Batterbee, assistant under-secretary at the Dominions Office in the 1930s, surveyed evidence on discrimination against Catholics in Northern Ireland and concluded that 'the bias of the Northern Ireland authorities is bound to be in favour of those who are supporters of the present regime: it is everywhere inimicable to good and impartial administration where government and party are as closely united in Northern Ireland' (cited in Boyce, 1988: 89–90).

There were also reasons of state why British policy-makers persistently avoided making dramatic choices over the status of Northern Ireland after 1921. The integration of Northern Ireland into Britain would have guaranteed poor relations with the Irish

Free State; whereas repartition or forced Irish unification might have renewed the bloody conflicts of the early 1920s. Northern Ireland remained therefore both a problem and an issue for negotiation between the British and Irish states throughout the 1920s and 1930s. The external interests of the British state were clear: good relations, especially in defence, with their neighbour in the British archipelago and the maintenance of good relations with all dominions. However, the British could not or were not prepared to deliver Irish unity, at least until they were threatened by German conquest. Yet they were also not prepared to resolve the status of Northern Ireland in the 1920s and 1930s as long as it might jeopardize Anglo-Irish relations. Only in 1949, following the declaration of an Irish Republic, and the experience of Irish neutrality during World War II, did the British government 'clarify' the status of Northern Ireland in the Ireland Act: 'Northern Ireland remains part of His Majesty's dominions and of the United Kingdom and it is hereby affirmed that in no event will Northern Ireland or any part thereof cease to be part of His Majesty's dominions and of the United Kingdom without the consent of the parliament of Northern Ireland.'

British equivocation over the status of Northern Ireland, determined by 'reasons of state', therefore created a climate in which hegemonic control made common sense to Ulster Protestants. The Act of 1949 lifted the threat of repartition (note the reference to 'any part thereof'), and formally consolidated control over Northern Ireland's status in the hands of its own parliament. However, given that the British constitution was very flexible, and that every Act of Westminster was as reversible as any other, Unionist fears were only marginally eased. They knew that they were not regarded as really British, and that there were always going to be circumstances where their status would be negotiable if it was in the interests of the British state. Moreover, by that time the system of hegemonic control was entrenched and had a logic of its own.

Irish nation-building failure in an almost mimetic version of British failure reinforced the system. The Stormont regime owed its existence to the refusal of Ulster Protestants to identify with the Irish nation. They perceived the evolution of independent Ireland as a complete vindication of their fears, and as a justification of the political development of Northern Ireland. The lament of the poet and senator William Butler Yeats during the 1925 debate over the illegalisation of divorce in the Irish Free State was prophetic: 'If you

show that this country, Southern Ireland, is going to be governed by
Catholic ideas and Catholic ideas alone, you will never get the North.
You will create an impassable barrier between North and South,
and you will pass more and more Catholic laws, while the North
will, gradually, assimilate its divorce and other laws to England.
You will put a wedge into the midst of this nation . . .' (cited in
Kennedy, 1988: 159–60). Yeats's analysis and prediction can be
generalized if we replace the word Catholic in the above quotation by
the omnibus expression 'Gaelic-Catholic-anti-British'. Irish cultural
nationalism grossly offended those Protestants who claimed cultural
sensibilities.

It is now increasingly accepted, at least in revisionist Irish
historiography, that Irish nationalism mirrored, albeit in a less
extreme and unjust way, the exclusivism and sectarianism of Ulster
unionism (Bowman, 1982; O'Halloran, 1985). What is not so widely
recognized is that the conditions under which the Irish Free State
was created and developed had unintended consequences which
facilitated the consolidation of hegemonic control in Ulster. The
Irish civil war was fought by Irish nationalists over the terms of the
Anglo-Irish Treaty, but not over the terms which referred to Ulster.
Both sides assumed that the Ulster question would be satisfied by the
Boundary Commission in ways which would make Northern Ireland
unworkable. The terms which provoked the civil war were those
which affected the scope and extent of Irish 'statehood': its degree
of substantive and ritual subordination to the British empire. The
geographical scope of the state was not an issue. The war was fought
between the pro-Treaty forces who argued that the Treaty gave the
Irish Free State the freedom to achieve freedom, and anti-Treaty
forces who argued that it did not. This war of Green against Green
(Hopkinson, 1988) occluded the Ulster question, and facilitated the
consolidation of hegemonic control by the UUP. The victors of the
war in the Irish Free State were in no mood to renew instability
through prosecuting another war for Northern Ireland and accepted
British money in return for burying the report of the Boundary
Commission of 1925, and tacitly accepting partition.

Although the civil war was won by the pro-Treaty forces, it
established the central axis of competition between the parties which
emerged in the new state. The two main parties, Fianna Fáil and Fine
Gael, carried on the civil war by parliamentary means, competing over
which of them would best establish the freedom of the Irish state, i.e.

which of them would best stand up for the Irish against the British state. This party-competition had three mutually reinforcing effects in the years before 1949. First, the external activities of the Irish Free State were directed towards the repeal, rewriting, and alteration of those terms of the Treaty which affected Anglo-Irish relations, and were regarded as intolerable violations of Irish sovereignty. Second, the internal activities of the Irish Free State were directed towards establishing achievements which had been made possible by independent Irish statehood: i.e. distinct cultural, social, and economic policies. Finally, both these external and internal state-building activities, almost inevitably, cut against the logic of contending that Ulster Protestants were part of the Irish nation, and served to reinforce partition. The less Ireland remained within the symbolic trappings of the British empire and the more its internal policies reflected the cultural values of its Catholic majority, the greater the likelihood was that hegemonic control would be entrenched north of the border. Irish state-building, logically but unintentionally, took place at the expense of pan-Irish nation-building. The symmetry is evident: British state-maintenance also took place at the expense of pan-British nation-building in Northern Ireland. Hegemonic control was the joint by-product of these nation-building failures. In the next chapter we explain why it proved unsustainable.

Appendix 3.1   The relative reduction (r) in the effective number of parties caused by PR(STV) in 1925 compared with plurality-rule in 1929

The effective number of parties in a competitive political system, N, is the reciprocal of the Herfindahl–Hirschman concentration index (HH). The latter is defined as $\Sigma\ p_i^2$ where p is the fractional share of the ith party and Σ stands for the summation over all parties. The effective number of parties in votes, Nv, is thus measured by $1/HHv = 1/\Sigma(pv)_i^2$; whereas the effective number of parties in seats, Ns, is measured by $1/HHs = 1/\Sigma(ps)_i^2$. The relative reduction in the effective number of parties from votes to seats, **r**, expressed as a percentage, is measured by $(Nv–Ns)/Nv \times {}^{100}\!/_1$ (Taagepera and Shugart, 1989: 77–91 and 273). In 1925 **r** was 13.22% (see below), whereas in 1929, after the abolition of STV it was 45.46% (see below).

(i) The Northern Ireland parliamentary general election 1925[36]
Source of election data: Elliott (1973: 89)

Party	Percentage of the vote *	Percentage of seats
Ulster Unionist Party	55.0	61.54
Independent Unionists	9.0	7.69
Nationalists	23.8	19.23
Republicans (Sinn Féin)	5.3	3.85
N. Ireland Labour Party	4.7	5.77
TT (Belfast tenants assoc)	0.9	0
UTA (farmers' assoc)	1.3	1.92

HHv = 0.37; Nv = 1/HHv = 2.70; HHs = 0.4268; and Ns = 1/HHs = 2.343. Therefore **r** = 13.22%.

(ii) The Northern Ireland parliamentary general election 1929

Party	Percentage of the vote	Percentage of seats
Ulster Unionist Party	50.6	71.15
Independent Unionists	14.3	5.77
Nationalists (Nat League)	11.7	21.15
Independent Nationalist	1.3	0
N. Ireland Labour Party	8.0	1.923
Independent Labour	0.8	0
Liberal	6.3	0
Loc Opt (temperance movt)	3.4	0
TT (Belfast tenants assoc)	2.4	0
Independent	1.2	0

HHv = 0.302; Nv = 1/HHv = 3.306; HHs = 0.5546; and Ns = 1/HHs = 1.803. Therefore **r** = 45.46%.
Note: *   =   percentage of the first-preference vote.

Notes

1. The Soviet Union and Yugoslavia were examples of countries in which ethnic contests for state power were made 'unworkable' under Communist hegemony. Since the collapse of this hegemony ethnic contests for state power multiply daily.

2. This concept is derived from Lustick (1979, 1987), though our definition, as he has pointed out in correspondence, differs from his. But he maintains that we use our definition consistently.

3. The Stormont parliament was not built until 1932, but we follow custom in referring to the period from 1920 as the Stormont era.

4. The Westminster model was extensively imported into the 1922 constitution of the Irish Free State and the Constitution of Ireland of 1937. This heritage, although tempered by the entrenchment of basic rights and proportional representation, is partially responsible for the ease with which Catholic majoritarianism has affected public law and public policy in the Republic of Ireland.

5. The absence of legitimacy was more important than the absence of party alternation. We reject the thesis that the failure of Great British political parties to compete in Northern Ireland was 'the fundamental reason for the continuing conflict in the province' (Roberts, 1987: 218). We explain later why Great British political parties did not organize in Northern Ireland (pp. 142-4), and why it would not make much difference if they did so now (pp. 297-9).

6. In 1945 the Northern Ireland Cabinet objected to a BBC Radio programme about parliament because they feared opposition MPs would have been presented with a platform to air their views (Birrell and Murie, 1980: 66).

7. On the rare occasions when the Senate rejected bills from the Commons, the latter yielded (Calvert, 1968: 156–7).

8. Canadian experience with their 1960 Bill of Rights suggests that judges schooled in the Westminster tradition cannot appreciate why one parliamentary statute can – or should   be used to overturn another. Only when a Charter of Rights was entrenched in the Canadian Constitution in 1982 and made incapable of amendment by the federal parliament alone have judges and lawyers been willing to challenge legislation (Mandel, 1989).

9. The more legitimate courts in the Irish Free State and the Republic of Ireland were confronted with cases challenging the constitution far more frequently than their northern counterparts: ninety-six challenges to the two Irish constitutions occurred between 1919 and 1970, by comparison with six in Northern Ireland (Barrington, 1972: 40).

10. Apologists for unionism mislead by glossing over this important distinction: thus Stewart persuades his readers that Stormont was not that bad: 'Not only did Stormont not enact discriminatory laws against Catholics; it was expressly forbidden to do so . . .' (Stewart, 1986: 177; and see pp. 133-4).

11. This tactic was used in Canada before 1982. Litigants opposed to provincial or federal legislation argued before the courts, often successfully, that the offending legislation was not in the jurisdiction of the level of government which had passed it.

12. Thus a Stormont statute which imposed hygienic controls on milk production was held to be legal even though it also affected cross-border trade in milk – an issue for Westminster's jurisdiction (Newark, 1955: 30). However, in 1972 the Northern Ireland divisional court did invalidate a section of the Special Powers Act by ruling *ultra vires* the power which it gave to members of Her Majesty's forces to disperse assemblies of three or more persons.

13. A justiciable Bill of Right or a less benighted judiciary might have weakened majoritarianism. In principle courts are less likely than legislatures and governments to distinguish between majorities and minorities, and more likely to make decisions based on the equality of plaintiff and defendant, and on the merits of the arguments presented. Judges are not paragons of impartiality, but they are less exposed to direct majoritarian pressures.

14. In federations constitutional amendments affecting competences require the consent of both levels of government (Wheare, 1963: 30–1).

15. Administrative actions helped prevent disputes arising between the two levels of government. Stormont's draftsman made sure that bills were within the parliament's competence (Newark, 1955: 29), and the Northern Ireland Attorney General had to certify the validity of bills before they received the royal assent. Consequently clashes over the division of powers were few (Kilbrandon, 1973: para. 158).

16. On another occasion the British government and the Westminster Speaker agreed that debate on religious discrimination in Northern Ireland was unnecessary because remedies were available in the courts (Calvert, 1968: 101)!

17. Our evaluation of the election systems in Northern Ireland between 1921 and 1969 (p. 148) ignores the votes cast in QUB elections. QUB votes were 'double-votes', since graduates of QUB could also vote in normal parliamentary constituencies. However, we have counted the four QUB seats as part of the percentage of seats won by the contending parties.

18. Northern Ireland Parliamentary Debates (Hansard) House of Commons, vol. 8, col. 2276.

19. Some sociologists accuse political scientists of an erroneous preoccupation with voting-systems in explaining political competitiveness (O'Dowd *et al.*,

1980: 28). However, PR(STV) increased the number of candidates and political parties vying to win seats in Northern Ireland, both before 1929 and after 1973. Had PR been maintained after 1929 the UUP's hegemony might well have been broken, and opened the road to political realignments. No sane political scientist would claim that PR(STV), in and of itself, can fundamentally alter ethnic voting-preferences (in this case voting within an ethnic bloc).

20. Compare this result with the Anglocentric view that 'in its composition the Northern Ireland parliament reflects the views of the people with no more distortion than is normally to be found in democratic parliaments. Its real peculiarity is that, being elected mainly on the constitutional issue, it has no alternation of parties in office' (Barritt and Carter, 1972: 43). Writing originally in 1962 it did not occur to Barritt and Carter that plurality rule (a) distorted 'the views of the people' more than the PR systems used to elect democratic parliaments in most of the rest of western Europe and the Republic of Ireland; (b) focused electoral competition on 'the constitutional issue'; and (c) sustained the UUP as a hegemonic party.

21. A good discussion of the spatial dimensions of voting in Northern Ireland can be found in Osborne (1982).

22. Roland Moyle, parliamentary private secretary to James Callaghan in 1969–70 (interview with B. O'Leary, 3 Jan. 1991). 'The way the old Home affairs department in Northern Ireland ran the police, my God, I mean the police were the creatures of the 'mini-aristocracy'. The stories one heard about the RUC inspectors. When one visited Fermanagh to see the prime minister Brooke he had to go through the side door like a servant' (Merlyn Rees, interview with B. O'Leary, 18 Dec. 1990).

23. Brooke is quoted addressing the Derry Unionist Association in the *Londonderry Sentinel* of 20 Mar. 1934. When questioned about this statement in Stormont, Craig declared: 'There is not one of my colleagues who does not entirely agree with him and I would ask him not to withdraw one word' (Farrell, 1976: 90–1).

24. To pre-empt potential feminist critics: the ethnic pattern in female-employment opportunities is discussed later (pp. 263-5).

25. Census-data between 1926 and 1951 do not allow an evaluation of the relative positions of Catholics and Protestants: our thanks to David Smith of the PSI.

26. There was 'a striking unevenness' in the distribution of Catholics across industries (Rowthorn and Wayne, 1988: 34; and see Table 3.1). They were scarcely present in well-paid engineering occupations. Few Catholics were found in the growing banking, finance, and insurance industries. They were present in low-pay industries: such as construction, clothing, and footwear.

27. It should be emphasized, as it was in the Cameron Report (1969), that some of the few Nationalist-controlled local councils practised a reciprocal discrimination in housing.

28. Another estimate in 1972 put the Catholic share of senior civil-service positions at 5 percent (Donnison, 1973).

29. Hewitt (1981) emphasizes that working-class Protestants were disenfranchised in local government and that gerrymandering was not as widespread as the civil-rights movement maintained, but his attempt to suggest that Northern Ireland's democracy was relatively 'normal' overlooks how the Westminster model can be employed to sustain political domination and reproduce historical inequalities.

30. Stewart cites as the exception the ban placed on the publication and distribution of republican and IRA literature.

31. Blacks in the southern states of the USA were subject to more brutal and oppressive local hegemonic control. For a comparison between Northern Ireland and other territories where minorities were subject to domination see F. Wright (1987).

32. The proposal prompted Craig to make an extraordinary riposte: dominion status for Northern Ireland was preferable to subordination to a Dublin parliament.

33. Craig's telegrams to Chamberlain express this outrage with brutal frankness (Fisk, 1983: 207–10). He suggested that de Valera was a German collaborator and that the British government should invade Eire. Other Unionist leaders were more circumspect: Brooke thought that some Unionists would have felt obliged to accept Irish unification to support the British empire in its hour of need (Barton, 1988: 160 ff).

34. There is continuous controversy as to whether Loyalist/Protestant ideology is primarily economically, religiously, or politically motivated (e.g. Bell, 1976; Bruce, 1986; Nelson, 1984; and Stewart, 1986).

35. There was one means through which British nation-building with respect to the Irish was actually followed, and more or less successfully. The Irish in Britain (i.e. in England, Scotland, and Wales) were given full citizenship rights, even after the declaration of the Irish Republic in 1949.

36. See Note 17 above.

4
Losing control:
the collapse of the unionist
regime, 1963–72

The Irish question . . . was almost as dead as Captain Boycott.
(R. J. Lawrence, 1965: 75)

*The advice that came to me from all sides was on no account
to get sucked into the Irish bog.*
(James Callaghan, 1973: 14)

Northern Ireland's status as part of the Union was apparently
consolidated by the Ireland Act of 1949, and the Stormont regime
coped easily with a small-scale IRA campaign waged from 1956
until 1962. Northern Ireland appeared stable when Terence O'Neill
replaced Lord Brookeborough as prime minister in 1963. Why then
did hegemonic control collapse within a decade, and the Provisional
IRA emerge as a powerful force? There are three typical explanations
of the fall of Stormont: two concentrate on exogenous factors, and
one stresses endogenous causes.

Unionist commentators blame Stormont's collapse largely on
Irish irredentism. In their view it was destroyed primarily by a
rebellion. The protesting Catholic minority are seen as disaffected
nationalists, a fifth column of the Irish Republic, and the civil-rights
campaign of 1967–9 as tactical nationalism. Unionist security forces
were provoked by Marxist or Republican (or Marxist–Republican)
revolutionaries in a planned campaign to destroy Stormont and
achieve a united Ireland (Wilson, 1989: 154, 157). Nationalist
militants were succoured by the Irish Republic: spiritually, by the
territorial claim to sovereignty embedded in the 1937 constitution;
physically, by the promise of a 'safe haven' south of the border; and

militarily, by shipments of arms from leading members of the Irish government.

Left-wing nationalists agree that Stormont collapsed because of a minority rebellion, but explain the intervention of British troops and the abolition of Stormont by the external interests of British imperialism or the British capitalist state (Farrell, 1980; O'Dowd *et al.*, 1980: 204). The British had used Stormont to suppress nationalists, but when it was destabilized by a legitimate mass democratic movement they intervened to shore up Stormont with a massive security presence, and when reconstructing Stormont proved futile, they opted for direct rule.

Conventional endogenous explanations account for the breakdown of the Stormont system through reference to endemic ethno-religious divisions. Sometimes no attempt is even made to explain the timing of the collapse: the cohabitation of the same space by two antagonistic communities is presumed to have meant that sooner or later the Stormont system would disintegrate.[1] But some do make an effort to explain why the system shattered in the late 1960s. Those for whom religion is the crucial cause of conflict see the ecumenical movement flowing from the Second Vatican Council of the Roman Catholic Church (1962–5) as a pivotal event which intensified the insecurities of Protestants and made them resistant to political change (Bruce, 1986: 89–92). Others put forward a version of the 'Great Man' theory of history: the interaction between the reforming Terence O'Neill, with his personal exposure to what they consider liberal and cosmopolitan English culture, and the atavistic, sectarian, and parochial politicians with whom he had to work, unleashed a chain of events which ended in the abolition of Stormont (Rose, 1971: 97; Bruce, 1986: 69–71).

All three explanatory strategies make partisan points, whether or not that is the intention of their proponents. Unionists absolve Stormont of much of the responsibility for the unrest, belittle minority grievances, and delegitimize the civil-rights movement; nationalists exonerate militant republicans of any blame for the outbreak of violence, casting the IRA in a purely reactive role; while the endogenous school depicts the role of external actors as either irrelevant or benign, and overstates the salience of religion and an alleged great man. The collapse of Stormont is better explained by a number of environmental changes which affected the motivations of political actors both outside and inside Northern Ireland.

The exogenous background to 'O'Neillism'

The political and economic development of the Irish state in the 1950s and 1960s decisively contributed to the collapse of hegemonic control. Until 1949 it had seemed that constitutional nationalism might succeed by mobilizing international pressures. Churchill had (tentatively) offered Northern Ireland to de Valera in 1940 in return for the Republic's participation on the allied side; after 1945 a number of the governing Labour party's MPs were sympathetic to a united Ireland; and there were efforts in the US Congress to make Marshall Aid to the UK dependent upon Irish reunification. However, when the Dublin government declared its intention to make the Irish Free State a Republic Westminster responded in the following year with the Ireland Act, dashing the prospects of constitutional nationalism.

Besides failing to recover 'unredeemed' Irish territory the Republic emerged out of the war-time emergency still protectionist, and with chronic emigration. By the 1950s its per capita emigration-toll was approaching the level of the immediate post-famine years. Driven largely by these economic concerns and by an international climate of trade-liberalization, the Republic's government embarked upon a major change in its development strategy in 1958. The Irish state decided to encourage international and multi-national capitalist investment. The change in direction was solidified in 1959 by the departure of de Valera who became President, and his replacement as Taoiseach by the more pragmatic Sean Lemass.[2] The post-1958 strategy-shift was driven by political considerations within the Republic but it had significant spillover effects on Northern Ireland.

The jettisoning of autarky had implications for irredentism, which seemed bad for business. Good relations with Northern Ireland, the UK, and the EEC became imperative for the success of the new economic strategy. The resolution of the national question would have to await economic development. Fianna Fáil, the party which managed the transition from protectionism to economic liberalism, rationalized the volte-face by claiming that without advanced economic development Ulster Protestants would continue to find unification an unattractive prospect. Its leadership developed a 'technocratic anti-partitionist' strategy (Lyne, 1990), claiming that through economic growth Irish unity would be accomplished.

Cross-border co-operation increased in the fishing industry, railways, tourism, and electricity generation, collaboration encouraged by civil servants in Dublin and Belfast.

The IRA campaign of 1956–62 did not disturb the thaw in north-south relations. The Republic co-operated with Stormont and introduced internment under its Offences Against the State Act. 'Operation Harvest' and its sequels ended with the IRA dumping its arms and berating the nationalist population for failing to give it sufficient support (Bowyer Bell, 1979: 289–336).[3] The IRA campaign had fizzled out long before the formal cessation of hostilities. Lemass directed friendly speeches northwards,[4] and eventually encouraged the Nationalist party to abandon its abstentionist policy and become the formal opposition at Stormont. The Northern minority was on its own: improvements in its position would have to come from within the British political system. In 1965 Lemass risked visiting O'Neill in Stormont. This visit conveyed an implicit recognition of Northern Ireland, even if it aroused the suspicions of loyalists like the Reverend Ian Paisley. The 'summit' meeting, the first between the two Prime Ministers on the island for forty years, was accompanied by others at ministerial and official levels. Lemass's initiative helped break the mould in Northern Irish politics, depriving unionists of the argument that the Irish state, the IRA, and the northern minority were in coalition against their regime, and created the space for O'Neill's rhetoric of 'community reconciliation'.[5]

The abandonment of autarky also had ramifications for Anglo-Irish relations. After the formation of the EEC, both the UK and the Republic began adapting their relationships in preparation for entry, signing a free trade agreement in 1965. Their simultaneous entry into the EEC, eventually ratified in 1973, would have occurred in 1967 but for President de Gaulle's exercise of the French veto. These improvements in British–Irish relations made it more difficult for the British government to resist the pressure from the Catholic minority for reform in Northern Ireland, and made Unionist justifications for hegemonic control seem threadbare and self-serving. The fact that the Irish government did not switch back to full-blooded irredentism when armed conflict broke out in 1968–9 (despite the temptations and a murky arms-running scandal involving some key government ministers[6]) increased international pressure upon British policy-makers to reform Northern Ireland.

The development of the post-war British state also had unintended consequences which undermined the foundations of hegemonic control. The British welfare state was dramatically extended after World War II by the Labour government. Despite the conservatism of the UUP government and its belief that the welfare state would exacerbate the fecklessness of the Catholic minority, the new welfare programmes were applied in Northern Ireland, and for straightforward reasons (Harkness, 1977). The anti-partitionism within the British labour movement made it dangerous to incur the wrath of a Labour government committed to increased state intervention in society. In any case the British government made their new welfare programmes extremely attractive by offering to make up whatever shortfall would exist if the Northern Ireland government provided services at UK standards while imposing tax rates similar to Britain. Had the UUP government followed their ideological beliefs and refused to implement Labour's welfare-state programme it would have posed dangers for Protestant inter-class solidarity and played into the hands of third parties like the NILP.

Brookeborough's Cabinet's decision to extend the welfare state and its social benefits to Northern Ireland was not motivated by a desire to increase support for the Union among the minority population.[7] That would have entailed a major deviation from the strategy of hegemonic control, and would have been inconsistent with other policies which denied British civil rights to Catholics and discouraged them from joining the UUP. Unionists continued to believe that most Catholics were unreconstructed rebels. Nevertheless the application of the welfare state to Northern Ireland had consequences which served to undermine control. It opened up obvious disparities between the standard of living in the two parts of Ireland, weakening the northern minority's formal enthusiasm for joining an independent and united Ireland,[8] and paved the way for Catholic demands for British rights in the late 1960s. Catholics began to interact more with state institutions and to expect more from them.

The most significant post-war welfare-state legislation had been in education, which had a time-lag before its consequences were felt. Catholics went on to secondary education and universities in greater numbers in the 1950s and 1960s. Their proportion of the Queen's University, Belfast, student body, for example, increased between 1961 and 1972 from 22 to 32 per cent, close to their proportion of the total population (Foster, 1988: 584). The civil-rights movement of the mid- and late 1960s was spearheaded by a new Catholic middle class, partially built by the British welfare state (Arthur, 1974: 23; Buckland, 1981; Cameron, 1969; Farrell, 1976; Purdie, 1990). The leaders of the civil-rights movements and the student-based movement, the People's Democracy, were overwhelmingly composed of the Catholic middle class or Catholic students. These new organizations, even if their importance has been exaggerated in comparison with local and traditional Catholic organizations, were new in their rhetoric and objectives, and dominated by graduates. The same is true of National Unity which challenged the Nationalist Party in the early 1960s. The leaders of these new organizations, who attracted public, British, and international attention, developed the slogan of 'equal citizenship' which proved so corrosive for Stormont's reputation. They embraced a rhetoric of civil rights which partially displaced traditional nationalism. One reason they did so was because the youngest amongst them had been brought up as citizens in the new British welfare state, which had unintendedly made Northern Irish Catholics more British.

Moreover by easing economic domination, the growth of the welfare state weakened a key facet of the control system. British social services erected obstacles to the brutal forms of control which exist in places like Israel (Smooha, 1980) and existed in South Africa before de Klerk's reforms. In independent hegemonic regimes, the economic dependency of the subordinated is nearly absolute, co-option is rife, and threats of economic retribution are often sufficient to ensure quiescence. However, in Northern Ireland no religious discrimination could be made in the allocation of welfare benefits (as opposed to services), since entitlements were mostly determined by Westminster and Whitehall. There were demographic implications. Unemployment and other welfare benefits slowed down minority emigration, thus sustaining a larger minority than would otherwise have been the case. The Catholic share of the Northern Ireland population had been static in the 1926 and 1937 censuses (at 33.5 per cent) but started to rise marginally in the post-war years (to 34.4 per cent in 1951, 34.9 per cent in 1961, and 36.8 per cent in 1971 (Compton, 1985: Table 1). This change had obvious consequences for Catholic confidence and Protestant insecurities during the protests of the late 1960s and early 1970s.

Finally, the growth of the welfare state entailed growing met-
ropolitan interest and clout in Northern Ireland. The Stormont
government's failure to manage its economy successfully, as shown
by an unemployment rate high above the UK average throughout
the late 1950s and 1960s, entailed an increasing subvention from
Whitehall. The inertia of Brookeborough, and his government's
apparent capture by economic élites in declining traditional industries led British officials to co-operate with UUP backbenchers in
replacing him with his 'progressive' Minister of Finance, Terence
O'Neill (MacDonald, 1986: 71). Fiscal dependency also made the
UUP government susceptible to pressure from the new Labour government elected in 1964. It was suggested that some of Stormont's
powers should be transferred to Westminster (Buckland, 1981: 107).
The Labour government was also interested in Northern Ireland for
other reasons. Harold Wilson had a large number of Irish voters in
his Huyton constituency, was keenly aware of his party's sizeable
Irish support, and had a desire to make his mark by tackling difficult
problems (Bew *et al.*, 1979: 179–80). He had expressed interest in
promoting reforms in Northern Ireland in speeches before the 1964
election campaign, and along with other ministers had indicated that
he shared the aspiration for a united Ireland. His memoirs make
clear that the new UK Prime Minister was intensely irritated by
the fact that the Ulster Unionists who returned all 12 of Northern
Ireland's MPs to Westminster in the 1964 election continued to
take, as they always had done, the Conservative whip (Wilson,
1971: 232). Labour's wafer-thin majority between 1964 and 1966
was jeopardized by the 'Ulster Tories'. In 1965 the Campaign for
Democracy in Ulster, made up of backbench Labour MPs, was
founded by Paul Rose to promote concern about abuses of human
rights in the region: it could count on as many as 100 Labour MPs
for support (Buckland, 1981: 108). In 1966 Wilson informed O'Neill
that the subvention was becoming hard to justify if the position of the
minority could not be improved (Wilson, 1971: 270).

The endogenous background to 'O'Neillism'

These developments in the Republic and Great Britain impinged
upon Northern Ireland in ways which presaged the breakdown of
hegemonic control. External developments were transforming the

politics of both ethnic blocs, but internal forces prompting change
were also at work. Traditional nationalism had failed Catholics in
the 1950s. Constitutional nationalism, articulated most recently in
the Anti-Partition League of 1948–9, had done nothing to alter
Northern Ireland's constitutional status or to improve Catholics'
socio-economic position. Voting for Sinn Féin candidates in elections in the 1950s[9] expressed alienation but achieved nothing, apart
from encouraging the IRA to believe that an insurrectionary strategy
was viable.

The apparent futility of either brand of traditional nationalism
and the changed attitudes induced by the welfare state promoted
revisionism among the Catholic population (McKeown, 1986: 1–38;
McKeown, 1984: 15 ff.). The Catholic middle class, while not
abandoning their nationalist sentiments, began to seek the reform
of Northern Ireland as their first goal; and before long for many
it became the overriding goal. A succession of groups emerged
seeking to advertise and change the position of the minority
under the Stormont regime. National Unity was formed in 1959
by those Catholics frustrated by single-issue anti-partitionism, and
by the way in which the Nationalist party neglected social and
economic questions (McAllister, 1975). While it aspired to a
united Ireland, it accepted the existence of Northern Ireland, and
demanded reform rather than concentrating on anti-partitionism. It
forced the Nationalist party to propose policies aimed at improving
the economic and social conditions of Catholics within Northern
Ireland (Buckland, 1981: 109).

In 1965 National Unity spawned a new organization, the National
Democratic Party. New attitudes within the Catholic community led
to the formation of the Campaign for Social Justice (CSJ) in 1964,
which addressed discrimination. By 1965 it had affiliated with the
National Council for Civil Liberties in London and cultivated the
Campaign for Democracy in Ulster. When adequate redress of
Catholic grievances was not forthcoming by 1967, the Northern
Ireland Civil Rights Association (NICRA) was formed with similar
aims to the CSJ, but instead of being an intellectual ginger-group it
employed the tactics of the US civil-rights movement. While CSJ
and NICRA were predominantly movements led by the middle
class, Belfast's working-class Catholics were also shifting towards
individuals, organizations, and parties prepared to put the reform of
Northern Ireland ahead of a united Ireland: electing Gerry Fitt at

the head of Republican Labour to Westminster in 1966, and Paddy Devlin of the NILP to the Stormont parliament in 1969.

Physical-force nationalism had failed even more abysmally than its constitutional counterpart. The IRA campaign of 1956–62 was a fiasco. 'Volunteers' were interned in both the North and South. They won no sustained international publicity or sympathy, and so little support from Northern Catholics that they felt obliged to abandon armed struggle. They had failed completely to mobilize the Catholic population, especially in urban areas, and acknowledged this in their cease-fire announcement. Indeed the UUP government felt so confident about its defeat of militant republicanism that it released all internees before the IRA announced its formal end to hostilities (Buckland, 1981: 105). In the wake of this crushing defeat some republicans dropped out in disillusion while others embarked upon the political rather than military road, eventually becoming more Marxist-Leninist than Catholic. The new republicanism eventually produced the Republican Clubs, a number of Wolfe Tone Societies, and much later the Workers Party. These groups supported the reformism of the civil-rights movement. By 1967 the IRA, as a military organization, was close to extinction.

The new participatory attitude among Catholics posed serious problems for the UUP's hegemonic control. Abstentionist defeatism was no longer the minority's preferred option. The legitimacy of hegemonic control rested on the notion that Catholics were nationalist rebels who had to be maintained in economic and political inferiority. Without a plausible national-security justification, heg emonic control was simply naked domination, and more difficult to sustain at home and abroad.[10] Controlling nationalists who wanted to destroy the state was more ideologically defensible than controlling Catholics who wanted just treatment. In the past Unionist solidarity had been bolstered by the Republic's verbal bellicosity, as in 1937 and 1948–9, and by the obvious unwillingness of the minority to accept Northern Ireland. However, the Republic's unwillingness to provide good excuses and some Catholics' willingness to play the political process spelled the end of an era.

The final environmental factor prompting the changes which resulted in 'O'Neillism' was the regional economy. Traditional industries (linen, shipbuilding, and agriculture) were in serious decline by the 1960s (see Table 4.1 (a)). Employment in the shipbuilding industry, the major employer of the skilled Protestant

Table 4.1
(a) Employment in Northern Ireland's traditional sectors, 1950–73
Source: NIO (1974: 6)

Sector	1950 labour force	1973 labour force	net loss (per cent)
Agriculture, forestry & fishing	101,000	55,000	46,000 (45.5)
Textiles	65,000	19,000	46,000 (70.7)
Shipbuilding	24,000	10,000	14,000 (41.7)

(b) The shifting pattern of sectoral employment, 1926–71
(shares in per cent)
Source: Kennedy et al. (1988: 99)

Sector	1926	1961	1971
Agriculture	29	16	11
Industry	34	42	42
Services	37	42	47

working class, fell by 40 per cent between 1961 and 1964 alone (Bew *et al.*, 1979: 135). Despite finding new sources of industrial and (mainly public-) service employment (see Table 4.1 (b)), Northern Ireland had much higher unemployment than any other region of the UK. A sympathetic unionist commentator declared that unemployment was the 'one problem that had defied solution' (Lawrence, 1965: 101). In these circumstances the Northern Ireland Labour party did well in competition with the UUP. The NILP had not won a seat at Stormont since its reorganization in 1949, but took four at the 1958 election, polling 16 per cent of the total vote, and retained them with its highest number of votes ever in the subsequent election in 1962, when it won 26 per cent of the total vote. The NILP posed a straightforward threat to the UUP's electoral hegemony, especially in the Belfast urban area.

'O'Neillism' and its consequences

Against this setting O'Neill became Northern Ireland's fourth prime minister. He adopted the strategies being employed in Great Britain to deal with the decline of traditional industries: regional planning, new-town development, and infrastructural investments which would boost economic growth ('regional Keynesianism'). A six-year plan was adopted in 1964 to counter the traditional concentration of industry around Belfast, and to disperse both industry and the labour force more widely around the region. Central to the new approach was the construction of economic infrastructure, including two motorways, new house-building programmes, a series of new growth-centres including a new city, a second university, and a centralized and rationalized public administration. The preoccupation with economic modernization had repercussions for border politics: in a move towards corporatist industrial relations, O'Neill recognized the Dublin-based Irish Congress of Trade Unions for the first time in 1964, and to enhance economic co-operation friendlier relations were pursued with the Republic. To create an atmosphere conducive to external investment, O'Neill promoted better 'community relations'.

There are various explanations of why O'Neill avoided the overt sectarianism of his predecessors. His time at Eton and his stint in the Guards, allegedly exposed him to liberal and cosmopolitan British culture and separated him from the narrow-minded bigots in the grass roots of the UUP and the Orange Order (Bruce, 1986: 69). One Anglophile believes that: 'because his early family life was primarily spent at school in England, abroad and in the Army, O'Neill lacked the intensely parochial look conventionally found among politicians in the province. Instead of looking in and back, he looked forward and out' (Rose, 1971: 97). However, even if one accepted the assumptions underlying these arguments, they are scarcely compelling. The superficiality of O'Neill's liberalism was demonstrated by a condescending speech made a few days after his resignation in 1969: 'It is frightfully hard to explain to a Protestant that if you give Roman Catholics a good job and a good house they will live like Protestants, because they will see neighbours with cars and TV sets. They will refuse to have eighteen children, but if the Roman Catholic is jobless and lives in a most ghastly hovel he will rear eighteen children on national assistance. It is impossible to explain this to a militant Protestant . . . He cannot understand, in fact, that if you treat Roman Catholics with due consideration and kindness they will live like Protestants, in spite of the authoritarian nature of their church' (cited in Buckland, 1981: 112).[11]

If we examine the political environment in which O'Neill operated, it is better to describe his motivations and actions as pragmatic rather than liberal. Traditional sectarianism would have done nothing to resolve the region's economic problems and might have dissuaded external investors from spending in Northern Ireland. Growing financial dependence on Westminster[12] and the interest of key elements of the Labour government in the region made traditional sectarianism a course fraught with danger. The *rapprochement* between Britain and the Republic posed a threat. Beating the sectarian drum had reduced plausibility given the acquiescence of the minority population, the collapse of the IRA, the conciliatory approach of the Republic's government, and the arrival of the ecumenical movement. A rhetorical alternative to sectarianism was 'thinkable' and sane.

'Modernization' had the potential to solve the UUP's problems. By tackling the NILP, using that party's own language and policies, O'Neill could present the UUP as the 'natural' party of government. Modernization could do for O'Neill what the abolition of PR had done for Craigavon in 1929. By 1965 he was able to win a Stormont general election in which the NILP share of the vote fell significantly. While some observers allege that O'Neill 'sought nothing less than a fully legitimate regime in which Catholics would support the Constitution as well as comply with its basic laws' (Rose, 1971: 97), few Catholics, past or present, swallowed this notion. O'Neill's concessions were symbolic rather than substantive, and when they came they were forced out of him. There was talk in 1964 of 'building bridges' between the two communities, revolutionary language given the intransigence of his predecessor, but only of benefit to Catholics if acted upon. A public condolence was sent to Cardinal Conway on the death of Pope John XXIII in June 1963; Catholic schools were visited for the first time by a Northern Ireland premier; and photographs were taken of the Prime Minister meeting priests and nuns. The invitation to Lemass also promised reconciliation. However, these gestures and the rhetoric accompanying them merely whetted the minority's appetite for reforms.

When it came to substance O'Neill disappointed. The Lockwood Committee on higher education, established in November 1963 without Catholic representation, revealed in early 1965 that the second university would be located not in predominantly Catholic and depressed Derry/Londonderry but in solidly Protestant and prosperous Coleraine. In the same year the government accepted the Matthew Report recommending the construction of a new city but, besides situating it between the predominantly Protestant towns of

Portadown and Lurgan, named it 'Craigavon' after the first Unionist Prime Minister. Infrastructural changes did not help nationalist areas: Derry/Londonderry and Newry lost rail connections while the new motorways went to Protestant Ballymena and Lurgan. Little attempt was made to promote Catholics to public bodies, a tendency which the *Belfast Telegraph* claimed 'made a nonsense of the prime minister and all that is said about a bridge-building policy' (Harkness, 1983: 149).[13] Catholics were not invited into the higher echelons of the regime, and the UUP, still tied to the Orange Order, did not attempt to attract Catholic members or support (Darby, 1976: 15–16): O'Neill was not to seek Catholic endorsement for the UUP until three months before his resignation. While the public commemoration of the fiftieth anniversary of the Easter Rising was allowed in 1966, a Protestant backlash prompted the government to ban the Republican Clubs and the centenary celebrations of the Fenian rebellion of 1867.

The instruments of hegemonic control were left unaltered. No move was made to reform the local government gerrymanders, or to end discriminatory housing policies which underpinned gerrymandering. While the business and university votes were abolished for Stormont elections in 1968, no attempt was made to introduce universal suffrage at the local level. Trade unionists concerned about the discrepancy between the local government franchise in Northern Ireland and Great Britain were told by the UUP that it was Great Britain which was out of line! (Buckland, 1981: 117–18). A white paper, *The Reshaping of Local Government: Statement of Aims,* released in December 1967, was concerned more with the structural inefficiencies of the local government system than with minority grievances. Nor were any steps taken to remove or reduce economic discrimination: the Minister of Home Affairs refused a private member's attempt to pass a Bill of Rights because it would allow 'disappointed office-seekers to air their frustrations' (Palley, 1972: 410). The Special Powers Act and the B-specials remained in place, along with offensive legislation like the Flags and Emblems Act. The judiciary remained overwhelmingly Protestant,[14] and the police actually became more Protestant: the proportion of Catholic officers dropping from 12 per cent in 1961 to 9.4 per cent in 1972.

The breakdown of hegemonic control in Northern Ireland exemplifies de Tocqueville's thesis that when a bad government seeks to reform itself, it is in its greatest danger (Arthur, 1980: 107; Wilson,

1989: 152). O'Neill raised minority-expectations (pushed higher by the election of a Labour government at Westminster), but he could not satisfy them, or chose not to do so.[15] The reluctance of Stormont to reform led to disillusionment and growing public protests by many Catholics, the transition occurring with the establishment of the NICRA in February 1967 out of the joint efforts of the Wolfe Tone Societies and the CSJ.

O'Neill's base within the UUP was insecure, and it was not long before charges were being heard about 'Lundyism from above'. He was out of touch with his party's grass roots, had not been elected,[16] and preferred the advice of technocrats to that of his party headquarters. He was aloof[17] and perhaps inept, avoiding consultation with his Cabinet before taking the momentous decision to invite Lemass to Belfast,[18] and setting up a new government department while most of his colleagues were on holidays. O'Neill's trust in civil servants threatened his Cabinet colleagues who were concerned about his 'presidential' style (Buckland, 1981: 133). Style was not his only problem; policy also mattered. Organizational modernization threatened the local government system. This rationalization would have reduced the numbers of councils and their functions and undermined Unionist clientelism. It caused grave anxieties to those who ran local power-bases, especially in western Northern Ireland, and they were to become key figures opposing O'Neill. By encouraging external investment O'Neill alienated some local entrepreneurs; and Belfast workers, redundant through the decline of traditional industries, were unenthusiastic about the Prime Minister's plans to decentralize economic activity (Wright, 1973). O'Neill faced general opposition from traditional unionists whose perception of rapid change was exacerbated by Brookeborough's long and intransigent tenure of office. They believed that the old ways had worked. With their siege-mentalities fully intact and the memories of the 1956–62 IRA campaign fresh in their minds, they saw the new behaviour of the minority and the conciliatory approach of the Republic's government as either a subtle republican plot or a demonstration of a new self-confidence amongst the minority – which was more a cause for concern than celebration. They did not share the view that the threat to Northern Ireland's existence had been reduced. Protestant fundamentalists led by Paisley believed that the ecumenical movement stemming from the second Vatican Council had made their situation more perilous, and were in the vanguard of the early opposition to O'Neillism (Bruce, 1986: 89–120). They regarded O'Neill and his symbolic olive branches to the Catholic community as the secular arm of the ecumenical movement.[19] Their anxieties were strengthened by Harold Wilson's Labour government,[20] and they argued for defiance and solidarity rather than concessions, even symbolic ones, to the minority.

O'Neill had simultaneously increased unionist disunity and minority expectations, undermining the control system. While Catholic opposition remained lobby-based rather than 'on the streets', the Prime Minister could hold his unionist opponents in check. Indeed, in the Stormont election of 1965 he succeeded in rolling back the threat from the NILP. O'Neill's decision not to ban the Republican commemoration of the fiftieth anniversary of the Easter Rising in 1966 aroused some Protestant opposition and allowed them to juxtapose their sacrifice at the Somme with the republican 'stab in the back' during 1916. However, O'Neill's unwillingness to confront these Catholic displays of 'defiance' was seen as encouraging rebellion, and his condemnation and jailing of Protestants who took the law into their own hands, like Paisley, confirmed and reinforced traditionalists' impressions that he was a traitor. In September 1966 O'Neill disclosed a backbench plot against him, naming backbenchers Desmond Boal, John McQuade, Austin Ardill, and John Taylor as the culprits, and fuelled speculation that a number of his ministers, including Harry West and William Morgan, and deputy Prime Minister Brian Faulkner, opposed him (Harkness, 1983: 148).[21] By April 1967 O'Neill had to sack Agriculture Minister West, a key figure in western unionist opinion (and a future leader of the UUP), ostensibly over a conflict of interest. In the same period the RUC uncovered a loyalist plot to kill O'Neill (Moloney and Pollack, 1986: 150).

However, not until the creation of the NICRA and Catholic mass-protests did O'Neill and O'Neillism come under serious fire within the Protestant community. NICRA's platform consisted of those grievances which O'Neill had neglected to touch: universal suffrage at the local government level, anti-discrimination legislation covering public employment, subsidized housing allocated according to need, repeal of the Special Powers Act, and the disbanding of the USC. The minority were appealing to the metropole for their rights as British citizens (Rose, 1971: 156). This appeal to the central government copied the tactics of blacks in the deep south of the USA

– a tool denied to other subordinated ethnic communities like South African blacks or Palestinians in Israel. There was an extensive range of opinion and divisions within the civil-rights movement; it was no mere republican/communist front (Purdie, 1988, 1990). Irish nationalism remained important amongst Catholics in the 1960s and simplistic economic or deprivation theses about their behaviour will not do, but those who have advanced the thesis that the civil-rights movement was merely nationalism in tactical guise (e.g. Hewitt, 1981; and Wilson, 1989: 153–4) simultaneously underestimate the scale of direct and indirect discrimination in Northern Ireland, and downplay the support which existed among the minority for a reformed Union.[22] While the non-violence of the civil-rights movement may have been tactical, it was a tactic which was not being used by all, or indeed by most, to win a united Ireland. It was supported amongst other reasons because it (i) set exemplary standards for future co-existence between the two ethnic communities; (ii) would avoid injuries and death; and (iii) make the majority listen while denying it an easy excuse to crush or dismiss the campaign (F. Wright, 1987: 165–6). It was the violent response to the civil-rights movement which led many Catholics to return to a less complicated nationalism.

The civil-rights platform had an obvious appeal to the British government. Redressing minority grievances entailed relatively low costs. However, the campaign posed novel problems for the governing UUP, opening up splits between reformers and hard-liners. With the absence of visible and serious irredentist activity from any quarter, the regime was deprived of one key source of legitimation: the threat of armed nationalist insurrection. Stormont had easily coped with armed subversion, by superior force and a panoply of repressive legislation, but these measures were too blunt in the new circumstances, especially given the region's lack of economic and political autonomy and the development of international broadcasting media. Whereas independent hegemonic regimes with autarkic economies could treat non-violent protest indistinguishably from violent protest – as South Africa did in 1960 and 1976 – Stormont, like state-governments in the southern USA, was more constrained.

The first major civil-rights march took place from Coalisland to Dungannon on 24 August 1968 (de Paor, 1971: 170–187). The success of this gathering prompted NICRA to organize another in Derry/Londonderry on 5 October. The march provoked atavistic outrage amongst Protestants: control of sacred territory was being challenged. Unionist opposition to O'Neill, which had been largely confined to parliament and the party's constituencies, spilled onto the streets. William Craig, the Minister of Home Affairs, willingly capitulated to the Protestants by ordering the civil-rights marchers to keep within nationalist areas. This attempt to reassert traditional territorial control, while dubbing the march as sectarian, served to escalate tension and, when the marchers refused to be cowed, the Protestant RUC ran amok. The televised scenes were conveyed around the world, and the message brought back to London by an injured delegation of visiting Westminster MPs who were present at the march.

O'Neill announced reforms, at Wilson's prompting, in November 1968. He included a promise to ensure the impartial allocation of public housing; the appointment of an Ombudsman to investigate minority grievances; the replacement of the Londonderry Corporation by a Development Commission; the reform and reorganization of the local government system; and the repeal of all or parts of the Special Powers Act. He promised these reforms would be implemented by 1971. The package antagonized unionists but did not go far enough for Catholics. Craig was fired in December after attacking the package, while Paisley under the slogan 'O'Neill must go!' stepped up his extra-parliamentary campaign. Radicals among the minority, exhilarated by their success, wanted to press further. The student-based People's Democracy organized a further march from Belfast to Derry/Londonderry in January 1969, providing an opportunity for loyalist extremists, including some in the security forces, to ambush the marchers at Burntollet bridge. O'Neill reacted by condemning the marchers and threatening the further use of the B-specials, thereby alienating Catholics; and a few days later, by setting up a commission of inquiry, thereby infuriating Protestants, and prompting the resignation of two leading ministers, supported by twelve backbenchers. The premier's response was to dissolve Stormont and call a general election for 24 February 1969.

From the Prime Minister's perspective the election was a failure even though the UUP's share of the vote – if we combine the tally of its official and unofficial candidates – was over 61 per cent. Of the 39 elected UUP MPs (36 official and 3 unofficial), 12 were opposed to O'Neill including his foremost critics, William Craig and Brian Faulkner (see Table 4.2). The UUP had

Table 4.2 The Stormont election of February 1969
Source: Flackes and Elliott (1989: 304–10)

Party/movement	votes	% poll	seats
Ulster Unionist Party (pro-O'Neill)	245,925	44	27
Ulster Unionist Party (anti-O'Neill)	95,696	17.1	12
Independent/Protestant Unionists	34,923	6.3	0
Northern Ireland Labour Party	45,113	8.1	2
Republican Labour	13,155	2.4	2
Nationalists/National Democrats	68,324	12.2	6
Civil-rights Independents/People's Democracy	45,622	8.1	3

Notes: (i) The turn-out was 71 per cent. (ii) 7 of the 52 seats were uncontested (5 UUP, 2 Nationalist). (iii) The UUP vote was split both between pro- and anti-O'Neill candidates and official and unofficial candidates.

split and so had its supporters, and O'Neill resigned within two months. The Catholic electorate, radicalized by Burntollet, elected three civil-rights leaders, John Hume, Ivan Cooper, and Paddy O'Hanlon, over sitting Nationalist MPs who had not encouraged demonstrations, and voted in considerable numbers for the semi-Trotskyist positions articulated by the People's Democracy. The fragmentation of the Catholic vote was even more extensive than that amongst Protestants, permanently weakening the Nationalist party, which had also been challenged by the National Democrats. Just over a year later the Social Democratic and Labour Party (SDLP) would be founded out of these fragments: merging the independent civil-rights MPs, the Nationalist MPs, Paddy Devlin from the NILP, and Gerry Fitt from Republican Labour; and absorbing the supporters of the Nationalist, National Democratic, and Republican Labour parties. It presented itself as a left-of-centre party which favoured civil rights for all, a just distribution of wealth, and pledged itself to work for Irish unity by consent. The NILP vote shrank dramatically in the February 1969 election. Although it drew support from both Protestant and Catholic districts, it did best in the predominantly Catholic Falls constituency, where Paddy Devlin won a seat. O'Neill himself was nearly humiliated in his own Bannside constituency, narrowly defeating Paisley. Further civil-rights demonstrations and the bombing of public infrastructure, which was blamed on the IRA but later found to be the work of the UVF, prompted the premier's resignation on 28 April 1969. The UUP's parliamentary representatives elected to replace him by his cousin Sir James Chichester-Clark, who defeated Faulkner by one vote.

The palace transition did not stop the minority revolt or the loyalist counter-attacks. During the summer marching season, police protection of Orange marches sharply contrasted with their earlier willingness to ban civil-rights marches. Escalating tensions culminated in Derry/Londonderry on 12–14 August with violent clashes between Catholics and the police forces, both the RUC and B-specials. The violence in Derry/Londonderry was replicated in Belfast where Protestant mobs and the police attacked Catholic areas, the latter killing six people on 14 August. British intervention occurred against this background. The key instruments of Unionist control, the local security forces, were thoroughly discredited. The RUC and the USC (B-specials) had been shown by the world's media to permit (and indeed to participate in) attacks against civil-rights demonstrations. Strategically-minded Catholic actors played these developments consciously. If they were reformists they sought to expose the 'violence in the system' to encourage the British to dismantle hegemonic control, and if they were revolutionaries they hoped to precipitate a more thoroughgoing crisis for either republican or socialist purposes.

British intervention: the politics of embarrassment

Why did the British centre (i.e. Westminster, Whitehall, and the élites of the parties of government) listen and eventually intervene? After all the centre had turned a blind eye in the 1920s, 1930s, the late 1940s, and the mid-1950s, when Catholic discontent or nationalist mobilization was effectively crushed. 'Up until then the official doctrine, that's still in being today, was that Ireland's a pretty ghastly place for any British politician to be involved in and that because of Lloyd George's settlement in the 1920s it had been got out of British politics at Westminster and the more it stayed that way the happier everybody would be . . . that's paraphrasing, but it's not inaccurate'.[23]

So what changed? First, Westminster and Whitehall were being explicitly addressed. Until the 1960s the Catholic minority had articulated their grievances either through (but mostly at) the Irish government or at the Irish diaspora in America. They had hoped for change from outside rather than within the UK. Their decision to address the centre in the 1960s implied some degree of willingness to work the UK system, and accordingly made it more difficult for them to be ignored. The British government reacted positively to being told backwoods Ulster Protestants were the problem rather than the British state. Second, contingent developments opened Westminster's ears and eyes. As in the USA national and global television made the exercise of hegemonic control over a local minority embarrassingly visible. The power élites of regimes whose international rhetoric suggested that they were homesteads of Western human rights were confronted with their own squalid backyards. Third, the growing British–Irish *rapprochement* and Britain's decline as a world-power made it difficult to ignore the appeal of the Republic that something be done to protect the minority.

Jack Lynch, the Republic's Taoiseach, made a crucial speech on 13 August 1969, in which he was heard to say that 'we would not stand idly by',[24] definitely called for an eventual ending of the partition of Ireland, announced the movement of troops and field-hospitals to the border, and asked the British government to request that a UN peace-keeping force be sent to Northern Ireland. British troops went into the Bogside the following day.

It had become clear to the British authorities that there were few if any alternatives to direct intervention. The Unionist coercive apparatus could no longer maintain stability: the RUC's 3,000 full-time policemen were exhausted by the August riots (whether from strenuous participation or control-activities). Unlike the deep south of the USA there were no federal/metropolitan organizations in Northern Ireland which could be used by Westminster to bypass local intransigence and address minority grievances. Northern Ireland did not have a justiciable Bill of Rights policed by Great British courts, and the Catholics were thereby deprived of a 'march and litigation strategy' (F. Wright, 1987: 197). Similarly, the constitutional powers by which Great Britain could legislate for Northern Ireland had fallen into abeyance. Nevertheless the decision to send troops was taken reluctantly (Wilson, 1971: 871–2). Pressure had been put on the Unionist government to make reforms before 1969 precisely to prevent this step. The UUP government was informed that it should exhaust its own coercive resources before calling on the British government, a decision which gave it a *carte blanche* to use CS gas and deploy the B-specials with the explosive consequences which followed in the street-battles of August 1969. Chichester-Clark requested that British troops be sent to Derry/Londonderry during the night after Lynch's speech; and having foreseen this request Harold Wilson and James Callaghan, the Home Secretary, duly obliged.

After August 1969 Callaghan and Westminster were determined to keep British involvement to a minimum, and to withdraw as soon as appropriate. This approach ruled out the strategic option of abolishing Stormont and integrating Northern Ireland into the rest of the UK – which would have caused difficulties with the Republic and many Catholics in Northern Ireland, and annoyed the pro-nationalist wing of the Labour party. More fundamentally, integration would have involved permanent embroilment in the Irish question, a commitment British officials had studiously resisted since 1921. Home Office officials counselled Callaghan that taking over the government of Northern Ireland would be the 'last thing' he should want (Callaghan, 1973: 22). The Labour government was even unwilling to establish a Whitehall ministry for the region which would exist in parallel with Stormont (ibid · 66) Given the practical problems involved in foisting a united Ireland on the unionists, and that Wilson's draft communiqué of 18 August 1969 with Chichester-Clark had declared that 'the border is not an issue' (Wilson, 1971: 875), London's options were narrowed to working for reform and the promotion of accommodation. British policy-makers felt that the UUP could be persuaded and cajoled into making enough concessions to conciliate the minority while retaining its own political base.[25] The dramatic failure of this policy between 1969 and 1972 resulted in the implementation of direct rule.

Reforms were canvassed and passed between August 1969 and June 1971 which conceded the merits of the entire package of demands made by the civil-rights movement. Professional public administration on the Great British model was to replace clientelism in local government. The local government system would be reformed, and its franchise would be based on 'one person one vote'. Commissions of inquiry were established which reported unfavourably on the Stormont regime (Cameron, 1969; Hunt, 1969). The most important reforms included the disarming of the RUC, the disbanding of the USC and its replacement by a locally recruited force under the command of the British Army's

GOC (NI), the creation of an independent Police Authority, and the establishment of a housing executive in late 1969 – to take over the housing functions of the local authorities – and a Commissioner for Complaints in November 1969 – to deal with complaints of discrimination by local authorities – the local counterpart of the Parliamentary Ombudsman who had been created in June. Reforms to the public prosecutions system took longer but were implemented by 1972, with the appointment of a Director of Public Prosecutions independent of the police force. Legislation making incitement to religious hatred a statutory offence was passed in July 1970, and a Ministry of Community Relations was created along with a Community Relations Commission. Local government reforms accepted in December 1970 included universal suffrage and the creation of an independent commissioner to draw up electoral boundaries. Finally, in June 1971, Faulkner – the Prime Minister who succeeded Chichester-Clark – announced the establishment of three parliamentary committees, to be appointed proportionally from all parties represented in Stormont, to review government policy in social, environmental, and industrial services.

However, British intervention and British-induced reforms sent shock waves through the unionist community while failing to satisfy Catholics. Traditional distrust of London, which had persuaded unionists to regard devolution as a bulwark of the Union, was exacerbated by the united Ireland sympathies of Harold Wilson and Labour's sympathies for the minority. The disbanding of the B-specials especially annoyed working-class Protestants, provoking serious riots in October 1969. Protestant insecurities and anger were massively reinforced by the offensive launched by the Provisional IRA, which had grown out of the vigilante groups organized to defend Catholic areas in 1969. The danger of unionist moderates being outmanœuvred by extremists within their bloc became apparent with electoral victories by loyalists in two Stormont by-elections in April 1970 and in the June 1970 Westminster general election.[26] Chichester-Clark's position was so weak after Paisley's 1970 by-election victory that he was replaced as vice-chairman of his own UUP branch at Castledawson by a local bus driver. There were three different Prime Ministers in three years: O'Neill, Chichester-Clark, and Faulkner. Faced with outflanking pressures, and deprived of some of its moderate elements when the biconfessional Alliance Party of Northern Ireland (APNI) was formed in 1970, the UUP government called for spectacular security measures to control violence emanating from the minority community.

For Catholics, the institutional nature of the reforms had little immediate effect upon their daily experience or life-chances, and consequently did not arouse their enthusiasm. The replacement of the B-specials by another locally recruited force with the partisan title of the Ulster Defence Regiment seemed cosmetic. The disarming of the RUC did not last even a year. Democratization of local government was rendered almost superfluous by the radical restructuring already in train which was transferring most local government powers to appointed boards and to Stormont – where the UUP still enjoyed a monopoly of power. Unemployment remained high among the minority while the prospects for improvement in housing were seriously affected by the need to rehouse the families forced out of their neighbourhoods in the summer of 1969 – a process which continued until 1971. More fundamentally, what may have satisfied Catholics in 1967–8 was no longer enough by 1970–1. Their expectations raised by British intervention, moderates wanted an end to the majority's exclusive control of the Stormont system, whereas nationalist radicals, including the militants of the Provisional IRA, wanted a united Ireland.

The British Conservative government, surprisingly elected in June 1970, opted to support centrists in the UUP by attempting to balance reforms with repression in Catholic urban areas. The new Conservative government confirmed nationalist stereotypes: the Conservative party's long record of sympathy with the UUP and the surviving formal links between the two parties had not been forgotten. A curfew in the Falls Road was followed by further hard-line measures including new special legislation and a threat in early 1971 that the army would shoot petrol-bombers. Home Secretary Reginald Maudling declared in July 1971 (what republicans were already proclaiming) that it had become a function of the British Army to 'maintain the constitution of Northern Ireland' (cited in de Paor, 1971: xvii).[27] Faced with the Provisionals aggressive campaign to bring down Stormont and terminate the British presence in Ireland, the UUP government demanded the use of the tried and trusted mode of repression, internment without trial. They told the Conservative Cabinet that they would continue to reform Northern Ireland provided they were able to repress nationalist insurrection: without internment they could not command the support of their own community. Edward Heath's government granted this request on 9 August 1971.

Internment, however, proved to be a political and military disaster. It unified most Catholics, prompted civil and armed disobedience, brought a propaganda coup for the Provisional IRA, international embarrassment for the British, and was the catalyst for even greater violence. The wrong people were arrested and some internees were tortured or suffered 'excessive maltreatment' as the official inquiry put it (Compton, 1971). In July 1971 the newly formed SDLP had left Stormont, withdrawing its consent from the institutions of government; after internment the party sponsored a civil-disobedience campaign which led Catholics to withhold rents and rates on a massive scale; and in the autumn they participated in an alternative parliament, the 'Assembly of the Northern Irish people': the 'Dungiven parliament'. Hegemonic control was over. Revolt was thinkable, although it remained to be seen whether it was workable.

The radicalization of the minority community which preceded (but was dramatically enhanced by) internment allowed loyalist politicians (and some unionist commentators) to claim vindication: the Catholics had been republican all along. However, because internment failed to destroy the P(IRA), but rather caused a violent escalation, the disintegration of the governing Unionists continued. The opponents of reform became increasingly well organized around Paisley and Craig. Paisley's Democratic Unionist Party (DUP) was formed in September 1971. Although Craig's Vanguard Unionist Progressive Party was not formed until March 1973, the Vanguard movement was created at the beginning of 1972. Protestants joined paramilitary groups in great numbers during 1971–2 (Buckland, 1981: 153–54) and started to engage in ethnic murders (see Ch. 1: 26 ff.). The fracturing of the UUP, the radicalization of the minority, and the deteriorating military situation increased the international embarrassment of the British government. Their embarrassment was raised to fever pitch on 30 January 1972 when British paratroopers shot dead thirteen unarmed civilian civil-rights demonstrators marching in Derry/Londonderry in protest against internment. The demonstration had been banned by the Unionist government, but the paratroopers were responsible for what became known as 'Bloody Sunday'. Having made Faulkner an offer he was bound to refuse – devolved government but stripped of its security powers – the Conservative leadership of Heath, Maudling, Carrington, and Whitelaw chose an option they had not been prepared to consider previously. The suspension of Stormont and direct rule were announced in March 1972.

When confronted by the demands of the civil-rights movement in the 1960s the UK government had discovered their inability to influence the Northern Ireland government without direct involvement through §75 of the Government of Ireland Act, a step British officials referred to as their 'hydrogen bomb' (Rose, 1989: 143). But back-room arbitration failed. Reforms, made under British pressure, were presented as originating from the Stormont government in the hope that devolution could be rescued without more fundamental constitutional restructuring. However, the tactic failed. Unionists, used to fifty years of near sovereignty in domestic affairs, were reluctant to co-operate in ending their hegemony: indeed Faulkner protested that Northern Ireland was not 'a coconut colony' (*Irish Times*, 28 March 1972).

Conclusion

The evolution and timing of the outbreak of the present Northern Ireland conflict are under explained by the internal-conflict paradigm which has come to dominate research on the subject (Whyte, 1988, 1990); and are insufficiently accounted for by the partisan histories of unionists, nationalists, and Marxists. The establishment and maintenance of a system of hegemonic control owed much to forces exogenous to Northern Ireland. Its collapse after 1963 must likewise be partially explained as the outcome of external developments in the British and Irish states, developments which had little to do with British imperialism or Irish irredentism (neither of these 'national character-traits' being noticeable during the 1960s). The Stormont regime was only capable of surviving as long as it was externally supported by historically specific patterns of British and Irish state-development. The limits to hegemonic control lay outside Northern Ireland. Chapter 5 shows that the politics of antagonism would take new twists with its collapse.

Notes

1. Thus one of the most distinguished historians of Northern Ireland argues that Stormont's collapse was inevitable: 'In the face of all these difficulties – a ramshackle political structure, a dearth of political talent, a divided society, a decaying economy and an irredentist neighbour – the wonder is not that the 1920 settlement eventually collapsed in violence in 1972 but that it lasted so long' (Buckland, 1981: 30).

2. The office, role, and interpretations of Irish Prime Ministers are discussed in Farrell (1971) and O'Leary (1991a).

3. Nationalists voted for republican candidates in the 1955 Westminster parliamentary elections – giving them 152,310 votes, or 23.7 per cent of the regional poll. Two jailed IRA men won the traditionally nationalist seats of Mid-Ulster and Fermanagh–South Tyrone. These results persuaded the IRA to launch a military offensive in 1956. However, by the time of the 1959 Westminster elections republican support had fallen to 11 per cent, largely because the Nationalist party decided to contest them.

4. In 1963 Lemass conceded that a united Ireland should be federal in form, with considerable autonomy for the northern state (de Paor, 1971: 138).

5. Lemass took a pragmatic view of the Republic's constitution. Before he retired he set up a Dáil committee which in 1967 proposed altering Articles 2 and 3 to make them 'aspirational' rather than outright declarations of Irish sovereignty.

6. See Kelly (1971) and MacIntyre (1971).

7. Unionists tried to distort the application of Westminster's welfare state policy by denying its benefits to large families in Northern Ireland – which were disproportionately Catholic. In 1956 Westminster made new provisions for family allowances, with increasingly larger payments for each child after the second. The Northern Ireland government's initial legislation reversed this flow of funds, so that larger allowances would be paid for the second and third children than for subsequent children. Under pressure from unionists concerned with alienating Westminster the government backed down (de Paor, 1971: 129–30).

8. In 1964, with a population less than half of the Republic's, Northern Ireland had 95,000 children in secondary education compared to 85,000 in the Republic. Expenditure on higher education was three times higher in Northern Ireland; welfare payments were 50 per cent higher; while 'the difference between the health services was so great that little comparison was possible' (Buckland, 1981: 103).

9. See Note 3.

10. Thus international support for Israel and the domestic cohesion of Israeli Jews are directly related to the perceived 'external' Arab threat.

11. The sentiments reflected in this speech do not square with the belief that

O'Neill 'had no sympathy with what he saw as parochial unionism' (Bruce, 1986: 68–71). O'Neill has been more aptly described: 'The Prime Minister's moderation lay in avoiding bigotry' (Arthur, 1974: 17)..

12. Between 1963 and 1968 British payments to Northern Ireland for the welfare state and agricultural subsidies increased from £46 million to £72 million (Buckland, 1981: 103).

13. In 1967 3 out of 33 people on the Youth Employment Services Board were Catholic; 2 out of 22 on the Hospitals Authority; and 2 out of 24 on the General Health Services Board. In 1969 it was estimated that the membership of 21 boards was 85 per cent non-Catholic (Harkness, 1983: 149).

14. Two of three judges in the Northern Ireland Court of Appeal had held the post of Attorney-General in UUP governments (Buckland, 1981: 116).

15. In the Loyalty Survey, carried out in 1968, Catholics felt that Northern Ireland politics were changing for the better, and felt this way more than Protestants. Of all Catholics interviewed 65 per cent believed things were changing for the better, 27 per cent saw no change, and only 4 per cent felt matters had become worse (Rose, 1971: 474 ff.).

16. It is questionable whether O'Neill would have won an election within the UUP (Buckland, 1981: 106; MacDonald, 1986: 72).

17. O'Neill's exposure to upper-class English 'liberal and cosmopolitan' culture may explain his aloofness better than his alleged liberalism.

18. Faulkner pin-pointed this decision as the start of the decline in unionist support for O'Neill (Faulkner, 1978: 40). While Lemass, by implicitly recognizing Northern Ireland, had arguably taken the more dangerous step, he had prepared the ground with his colleagues (Foster, 1988: 585).

19. 'Catholic schools were places in which soul-damning heresies were transmitted, and to visit them was to recognize that Catholicism was a permitted variant of the Christian church' (Bruce, 1986: 91).

20. Wilson returned the remains of Roger Casement, who had been executed by the British authorities for treason for his role in the Easter Rising of 1916, to the Republic.

21. All these figures subsequently made their names as key unionist die-hards: Faulkner became the last prime minister under the Stormont regime; West became leader of the UUP in 1974; Taylor a key figure in the UUP; Boal and McQuade leading lights in the DUP; and Ardill the first deputy leader of William Craig's Vanguard party (see Ch. 5: 187). Having made or finished their careers, Faulkner, West, and Ardill were subsequently to travel to Damascus. As they aged they became pillars of moderation.

22. Asked in 1968 if they approved or disapproved of the Northern Ireland constitution (admittedly an imperfect and complex question) almost as many Catholics approved as disapproved (33 per cent as against 34 per cent) (Rose, 1971: 477). A *Belfast Telegraph* poll in 1967 showed that 70 per cent of the minority supported the continuation of the link with Britain in one form or

another, and only 30 per cent wanted an independent united Ireland (Whyte, 1990: 77). The Cameron Commission reported that nationalism amongst the minority was less important than it had been (Cameron, 1969: para. 11). Rose's survey suggests the same: 30 per cent of Catholics said that they would approve 'if nationalists agreed to stop debating partition and accepted the present border as final' (1971: 483).

23. Roland Moyle, former minister of state at the NIO (1974–6), accompanied James Callaghan during the British intervention of 1969 (interview with B. O'Leary, 3 Jan. 1991).

24. In fact he said that 'the Irish government can no longer stand by and see innocent people injured'. Lynch was attacked by Chichester-Clark for his 'inflammatory' broadcast: although it appears that Lynch's prime concern was to manage the divisions within his own party rather than to inflame passions.

25. 'As no alternative instrument of government existed, it seemed to me better to win the agreement of the Ulster Unionists to what was necessary than to use the power of parliament to dismiss them' (Callaghan, 1973: 24).

26. In the 1970 Westminster elections for the first time the UUP won only eight of the twelve seats. Ian Paisley won North Antrim, Bernadette Devlin and Frank Maguire (Unity) won mid-Ulster and Fermanagh and South Tyrone, and Gerry Fitt (Republican Labour) won west Belfast.

27. Former NIO ministers unite in indicting Maudling's tenure of the Home Secretaryship as a disaster for Northern Ireland. Merlyn Rees refers to Maudling's time in office as 'the mouldering years' (interview with B. O'Leary, 18 Dec. 1990).

5
Deadlock, 1972–85: the limits to British arbitration

We have now got into something which we can hardly mismanage

Richard Crossman (1977: 620)

As Secretary of State for Northern Ireland I found myself performing a dual role, as a Governor-General representing the Queen and as such the enemy of every Republican in the province, but also . . . acting like a referee in a boxing ring whose authority seemed to be resented equally by both sides.

James Prior (1986: 181)

Arbitration of ethnic conflicts entails the intervention of a 'neutral authority above the rival subcultures' (Lehmbruch, 1975: 378). It differs from other methods used to stabilize antagonistic societies because it involves conflict-regulation by agents other than the contending parties. The (at least alleged) disinterestedness of the arbiter makes it possible to win the acquiescence if not the support of the contending ethnic communities; and thereby dampens the violence which might otherwise occur. An arbiter provides governmental effectiveness.[1] Arbitration, in principle, can establish the conditions for longer-term conflict-resolution (partition, power-sharing, or even peaceful assimilation); or it can form a prelude to the reconstruction of the old system of control or a new one - if the arbiter hands power to a different ethnic community. The prerequisite for agreed arbitration is that the arbiter's claim to neutrality be broadly accepted by the major contending communities. Not all professed arbiters pass this test. Since 'neutrality' is rhetorically superior to 'partisanship', and useful for domestic and international consumption, the self-presentations of arbiters must be treated with scepticism: few observers credited Syria's intervention in Lebanon or Soviet federal intervention in Nagorno Karabagh with impartiality.

Arbitration of ethnic conflicts is of two broad types, internal and external, each of which can be performed by different kinds of agent. Internal arbitration can be executed by an individual who is not a member of the main antagonistic communities. It can be fulfilled by statesmen with the moral authority to transcend their ethnic origins: for example, Mahatma Gandhi in the Indian subcontinent. It can be managed by someone who can claim a connection with all the major ethnic groups: for example Siaka Stevens in Sierra Leone.[2] Internal arbitration can also be performed by credible non-partisan institutions as opposed to individual agents. The monarchy played the role of arbiter between the Hutu and Tutsi tribes in Burundi before 1966 (Lemarchand, 1991: 3). Federal governments and supreme courts can arbitrate ethnic conflict as happened in the southern states of the USA under the Kennedy and Johnson presidencies. Finally, internal arbitration can be performed by a political party. One of the key justifications for one-party states in Africa and Asia, aside from Marxist-Leninist doctrine, has been the controversial thesis that arbitration can occur within a monopolistic political party. The one-party state claims to absorb key members of the rival ethnic communities and regulate their rival aspirations. This argument for 'control by consent' was advanced by Nkrumah in Ghana in the 1960s, Nimeiri in Sudan in the 1970s, and Mugabe in Zimbabwe in the 1980s. In a competitive political system internal arbitration can also be performed by a pivotal political party, one judged to be sufficiently disinterested by the other contending factions to be able to chair a cross-ethnic coalition: the APNI has long sought to perform this role in Northern Ireland.

External arbitration by contrast suggests that ethnic conflict cannot be successfully managed within the relevant political system. External arbitration can be performed by a single external agent or state, a bi-national authority, or a multi-national force. Bi-national arbitration occurs when two states jointly arbitrate, as in the notion of joint British and Irish authority which many have recommended for Northern Ireland. Multi-national arbitration, as originally envisaged for United Nations' peace-keeping forces, is performed with intermittent success in Cyprus and parts of the Middle East and Africa.

British arbitration

The British government's self-portrait of itself as a neutral arbiter in Northern Ireland after 1972 was not novel. In retreat from empire, mandates and protectorates, British governments had maintained they were neutrally arbitrating the rival claims of Muslims and Hindus in the Indian subcontinent, Jews and Arabs in Palestine, Turkish and Greek Cypriots, and, lest it be forgotten, Irish nationalists and Ulster unionists before 1921. After 1972 arbitration in Northern Ireland had major attractions for Westminster and Whitehall élites. It was in keeping with the rhetoric of traditional British policy: Lloyd George had described Britain's position between the 'Irish factions' as one of 'benevolent neutrality' (O'Malley, 1983: 205). Arbitration seemed apposite 'crisis-management', much less drastic than engineering a united Ireland and British withdrawal, integrating Northern Ireland with the rest of the UK, or imposing a new partition, all of which had potentially disastrous consequences. It was internationally acceptable, in the USA, and to a less extent in the Republic of Ireland - which demanded that the British government act to redress minority grievances. It promised international respectability and the benefits of ambiguity: the British government could portray itself as an 'outsider' or 'insider' as the occasion demanded. Moreover, the disinterested pursuit of rational compromise would ensure that Irish politics was kept from the centre of the political stage, an objective shared by successive generations of the British governing class since 1868. Arbitration therefore had presentational advantages even if it did not produce notable successes.

Throughout the years from the eruption of the civil-rights demonstrations until the signing of the Anglo-Irish Agreement in 1985, British governments portrayed themselves as unswayed by the partisan preferences of the rival subcultures in Northern Ireland, and able to act autonomously to protect both their interests. When the Labour government introduced the troops in 1969, one of its proclaimed purposes was to keep the warring factions apart: the troops were to be 'pigs in the middle' (Hamill, 1985). When the Conservative government suspended Stormont in 1972 they set up a co-ordinating Northern Ireland Office (NIO), deliberately hiving off functions previously scattered amongst Whitehall departments, and envisaged its role as the department for pursuing the public interest of Northern Ireland.

Since 1972 the government of Northern Ireland has been carried out largely through the office of the Secretary of State[3] presiding through the NIO (apart from a five-month period of a power-sharing devolved government in 1974). The incumbent of the office of Secretary of State for Northern Ireland has never been someone born there, has never been elected from one of its constituencies, and has always been an English Conservative or Labour MP.[4] As representatives of Great Britain's political parties the successive Secretaries, at least in their own minds, have had reasonable claims to being neutral between Catholicism and Protestantism, or Irish nationalism and Ulster unionism. All of them have claimed to be impartial arbiters: William Whitelaw (1972–3); Francis Pym (1973–4); Merlyn Rees (1974–6); Roy Mason (1976–9); Humphrey Atkins (1979–81); James Prior (1981–4); Douglas Hurd (1984–5); Tom King (1985–9); and Peter Brooke (1989–92). British Prime Ministers have made deliberate efforts to include both English and Welsh Catholics and Protestants amongst Northern Ireland's junior ministers to emphasize the 'balanced' nature of their administrations. Bi-partisan agreement between the two main Great British political parties facilitated their efforts to present themselves as arbiters, and did not cease until 1981 when Labour changed its policy to favour the unity of Ireland by consent (NEC, 1981).

Until 1985 British arbitration rested on three fundamental policy-premisses. First, *encouraging the rival subcultures to work together towards an internal political accommodation, while retaining the position of 'honest broker'*. The 'neutrality' of this stance rested on the refusal to countenance 'majority rule' (the anti-unionist premise) in anything resembling its pre-1972 manifestation, or to contemplate coercing unionists into a united Ireland (the anti-nationalist premise). It was hoped that arbitration would establish an atmosphere conducive to the sharing of power by nationalists and unionists in a devolved Northern Ireland government, or consociationism[G]. Second, *reforming Northern Ireland* initially entailed 'modernizing' the region along the lines of the post-war British consensus. Professionalized administration of the welfare state would replace the parochial, clientelist, and supremacist sectarianism which had marred the conduct of state agencies before 1972. Economic growth and equal opportunities in the public and private sectors would enable Catholics and Protestants to transcend their traditional ascriptive social relations, as had happened elsewhere in the UK, notably in Central Scotland. In the 1980s, 'reforming Northern Ireland' entailed the partial application of Thatcherite recipes of economic rationalization and privatization, but the commitment to an impartially administered welfare state remained. Third, *impartial security policies based on criminalisation* underlined arbitration. British policy-makers stressed their peace-keeping role. Security policy was taken from Stormont's control because it was a potentially lethal instrument of ethnic partiality. After some initial hesitation Conservative and Labour administrations decided that political violence was to be treated as criminal violence; and dealt with by legal processes as 'normal' as circumstances permitted. Disinterested criminalisation of nationalist or loyalist violence would allow the British to keep their arbitration credentials intact.

This chapter reviews the experiment in British arbitration after 1972 and explains its unravelling between 1979 and 1985. British arbitration would eventually be replaced by a limited form of *joint* arbitration by Britain and the Republic of Ireland through the institutions of the Anglo-Irish Agreement. However, we first analyse how the Northern Ireland party-system evolved after the fall of Stormont, because its transformation was to become one of the major obstacles to successful arbitration.

The evolution of party-competition and the party-system, 1969–85

The support for political parties, expressed as a percentage of the total vote (or as a percentage of the total first-preference vote) in the region-wide elections held in Northern Ireland between 1969 and 1985, is shown in Table 5.1. The table breaks down parties and their support into four categories: the unionist bloc, the nationalist bloc, the bi-confessional bloc, and a residual category.

After 1972 *the unionist bloc* remained characterized by its overriding commitment to the Union and its essentially Protestant appeal. However, it experienced considerable fragmentation. The divisions opened up by 'O'Neillism' in 1969 were exacerbated by the reintroduction of proportional representation (STV) in 1973 for local government and assembly elections, and subsequently in 1979 for European elections. The UUP splintered into multiple parties between 1969 and 1976, but eventually realigned around two

Table 5.1 Party support in elections in Northern Ireland, 1969–85

Source: O'Leary (1991d: 343)

Election		unionist bloc			nationalist bloc			bi-confessional bloc			residual
		UUP	DUP	Other U	SDLP	SF	Other N	NILP	APNI	WP	Other
1969	S	61.1	-	6.3	-	-	18.8	8.1	-	-	5.7
1970	W	54.3	-	4.5	-	-	23.3	12.6	0	-	5.1
1973	LG	41.4	4.3	10.9	13.4	-	5.8	2.5	13.7	-	8.0
1973	A	29.3	10.8	21.8	22.1	-	2.0	2.6	9.2	-	1.0
1974 Feb	W	32.3	8.2	23.7	22.4	-	4.5	2.4	3.2	-	3.3
1974 Oct	W	36.5	8.5	17.1	22.0	-	7.8	1.6	6.3	-	0.2
1975	C	25.8	14.8	21.9	23.7	-	2.2	1.4	9.8	-	0.4
1977	LG	29.6	12.7	8.5	20.6	-	4.1	0.8	14.4	-	8.3
1979	W	36.6	10.2	12.2	19.9	-	8.2	-	11.8	-	2.1
1979	E	21.9	29.8	7.3	24.6	-	6.7	-	6.8	-	2.9
1981	LG	26.5	26.6	4.2	17.5	-	5.3	-	8.9	1.8	8.2
1982	A	29.7	23.0	6.7	18.8	10.1	-	-	9.3	2.7	0.7
1983	W	34.0	20.0	3.0	17.9	13.4	-	-	8.0	1.9	1.6
1984	E	21.5	33.6	2.9	22.1	13.3	-	-	5.0	1.3	0.3
1985	LG	29.5	24.3	3.1	17.8	11.8	2.4	-	7.1	1.6	1.8

Notes:

(i) Type of election is indicated by letter: S = Stormont Parliament; W = Westminster Parliament, LG = Local Government; A = Assembly; C = Convention; and E = European Parliament.

(ii) The symbol (-) indicates the party did not exist or did not contest the election.

(iii) 'Other Nationalist' includes the Republican Clubs until 1979.

(iv) The 'bi-confessional bloc' consists of parties who endorse the Union (NILP and APNI), or who accept it for the medium–long term (WP), but draw bi-confessional support. Thus the APNI, though it endorses the Union, and is therefore 'unionist', is not classified as part of the unionist bloc because its support is bi-confessional.

(v) The Workers' Party is separately classified from 1981 in the 'bi-confessional bloc'.

principal organizations, the UUP (now often known as the OUP, or the Official Unionists) and the DUP. Unionist party-organizations which emerged but faded without enduring impact between 1969 and 1976 included the Vanguard Unionist Party (VUP) founded by William Craig (which was militantly loyalist), the Unionist Party of Northern Ireland founded by Brian Faulkner (which was in favour of power-sharing), and the Ulster Loyalist Democratic Party (which acted as a front for the UDA). The Alliance Party of Northern Ireland (APNI), founded in 1970 by former members of the UUP, middle-class professionals, and a former nationalist MP, became a bi-confessional party. However, since it drew Catholic as well as Protestant support, recognized the importance of reconciling two traditions in the region, and sanctioned the establishment of institutionalized co-operation with the Republic of Ireland, we do not classify it as part of the unionist bloc.

In the 1970s and early 1980s the UUP and the DUP differed between themselves, and internally, over the merits of integration and devolution as means of resolving the political crisis. However, they both remained vehemently opposed to the institutionalization of any significant 'Irish dimension'; and lobbied vigorously for 'more security', arguing at various times for 'selective internment', 'administrative detention', 'shoot-to-kill', and 'cross-border hot-pursuit of terrorists into the Republic of Ireland'. The DUP grew at the expense of the UUP until 1981 (see Figure 5.1). Moreover, its leader Paisley won a huge first-preference vote in every European election after 1979, making him the most popular unionist politician amongst Protestants. However, the UUP halted the DUP's growth in the early 1980s and would make a comeback in the late-1980s (see Ch. 7: 257-9).

Figure 5.1 shows that the percentage share of the unionist bloc declined over time. In all the elections held between 1969 and 1979 its mean vote was 59.81 per cent, and its median vote 60.5 per cent, whereas in the elections held between 1981 and 1989 its mean vote was 55.6 per cent, and its median vote 56.9 per cent. The departure of some middle-class Protestant (and a small number of Catholic) unionists to vote for the pro-power-sharing APNI reduced the size of the unionist bloc in the mid-1970s; and even though the APNI did less well in the early 1980s its existence ensured that the unionist bloc's electoral share had come to hover at just over half of the voting electorate by the late 1980s (see Ch. 9: Table 9.1).

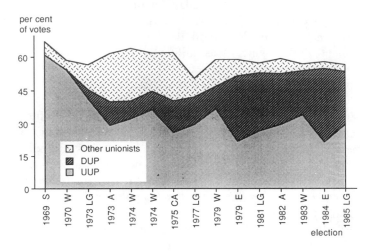

Figure 5.1 The unionist bloc, 1969–85
Source: Table 5.1

The volatile distribution of the vote within the unionist bloc was more marked than the gradual decline of its overall vote-share. Figure 5.1. shows that unionist fragmentation between 1970 and 1975 rapidly gave way to two-party competition within the unionist bloc between the UUP and the DUP. Five features of UUP/DUP competition, displayed in Table 5.2., merit comment.

First, in the European parliamentary elections (which have the highest turn-out in the UK) Paisley's performance far exceeds support for his party in other elections, emphasizing his charismatic status with Protestants. Northern Ireland has three European seats so these elections are a personal popularity contest for party leaders. Second, in Westminster elections the UUP consistently outpoll the DUP. The Westminster parliament is still elected under plurality rule, and therefore incumbent UUP MPs benefit from the fear that a vote for a DUP candidate would let in a nationalist challenger. The logic of plurality rule in Westminster elections obliges Paisley, often against the wishes of his party colleagues, to permit the UUP a free-run in certain constituencies. Third, competition between the UUP and the DUP was fiercest in local-government district and the regional assembly elections held in 1973, 1975, and 1982. In these elections PR(STV) permitted freer party-competition, and

Table 5.2 UUP and DUP competition before 1985
Source: Table 5.1. Key as in Table 5.1.

Year/ Election		UUP share (per cent)	DUP share (per cent)	UUP – DUP	(DUP)/ (UUP+DUP) as per cent
1969	S	61.1	(-)	(-)	(-)
1970	W	54.3	(-)	(-)	(-)
1973	LG	41.4	4.3	+37.1	9.4
1973	A	29.3	10.8	+18.5	26.9
1974 Feb	W	32.3	8.2	+24.1	20.2
1974 Oct	W	36.5	8.5	+26.0	18.8
1975	C	25.8	14.8	+11.0	36.5
1977	LG	29.6	12.7	+16.9	30.0
1979	W	36.6	10.2	+16.4	21.8
1979	E	21.9	29.8	−7.9	57.6
1981	LG	26.5	26.6	−0.1	50.1
1982	A	29.7	23.0	+6.7	43.6
1983	W	34.0	20.0	+14.0	37.0
1984	E	21.5	33.6	−11.1	61.0
1985	LG	29.5	24.3	+5.2	45.2

Paisley's charisma was of less value to his party. Fourth, the UUP's better performances in Westminster elections and the DUP's better performances in local government or regional elections help explain why the DUP leadership became more enthusiastic about devolution than the leadership of the UUP, and why the UUP, over-represented at Westminster, became more consistently in favour of the administrative integration[G] of Northern Ireland into the UK.[5] Finally, vigorous competition between the UUP and the DUP undermined British arbitration between 1972 and 1985 because both parties rejected 'power-sharing' with equal vehemence as 'foreign' and 'non-British'.

After 1972 *the nationalist bloc* remained characterized by a commitment to the political unification of the island of Ireland, and its essentially Catholic appeal. Its internal differences were primarily over what kind of accommodation should be reached with Ulster unionists, how to achieve Irish territorial unification, and the nature of any post-unification Ireland. The Nationalist party never recovered from the impact of the 1969 elections, and new organizations emerged to displace it, determined to have a modern

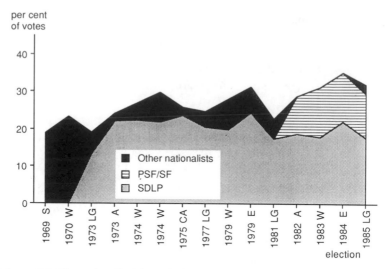

Figure 5.2 The nationalist bloc, 1969–85
Source: Table 5.1

party structure rather than rely on clerical or élite-based clientelism. Nationalist organizations which emerged but faded without decisive impact before 1985 included the Republican Clubs, established by the Official IRA's politically minded members (and which we count as part of the nationalist bloc until 1979), and the Irish Independence Party (IIP), which chided the SDLP for being insufficiently nationalist.

The largest party in the nationalist bloc became the SDLP, which consolidated its position after contesting its first regional elections in 1973 (see Figure 5.2). Constitutionally nationalist, and committed to the unification of Ireland by consent, the SDLP became a member of the social democratic Socialist International. Its support was primarily drawn from the Catholic population, but was disproportionately concentrated amongst the better-off Catholics, those who live west of the River Bann which divides Northern Ireland in half, and the over-30s. The SDLP's electoral fortunes declined slightly in the early 1980s but it re-established its position after the Anglo-Irish Agreement (Ch. 7: Table 7.2, and see Ch. 9: Table 9.1).

Sinn Féin, the second largest party in the nationalist bloc, began life as Provisional Sinn Féin (PSF) in 1970, and as the explicitly political counterpart of the Provisional IRA. It consistently supported the 'armed struggle' of the IRA. PSF was legalized by the British

Table 5.3 SDLP and (P)SF competition before 1985
Source: Table 5.1.

Year/ Election		SDLP (per cent)	(P)SF (per cent)	SDLP – (P)SF	(PSF)/ (SDLP+PSF) as per cent
1969	S	(-)	(-)	(-)	(-)
1970	W	(-)	(-)	(-)	(-)
1973	LG	13.4	(-)	(-)	(-)
1973	A	22.1	(-)	(-)	(-)
1974 Feb	W	22.4	(-)	(-)	(-)
1974 Oct	W	22.0	(-)	(-)	(-)
1975	C	23.7	(-)	(-)	(-)
1977	LG	20.6	(-)	(-)	(-)
1979	W	19.9	(-)	(-)	(-)
1979	E	24.6	(-)	(-)	(-)
1981	LG	17.5	(-)	(-)	(-)
1982	A	18.8	10.1	+8.7	34.9
1983	W	17.9	13.4	+4.5	42.4
1984	E	22.1	13.3	+8.8	37.6
1985	LG	17.8	11.8	+6.0	39.8

government in 1974 in an effort to persuade the party to contest elections to a Northern Ireland convention in 1975 – the hope being that
it would win little support and thereby undermine the Provisionals.
However, PSF did not abandon 'principled abstentionism' until after
hunger strikes in 1980–1 provoked mass sympathy for militant
republicanism. Since 1982 it has contested all elections in the region.
Its rapid growth, under a leadership which had been imprisoned or
interned for paramilitary activities, mobilized the poorest, youngest,
and previously abstentionist sections of the Catholic electorate, and
also ate into the SDLP's support-base (see Table 5.3). Sinn Féin's
growth within the nationalist bloc undermined the British policy of
arbitration, even more than the DUP's growth within the unionist
bloc; and it was a vital ingredient in the decision to negotiate the
Anglo-Irish Agreement.

The most obvious long-term trend in the nationalist bloc was its
growth. Figure 5.2 shows a clear upward trend.[6] It grew under British
arbitration by contrast with the Stormont period. Although not everybody who voted nationalist was uncompromisingly committed to a
pan-Irish solution, the Catholic population became both *absolutely*

and *relatively* more nationalist in its voting behaviour after 1969, for four distinct yet potentially compatible reasons. Demographic explanations suggest that because the Catholic population has been growing the nationalist vote has risen in tandem. However, the nationalist vote rose from just below a fifth to just over a third of the electorate in the twenty years 1969–89, whereas, at most, the Catholic population (as opposed to the electorate), rose from just over a third to two-fifths of the total population between 1961 and 1981. Therefore, even if the Catholic demographic surge boosted nationalist voting, it is still true that nationalist voting increased within the Catholic electorate. Psephological explanations suggest that the change in the voting system to PR(STV) increased Catholic voting-participation. However, the nationalist vote also increased in Westminster elections, where the STV system is not in operation. Institutional explanations point to (i) the legalization of PSF in 1974, (ii) increases in the number of Westminster seats after 1979, and (iii) recent reforms giving Irish citizens the right to vote in Northern Ireland in the same way as British citizens as all being of some consequence in increasing the available nationalist electorate. One of these institutional changes was very important: had Sinn Féin remained illegal nationalist abstention would have remained higher. The change in the number of Westminster seats helps explain the rise in nationalist voting at Westminster elections since 1979 (the greater the number of seats the greater probability that one's vote will make a difference), but it can have been only a minor factor, and does not apply to the other elections. The change in the status of 'I' voters applied only to local government elections after 1989, and therefore cannot be responsible for the long-run growth-trend in nationalist voting. Finally, political explanations point to increased nationalist voting as symptomatic of the polarization of Northern Ireland, under the impact of paramilitary campaigning, counter-insurgency operations by the security forces, and the failure of British reform programmes. Political explanations suggest that increased nationalist voting in the 1980s was the joint product of Sinn Féin's mobilization of previously abstentionist voters, and the failure of British reforms to win the 'hearts and minds' of the Catholic population. Figure 5.2. shows how Sinn Féin's decision to participate in Northern Ireland elections boosted the total nationalist vote. Whatever the explanations nationalist voting rose and, *ceteris paribus*, seems destined to continue to rise, especially if current demographic trends continue.

The non-confessional or, more accurately, *the bi-confessional bloc*, was characterized by the (nominally) non-ethnic and non-religious appeal of its parties. The NILP had sought bi-confessional support before 1969, and after this date it was joined by the APNI, and the Workers' Party (WP), which metamorphosed from the Republican Clubs in the early 1980s and sought support as a non-sectarian Marxist party. The NILP, the APNI, and the Workers' Party are all tacitly unionist, because they accept the Union, at least for the time being, but their political appeal, rationale, and bi-confessional support count against classifying them as dissident components of the unionist bloc.[7] They make no apologies for and do not wish to return to anything like the Stormont regime; nor do they wish to set the existing Union in concrete. Both the APNI and the WP recognize the importance of an 'Irish dimension' in winning nationalist consent to any future governmental arrangements for Northern Ireland; and the (collapsing) Workers' Party remains organized as an all-Ireland party, with units in the Republic and Northern Ireland.

The bi- or non-confessional bloc was squeezed after 1969, even though the APNI experienced a surge of support in the mid- and late 1970s. The fortunes of the NILP, the APNI, the WP, and the residual category in Table 6.1 suggest a steady decline of the non-polarized electorate. The NILP, unlike the APNI and the WP, disappeared off the party-political horizon in the 1970s: its working-class Protestant support went either to the UUP or the DUP, and its working-class Catholic support went to the SDLP. The APNI's initial growth was not sustained, and the WP failed to make any serious inroads into the working class electorate. The failure of the non-confessional bloc to grow in the 1970s and its crumbling in the early 1980s meant that the only pillar upon which British arbitration could rest was disappearing into the sands. British arbitration contributed, as we shall show, to the weakening of the bi-confessional bloc and the rise of the ultras in the unionist and nationalist blocs.

Arbitration and reform in an ethnically divided society

The Northern Ireland parliament was prorogued on 30 March 1972 by the Northern Ireland (Temporary Provisions) Act and its legislative powers transferred to Westminster. More permanent arrangements were contained in the Northern Ireland Constitution

Act of 1973. The Conservative government proposed a fundamental compromise. For unionists, their right to self-determination was affirmed by the Constitution Act (§1) which stated that a united Ireland could be achieved only by the consent of a majority in the region.[8] Nationalists' right to an important role in any devolved government was made clear by the rejection of majority rule, and the scrapping of the pre-1972 requirement that government ministers take an oath of allegiance to the Crown. The Act required the Secretary of State to appoint an executive mostly from sitting members of a new legislature and 'likely to be widely accepted throughout the community' (§2). The executive would have to be power-sharing in form, containing members from both the majority and minority communities. In addition each executive member was to be advised by consultative committees which would reflect the balance of parties in the assembly. To facilitate power-sharing the Northern Ireland Assembly Act provided for the reintroduction of proportional representation (STV) for region-wide elections, as an act of fairness to nationalists/Catholics, and in the hope that it would break up the UUP monolith.

The British government indicated its resolve permanently to broker the conflict, even if an agreed devolved government were to be established – a marked shift from its absentee policy after 1920. The proposed devolved legislature was downgraded and retitled. It was to be an assembly rather than a parliament, and unicameral rather than bicameral. Its 'legislation' would be termed 'measures' rather than 'acts', even though they would have the same force. The prime minister, Cabinet, and ministries of the Stormont system were replaced by a 'chief executive', an 'executive', and 'departments'. The Secretary of State was to scrutinize and approve the legislative output of the new assembly, and prevent the lack of supervision which had taken place before 1969. Some powers which had been abused by Stormont – the appointment of magistrates and non-supreme court judges,[9] public prosecutions, and the franchise for local and assembly elections – were put under Westminster control. Others, notably security powers, were provisionally retained by Westminster, although they could be transferred to the Northern Ireland legislature if political conditions permitted. Moreover §4 of the new act, like §75 of the Government of Ireland Act, maintained the right of the UK parliament to legislate for Northern Ireland in respect of any matter.

Accompanying these reforms were a number of civil-rights measures designed to remove sectarian bias in the distribution of public goods which had prevailed under the Stormont regime. The establishment in 1971 of a Housing Executive to take control of public housing from the local authorities would lead to an impartial allocation of one vital resource.[10] There was also fairer administration of education and health services after the establishment of government-appointed area boards. The government announced the appointment of an independent Director of Public Prosecutions, and an end to the use of extreme interrogation methods perfected in Aden and Yemen and deployed in the wake of the introduction of internment in August 1971. It also scrapped rubber bullets in favour of the plastic variety, and indicated its desire to phase out internment.

The nationalist bloc had to be convinced of British bona fides. However, the political compromise of no united Ireland for unionists on the one hand and power-sharing for nationalists on the other was the equivalent of 'a quarter of a loaf is better than none'. The unionist veto on Irish unity could be employed to maintain their side of the British compromise intact, but a unionist refusal to co-operate in power-sharing could deny nationalists their portion of the compromise. Similarly, British promises to supervise the activities of a power-sharing devolved government were welcome but of no use if such a government failed to materialise. Moreover little was done to reduce rapidly or effectively the glaring economic inequality between Protestants and Catholics which undergirded minority grievances. Individual posts and agencies, such as Parliamentary Commissioners for Administration and for Complaints in 1969, a Local Government Staff Commission in 1973,[11] and a Standing Advisory Commission on Human Rights (SACHR) in 1973,[12] were established to monitor and recommend the correction of abuses but with inadequate powers and resources. There was an attempt in the Constitution Act (1973) to improve the ineffective anti-discrimination clauses of the Government of Ireland Act, but the new provisions suffered from much the same weaknesses (Ch. 3: 116-7). Legislation which discriminated against persons on the grounds of their religion was extended to include political opinion (§17) and made retroactive to 1921; and it was made unlawful for the Northern Ireland executive, departments, district councils, library, education, health and social services boards to discriminate on the grounds of either religious or political belief (§19). Nevertheless the measures lacked teeth. The new 'protections' against discrimination in fact inhibited affirmative action programmes.[13] They were not entrenched in ways which might have encouraged judicial activism. In consequence, they were little more relied upon by the minority than their 1920 antecedents.[14] The new constitutional act, like its 1920 predecessor, made no provision for the protection of civil rights other than against discrimination, or for promotion of communal rights – such as the right to speak the Irish language or have it displayed on street signs. Consideration was given to a bill of rights, and supported in outline by all the parties in Northern Ireland, the Irish government, the Gardiner Committee, and the SACHR. However, the British government knew that a bill of rights would restrict its ability to manage security, did not wish to encourage demands for a bill of rights in Great Britain, and thought that one restricted to Northern Ireland would create the awkward possibility that British legislation would be unconstitutional there but not elsewhere in the UK (McCrudden, 1989: 321–2). In addition to these shortcomings, the early achievements of the civil-rights movement, such as universal suffrage for local government elections and an end to gerrymandering of local government boundaries, were undermined by the emasculation of local government in the Macrory reforms proposed in 1970 and implemented in 1972.[15]

More damagingly the government felt obliged, in the light of the high levels of violence in the early 1970s, to maintain intact an array of repressive security measures. It started direct rule with its credentials as an impartial arbiter severely impaired. The British Army, especially after the Falls Road curfew of 1970, internment in 1971, and Bloody Sunday, was regarded as having two faults by Irish nationalists: it was British, and it was an army. The Diplock Report (1972), which stemmed from British attempts to find a replacement for internment, recommended options which were only mildly less Draconian: the suspension of the right to a jury-trial for certain indictable offences, new relaxed rules on the admissibility of evidence and on the onus of proof, and wider powers of arrest for the security forces. These recommendations, which involved considerable digressions from British common law, were duly incorporated in the Emergency Provisions Act 1973, which in addition retained the power of internment. While it resulted in the repeal of the controversial Special Powers Act, it was widely and correctly recognized as containing many of the same abuses: up to one half of the new act was directly inspired by the older legislation (Hogan and Walker, 1989: 27).

These measures would have been consistent with arbitration had the British been only peace-keepers. However, they were involved in quelling a minority rebellion against *British* rule, and security measures were for the most part directed against the *Irish* minority which resisted British rule. Although internment began in August 1971, the first loyalist was not arrested until February 1973. While internment operated, 2,060 republicans as against 109 loyalists were detained (Hogan and Walker, 1989: 93–4), at a time when loyalist violence was as vigorous as that of nationalists (Ch 1: 28-32).

Consociational initiatives, 1972–5

The government sought a power-sharing or consociational settlement as the jewel in its arbitration strategy. A consociation has four institutional traits (Lijphart, 1977). First, a power-sharing coalition government of political parties enjoys the support of more than a simple majority of those who vote. Second, there must be community autonomy, permitting the rival ethnic communities self-administration where feasible – for example in the running of their schools. Third, there must be proportionality in the public sector – in elections, assembly committees, public employment, and in the allocation of public expenditure. Finally, mutual veto or concurring majority principles must operate, giving the minority the ability to protect its most important interests.

British policy during 1972–5 amounted to a reinvention of consociational ideas, although they did not envisage affirmative action to ensure full proportionality of the two communities in public-sector employment or in receipt of public expenditure. Success in promoting a consociational endeavour, however, requires not simply that the rival élites be willing to consider such a compromise, but also that they are capable of retaining the support of their followers, and that their ethnic bloc is not divided in a way which inhibits compromise.[16] Northern Ireland, however, no longer possessed an élite-dominated political culture. The UUP forced out two of its leaders between 1969 and 1971, and removed Faulkner when he risked power-sharing in 1973–4. Even Paisley did not have an unassailable position within the DUP.[17] Nor did the minority leaders enjoy appreciably greater security of tenure, the Nationalist leader, Eddie McAteer, had been eclipsed during the turbulence of 1968–9, and those who replaced him had to jockey carefully for position. Intra-bloc rivalries in the electoral arena also militated against compromise. Vanguard and the DUP acted as restraints on the UUP's willingness and ability to negotiate. The 1973 Assembly elections, conducted under PR,[18] split the unionists into *six* different groups. Those supporting discussion of power-sharing, Brian Faulkner's 'Official Unionists', won twenty-four seats, whereas unionist candidates opposed to power-sharing won twenty-six.

While the SDLP emerged as the dominant political party in the nationalist bloc 'the effect of the post-68 mobilisations had been to create a whole range of local defence groups, community associations and smaller leftish and republican groups which, together with the Provisionals, unceasingly criticised the SDLP and argued that it would shortly be absorbed and coopted' (Bew and Patterson, 1985: 54–5). British security policies and the inadequacy of British reforms erected obstacles to compromise for the SDLP leadership. The party refused to take part in talks called by Whitelaw at Darlington in October 1972, recommended that its supporters not support the police in 1973, and supported a rent-and-rates strike against internment. It boycotted the border poll, undermining the legitimacy of any internal settlement, and insisted that any power-sharing devolved government be accompanied by an institutionalized 'Irish dimension'. When the SDLP did enter talks with the Secretary of State and decided to contest the 1973 elections for the new assembly, it came under immediate criticism from the People's Democracy, the Officials, and the Provisionals.

In these unlikely circumstances a consociational settlement was negotiated in late 1973, and confirmed at Sunningdale, England, in December 1973. It created a power-sharing executive in which Faulkner's Official Unionists, the SDLP, and the Alliance formed a coalition government, with Faulkner as chief executive and Gerry Fitt of the SDLP as deputy chief executive. The Sunningdale agreement envisaged the creation of a Council of Ireland, at the SDLP's insistence but with the support of both the British and Irish governments. The Council of Ireland was to comprise a cross-border body – drawn from seven members of the Northern Ireland executive and seven members of the Irish government, a secretariat, and a consultative assembly with 30 members of the Northern Ireland assembly and 30 members of Dáil Éireann. Unanimity was to be the basis of the Council's resolutions, and thus mutual vetoes were to operate. The Council was to be experimental, vested with minor consultative and research functions, but was to have a 'harmonizing' role, and the door was left open for it to expand into institutions capable of forging a united Ireland.

Faulkner and his unionist negotiators at Sunningdale hoped to win acceptance for the Council of Ireland among their supporters by emphasizing potential security benefits from co-operation with the Irish government, the mainly symbolic nature of the Council, the unionist veto over any proposals inimical to their interests in the Council, and the recognition of Northern Ireland's status contained in Article 5 of the agreement: 'The Irish Government fully accepted and solemnly declared that there could be no change in the status of Northern Ireland until a majority of the people of Northern Ireland desired a change in that status.' However, Faulkner proved incapable of selling the Council of Ireland to the unionist bloc, and many of his own supporters. The IRA intensified its campaign, so did loyalist paramilitaries, and Sunningdale brought no 'peace dividend'. The Irish government, like the SDLP, partly trapped by British security policies, refused to facilitate the extradition of suspected terrorists to the UK, insisting instead that they be tried where apprehended.[19]

These actions heightened unionist anxieties. Sunningdale and the Council of Ireland strengthened the position of the anti-consociational unionists and led to their consolidation in a broad electoral front, the United Ulster Unionist Council (UUUC), formed in December 1973. The British general election of February 1974, called in the midst of Edward Heath's attempts to defeat a miners' strike, intervened at a critical and early stage in the consociational experiment, and to the benefit of the UUUC.[20] Plurality rule meant that the biggest bloc would do best in the Westminster elections. However, the nationalist and unionist coalition partners in the executive stood candidates against each other and therefore the UUUC anti-Sunningdale unionists were able completely to rout Faulkner's unionists. The UUUC obtained 51 per cent of the popular vote but eleven of Northern Ireland's twelve seats at Westminster. Poll evidence showed that strong Protestant support for the power-sharing experiment had dropped after the general election to 28 per cent of their bloc.

However, the SDLP, accused by republicans of legitimising hardline security measures against its own community, was neither willing nor able to save Faulkner by making concessions over the Council of Ireland. The possible trade-off of the abandonment of internment in return for the suspension of the Council of Ireland was not possible, because the British government maintained that internment could not be ended until 'the security situation' improved: a 'catch 22' policy given that internment was partially responsible for violence.

Ulster Protestants' concerns were exacerbated by the election of a new Labour government regarded as sympathetic to the notion of a British withdrawal. Furthermore a constitutional challenge brought by an extreme nationalist in the Republic of Ireland to Article 5 of the Sunningdale settlement produced an outcry. The Irish Supreme Court ruled that the Irish government had not recognized the *de jure* status of Northern Ireland as part of the United Kingdom, because such recognition would have contradicted Articles 2 and 3 of Ireland's 1937 constitution (*Boland* v. *An Taoiseach*). The Irish government had merely recognized Northern Ireland's *de facto* status as part of the UK; and the Irish Attorney General declared that 'any person living in this island and knowing our history could not possibly construe the Sunningdale declaration as meaning that we did not lay claim over the six counties' (Irish Times, 22 April 1974).

The position of Faulkner's Unionists on the executive was becoming untenable. A strike organized by the Ulster Workers Council (UWC) in May 1974, and allowed to boomerang by an incompetent response from the NIO and the newly appointed Secretary of State Merlyn Rees (Fisk, 1975), led to the collapse of the power-sharing executive and the Sunningdale agreement, and to a period of direct rule from Westminster which has continued ever since. Internal squabbling in the executive over the Council of Ireland confirmed key army and NIO policy-makers in their view that its disintegration was imminent and that decisive action should not be taken against the UWC. However, the failure of the Labour government to 'stand up to the loyalists' confirmed nationalists in their estimation that Britain was incapable of being a neutral arbiter. The SDLP, already bitter at the failure of Britain to end internment and make key reforms in policing and job-discrimination, was convinced that the strike could have been destroyed by resolute British action, and treated the NIO's inaction on all three fronts as proof of the need for a strong Irish dimension. Loyalists, on the other hand, were euphoric about their ability to confront and defeat the British and Irish establishments: Dublin was no longer 'a Sunningdale away'.

The prospects for future accommodation looked grim. Nevertheless the Labour team at the NIO, some of whose members saw grounds for optimism in the 'proletarian' activism of the Protestant workers,[21] called a constitutional convention under a revised Constitution Act (1974). Elections would be held for the convention in 1975. British policy-makers decided to remain in the background as mediators rather than directors of initiatives. The NIO's back-seat role left the internal parties to design their own agreed mode of government, but which would nevertheless 'command the most widespread acceptance throughout the whole community' (Rees, 1985: 183–210, 251–82).

In the elections to the convention unionists opposed to power-sharing *and* an Irish dimension won an absolute majority of the votes cast. The most vigorous factional competition occurred between the DUP and the VUP in their contest to win the 'not an inch' vote. The VUP leader Craig's close association with the overthrow of the power-sharing executive contributed to his party gaining 14 seats to the DUP's 12. Surprisingly, despite these results and the terrible violence surrounding the deliberations of the convention, Craig eventually suggested a temporary power-sharing deal with the SDLP. He justified it as a response to the crisis and as compatible with the Westminster model of government, which had allowed temporary coalitions during the depression and the two world wars. What happened to Craig demonstrates that even the hardest of hardline politicians in Northern Ireland, with the most impressive credentials of ethnic intransigence, are not sufficiently autonomous to guarantee the support of their followers. Craig had been regarded as more extremist than Paisley, because he was willing to consider a unilateral declaration of independence for Northern Ireland, advocated a 'shoot-to-kill' policy for the security forces when confronted by law-breaking republicans, and was involved in paramilitary mobilization. However, after his offer to the SDLP, he was ostracized by the UUUC and the majority of his own party members in the convention. The latter immediately created a separate faction loyal to the UUUC. Their former leader was dispatched into the political wilderness, never to recover. He lost his Westminster seat in the 1979 election to the DUP's deputy leader, Peter Robinson, and was rarely heard of again. His fate remains a warning to other potential 'Lundys' within the unionist camp.

The SDLP's willingness to compromise on Craig's initiative was never fully tested since it was withdrawn before negotiations had reached a critical point. A cynical observer remarked that the UUUC's behaviour meant that the SDLP 'had reasonableness thrust upon them' (Rose, 1976: 132). Not surprisingly the final convention report, reflecting the aspirations of the UUUC majority, called for the establishment of a majoritarian executive, and described the SDLP as fundamentally republican and incapable of being loyal members of any sort of Northern Ireland government. The convention was accordingly dissolved in March 1976. No end to direct rule appeared in sight.

A second start: criminalisation, Ulsterisation, and normalisation, 1976–81

The collapse of the convention and the continuing violence led to a re-evaluation of British arbitration. New security and reform initiatives, which had been considered while the convention met during 1975–6 were attempted (Rees, 1985); reflecting an in-built tendency for British policy-makers to partition their consideration of 'party-political' and 'security' issues. Under Rees's successor, Roy Mason, wide-ranging political initiatives were shunned lest they heighten expectations and create instability. After 1976 'benevolent' good government was tried as a longer-term strategy and not simply as a prelude to a devolution settlement.

Criminalisation, Ulsterisation, and normalisation were the key themes in this second start. They stemmed from the 1975 Gardiner Report which recommended that internment lapse, that suspects be dealt with through the courts, and that the 'special status' category for prisoners interned without trial be phased out. They were occasioned by the failure of the government's cease-fire negotiations with the PIRA in 1975. Gardiner's recommendations were adopted in 1976. A policy of 'police primacy' in which the RUC would take over many tasks conducted by the army was piloted, and began to take serious effect from 1977. 'Criminalisation' and 'normalisation' were designed by a government anxious that its role be externally regarded as impartial and legitimate. In addition, a

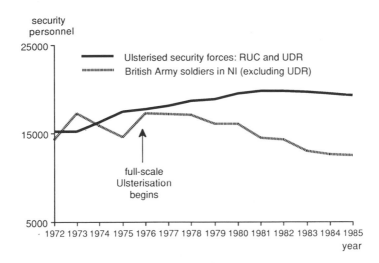

Figure 5.3 The Ulsterisation of the security forces
Source: adapted from IIP (1990: Table B9)

reduction of British troops stationed in Northern Ireland and a lower
profile for those remaining led to the planned 'Ulsterisation' of the
security forces and a greater role for what were proclaimed to be
the 'reformed RUC' and the 'modern UDR' (see Figure 5.3).[22]

The success of criminalisation was dependent on the British
arbiters being seen to be relying on normal legal processes. However,
the government continued to depend on Diplock courts, to use
extraordinary powers of arrest provided by special legislation, and
to derogate from the European Convention on Human Rights on the
grounds that there was an emergency. Moreover, the abandonment
of internment led to increased reliance on confessions, extracted
by dubious 'questioning' techniques (Taylor, 1980). Criticism by
Amnesty International (1978) and an enquiry by the Bennett Committee (1979) resulted in new controls on police conduct and a
decline in complaints. As a consequence, however, confessions,
as the key method of securing convictions, were replaced by
accomplice-evidence, often uncorroborated, and in conflict with
common law practices in Great Britain. By the early 1980s the RUC
had perfected a new method of securing convictions. They cultivated
the 'supergrass', an accomplice who would implicate large numbers
of his erstwhile colleagues in return for a new identity, a new home,

and substantial remuneration (Greer, 1986, 1987; Hogan and Walker, 1989: 123–6). The fact that 15 out of 25 supergrasses operating in this period subsequently retracted their evidence (which helped convince the judges to condemn it) did little to improve minority impressions of the administration of justice - although in fairness the RUC produced loyalist as well as nationalist supergrasses.

Normalization gave a greater role to the police, but involved training them to do the job of the military and equipping them appropriately. 'Normal British policeman' could not be half-way between an army and a constabulary. The sleight of hand involved in 'police primacy' did not convince the minority, who refused to regard the flak-jacketed, heavily armed, armoured land-rover-borne RUC as a normal police force. The use of plastic bullets to disperse demonstrators, causing several fatalities, did not suggest that the RUC was a normal police force. Little use was made of the normal police methods of gathering intelligence – maintaining close relations with the relevant community – and the RUC was forced to rely on military snatch-operations in Catholic areas. In addition, the British Army continued to operate in a major back-up role, but almost exclusively in republican areas, and therefore highlighted the partisan nature of British arbitration.

While Ulsterisation had obvious advantages for the British government, in that it led to fewer British soldiers being killed than would otherwise have been the case[23] (and for working-class Ulster Protestants who held the vast bulk of the jobs in the nearly 20,000 RUC and UDR establishments), the benefits for the minority were not obvious. Once more they were being policed and soldiered by the local majority. The UDR looked suspiciously like a reformed B-specials; and sectarian atrocities by renegade elements of the UDR made it impossible for the SDLP to support the security forces without what some saw as equivocation. The SDLP spokesperson usually declared that s/he supported the security forces when they acted impartially within the law. Ulsterisation had one other effect which did little to promote the prospects for political accommodation. Since the indigenous security forces, i.e. Ulster Protestants, began taking the brunt of nationalist paramilitary actions, the willingness of unionist politicians and their supporters to seek a settlement with the nationalist minority diminished. In 1985, sixteen years after the onset of sustained violence, and eight years after 'Ulsterisation' and 'normalisation', ethnic attitudes on the police, the legal system, and

Table 5.4 Ethnic attitudes on law and order, June 1985
Source: *Belfast Telegraph*, 2.6.1985

	Protestants (per cent)	Catholics (per cent)
The RUC discharges its duty unfairly/very unfairly	4	53
The RUC discharges its duty fairly	59	43
The RUC discharges its duty very fairly	37	4
The legal system dispenses justice unfairly	36	68
The legal system dispenses justice fairly	64	32
The use of plastic bullets is unacceptable	14	87
The use of plastic bullets is acceptable	86	13

the use of plastic bullets remained as polarised as ever, tempered only by some evidence of Catholic confidence in the RUC (see Table 5.4).

Criminalisation backfired more spectacularly than Ulsterisation. The withdrawal of 'special category' status in March 1976 was followed from September 1976 by a 'blanket protest': republican prisoners convicted of scheduled offences through the Diplock courts demanded 'political status' and refused to wear normal prison clothing and donned blankets instead. They later proceeded to a 'dirty protest' in which they smeared their excrement on cell walls. The dirty protest was followed by two hunger strikes in 1980 and 1981, ten men led by Bobby Sands dying in the latter year (Beresford, 1987; O'Malley, 1990a). Thatcher's hardline refusal to make any concessions to the prisoners which would suggest in any way that they differed from ordinary criminals satisfied unionists and Conservative backwoodsmen, but caused a predictable wave of revulsion within the Catholic community, including those who did not support the IRA. In a Westminster by-election created by the death of Frank Maguire (an independent nationalist MP for Fermanagh–South Tyrone), Bobby Sands, the leader of the IRA prisoners in the H-block prisons, defeated Harry West of the UUP in a straight fight. The local SDLP constituency party refused to run a candidate against Sands. The solidarity of the nationalist vote for Sands was ominous: and after he went on to be the first prisoner to die, his election-agent Owen Carron retained his seat as a 'proxy political prisoner'. The dirty protests and the hunger strikes allowed PSF to emerge as a serious political force, mobilizing the abstentionist nationalist electorate. Two other hunger strikers were elected to Dáil Éireann in the June 1981 general election in the Republic of Ireland. The hunger strikers had legitimated the IRA in the eyes of some of the world's media as an authentic national liberation movement.

Criminalisation, normalisation, and Ulsterisation might have stood a better chance of success if the British government had been successful in reforming Northern Ireland's discriminatory economy. The Fair Employment (Northern Ireland) Act 1976 was designed to enforce the anti-discrimination provisions contained in the 1973 Constitution Act. It outlawed discrimination on religious and political grounds in the public and private sector, and established a Fair Employment Agency (FEA) to promote equality of opportunity. The FEA was made responsible for receiving and investigating complaints, and for conducting its own inquiries into the availability of equality of opportunity. However, even though the agency proved a failure as a means for correcting employment disparities (McCrudden, 1982), the FEA at least presided over an outpouring of reliable statistics and research on the scale of economic inequality.

Table 5.5 demonstrates the consistent nature of the unemployment disparities in a period when the Fair Employment Act was supposed to reduce them. Throughout the period 1971–87 Catholic males were about two and a half times more likely to be unemployed than Protestants (see Cormack and Osborne, 1991; Osborne and Cormack, 1986; Smith and Chambers, 1991). While the Northern Ireland male unemployment rate remained consistently much higher than that in Great Britain (19 per cent compared to 11 per cent in 1981), the rate among male Protestants (12 per cent in 1981) was roughly equivalent to the Great British average while that for male Catholics (31 per cent in 1981) was dramatically higher. Northern Ireland's Protestants, both males and females, were far more British in their employment rates than their Catholic co-citizens.

The Fair Employment Act, and related policies of attempting to shift jobs to Catholic areas and training Catholics to do them, did not produce significant results before 1985. An authoritative 1987 study which considered the effects of the 1976 Act in promoting equality of opportunity found that inequalities between Catholics and Protestants remained substantial and in some instances had increased (Smith and Chambers, 1987a, 1987c; and see Ch. 7: 262 ff.). Job discrimination was still considered appropriate in certain quarters,

Table 5.5 Per cent unemployment by religion and sex in Northern Ireland, compared with the Northern Ireland and Great British averages

Source: McCormack and O'Hara (1990: 6)

Year	MALE					FEMALE				
	Catholic	Protestant	NI average	GB average	Catholic/ Protestant ratio	Catholic	Protestant	NI average	GB average	Catholic/ Protestant ratio
1971 census	17.3	6.6	10.3	5.5	2.6: 1	7.0	3.6	4.7	4.7	1.9: 1
1981 census	30.2	12.4	19.1	11.3	2.4: 1	17.1	9.6	12.6	7.4	1.8: 1
1983–4 chs*	35	15	24	14	2.3: 1	17	11	13	10	1.5: 1
1985–7 chs*	36	14	22	12	2.6: 1	15	9	11	9	1.7: 1

Note: * = continuous household survey.

a view encouraged by some unionist politicians and academics, especially in any job with a security-dimension; investigations into discrimination had had little effect upon employers; monitoring of the composition of work-forces, without which the difficulty of combatting inequality increases considerably, was not compulsory. Little had been done to eradicate informal recruitment practices, and even when employed Catholics continued to have worse jobs than Protestants in most sectors, although they had made some headway in the Northern Ireland civil service.

The differential in ethnic employment levels and status in Northern Ireland might not have been as grave as in some other divided societies, say South Africa or the southern United States, but it exacerbated traditional antagonisms, fuelled Sinn Féin's arguments, and gave support to the IRA's argument that Northern Ireland was unreformable. Resolute state action, aimed at ending discrimination and redressing disparities between the minority and majority in a positive-sum fashion, would have gone some way towards reducing tensions under British arbitration.[24] However, the resolve amongst the British political élite was missing. Roy Mason (Secretary of State, 1976–9) declared that he was more worried about the region's economy than its political or security problems. However, despite the government's recognition that Northern Ireland had a 'dual economy' (Bew and Patterson, 1985: 90) little was done to promote sustained economic development or to eradicate structural economic inequalities. Mason's 'bread and circuses' increased expenditure on social security and leisure centres throughout Northern Ireland but were little better than opiates. For most nationalists, the reform of Northern Ireland under direct rule seemed rhetorical rather than substantive.

Arbitration had increased militancy within both ethnic blocs rather than reduced it. Direct rule appeared structurally if not intentionally biased. It meant *British* rule of Northern Ireland, and as that was far more palatable for unionists than sharing power with nationalists, they had no incentive to contemplate a major shift in political behaviour. Unionist contentment with the status quo manifested itself in a number of ways. In 1977 a loyalist strike to achieve majority rule and stronger security measures proved ineffective because direct rule, unlike power-sharing and the Council of Ireland, did not threaten unionists. Opinion polls in the late 1970s showed that unionists were considerably happier than nationalists with direct rule. A *Fortnight* poll published in October–November 1980 asked Protestants and Catholics to rank power-sharing, direct rule, and a system in which the minority would have substantial veto-powers. Whereas 57 per cent of Protestants preferred direct rule, a mere 15 per cent of Catholics did the same; and whereas 79 per cent of Catholics preferred power-sharing this view was shared by only 26 per cent of Protestants.[25] Most significantly direct rule allowed the unionists the luxury of disunity and an internal debate not on concessions to the minority but on the relative merits of majority-rule devolution versus integration. The UUUC broke up after the 1977 strike, which had not been supported by the UUP; and some unionists, inspired by Enoch Powell, openly saw direct rule as a stepping-stone towards full integration with the 'British mainland'. They opposed any form of devolution and argued variously for an end to the 'order in council' system for passing Northern Ireland legislation, the creation of a Northern Ireland Select Committee, and the establishment of a Northern Ireland regional council on the model of Scottish local government.

The structural bias of 'British' arbitration in favour of unionism was exacerbated by the pivotal position held by ten Unionist MPs in the House of Commons between 1976 and 1979, when the Labour government lacked a parliamentary majority. Prime Minister Callaghan's expedient concession of five extra Westminster seats to Northern Ireland won unionist support but impugned British neutrality.[26] Roy Mason's reluctance to undertake a consociational initiative, his temporary embrace of integrationist proposals close to the unionist position, his undisguised dislike of the SDLP and 'greens', and his general handling of direct rule won him praise from the Orange Order, a certain kiss of death for a professed arbiter (Bew and Patterson, 1985: 103).[27] It was apt perhaps that the Labour government was brought down in May 1979 as a result of abstentions by Frank Maguire, an independent nationalist MP, and Gerry Fitt, the SDLP's leader, who explained his abstention on the vote of no confidence as a direct retaliation for Mason's conduct in Northern Ireland.

The second wave of consociational initiatives, 1979–82

Arbitration became less attractive to the new Conservative policy-makers elected in 1979 because it became obvious that it impeded an agreed settlement, indeed any settlement, and because the British government's Northern Ireland policies became progressively discredited, domestically and internationally. Since both major British parties had vied for unionist support in the period preceding the dissolution of parliament in 1979, the Speaker of the US House of Representatives, Tip O'Neill, claimed that they were treating the region as a 'political football', a remark which brought 'shocked denials' from those who felt it too close to their bones.

The non-partisan credentials of the Conservatives were not more impressive than Mason's administration. Apart from the Heath interlude, relations between the Conservatives and the UUP had been very good. One UUP MP, Enoch Powell, was a former senior Tory, once tipped for the party leadership. Other Conservatives like Sir John Biggs-Davison and Ian Gow were closely linked to the UUP, and Prime Minister Thatcher, and often spoke like the political heirs of those who had threatened civil war rather than coerce Ulster in 1912. The Conservative spokesman for Northern Ireland before his assassination by the INLA in 1979 had been Airey Neave, a friend of senior unionists, an advocate of stronger security measures and a supporter of integration[G]. Integrationist proposals formed a part of the manifesto on which the Conservatives contested and won the 1979 election.[28] Most significantly Margaret Thatcher was too close to the UUP to be accepted as impartial. Her position on law and order, especially the latter; on British patriotism; and even her emphasis on private enterprise, were all closer to the values, or at least self-perceptions of unionists than nationalists.

The failure of criminalisation, the shortcomings of reform, and the obstacles to consociationalism posed by arbitration provoked a new departure within the SDLP. The formation of the IIP in 1977, a more ultra-nationalist party, raised the spectre of an electoral challenge to the SDLP's leadership of the nationalist bloc. In 1977 the SDLP's party platform adopted an increased emphasis on the Irish dimension, a stance which led to the expulsion of one of the party's most prominent socialists, Paddy Devlin. John Hume, the party's leading thinker, winner of a European parliamentary seat in 1979, and its future leader, despaired of an internal settlement, and began to build an international constituency to support his party's position.

In September 1979, the new Secretary of State, Humphrey Atkins, announced that the government intended to convene a conference of the main Northern Ireland parties. In November the government presented a flurry of suggestions on how minority interests could be safeguarded within a Northern Ireland government and assembly. The White Paper, which did not propose a discussion of the Irish dimension, was condemned by the SDLP, which precipitated the resignation of Fitt, and his replacement by the less pliant and more nationalistic Hume. The SDLP only agreed to take part in the conference after being permitted by Atkins to discuss the Irish dimension and put forward their own devolution proposals. The UUP, miffed at the government's volte-face on its manifesto commitment, refused to take part and condemned the conference as an attempt to give a veto to minority interests, which it was! The DUP was more receptive to Atkins's proposals but its manœuvrability was overestimated and its motives misunderstood by a government engaged in wishful thinking.

Unionist intra-bloc rivalry was more intense in 1979–80 than at any time since Sunningdale. The DUP's tripling of its Westminster seats at the May 1979 general election, followed by Paisley's huge triumph in the June 1979 European election, posed a major challenge to the UUP, and over the next year, in Hume's words, it sought to 'out-Paisley Paisley'. The UUP depicted the DUP as a party prepared to sit at the same table as nationalists, and Paisley's desire for devolution led Powell to describe Paisley as an inveterate enemy of the Union. Paisley's willingness to enter discussions, however, was not motivated by a desire to compromise with the SDLP, but by the classic grounds accepted by unionists in 1921; they needed their own parliament as a 'bulwark of the Union' and that ruled out power-sharing with nationalists. Nevertheless, the government welcomed Paisley's decision to participate in talks and courted him as a moderate in the belief that his new-found status as the leader of the Protestants, his personal ambition to be prime minister of Northern Ireland, and the DUP's desire to consolidate its success would make him amenable to compromise. British policy-makers suffered from two misconceptions: 'the DUP was a normal political party capable of change and compromise . . . [and] that Paisley was a leader in the sense that he could deliver his grassroots, rather than merely articulate their belligerent brand of unionism' (Moloney and Pollack, 1986: 340, citing Smyth, 1983).

The Conference began in January 1980 but was adjourned in March without progress. A further White Paper in July proposed two constitutional models: one which amounted to a power-sharing executive; the other which allowed for the possibility of a majoritarian executive but provided blocking powers for the minority within the assembly. Predictably the unionists rejected the former whereas the SDLP rejected the latter. By November of 1980 the government admitted the initiative had failed, and Paisley was once more on the war-path leading 'Carson-trail' rallies against the Anglo-Irish 'joint studies' set up within the framework of a British–Irish inter-governmental council agreed by Thatcher and Charles Haughey, the new Irish prime minister, in December 1980.

In the wake of the massive outpouring of nationalist discontent during the 1981 hunger strikes the new Secretary of State, James Prior, announced a new consociational initiative in April 1982. The devolution of power from Westminster was made conditional upon 'broad cross-community support' – operationalized as 70 per cent of the new assembly. Power would be devolved incrementally in policy-areas where agreement could be secured, which gave rise to the phrase 'rolling devolution'. Prior's initiative was intended to promote power-sharing, and, if that proved fruitless, to put a democratic gloss on direct rule - the Assembly would enjoy some scrutinizing, advisory, and debating functions in the absence of agreed devolution.

Prior's initiative was a failure. The Irish government of Haughey was hostile; the Irish opposition under FitzGerald was critical; and Thatcher undermined her own Secretary of State as Prior complained to one of the authors. The SDLP was antagonized because power-sharing seemed to be no longer regarded as a non-negotiable right; and because there was no concrete manifestation of an Irish dimension.[29] PSF, riding high on their post hunger-strike support, contested the assembly election on an abstentionist ticket and secured 10.1 per cent of the vote. Faced with this electoral threat and with both unionist parties seeking to outdo each other in their refusal to compromise, the SDLP abstained from the assembly, effectively destroying the initiative. The key party required to make power-sharing work was not even present at the assembly, and Sinn Féin's breakthrough cast a dark shadow on British claims to neutrality: one third of the nationalist community supported a war to expel them from Northern Ireland.

The assembly became a talking shop, a forum in which the rival unionist factions competed with each other. The UUP espoused integrationist proposals (which envisaged enhanced local government) while the DUP continued to support majority rule. The assembly eventually ended up being used as a propaganda forum from which unionists denounced the Anglo-Irish Agreement, and consequently was wound up in the summer of 1986 (O'Leary, Elliott, and Wilford, 1988). Sinn Féin's momentum continued into the 1983 Westminster elections, with the party winning the seat of West Belfast from the former leader of the SDLP, and increasing its support to 13.4 per cent of the poll and 42 per cent of the nationalist bloc. The absence of power-sharing, the delegitimization of the criminalization strategy, and the failure to reduce the serious economic disparities between Catholics and Protestants allowed Sinn Féin to declare that Northern Ireland was unreformable, and Haughey to call it a 'failed political entity'. The spectacle of 100,000 Catholics supporting a party which condoned the murder of Protestant members of the security forces did nothing to enhance the prospects for internal accommodation.

The SDLP turned the growth of unconstitutional nationalism to its advantage: it encouraged all Irish constitutional nationalist parties (north and south) to develop an agreed negotiating strategy with the British government, to circumvent the unionist veto and stall Sinn Féin. The Republic's parties, worried by the growth of Sinn Féin, accepted the SDLP's proposals and established the New Ireland Forum which would deliberate during 1983–4, and eventually recommend four ways forward for a new Ireland: a unitary Irish state, a federal Ireland, joint British and Irish authority over Northern Ireland, and open discussions with the British government on the best way to progress. The Forum's proposals were conveyed to the British government by Irish Prime Minister FitzGerald, but received what seemed like a curt public dismissal from Prime Minister Thatcher in November 1984.[30] However, this reaction was not as absolutist as it seemed.

Searching for a way out of international and domestic embarrassment

Arbitration had promised international respectability for the British position but by 1983–4 it increasingly lacked credibility. The representatives of the newly elected European parliament discussed Northern Irish affairs in a critical vein after 1979. The hunger strikes were a 'watershed in European perceptions of the Northern Ireland problem' (Guelke, 1988: 158), and touched off adverse criticism of British policy in the Continental press. The European Commission of Human Rights condemned the inflexible nature of the British reaction to the strikes (McCrudden 1989: 323). European parliamentarians, disposed to policies which would erode boundaries within the community, sided largely with the SDLP's and Fine Gael's social and christian democratic brands of constitutional nationalism. The European parliament condemned the use of plastic bullets in 1982, and in February 1983 established an inquiry into the political and economic problems of Northern Ireland. Its report, released in December 1983, implicitly rejected Britain's neutrality by supporting the establishment of joint Anglo-Irish machinery to deal with the 'constitutional oddity' of Northern Ireland (Haagerup, 1983–4).

More significant, for the British government, was American dissatisfaction with their arbitration.[31] American intervention in Northern Ireland's affairs had not been apparent before 1976 because Britain's emphasis on power-sharing and an Irish dimension was welcomed by the Irish-American élite. Edward Kennedy had even suggested that Whitelaw be nominated for the Nobel Peace Prize for his role in negotiating the Sunningdale agreement (Guelke, 1988: 138). However, the collapse of the executive and the entrenchment of direct rule under Mason ended this *rapprochement*, and the differences between the Irish-American political élite and the British government were exploited by the SDLP and successive Irish governments. In 1977 President Carter took the unprecedented step of indicating that the internal politics of Northern Ireland was a legitimate concern of American foreign policy, and expressed support for a peaceful settlement involving the Irish government. On St Patrick's Day 1978, the 'four horsemen', Senators Kennedy and Moynihan, Speaker O'Neill, and the Governor of New York, Hugh Carey, issued a joint statement criticizing the lack of political progress under direct rule and the violation of human rights by the security forces. The following year they condemned British policy, especially police interrogation methods, and called for consideration of an Irish confederation. In the same year, the State Department suspended shipments of arms to the RUC, fearing embarrassment over pending congressional hearings which would have aired the Amnesty International and Bennett Reports. In the early 1980s Irish Americans launched a campaign to correct the disadvantaged economic position of the minority in Northern Ireland. The Democratic presidential platform in 1984 declared its support for a ban on commercial transactions with firms practising religious discrimination in Northern Ireland. In November 1984 the 'MacBride principles' were developed, aimed at persuading American companies investing in Northern Ireland to adopt affirmative action programmes to reduce employment disparities between minority and majority (McCormack and O'Hara, 1990: 42–5). By mid-1985 they had been endorsed by the American Labor Federation, the AFL-CIO and by the American Council of Churches. In November 1985 Massachusetts adopted legislation requiring compliance with the MacBride principles, and other states began to follow suit. These different modes of American pressure helped persuade the British of the merits of formal and deeper co-operation with the Republic of Ireland. Each time Thatcher visited the United States before 1985, Northern Ireland was raised, often by Reagan himself, partly because of skilful diplomacy by the Irish government and the SDLP's contacts with Irish-American politicians (FitzGerald, 1991: 527, 535, 561–2). Reagan continued a promise made by Carter to provide aid in the event of a settlement and praised the New Ireland Forum Report; while his administration criticized Thatcher for her apparent rejection of its proposals in November 1984.

The other benefit of arbitration, quarantining Northern Ireland from partisan politics in Great Britain, also unravelled as the Labour party at its 1981 conference expressed its support for a united Ireland by consent (NEC, 1981), and two years later the Liberal party conference passed a resolution calling for the withdrawal of British troops. The Kilbrandon Report (1984), commissioned by the British–Irish Association, supported wider involvement of the Republic in Northern Ireland, and was implicitly critical of British policy.

This domestic and international criticism, combined with the rise of Sinn Féin, explain why the British government, increasingly impatient with its thankless role as arbiter, began to explore with the Irish government other long-run strategies of conflict-management. An 'Anglo-Irish framework' was first developed in two intergovernmental summits in 1980. The background involved the failure of local politicians to agree to an internal settlement, American pressure, and London's need to muzzle the Irish government over its handling of the hunger strikes. At the second summit meeting in December 1980 an agreement was reached by Thatcher and Haughey to give consideration to 'the totality of relationships within these islands'.[32] Joint studies began on economic, security, and political co-operation between the two governments, initiating the interactions between officials which would end in the Anglo-Irish Agreement.

A prime ministerial summit meeting in November 1981 led to formal agreement on the creation of a British–Irish Intergovernmental Council. A series of bilateral meetings between the two governments were held between 1982 and 1983 within the framework of the council. However, progress was limited owing to the Republic's neutrality during the Falklands war and because of Prior's decision to undertake his 'rolling devolution initiative'. Formal interactions resumed at a summit meeting in November 1983 between FitzGerald and Thatcher. The two governments began to negotiate on a major new initiative, a convergence overshadowed by Thatcher's outspoken rejection of the terms of the Forum Report in the Chequers press conference which took place a year later. Solitary British arbitration was coming to an end.

Notes

1. Arbitration is distinguishable from mediation because the arbiter makes the relevant decisions, whereas mediators merely facilitate them.

2. Garret FitzGerald (Irish prime minister, 1981, 1982–7), attempted to capitalize on his mixed parentage. Since his mother was a northern Irish Protestant, whereas his father was a southern Irish Catholic, he claimed to comprehend both traditions in Ireland. However, his claim to 'neutrality' was not credible to unionists, who observed that both his parents had been nationalist revolutionaries.

3. The Ministry of Defence remains responsible for the Army and the UDR, and the intelligence services report direct to the prime minister.

4. Peter Brooke, who became Secretary of State in 1989, has the dubious advantage for an arbiter of being related to Sir Basil Brooke, Northern Ireland's third prime minister.

5. These tendencies explain why we favour a change to a PR for Westminster elections (McGarry and O'Leary, 1991b: 297).

6. The upward trend would be higher had we not removed the Workers' Party from the nationalist bloc after 1981, even though we counted the Republican Clubs as a component of the nationalist bloc as late as 1979.

7. The Conservative party, which has organized in Northern Ireland since 1989, is fairly seen as a dissident faction within the unionist bloc.

8. A border poll held in 1973, boycotted by the SDLP, demonstrated that there was no such consent: 57.5 per cent of the total electorate declared that they wanted to remain part of the UK.

9. The Government of Ireland Act reserved the appointment of the supreme court to Westminster.

10. The PSI survey of 1986 confirmed that public opinion believed that the public housing system is now fair. However, the PSI analysis showed that this consensus is at odds with the facts: the housing system does not deliver equal opportunities to Protestant and Catholic applicants, and favours Protestants (Smith and Chambers, 1991: 330–67).

11. The 'effectiveness' of this body can be seen in a report published by the FEC in 1990: of a total of 66 senior officers employed by 5 unionist-controlled district councils in 1990, 2 were Catholics (*Fortnight*, Oct. 1990: 6).

12. The SACHR is an advisory body. The Secretary of State is not obliged to consult it, let alone take its advice.

13. The Canadian Charter of Rights and Freedoms (§15) prohibits discrimination on the basis of religion, language, age, and gender, but explicitly allows affirmative action programmes to aid disadvantaged minorities.

14. The provisions were used successfully to challenge a unionist council's discriminatory action against the GAA (*Purvis* v. *Magherafelt District Council*).

15. The proposals were originally welcomed by NICRA – as an attack on unionist discriminatory bastions.

16. Detailed analyses of the failure of consociational initiatives in Northern Ireland after 1972 can be found in McGarry (1990) and O'Leary (1989).

17. In 1971, after causing much consternation among his supporters, he retracted a statement that an accommodation with the Irish Republic might be possible if the influence of the Catholic Church there was reduced (O'Malley, 1983: 192).

18. Paisley told his party's tenth annual conference that the introduction of PR, which he denounced at the time as 'un-British', came by the 'Providence of God' (Arthur and Jeffery, 1988: 52).

19. A Criminal Law Jurisdiction Act was passed by both governments in 1975–6 enabling the trial of a suspected perpetrator of a terrorist offence committed in the other's jurisdiction.

20. Whitelaw and Pym, Secretaries of State between 1972 and 1974, both advised Heath against calling a general election, because they thought the

Conservatives might lose and because of the destabilizing repercussions for Northern Ireland (interviews with B. O'Leary, 15 Jan. 1991 and 4 Mar. 1991).

21. Merlyn Rees and his deputy Stan Orme naïvely equated trade union action with 'socialism'. The ethnic exclusivism of the UWC's socialism did not lead Rees to draw parallels with national socialism but led him to talk of 'Ulster nationalism' (Rees (1985); and interview with B. O'Leary, 18 Dec. 1990). Rees's colleague and minister of state at the NIO, Roland Moyle, has a different memory of loyalist trade unionists: 'you'd have a meeting with the shop stewards in Northern Ireland, and you'd see all these characters walk in in their blue overalls and their AUEW and TGWU badges on, and you'd think "Good, I'm among friends", but by the time you'd been talking to them for about fifteen minutes you wondered whether you were talking with an escaped fraction of Hitler's Nazi party' (interview with B. O'Leary, 3 Jan. 1991).

22. Roland Moyle commented: 'I always had the personal reservation, and I don't suppose I did much about it, that "Ulsterisation" was basically "Protestantisation" and "Protestantisation" was what the whole problem was about' (interview with B. O'Leary, 3 Jan. 1991).

23. Between 1969 and 1975, 125 members of the local security forces were killed compared with 248 British soldiers; whereas between 1976 and 1984 the figures were 238 and 137 respectively (calculated from IIP data-base).

24. Governments in Quebec, Malaysia, and South Africa (in respect of the Afrikaner–English cleavage among whites) have shown that state power can be used effectively to pursue affirmative action (Esman, 1987).

25. The 1978 Northern Ireland Attitudes Survey (the representativeness of which was very badly impaired) showed that majorities in both blocs regarded the British as even-handed 'on the whole'; but whereas 89 per cent of Protestants concurred, 70 per cent of Catholics agreed.

26. Northern Ireland was 'under-represented' in the Commons because of its former possession of a powerful devolved government; increasing its representation implied that a new devolutionary experiment was off the agenda.

27. 'He's probably the Protestants' favourite Secretary of State' (Roland Moyle, interview with B. O'Leary, 3 Jan. 1991).

28. Prior maintains that Neave had shifted from his 'integrationist' enthusiasms before he was assassinated (interview with B. O'Leary, 14 Nov. 1990).

29. According to Prior, Thatcher personally overruled his willingness to embrace an Irish dimension even though Francis Pym, former Northern Ireland Secretary, and Foreign Secretary during Prior's time at the NIO, had warned the cabinet committee that unless Prior's White Paper 'was reasonably "green" there was no way of selling it to the Republic or to the nationalists' (interview with B. O'Leary, 14 Nov. 1990).

30. In a Chequers press conference Thatcher said 'that is out!' to each of the Forum's three models. According to FitzGerald in the meeting which preceded

her press conference she had been much more constructive. He claims that the negative impact caused by Thatcher's 'out! out! out!' burst gave him leverage to increase the diplomatic momentum for an agreement (interview with B. O'Leary, 14 June 1989). He has since provided a full account of this episode (FitzGerald, 1991: 522–4).

31. 'I remember we had a discussion of the constraints on policy-making . . . and I thought the main constraint was none of the issues that had been discussed but the pressure of Irish people in the USA on the American attitude, and the pressure of Catholic communities in Europe . . . I don't know whether it was regarded as a bit too near the belt, but they were not officially regarded as a constraint on policy' (Roland Moyle, interview with B. O'Leary, 3 Jan. 1991).

32. Brian Lenihan, Haughey's foreign minister, claims responsibility for the phrase (interview with B. O'Leary, 18 Oct. 1989). He was criticized by the British for overplaying the significance of the summit.

6

The meaning(s) and making of the Anglo-Irish Agreement: an experiment in coercive consociationalism

The Anglo-Irish Agreement 'copper-fastens partition'.
(Gerry Adams, President of Sinn Féin, December 1985)

The Anglo-Irish Agreement 'rode to victory on the back of IRA terrorism'.
(Ian Paisley, DUP Leader, April 1986)

We have signed an agreement in which the Prime Minister of Ireland . . . has . . . accepted that for all practical purposes and unto perpetuity, there will not be a united Ireland.
(Tom King, Secretary of State for Northern Ireland, December 1985)

The Anglo-Irish Agreement has made Northern Ireland a shared colony.
(Jim Allister, DUP Chief Whip in the Northern Ireland Assembly, May 1986)

In the Anglo-Irish Agreement the British have conceded sovereignty over Northern Ireland to the Irish Republic.
(Harold McCusker, Deputy Leader of the UUP, February 1986)

The Anglo-Irish Agreement is a framework for a solution, not the solution.
(John Hume, SDLP leader, December 1985)[1]

On 15 November 1985 an international treaty was signed by the Irish Prime Minister Dr Garret FitzGerald and the British Prime Minister Margaret Thatcher at Hillsborough Castle, the former residence of the Governor General of Northern Ireland. What instantly became known as the Anglo-Irish Agreement (AIA)[2] was proclaimed as a major initiative to replace antagonism with accommodation. The official communiqués declared that the AIA would promote peace and reconciliation between the two traditions in Northern Ireland and across both parts of Ireland; and that it would consolidate better relations between Great Britain and Ireland. This chapter examines the meaning(s) and making of the AIA, while the next one examines its impact.

The content of the AIA and its rival interpretations

The AIA is an international agreement between the UK and the Republic of Ireland, lodged at the United Nations, which contains an agreed definition of how the status of Northern Ireland might be changed. Article 1 reads "The two Governments (a) affirm that any change in the status of Northern Ireland would only[3] come about with the consent of a majority of the people of Northern Ireland; (b) recognise that the present wish of a majority of the people of Northern Ireland is for no change in the status of Northern Ireland; (c) declare that, if in the future a majority of the people of Northern Ireland clearly wish for and formally consent to the establishment of a united Ireland, they will introduce and support in the respective Parliaments legislation to give effect to that wish'.[4] The electorate of Northern Ireland are therefore free to choose, by majority vote, presumably through a referendum, to remain part of the UK or in future to become part of the Republic of Ireland.[5]

In Article 2 the AIA established an intergovernmental conference (IGC) where both governments discuss public policy matters affecting Northern Ireland and are committed to making 'determined efforts . . . to resolve any differences'. The AIA also commits both governments to promote a devolved government in Northern Ireland based on the 'co-operation of constitutional representatives . . . of both traditions' which would 'secure widespread acceptance throughout the community' (Article 4). However, until this devolved government is achieved the Irish government is acknowledged as representing the interests of the nationalist minority in the intergovernmental conference (Article 5(c)).

The AIA contained thirteen articles in total, as the superstitious observed. Their content and the accompanying communiqué suggested a renewed British commitment to reform Northern Ireland, especially the administration of justice within its jurisdiction; and to guarantee equality by working 'for the accommodation of the rights and identities of the two traditions which exist in Northern Ireland', by protecting 'human rights' and preventing 'discrimination' (Articles 4(a) and 5). The two governments pledged themselves to political, legal, and security co-operation over Northern Ireland (Articles 5–8) and also to cross-border co-operation on security, economic, social, and cultural matters (Articles 9 and 10). Arbitration was to be renewed, but with Irish governmental support.

Reactions to the AIA varied widely (O'Leary, 1987a: 5–8). It was backed solidly in Great British and Irish public-opinion polls,[6] but opposed by the majority within Northern Ireland. The AIA was overwhelmingly supported in Westminster, winning the official support of all the major parties, although it was opposed by unionist MPs, some ultra-right Conservative MPs, and by a small number of ultra-left Labour MPs who thought it was insufficiently nationalist. The AIA was backed by Fine Gael, the Irish Labour Party, and the Progressive Democrats in the Republic, but only approved by Dáil Éireann against the opposition of Fianna Fáil. The AIA prompted the resignation of Senator Mary Robinson, later to be elected President of Ireland in 1990, from the Irish Labour Party, on the grounds that unionists had not been consulted about it.[7] Within Northern Ireland the AIA was vehemently opposed by the two main unionist parties, the UUP and the DUP, and by Sinn Féin. It was enthusiastically supported only by the SDLP, and after misgivings, by the APNI.

Interpretations of the AIA ranged dramatically. Minimalist supporters backed it for pragmatic reasons. It would establish inter-state institutions for managing civil unrest, provide mechanisms for dampening violence, and by quarantining the conflict help prevent destabilizing spillovers into the core Irish and British political systems. For them the AIA was fundamentally about containment: stopping Sinn Féin and the IRA. Maximalist proponents, by contrast, understood it as a principled framework for a long-run political solution. They differed over what that long-run solution should be, especially over whether it would lead to Northern Ireland's eventual integration into Great Britain or into the Irish Republic, but agreed in endowing the Agreement with heroic rather than pragmatic significance. It was variously interpreted as a prelude to the creation of an all-Ireland federal state (Palley, 1986); to the exercise of joint authority by the British and Irish governments over Northern Ireland (Kenny, 1986); and, most commonly, to the establishment of a power-sharing devolved government within the province under modified British sovereignty (O'Leary, 1987a, 1989; McGarry, 1988).

The opponents of the Agreement were also differentiated, and found in all parts of Britain and Ireland. Sceptics alleged that the AIA was little more than an exercise in symbolic politics, a venture which pretended to address the sources of the conflict, a continuous media-event which would restate existing problems in the guise of solving them.[8] Zealous critics by contrast contended that the AIA was a major constitutional turning-point. Ulster unionists lamented that it marked the end, or the beginning of the end, of the Union, as seen in the quotations at the head of this chapter from Jim Allister and Harold McCusker (see also Haslett, 1987; P. Smith, 1986). One iconoclastic former Irish minister shared these perceptions: 'The Anglo-Irish Agreement constitutes a deal between Irish Catholics and the British at the expense of Irish Protestants in their "Ulster" bastion . . . accompanied by a great deal of verbiage about "reconciling the two traditions" in Northern Ireland, . . . [and] cant . . . of the hollowest description' (O'Brien, 1988: xxxiii, xxxvi). Yet these pro-unionist viewpoints are difficult to reconcile with the fact that the Agreement was equally bitterly opposed by many Irish nationalists. Irish republicans asserted that the AIA effectively surrendered official Irish efforts to 're-integrate the national territory' as pledged in the Irish Constitution. They contended that it betrayed the spirit if not the letter of *Bunreacht na hÉireann* in return for implausible reassurances from 'perfidious Albion' that the northern minority would be treated better in future (Coughlan, 1986). The AIA in their eyes is the continuation of British direct rule in the region by other means: a shameful 'contract with the enemy' (Boland, 1988).[9] It was, in the view of Sinn Féin's president 'in the final analysis . . . about stabilising British interests . . . [by] insulating the British from international criticism of their involvement in Irish affairs' (Adams, 1986: 105).

Given these widely varied interpretations it is best to understand the AIA negatively. It is not three things which it is alleged to be. First, it is not joint authority, the exactly equal sharing of sovereignty of Northern Ireland by two separate states, although it could become a stepping-stone towards joint authority in the future. The articles of the AIA plainly did not give London and Dublin equal responsibility for all aspects of the government of Northern Ireland. Article 2 stated: 'There is no derogation from the sovereignty of the Irish Government or the United Kingdom Government, and each retains responsibility for the decisions and administration of Government within its own jurisdiction.' The Irish government had wanted joint authority, and having failed to obtain it FitzGerald told Thatcher during negotiations that 'it [is] with great reluctance that we [are] prepared to take on responsibility without power' (FitzGerald 1991: 543). The Agreement was not an acceptance by the UK government of the joint authority model sketched in the New Ireland Forum (1984c). The Forum report had offered three possible models of a new Ireland: first, a unitary state; second, a federal/confederal state; and third, joint authority.[10] The AIA in fact represented the British response to a fourth undelineated proposal in clause 5.10 of the Forum report: to wit, 'The Parties in the Forum also remain open to discuss other views which may contribute to political development' (1984c: 30). The UK did not cede sovereignty in the AIA, and in January 1986 a High Court judge ruled against a unionist claim to the contrary. However, the AIA manifestly represented *de facto* concessions on how Westminster's sovereignty would be exercised.

Second, the AIA did not 'put the Unionists on notice that reunification of Ireland will inevitably be enacted on an as yet undetermined date' as one constitutional lawyer asserted (Palley, 1986). The first clause of the Agreement simply repeated the often expressed policy of successive British governments since the abrogation of Stormont in 1972, and enshrined in §1 of the Northern Ireland Constitution Act of 1973, that Irish unification will not take place without the consent of a majority of the people of Northern Ireland. There was therefore nothing new about the 'notice' being given to the unionists about their constitutional status with regard to the Irish Republic, and indeed the AIA is a formal recognition by the Irish government of the British constitutional guarantee. The AIA makes Northern Ireland a conditional unit of the UK, part of the Union as long as a majority wish it to be so, but this feature of its constitutional status is nothing new: the same conditional guarantee was true of the Ireland Act of 1949 – even though the agent specified in the latter act was the Northern Ireland parliament, whereas the people of Northern Ireland are specified in the AIA. The 'notice' of constitutional significance embedded in the Agreement was different: the unionist identity, whilst guaranteed preservation, was downgraded to equality with the nationalist identity in the internal affairs of Northern Ireland.

Third, the AIA did not represent the *de jure* abandonment of the Irish Republic's constitutional claim to Northern Ireland as ultra-nationalists alleged. The Irish government had been prepared to propose a referendum on changing Articles 2 and 3 of the Republic's constitution, if the British government had been prepared to consider joint authority; but, according to the Irish Prime Minister it was the British who ceased to press movement on Articles 2 and 3 after they had ruled out joint authority (FitzGerald, 1991: 494–550). The AIA was carefully designed to make it immune to a constitutional challenge in the Irish courts: since it could legitimately be interpreted as an agreement over how the national territory might be 'reintegrated', it was not in violation of the letter of the Constitution. Indeed the Irish Supreme Court ruled in 1990 (*McGimpsey* v. *An Taoiseach*) that 'reintegration' remained a constitutional imperative, and the AIA could be construed as a means to that end. Article 1c states that 'if in the future a majority of the people of Northern Ireland clearly wish for and formally consent to the establishment of a united Ireland', then the two governments will introduce legislation to convert that wish into reality. It therefore specifies a mechanism – unity by consent of a majority of the population of Northern Ireland – through which 'reintegration' can occur. However, ultra-nationalists were correct to appreciate that the AIA represented the *de facto* abandonment of Irish unification as an immediate policy goal of Fine Gael and the Irish Labour Party – which was not the same thing as 'in perpetuity' as the Secretary of State for Northern Ireland, Tom King, tactlessly suggested on 3 December 1985 when the ink on the parchment was still fresh. King's gloss, designed to placate unionists, caused uproar amongst nationalists – the standard fate of British arbiters when they try to reassure unionists; and his subsequent retraction, after briefings by his officials, left both unionists and nationalists dissatisfied.

What was the constitutional significance of the AIA if it was not the creation of formal joint authority, and neither a formal notice to unionists of eventual reunification nor the formal abandonment of irredentist claims by the Republic? First, it formalized inter-state co-operation in conflict-management. Second, it signified that whilst the unionist guarantee remained – Northern Ireland would remain part of the UK as long as unionists constitute a majority – unionists would have no veto, tacit or explicit, on policy formulation within Northern Ireland. Third, the Agreement bound the Republic to a constitutional mode of reunification which is known to be practically infeasible in the medium term, although in the longer run, if demographic and attitudinal changes were to occur, Irish reunification might be feasible.

The Agreement formalized inter-state co-operation. The inter-governmental conference which it established is solely a consultative body. Although Dr FitzGerald claimed that the IGC's role 'was more than consultative, but less than executive' his argument was rhetorical: the IGC represented something less than his original ambition to have an Irish minister permanently established in Belfast as part of the government of Northern Ireland (interview with Dr FitzGerald, 14 June 1989; and see FitzGerald, 1991: 494 ff.). The IGC has no executive authority or capacity, no recognizable instruments of state, such as taxation, expenditure, or coercive powers, and has no formal policy-implementation function. On a minimalist construction it represented the formalization of the talks which the two governments had been having in the British–Irish intergovernmental council since 1980. Through the civil service secretariat, established to service the IGC at Maryfield in Belfast, this collaboration was institutionalized. The secretariat has become the key conduit for Anglo-Irish relations, a crisis-management centre, and to a less extent a forum for policy analysis before meetings of the IGC. However, the IGC fundamentally is no more than a policy-formulation forum which the Secretary of State for Northern Ireland can choose to take into consideration, concur with, or ignore in the government of Northern Ireland. The two governments are bound to make 'determined efforts . . . through the Conference to resolve any differences' (Article 2) but this provision does not constitute a justiciable Irish veto on British policy-making – and it has not worked as an Irish veto in practice. The policy-arenas open for discussion in the IGC are spelled out in Article 2a: (i) political matters; (ii) security and related matters; (iii) legal matters, including the administration of justice; (iv) the promotion of cross-border co-operation. The possible agenda is thus extremely wide-ranging, as the definition of political matters is infinite. Article 6 elaborates these four fields, and specifically entitles the Irish government to discuss the work of SACHR, FEA, the Equal Opportunities Commission (EOC), the Police Authority for Northern Ireland (PANI), and the Police Complaints Board (PCB). These five agencies were the fruit of British attempts to reform Northern Ireland before 1985, and a direct input for the Irish government was clearly intended as a 'confidence-building' measure for the nationalist population. Article 6 has ensured that the Irish government has been formally and informally consulted both on the work of these agencies and has vetted the personnel appointed to salient positions within them (unattributable sources).

The AIA signified a more crushing end to unionist ascendancy than the suspension of Stormont in 1972. The Union was preserved, but without an Ulster unionist veto on its structure or on policy-making: 'unionism without the Unionists' became the operative constitutional norm as one official put it. The unionists were denied formal access to major policy-formulation bodies unless they took advantage of the possibilities for devolution built into the AIA. The assembly set up under Prior's rolling devolution experiment of 1982 was not mentioned in the AIA, and its demise in June 1986 in the face of continued SDLP abstention, and unionist abuse of its facilities to attack the AIA, came as no surprise (O'Leary, *et al.* 1988). The framers of the Agreement, at least at official level, understood that unless Ulster unionists accepted it, and negotiated an agreed form of devolution with the SDLP, then the British government would act as spokesperson for unionism in the intergovernmental conference – leaving British ministers in the curious position of being both neutral arbiters and partisan spokespersons for unionists. On the other hand, through the offices of the Irish government, the minority, at least in its SDLP rather than Sinn Féin voice, was to have its grievances articulated in the IGC, even in the absence of agreed devolution. Unionists pointed to this structure as evidence of a fundamental lack of balance in the Agreement.

The fact that the Agreement gave the Irish Republic a *de jure* interest in the affairs of a minority within another state border was a symbolic affirmation of the legitimacy of the minority's complaints, both before *and after* 1972. Before the signing of the AIA the official British position had been to blame all the discreditable features of Northern Ireland upon unionist hegemony in the period of devolved government (1920–72). The British signature at Hillsborough implicitly affirmed that direct rule (1972–85) had not reformed Northern Ireland, and tacitly implied that on its own the UK government could not do so. The Agreement explicitly recognized that both an Irish dimension (the AIA and the IGC) and agreed devolution (Article 4) were necessary to complete the reform of Northern Ireland. Since these measures embodied two of the key demands the SDLP had made from its inception it is easy to see why the constitutional nationalist party regarded the Agreement as a framework for an eventual settlement because it put them on a more equal footing with the unionists. Paisley exaggerated when he suggested in May 1986 that the Agreement had made Hume the 'uncrowned king of Northern Ireland' but everybody could see why he could think so.

The AIA brought into the open the distinction between traditional nationalists who argued for Irish unity as a non-negotiable right of the majority of Irish people resident on the whole island of Ireland, and revisionist nationalists who argued that Irish unity could and should only be accomplished with the consent of a majority within Northern Ireland. The AIA bound the Irish state to revisionist nationalism in an international agreement, and by doing so crystallized divisions which have long been apparent amongst Irish nationalists. Fine Gael, the Irish Labour Party, and the newly formed Progressive Democrats supported the Agreement. Fianna Fáil, the most traditional nationalist party, opposed it in opposition but chose to work it when returned to government in February 1987 (O'Leary, 1987b; O'Leary and Peterson, 1990). For a brief interlude Fianna Fáil was left representing a brand of constitutional nationalism which disagreed with the IRA and Sinn Féin over means rather than ends. However, it was soon forced by the weight of Irish public opinion to endorse and operate the AIA.[11] Revisionist nationalism was thus entrenched in the Republic's party-system. The Agreement had placed on the Irish constitutional agenda the possible revision or amendment of Articles 2 and 3 to make them (a) aspirational rather than irredentist and (b) consistent with the spirit of Hillsborough.

Two final points should be made about the constitutional significance of the AIA. First, the AIA did not form part of the domestic law of the UK, and thus the manner in which the British government managed the IGC was not amenable to judicial regulation. The same is true of the position of the Irish government. Second, although the AIA was apparently permanent it necessarily exuded a transitional character;[12] it was considered a framework to promote a more general settlement to which unionists could eventually subscribe. Nothing in the AIA, international law, or political reality could prevent either government from negotiating a new agreement. Indeed from late 1989 talk emerged from both governments about their willingness to discuss a new British–Irish Agreement which would transcend the AIA. The AIA is, and was designed by its makers to be, a framework which permits other constitutional settlements to be built on top of it. It was made compatible with substantial, albeit necessarily agreed, devolution (Articles 4b and 4c). It forms the basis upon which joint authority, as envisaged by the New Ireland Forum or the Kilbrandon inquiry of November 1984, might be erected. However, *pace* unionists, the AIA is not and has not (yet) become joint authority, as our review of its impact in the next chapter confirms.

Why was the AIA signed?

The formal communiqué at Hillsborough declared that the promotion of peace and reconciliation was its main objective. What are we to make of this claim? Was it, in the words of disgruntled unionists, 'a mixture of the vilest cunning on the one hand, and the most enormous stupidity on the other' (*The Equal Citizen*, 3, 22 December 1986)? Was it statecraft or folly? There are three modes of explaining international relations in political science which illuminate the signing of the agreement: rational actor explanations, organizational process explanations, and governmental politics explanations (Allison, 1971). We shall evaluate each in turn.

Rational actor explanations

The rational actor approach to foreign policy analysis suggests that we should assume that the AIA was a rational decision reached by states in pursuit of their objectives, indeed the optimal outcome available to both signatories given their interests and power. These assumptions are common to three different accounts of the signing of the AIA: (a) the self-presentations of the British and Irish governments; (b) the 'imperialist' mode of explaining Britain's Northern Irish policies; and finally (c) the Machiavellian reading of the AIA which we endorse on the basis of interviews with some of the negotiators of the Agreement.

(a) *Self-presentations.*

The self-presentations of the two governments stressed that they were engaged in a disinterested act of statesmanship; they aimed to provide security and to create peace and reconciliation, the key ingredients for any stable state order. The two governments stressed different ingredients: the British government underlined the security dimensions of the AIA to both dissident Conservatives and Ulster unionists, whereas the Irish government highlighted the improved status of the nationalist minority. Increased cross-border security liaison, the Republic's accession to the European Convention on the Suppression of Terrorism, renewed efforts to facilitate extradition between Ireland and Great Britain, and the Irish government's support for an American bill to facilitate the extradition of suspected Irish terrorists figured prominently in British rhetoric. Multiple embarrassing incidents like the Glenholmes affair,[13] 'Stalkergate',[14] and the Ryan affair[15] did not stop the British government from claiming security successes from the increased harmonization of the intelligence services and resources of the RUC and the Gárda Síochána.

However, there was no overwhelming case for a security offensive by the British and Irish states before the signing of the AIA. The most intense phase of political violence was in the early 1970s, during the collapse of Stormont and the failure of the Sunningdale settlement (see Ch. 1: 28–32). Ulsterization had led to a considerable reduction in the numbers of Army personnel killed since the mid-1970s (see Ch. 5: 202-5). British counter-insurgency strategists had achieved their goal of 'acceptable levels of violence' within Northern Ireland before the signing of the Agreement, and the high-risk initiative embarked upon at Hillsborough put Catholic civilians at risk from outraged loyalist paramilitaries, caused ferocious conflicts of loyalty within the RUC and the UDR, and compelled the British into increasing the Army presence in Northern Ireland. Interview-sources suggest that British security advisers were sceptical of the security pay-offs from the AIA unless it were to contain specific provisions enabling 'cross-border' pursuits and easy extradition, and that very few of them were consulted in the process of negotiating the Agreement.

On the Irish side the terms of the AIA left the Fine Gael–ILP coalition government exposed to charges of violating the Republic's sovereignty, giving retrospective recognition to RUC cross-border pursuits, and abandoning a well-established constitutional freedom for the protection of political exiles. In the Irish general election of 1982 Haughey's deft playing of the 'green card' over RUC cross-border incursions had caused severe damage to Fine Gael, so there were good reasons for suggesting that the security dimensions of the Agreement, both explicit and tacit, were not in the short-run interests of the Irish government. As John Taylor of the UUP pointed out with sublime subtlety, the prospects of bombs on the streets of Dublin rose after the Agreement was signed (*Irish Times* 18 June 1986). Moreover, the Irish government's future presence at the intergovernmental conference would bind them against making wholesale criticisms of the RUC and the UDR; and Irish negotiators of the AIA were well aware of the British interest in tying the Irish government into more or less uncritical support of British security policy in Northern Ireland.

The AIA did not bring peace and reconciliation instantly with the two prime ministerial signatures. No one believed otherwise. The deliberate exclusion of the unionists from participation in the negotiation of the Agreement, whilst entirely practical, made their opposition to it all the stronger when it emerged. In the short run the Agreement would undoubtedly exacerbate rather than ameliorate the existing levels of polarization, and so it proved (see Ch. 7: 270–3). Though interview evidence suggests that both the British and Irish governments were genuinely surprised by the depth and scale of animosity towards the AIA amongst the Unionists, they expected an initial rise in the level of violence – i.e. increased insecurity (FitzGerald, 1991: 565). Peace and reconciliation were therefore hoped for in the longer rather than the shorter term.

(b) *The imperialist interpretation.*

Traditional Irish nationalists and 'green Marxists' assume that the Northern Ireland conflict is caused by British imperialism and will cease only with the latter's termination (McGarry and O'Leary, forthcoming: chs 1–2). They understood the AIA as the outcome of British imperialist interests (e.g. Adams, 1986; Boland, 1988; and Coughlan, 1986, 1991). The AIA was an attempt by the British state to re-establish its hegemony in Ireland. The method: to obtain the consent of the 'comprador' government of the twenty-six counties to British rule in Northern Ireland and to direct British intervention in the affairs of the twenty-six counties. The AIA was meant to demobilize the radical nationalist movement built by Sinn Féin, restore the social base and credibility of the SDLP, and create the conditions for a military and political counter-offensive against the IRA. Symbolic gestures towards nationalist sentiment were traded by the British government in return for the Irish government's support for Britain's real objectives: a security agreement on extradition, a Europe-wide offensive against terrorists, and the Irish government's support for an assault on the American havens of support for republicans.

This account of the AIA is found in the Sinn Féin press, *An Phoblacht/Republican News*, and in various booklets and pamphlets published by republicans, and echoed by some of the British ultra-left. It supposed well-defined objectives for the Agreement: the maintenance of British rule in Ireland, the incorporation of the Irish Republic's élites into the NATO ruling class, and the repression of Sinn Féin and the IRA. The circumstantial evidence they cited included the Irish government's decision to join the European Convention on the Suppression of Terrorism, the opening of discussions on EC defence arrangements which would violate the Republic's traditional conceptions of neutrality, and co-ordinated efforts by the Thatcher and Reagan administrations to ensure that the US Senate passed an extradition treaty against the opposition of a well-organized Irish-American lobby.

There can be no doubt about this 'evidence', only about its significance. This imperialist explanation of the AIA is difficult to falsify since it presumes secret state-strategies and motivations which will not be found in the public domain. However, it suffers from key implausibilities: it portrays the Irish Republic as a puppet-state, with the political leaders of Fine Gael and the Irish Labour Party as British marionettes; it fails to provide any rigorous rationale for why the British state, let alone British capital, should be so concerned to maintain Northern Ireland as part of the UK (see McGarry and O'Leary, forthcoming: ch. 2); and its implicit claim that Northern Ireland possessed major geo-political significance in 1985 is not credible. Fear of an Irish Cuba existed; indeed James Prior claimed that 'beyond the issue between Catholics and Protestants . . . lay the spectre of Marxism' (Prior, 1986: 235). However, most British and Irish politicians were classifying Sinn Féin as Marxists for propagandist reasons. Embarrassment rather than paranoia was more paramount in British policy-making in the run up to the AIA. Fear of Sinn Féin was far more extensive in the Republic than in Great Britain. Although FitzGerald was more genuinely worried about a Marxist insurrection in Ireland than Thatcher, he and his colleagues exaggerated their fears about Sinn Féin to enhance their bargaining position with their British counterparts.[16]

The 'imperialist' explanation of the AIA fails because it has an implausible conception of British objectives, based on an outmoded and falsely applied theory of imperialism. It is not wrong to maintain that the AIA was targeted at Sinn Féin, but the weaknesses in republican theories are best illustrated by their incomprehension of loyalist reaction to the AIA. They treat loyalist reaction to the AIA as either wholly irrational, or based upon a misperception of devious Albion which remains, as ever, on the loyalist side. These readings are sectarian and false: the loyalists are not without brains, and the AIA threatened their interpretation of the Union, if not in the way that the IRA would prefer. Outside of Sinn Féin and the British and Irish ultra-left the only personality to have consistently maintained an interpretation of the AIA as an imperialist plot is Enoch Powell who argues that the Hillsborough accord was part of an American machination to get the Republic of Ireland into NATO (Powell, 1986).[17]

(c) *The Machiavellian interpretation.*

The Machiavellian interpretation of the AIA portrays it as a rational power-game, designed to coerce the unionists into accepting a new version of the Sunningdale agreement of 1973–4. As we have shown British policy-making between 1972 and 1975–6, and after 1982, was in favour of voluntary power-sharing in a devolved regional government in Northern Ireland, and willing to consider an Irish dimension. The British government did not abandon these objectives during the negotiation of the AIA, as a senior British negotiator informed us, although at one stage Douglas Hurd, the then Secretary of State for Northern Ireland apparently advocated majority-rule devolution in exchange for an Irish say in the affairs of Northern Ireland (FitzGerald, 1991: 512).

The AIA was understood by many British and Irish negotiators as an attempt to create the conditions for power-sharing to work, to coerce key fractions of the unionist bloc to accept a power-sharing devolved government as the lesser of several evils. On the one hand the AIA confronted the unionists with an Irish dimension of far greater political salience than the Council of Ireland proposed at Sunningdale. But on the other hand the AIA offered them devolution as a mechanism for removing the agenda-setting scope of the IGC, provided they were prepared to bite the bullet of 'agreed devolution' which would mean power-sharing given that the SDLP could not settle for anything less.

The AIA, as intended, altered the structure of the incentives facing the political élites of both blocs. With the Irish dimension established, the SDLP's leadership would be freer to negotiate a power-sharing devolved government acceptable to unionists, precisely because the AIA would strengthen them against SF. And the unpalatable choices which the AIA would put before the unionists would divide them, and create a fraction sufficiently significant and autonomous to do business with the SDLP and the APNI after ultra-loyalism had been tried and defeated – at least that was the thinking in some officials' minds. Thatcher's remarks in an interview in Belfast soon after the signing of the Agreement lend credence to the Machiavellian interpretation: 'the people of Northern Ireland can get rid of the inter-governmental conference by agreeing to devolved government' (*Belfast Telegraph*, 17 December 1985). Thatcher's remark was misleading because within the terms of the AIA the 'people of Northern Ireland' did not have the choice she suggested, but it was revealing. The choice offered by the AIA to unionists was: negotiate a power-sharing devolved government which will make irrelevant the proceedings of the intergovernmental conference or allow the intergovernmental conference to become the bridgehead of a very significant Irish dimension.

The Machiavellian interpretation of the AIA makes sense. The political education of the British and Irish élites persuaded them that a voluntary internal settlement was impossible as long as salient fractions of unionists had no selective incentives to induce them to accept power-sharing, and as long as the SDLP felt threatened on its green flank by Sinn Féin.

Organizational process explanations

Unlike rational actor explanations, organizational process accounts do not leave us with perfectly lucid explanations of how rational actors reach optimal decisions in line with their preferences. The second standard mode of analysing foreign policy decisions suggests that governments should not be understood as unitary actors who pursue well-specified goals and objectives. Rather, any foreign policy-decision will bear the hallmarks of the state agencies involved, their standard operating procedures, their established repertoires for defining problems, and their pet-solutions.

On the British side the state agencies involved in the making of the Agreement were the Cabinet Office, the Foreign Office, the Overseas and Defence Committee of the Cabinet chaired by Margaret Thatcher, and to a less extent the Northern Ireland Office. The pertinent legal and intelligence services of the core executive were also consulted. Whilst the Northern Irish NIO officials were not influential, and indeed were deliberately kept in the dark for as long as possible, some of the NIO's most senior British officials were very important in the negotiating of the Agreement, as was Douglas Hurd, the Secretary of State who replaced James Prior in 1984 and Sir Geoffrey Howe at the Foreign Office. The jargon amongst NIO officials and FO diplomats for dealing with Northern Ireland included 'internal' and 'external' tracks.[18] The internal track meant the steady pursuit of the broadest possible agreement within Northern Ireland. The external track meant the pursuit of the maximum feasible good relations with the Irish Republic and the USA to ensure minimum feasible international embarrassment. Our interviews confirm Arthur's (1985) suggestion that Britain's Northern Irish policy-making procedures have been characterized by two features: quarantining Ireland from mainstream politics and maintaining international respectability. The imperatives of the two tracks have often conflicted, but the AIA clearly had both tracks built into it: agreed devolution and good relations with the Irish Republic. The AIA therefore made good sense to the British because it fitted their existing definitions of the 'problem' and their pre-established routines for managing it.

On the Irish side, since the partial success of the modernization programmes embarked upon in the late 1950s and early 1960s the standard modes of defining Northern Ireland's issues had altered amongst both administrators and the policy élite. Irish state officials, outside the ranks of Fianna Fáil, came to define Northern Ireland as a problem for the stability of their state, as a threat to their programmes of modernization, and as an anachronism rather than simply a question of burning injustice or uncompleted national revolution. For Irish state officials during the 1970s the conflict was managed through two strategic routines: playing the role of guardian of the Northern Ireland minority rather than prospective ruler of Northern Ireland and Ulster unionists; and increasing co-operation with the UK, through the EC and other forums to contain the conflict ('unique relationships amongst these islands', and 'interdependence is not dependence' provided the bureaucratic phrases which signified the new administrative codes). The AIA again fitted neatly with established bureaucratic routines of the Irish Republic. Fianna Fáil was the only major organization in the Irish Republic yet to have adjusted its rhetoric to the foreign policy routines of the Irish state, at least in opposition, but it too would play the game after 1987.

The organizational process story provides a plausible background explanation of the making of the AIA. Ensconsed in the vacillations of personalities and crisis-episodes, behind the zig-zags in British policy-postures highlighted by Bew and Patterson (1985: 39–131), buried under the rapid turnover in Irish governments during 1980–2, and indeed behind the aberration of Thatcher's reaction to the New Ireland Forum proposals, compatible strategies for managing the Northern Ireland conflict had developed in the agencies of both states. 1984–1985 was an opportune moment for the cementing of the two states' approaches, and after eighteen months of negotiations both the Thatcher and FitzGerald governments, in the mid-term of their respective tenures of office, determined for different reasons to make a symbolic initiative.

Governmental politics explanations

Foreign policy decisions are never solely tales of rational governmental actions or of the evolution of bureaucratic routines. They are also punctured by personalities, symbolism, and party manœuvering and post-hoc rationalization in an uncertain environment. The two key personalities in the making of the Anglo-Irish Agreement were Dr Garret FitzGerald and Sir Robert Armstrong, the British Cabinet secretary. The symbolic dimensions of a major initiative and agreement strongly appealed to FitzGerald who claimed to have entered politics to solve the Northern Ireland problem and to make the Irish Republic more pluralist. Armstrong, a taciturn and apparently unimaginative bureaucrat, is nevertheless widely credited with selling the AIA to Margaret Thatcher, and FitzGerald's memoirs are full of references to Armstrong being 'helpful' (FitzGerald, 1991: 469, 494 ff., 517). The British Prime Minister had hitherto shown only 'the most philistine of unionist prejudices' (non-attributable NIO source) but she had displayed a penchant for tackling head-on what she perceived, rightly or wrongly, to be the major crises of the British state, and a preparedness to break through existing conventional inertia. Escape from death at Brighton in October 1984 concentrated Thatcher's mind on the Northern Irish question in a way the IRA did not anticipate. There is nevertheless still some amazement amongst former British ministers and officials that Thatcher signed the AIA; and they unite in maintaining that Sir Robert Armstrong, another senior civil servant David Goodhall, backed by Foreign Secretary Sir Geoffrey Howe, sold the AIA to her as good for the Union, good for security, and as a historic and symbolic act of statecraft.[19]

The two premiers not only enjoyed the symbolism of a major initiative but shared a similar resolution to embark upon a 'leap into the dark', a propensity few of their predecessors had displayed, and their personal beliefs and styles must enter any complete explanation of the signing of the Agreement.[20] The AIA was good domestic politics in both states. Playing skilled statecraft brought temporary rewards in the opinion polls. The Irish coalition government enjoyed a brief renewal of support and enjoyed overwhelming approval for the agreement in opinion polls. Fianna Fáil's difficulties after their opposition to the AIA precipitated the formation of the break-away Progressive Democrats, and created an unexpected, and briefly enjoyed, party-political bonus for Fine Gael. However, many maintained at the time of the signing of the AIA that both leaders' preoccupation with symbolic politics would set in train a policy folly which would defeat their respective objectives.

Whatever the truth of these contentions the decisive actor in the making of the Agreement was the SDLP and its leader John Hume. Content that the British and Irish premiers obtain whatever short-run glory was on offer, the SDLP leader was reticent about his role in the AIA. But as the instigator of Anglo-Irish discussions and the New Ireland Forum, as the leader who advocated abstaining from Prior's rolling-devolution initiative on the grounds that a boycott would produce something more, and as an actively consulted adviser to the Irish government throughout the negotiations, Hume contributed more than any other political leader on the road to Hillsborough. Ulster unionists were more aware of this fact than the Republic's or British commentators who vied to credit the Agreement entirely to the efforts of the respective Prime Ministers, Cabinet secretaries, foreign ministers, and ambassadors. To Ulster unionists Hume was the evil genius behind the Agreement; certainly his party had the most to gain and lose from any agreement, and its relations with both governments were critical in its design.[21]

Conclusion: the nature of the experiment

The Anglo-Irish Agreement was signed as part of a jointly designed British and Irish Machiavellian master-plan to coerce unionists into accepting a power-sharing devolved government together with an Irish dimension, knowing that the intergovernmental conference could survive whatever strategy the unionists would use to undermine it. The AIA emerged at the confluence of well-established bureaucratic strategies, symbolic politics, and jockeying for position on the part of the SDLP. John Hume's description of the AIA as a 'framework' for a solution rather than a solution was correct, but it was a framework weighted in favour of the SDLP's favoured solutions.

Our explanations of the meanings and making of the Anglo-Irish Agreement are at odds with partisan unionist and nationalist contentions. The AIA was not the end of the Union. If unionists subsequently decided to behave in ways which encouraged British politicians to consider ending the Union that was not part of the British agenda during the negotiation of the Hillsborough accord. Had it been, Thatcher would not have signed it, and to have hidden such an agenda from her implies a very strong underestimation of her political abilities, one probably shared only by Edward Heath. The AIA was also not the formation of a system of joint authority, although it could form the basis for joint authority if a consociational settlement proved impossible to negotiate. But if joint authority eventually materialises from the AIA that will be because the parties within Northern Ireland fail to come to an internal settlement, and because the British government has despaired of persuading unionists to share local political power and accept the reform of the region together with an institutionalized Irish dimension. Finally, the AIA was not a surrender to British imperialism or a sell-out of Irish nationalism: it gained, for the first time, a voice for the Irish government in the affairs of Northern Ireland, and marked the widespread recognition by the vast majority of Irish nationalists that Irish unity, if it was ever to be accomplished, could come about if and only if a majority of the population of Northern Ireland could be persuaded of its merits.

Notes

1. All unreferenced quotations in this chapter are from two sources: first, the *Irish Times*, the most reliable paper of record in Ireland, and second, interviews of politicians and civil servants carried out by B. O'Leary in Belfast, Derry/Londonderry, Dublin, and London. The interviews were attributable and mostly on-the-record with politicians, but non-attributable and off-the-record with civil servants. The latter were usually more accurate in detail and recall. The interviews were carried out in 1985–6, 1988–9, and 1990–1, and have led one of the authors to modify the arguments he had previously advanced about the making of the AIA (O'Leary, 1987a).

2. The correct title of the Agreement in the British version is 'Agreement between the Government of the United Kingdom of Great Britain and Northern Ireland and the Government of the Republic of Ireland' whereas the correct

Irish version is 'An Agreement between the Government of the Republic of Ireland and the Government of the United Kingdom'.

3. Dr FitzGerald maintains that the poor grammar in this clause was maintained because the phraseology in Article 1(c) had been used in a communiqué issued by Thatcher and Haughey in 1980; he argues it was designed to persuade Haughey to accept the AIA as consistent with his own past policies (interview with B. O'Leary, 14 June 1989).

4. The text of the Agreement can be found in Appendix 1 of McGarry and O'Leary (1991b). A judicious legal interpretation is available in Hadden and Boyle (1989).

5. They are not, however, granted full self-determination since they are not free to choose independence or to partition the territory.

6. An MRBI poll conducted a week after the signing of the AIA found that 59 per cent of the Irish electorate approved of it; by February 1986 69 per cent approved of it; and by 1988 70 per cent thought it should continue (*Irish Political Studies*, 1986, 1: 144; 1987: 2: 155; 1989, 4: 158).

7. The unionists leaders were apparently offered the opportunity to see a draft of the AIA a couple of months before it was announced but on privy-council terms. They turned down the opportunity (non-attributable source). As Lord Prior puts matters: 'They certainly wished to be in a position to say they hadn't been consulted' (interview with B. O'Leary, 14 Dec. 1990).

8. Former Secretary of State Merlyn Rees did not vote for the AIA: 'I didn't make a song and dance about it, because what's the point? . . . I didn't like the involvement of the Foreign Office, it was something to please world opinion, to please the Americans . . . It's no good going from ignoring the minority to then ignoring the majority' (interview with B. O'Leary, 18 Dec. 1990).

9. In February 1986 a mere 13 per cent of the Irish electorate agreed that the agreement would put a united Ireland 'farther away' (*Irish Political Studies*, 2: 155).

10. Fianna Fáil preferred the first model; Fine Gael, the Irish Labour Party, and the SDLP preferred the second and third models.

11. In November 1985 32 per cent of the electorate agreed with Haughey's stand on the agreement; by February 1986 only 26 per cent did so (*Irish Political Studies*, 1986, 1: 144 and 1987, 2: 155).

12. The review which took place after three years, and was published in May 1989, examined the workings of the IGC rather than the principles of the AIA.

13. Evelyn Glenholmes, a suspected IRA paramilitary, walked free from a Dublin court in March 1986 because British officials bungled extradition procedures and compelled the Irish court to quash the British application.

14. The Stalker affair centred on whether the RUC, MI5, the Home Office, or others, conspired to obtain the suspension from duty of the Deputy Constable

of Manchester Police who had been given the task of investigating whether or not the RUC had a shoot-to-kill policy during 1982 – see Ch. 7: 247.

15. See Ch. 7: 248.

16. FitzGerald maintains that in the process of negotiating the AIA Thatcher objected to his talk of nationalist 'alienation' in Northern Ireland – because in her view it was a Marxist concept. He pointed out that the idea of 'alienation' was originated by Hegel, if not earlier (interview with B. O'Leary, 14 June 1989).

17. Powell believes the conspiracy goes back a long time: 'Britain in the mid- 1960s committed itself to deliver, if not the absolute achievement of an all-Ireland state, at any rate sufficient "progress" towards it – "progress" in that sort of context is a working cliché-tool of the British Foreign Office – to be accepted as a "payment on account" in NATO's bargaining with the Irish Republic' (transcript of address to the Carlyle Club at Peterhouse College, Cambridge, 1989 heard by B. O'Leary).

18. Stock phrases used unprompted in interviews by officials in the NIO in 1986 and 1988–9, and by former NIO and FO officials in 1990.

19. Lord Prior describes how Peter Utley, a leader writer on the *Daily Telegraph* and unionist sympathizer, was shaken by the superficiality of Thatcher's knowledge of Northern Ireland and her lack of interest in the subject just after the publication of the New Ireland Forum Report in May 1984 (Prior, 1986: 239, and interview with B. O'Leary, 14 Nov. 1990).

20. There are some juicy exchanges recorded in FitzGerald's memoirs: in September 1984 Thatcher told him 'we are walking on eggs', and in the aftermath of the Agreement she complained to him 'You've got the glory and I've got the problems' (FitzGerald, 1991: 507, 570).

21. However, the agreement had to be sold by Hume and the Irish government to sections of the SDLP which were thought to be more hardline, and unhappy at the lack of concrete concessions on the UDR and the administration of justice. A senior official, now in the Taoiseach's office, was given special responsibility to persuade Seamus Mallon, deputy leader of the SDLP, to accept the agreement (non-attributable sources).

7

The impact of the Anglo-Irish Agreement, 1985–9: the limits to coercive consociationalism

The journey of a thousand miles starts with a single step.
(Chinese proverb cited by Peter Barry, Irish Foreign Minister)

The Anglo-Irish Agreement had immediate and long-term goals.[1] Policy-makers believed 'something had to be done' to stop the rise in support for Sinn Féin. Both governments wished to break the stalemate which had prevented an internal political settlement in Northern Ireland. The Irish coalition government was anxious to promote the interests of the nationalist community in Northern Ireland, if only to protect the Irish party-system from the impact of Sinn Féin. Although not averse from gaining a foothold in the long march to Irish unification, its priority was peace before Irish unity (Mair, 1987). The British government was anxious that the Irish government share responsibility, if not power, for the management of Northern Ireland, to help reduce the international embarrassment caused by its most troublesome territory. Finally, both governments were concerned about security and wished to reduce the violence associated with the conflict.

This chapter evaluates the impact of the AIA until the end of 1989. First, we consider the development of exogenous co-operation between the British and Irish governments, both inside and outside the intergovernmental conference. Then we evaluate the endogenous impact of the Agreement in promoting a consociational settlement; in reforming social and legal justice in Northern Ireland, and its consequences for the regulation of political violence.

Co-operation and conflict in British–Irish relations

The most obvious development since the signing of the AIA was the institutionalization of British and Irish co-operation, confirmed in the 'Review of the Anglo-Irish Intergovernmental Conference' published in May 1989 (see McGarry and O'Leary, 1991: 311–17), and culminating in joint support for 'the Brooke initiative' to organize inter-party talks within Northern Ireland and across Ireland, which began in late 1989. Institutionalized 'intergovernmentalism' (Cox, 1987) included regular sessions of the IGC which covered the 'high' and 'low' politics of Northern Ireland, regular meetings and communications between NIO ministers and their counterparts in the Republic of Ireland, the working of the joint administrative secretariat at Maryfield,[2] and attempts to harmonize their statements and policies by both governments after they have engaged in serious negotiations or exchanges of view.

However, there have been many visible tensions in British–Irish relations since November 1985, some of which verged on crises in the eyes of the respective national media. In the Irish Republic the Fine Gael–Irish Labour Party sponsored referendum held on 26 June 1986 to permit civil divorce, was defeated by a vote of 63 per cent 'against' on a 63 per cent poll. It was a blow to FitzGerald's programme of constitutional transformation of which the AIA had been an integral component. Although the divorce proposal was badly worded, and insufficiently addressed to the interests of married women, the poll persuaded unionist observers that the pluralism in the Republic was still circumscribed by 'Rome rule'. Whilst an abundance of condoms, abortions, and divorces would not have altered unionists' attitudes towards the AIA or Irish unity, the referendum victory for the forces of Catholic reaction revealed that Irish state-development continued to take place at the expense of pan-Irish nation-building.

General elections and prospective changes of government in both countries threatened difficulties soon after the signing of the AIA. The Irish general elections of February 1987 and June 1989 were expected to produce majority Fianna Fáil governments. Fianna Fáil had initially opposed the AIA, and raised doubts about its constitutionality. However, the fear that it would repudiate or seek to renegotiate the Agreement proved hollow because it failed to win an overall parliamentary majority on both occasions, and in any case its leader, Haughey, who replaced FitzGerald as Irish Taoiseach, had decided he would work the AIA before the 1987 election (O'Leary, 1987b; O'Leary and Peterson, 1990). Haughey appointed the emollient Brian Lenihan as foreign minister and co-chairman of the IGC; and moved to repair his strained relations with Mrs Thatcher and the SDLP which had been irritated by Fianna Fáil's vote against the Agreement. However, controversy was created in the Irish general election of February 1987 when the Secretary of State for Northern Ireland, Tom King, used the occasion to encourage unionists to negotiate a devolved government – arguing that the election had led to 'a pause' in the operation of the AIA. This ploy was not an attempt to renege on the Agreement by the British government, but it was insensitive to the interests of the outgoing Irish government.

The two Irish general elections gave one decisive boost to the framers of the AIA. After a heated debate within its membership Sinn Féin had agreed in November 1986 that it would not only contest Irish elections but also take any seats which it won in Dáil Éireann:[3] it polled a derisory 1.9 per cent of the first preference vote in 1987, followed by a mere 1.2 per cent in 1989. The poor electoral performance of the party, now almost entirely dominated by a northern leadership and membership, meant that one objective of the AIA, halting Sinn Féin's growth throughout Ireland, had been rapidly realized. Sinn Féin's leadership had failed to realize that sympathy for 'armed struggle' in the Republic was slight; activated, if at all, by perceived British intransigence; and that empathy for the 'hunger strikers' did not mean unequivocal support for the IRA. Moreover its cadre had not developed the radical rapport with the urban poor in the Republic which it had built over a decade in Belfast and in Derry/Londonderry. They had a very crude appreciation of the domestic politics of the Republic, in which a programme of armed revolutionary nationalism, socialist autarky, and withdrawal from the EC stood little chance of success. Sinn Féin's hubris did both governments a favour.

The Westminster general election of June 1987 was much less of a threat to the AIA. All the major parties' manifestoes expressed support for its continuation. The unionists had hoped that a 'hung parliament' would enable them to negotiate the suspension of the

AIA, but the Conservatives' renewed majority shattered this wishful thinking, and the UUP lost Enoch Powell's seat to the SDLP's Eddie McGrady. Nevertheless the UK general election did affect the operation of the AIA because it prompted personnel changes, on top of those created by the new Irish government in February. With the departure of Nicholas Scott, after six years in the NIO, and simultaneous changes amongst leading civil servants, the major figures involved in the negotiation of the AIA had moved on. These changes contributed to the significant deterioration in the co-ordination of British–Irish relations in late 1987 and 1988 when several well-publicized episodes caused temporary crises.

Another danger to stable British–Irish relations was posed by disagreements between the two governments over the meaning(s) of the Agreement, especially Article 1. British efforts to reassure unionists about their status as Britons conflicted with Irish politicians' defence of the AIA against ultra-nationalist critics. Both governments remained in the curious position of wanting to say that only the other state has made major concessions on sovereignty in the AIA. The ambiguity of Article 1 was designed to make the AIA proof against a constitutional challenge in the Republic's Supreme Court (and did ensure its survival against court-challenges by unionists in 1988 and 1990) but it served to inflame both nationalists and unionists.

A continuing source of British–Irish conflict since the first meeting of the IGC in December 1985 has been over the objectives and priorities of public policy for Northern Ireland. Press releases, communiqués, and interviews permit informed judgements about the respective governments' objectives and priorities. Initially the British wanted improved security, especially in cross-border relations and extradition, as the primary objective to be pursued in the IGC. They wanted to reassure unionists that the AIA was not against their interests, and promoted the idea of a devolved government. They were prepared to move, very slowly, to reform Northern Ireland in ways which would meet some nationalist criticisms, but they did not wish to antagonize unionists by linking reforms to the implementation of the AIA. Increased IRA activity in 1987 and 1988, after large shipments of arms and materials were landed from Libya, strengthened the British emphasis upon security, crisis-management, and the defeat of the IRA, and reduced whatever commitment they had to reforming the administration of justice.

Irish objectives and priorities differed. According to Peter Barry, the first Irish foreign minister to represent the Irish government in the IGC, the Fine Gael–Labour government in 1985 primarily sought to reform Northern Ireland by advancing minority interests and aspirations, in the administration of justice, i.e. the courts, the UDR, and the police.[4] Although it shared the wish to see a devolved government established it was soon convinced that devolution could not be realized in the short term, given the unionists' hostility to the AIA. Finally, it sought co-operation on security. The minority Fianna Fáil government which succeeded in February 1987 and held office until June 1989 was sceptical of, if not opposed to, devolution, and suggested it be accompanied by a broader 'north–south settlement' as well as a British–Irish settlement embracing the 'totality of relationships' between the two islands. Foreign minister Lenihan claimed to have three equally important goals: the promotion of the welfare of the minority, easing the fears of the majority, and reforming Northern Ireland (*Irish Times*: 11 May 1987). The Fianna Fáil–Progressive Democrats coalition government, formed after the June 1989 election, by contrast, restored devolution as a formal objective of the Irish government. However, Gerry Collins, the new foreign minister was a leading light in Fianna Fáil, and considered a possible candidate to succeed Haughey as leader of 'The Republican Party'. He was therefore concerned to display a vigorous defence of Irish sovereignty and of the interests of the nationalist minority in Northern Ireland. These conflicting, and changing, objectives and priorities of both governments generated intermittent cross-national strain, and slowed the reforming momentum initiated by the AIA.

Where British–Irish relations showed most tension were in specific legal and security episodes which received global publicity. That these domains should be the epicentres of mini-crises is not surprising. Legal and security systems are at the heart of sovereignty. They are also run by agencies which core executives in liberal democracies have some difficulty in controlling, especially where there are constitutional restraints on executive influence. Finally law and policing are at the nub of ethnic conflict. In late 1987 the Irish government amended the Extradition Act, 1986, to ensure that prima-facie evidence that an offence had been committed would be required before suspects would be handed to the British. This amendment was passed after the refusal of the British government to change the court system in Northern Ireland to allow mixed courts or 'three-judge' courts to replace the single-judge Diplock courts – Dr FitzGerald maintained that these two issues had been linked in the negotiation of the AIA – and because of public anxieties about the treatment of Irish suspects in British courts. We are reliably informed that the Irish desire to change the administration of justice was vetoed in Cabinet by Lord Hailsham,[5] the Lord Chancellor, who had been lobbied by Lord Lowry, the Lord Chief Justice of Northern Ireland. Despite Irish successes in undermining British arguments in the IGC progress on the issue was blocked. Irish underconfidence in British justice was reinforced in January 1988 when the Court of Appeal rejected the appeal of those convicted of the Birmingham pub bombings in 1974, despite suspicions about both the forensic evidence and the nature of the confessions which formed the basis of the convictions. The Irish government did not blame the British government because English judges found the idea that the West Midlands police could behave illegally 'too appalling to contemplate' in the words of Lord Denning. However, it could, and did, complain vociferously when the British Attorney General, Sir Patrick Mayhew, decided, in the same week, it would not be in the national interest to prosecute certain RUC officers, despite evidence of a conspiracy to pervert the course of justice produced by inquiries into allegations that the police had engaged in 'shoot-to-kill' policies in the early 1980s (Stalker, 1988). Nationalists throughout Ireland reacted furiously: in their view Mayhew had decided to cover-up an issue discussed in the intergovernmental conference, and it appeared to the Irish side that the British authorities spoke with 'forked tongues' over their inquiry into the 'shoot-to-kill' allegations.

On 21 February 1988, Aidan McAnespie, an unarmed Catholic civilian and Sinn Féin supporter on his way to a GAA football match, was shot dead on the border by a British soldier in suspicious circumstances. The Irish government, dissatisfied with the British response, set up its own police inquiry. The fires of this event were fanned when it was disclosed that the only British soldier to have been sentenced for a manslaughter charge as a result of political violence in Northern Ireland since 1969 had been released by the Home Secretary in February 1987. Having served a much reduced three-year sentence, Private Thain was back serving with his former regiment. Then the Home Secretary, Douglas Hurd, apparently without consultation with the Maryfield secretariat, announced that the Prevention of Terrorism Act was to be made permanent, despite the fact that it contained 'internal exile' clauses offensive to Irish sensibilities and civil libertarians. The British Attorney General, badly briefed about the nature of the amendment to the Irish Extradition Act, accused the Irish government of breaching extradition agreements. The killing of three unarmed IRA terrorists by the SAS in Gibraltar on 6 March 1988, in circumstances where they might have been arrested, increased tension still further. The 'deaths on the rock' were eventually found in September to have been 'lawful killings' in a split verdict of 9–2 in a coroner's inquest held on Gibraltar, but suspicions remained that the IRA personnel had been executed with the express sanction of senior figures in Whitehall and Westminster. The funerals of the executed IRA personnel were subsequently attacked by a loyalist paramilitary, resulting in murders of two civilians and an IRA Volunteer on 16 March, and on 19 March two British soldiers who inadvertently drove into the funeral cortege of the IRA volunteer in Andersonstown, west Belfast, were lynched by members of the procession.

The culmination of these bloody and bizarre events forced both governments to get a tougher grip on their relations, and to agree on the need for closer and better crisis-management and crisis-avoidance. However, in December 1988 another major public row occurred when the Irish Attorney General refused to extradite Father Patrick Ryan, despite prima-facie evidence sufficient to warrant a prosecution on terrorist charges, because the public comments of Thatcher and other Conservative MPs had prejudiced his prospects of a fair trial. Ryan had previously been detained in Belgium in June, and following a three-week hunger strike had been deported to Ireland on 25 November. The Irish Attorney General invited his British opposite number to use the Republic's Criminal Law (Jurisdiction) Act, which enables the prosecution of suspects in one jurisdiction for offences committed in another. However, the British attempt to use this Act in the Ryan case failed in 1989 because of lack of evidence, and amidst rumours that key witnesses were not prepared to travel to Ireland.

These events, intentionally or otherwise, appeared to show to the Irish that security, counter-insurgency, and national sovereignty pre-rogatives mattered more to British governments than good relations with the minority in Northern Ireland and the Irish government, or the preservation of the rule of law by the security forces. Cases in Britain such as the Guildford Four, the Maguires, the Birmingham Six, and the Winchester Three, all falsely convicted by English courts of IRA-related offences in controversial circumstances, became *causes célèbres* in Ireland.[6] The eventual decision of British courts in 1990–1, after much pressure, to free the Winchester Three, the Guildford Four, and the Birmingham Six, and to review the convictions of the Maguires even though they had served out their sentences did something to restore Irish confidence in British justice, although the miscarriages of justice also confirmed Sinn Féin's propaganda. The Home Secretary subsequently announced a Royal Commission to inquire into the criminal justice system in 1991.

On the other hand the very same episodes appeared to show to some British politicians that Irish governments were insufficiently resolute in 'the fight against terrorism' and 'irrationally prejudiced' about British courts; and continual Irish insistence on procedural exactness over extradition was construed as obstructive. Irish officials in response claim that the British fail to realize that they have to work within a more exacting legal and constitutional system, under which procedural flaws will result in the failure of prosecutions. Though none of these episodes revealed a British or Irish desire to renege on the AIA, in the British case they certainly suggested a lack of co-ordination between government ministries and agencies dealing with Northern Ireland (the NIO does not handle all matters which affect British–Irish relations). FitzGerald put matters harshly in June 1989: 'The failure of the Irish to understand how stupidly the British can act is one of the major sources of misunderstanding between our countries . . . Their system is uncoordinated. Because there's a Northern Ireland Secretary people think there's a Northern Ireland policy – but there isn't' (McKittrick, 1989b). Both governments, in the jointly published 'Review of the Inter-governmental Conference', showed themselves sensitive to the charge that the IGC lacked strategic co-ordination and had degenerated into a forum for mere 'crisis management'. They resolved to order their affairs better in future and avoid the temptations of 'megaphone diplomacy', and there were some signs after 1989 that the public manners of the politicians from the two states had improved.

Party-political developments and the failure of coercive consociationalism

Party-political developments after Hillsborough were dominated by the implacable hostility of most unionists to the AIA. 'Ulster' meaning Protestant Ulster 'says No' has been the slogan of their resistance. Unionists rejected Article 1 of the AIA because it suggested a lack of commitment to the Union in Westminster. They condemned all the other articles because they give a 'foreign power' a say in the affairs of the UK. They refused to negotiate a power-sharing devolved government under Article 4 on the grounds that it would be discussed 'under duress', that it was not British to have permanent coalition governments, and because the intergovernmental conference, and its secretariat at Maryfield, would be left intact even if a devolved government were to be agreed.

The unionist campaign against the AIA began constitutionally (if one discounts an attempted assault of Secretary of State King by a crowd led by DUP councillors). They emphasized legitimate opinion-mobilization, and attempted to challenge the agreement's legality in the courts. When the British government rejected a call for a local referendum on the AIA fifteen unionist MPs co-operated in resigning their Westminster seats and forcing a 'mini-referendum' of by-elections in January 1986. The SDLP MP, John Hume, and the Sinn Féin MP, Gerry Adams, did not resign their seats. The SDLP gave the unionists the minimum of help: confining themselves to contesting four seats which were potential marginals, mid-Ulster, Fermanagh and South Tyrone, south Down, and Newry and Armagh. The unionists were obliged to run a token candidate called 'Peter Barry', the Irish foreign minister's name, in another four constituencies to avoid unopposed returns. The by-elections backfired when the unionists failed to win their target of half a million votes against the AIA. They polled 418,230 votes, but lost the Newry and Armagh seat to the SDLP's deputy leader Seamus Mallon. The SDLP percentage of the vote cast in the four constituencies they contested rose by 19.1 per cent, whereas Sinn Féin's percentage of the vote cast in the same constituencies fell by 24 per cent (see Table 7.1). The two governments were able to claim the swing within the nationalist bloc as evidence that the AIA was working: Sinn Féin had been halted and squeezed. However, the same by-elections showed the depth and breadth of unionist opposition to the AIA.

Table 7.1 The outcome of the January 1986 by-elections in which the SDLP and Sinn Féin competed
Source: constructed from data in Flackes and Elliott (1989: 344–7, 352–5)

	Sinn Féin			SDLP		
	1983	1986	1983–6	1983	1986	1983–6
	votes (%)	votes (%)	net gain (per cent)	votes (%)	votes (%)	net gain (per cent)
1. Fermanagh – South Tyrone	20,954 (40.2)	15,278 (27.2)	–13	9,923 (19.0)	12,081 (21.5)	+2.5
2. Mid-Ulster	16,096 (29.8)	13,998 (27.2)	–2.6	12,044 (22.4)	13,021 (25.3)	+3.1
3. Newry and South Armagh	9,928 (20.0)	6,609 (13.2)	–7.7	17,434 (36.8)	22,694 (45.7)	+8.9
4. South Down	4,074 (7.9)	2,936 (5.7)	–2.2	20,145 (39.2)	23,121 (44.9)	+5.7
Total votes (1+2+3+4)	51,052	38,821	–24	59,546	70,917	+19.1

The by-elections were neglected by the British media, then preoccupied with the 'Westland affair' which briefly threatened to topple Margaret Thatcher. The by-elections were followed by the decision of unionist MPs to boycott Westminster and the NIO. The facilities of the Northern Ireland assembly, which nationalists had boycotted since its formation in 1982, were used for political protests (O'Leary *et al.*, 1988). The last formal links between the Conservative party and the UUP were sundered. Mass demonstrations were called in which up to two hundred thousand unionists were mobilized and entertained by burning effigies of Thatcher and coffins representing the Union. A one-day general strike was called for 3 March 1986. In late February James Molyneaux and Paisley, the *leaders* of the UUP and DUP, for a brief moment, looked prepared to accept some fudge which Thatcher and King were prepared to offer about prospective negotiations, but were quickly brought back into line by their followers when they returned to Belfast. Despite evidence of widespread Protestant support for the strike, media reports branded the strike as wholly intimidatory, and Molyneaux felt compelled to dissociate the UUP from the strike organizers. Although an *Irish Times/MRBI* opinion poll showed 81 per cent of Protestants disapproving of the AIA in February 1986, unionist leaders, especially within the UUP, felt constrained over what means they could use to attack the British government without dividing their supporters.[7]

As the UUP and DUP were trying to restructure their campaign ultra-loyalist paramilitaries began co-ordinated attacks on RUC officers. They were capitalizing on evidence of hostility to the AIA within the rank-and-file of the RUC – openly articulated by the RUC Federation chairman. Inflammatory political rhetoric about 'our police' was followed up with knocks on the door. The attacks on the police, which peaked between March and May 1986, were accompanied by a renewed spate of loyalist sectarian murders of Catholics. However, as predicted by Andy Tyrie, the leader of the UDA, the unionist politicians played 'Pontius Pilate' on their paramilitary brethren, and washed their hands of the loyalist attacks. The wave of assaults on the RUC came to an end in May. However, they had some impact, because in July 1986 the RUC decided not to repeat their decision of the previous year to ban Orange marches through Catholic areas of Portadown, although they imposed order on the marchers.

The unionists' local-government campaign, as part of their dual strategy of constitutional mobilization and civil disobedience, went off half-cocked. They had threatened to make local councils ungovernable and not to set the rates (local property taxes). However, talk of 'Gideon's army'[8] waned as key unionist politicians folded under the threat of action by auditors in Belfast and elsewhere. Nor did the unionists' call for the withholding of rates by citizens and businesses proceed with much success: at least by comparison with the SDLP-sponsored rent-and-rate strike against internment. In June 1986 unionist politicians embarked upon a campaign in 'the mainland'. But the fate of Boyd Black, who stood in the Fulham by-election in April 1986 on a broadly unionist platform only to receive fewer votes than Lord Sutch of the Monster Raving Loony Party, and the 100 people who attended the first 'mass meeting' against the AIA at Liverpool, gave unionists some sense of their isolation from all but the lunatic fringe of English public opinion. The Friends of the Union, established in late May 1986 by leading figures in the Conservative party to co-ordinate the Great British campaign, showed no signs of having any decisive impact upon élite or public opinion: the unionists were on their own.

Unionist opposition to the AIA in 1986–7 won them nothing more than the diplomatic postponement for a couple of days of scheduled meetings of the IGC, whilst the assaults on the RUC lost them the sympathy of some right-wing Conservatives. However, although their opposition severely curtailed the British government's warmth about the principle and pace of prospective reforms, it could do little more. Unionists were not mobilizing against an internal power-sharing settlement in which other unionists were participating. They were mobilizing against the British government, against Margaret Thatcher and Tom King, a taller order than Harold Wilson and Merlyn Rees. The Conservative administration, the Army, and the bulk of the RUC's leadership were prepared for and had the motivated leadership to defeat any extended strike. 'Biting the hand that fed them' caused anxiety amongst Protestants aware that their material prosperity was dependent upon the retention of the British connection.

The stakes for unionists were strikingly different from those in 1974. Their range of options was no longer circumscribed to either internal power-sharing along Sunningdale lines or the continuation of direct rule. Instead they had four obvious and painful choices:

- first, 'stay in a state of permanent disaffection or rebellion against the British government until the AIA is repudiated';
- second, 'accept internal power-sharing with an Irish dimension and thereby reduce the role of the IGC';
- third, 'advocate the full electoral and administrative integration of Northern Ireland into the UK'; and
- fourth, 'exercise self-determination and call for independence'.

The first choice posed a simple problem: what if the British government never surrendered? Unionist obstinacy might lead to the evolution of full British and Irish joint authority, and would therefore be the politics of the self-fulfilling prophecy. The second choice had the built-in carrot of allowing power-sharing to reduce the importance of the IGC, but required sufficient unionist politicians from the UUP and DUP both to accept power-sharing and be confident that they would not be instantly outflanked and meet the fate of Brian Faulkner or Bill Craig. The third choice, increasingly popular with unionist public opinion between 1986 and 1988, nevertheless divided them because some trusted no British political parties after the AIA, some believed that devolution was the best way of protecting the Union, and others feared that British party-organization in the region would fragment the unionist vote.[9] The fourth choice would split unionists completely: they are after all unionists. They do not seek sovereignty over themselves. The overwhelming majority are not 'Ulster nationalists' and they would contemplate independence only if they are coerced into a united Ireland – and indeed many UUP and APNI voters would baulk at independence even if joint authority were imposed.

The DUP sat at these crossroads. Rhetorical demands for a nuclear strike on the Irish Republic indicated its members' feelings if not their intelligence.[10] The DUP were not sufficiently cohesive to raise independence as a threat, although their deputy leader Peter Robinson canvassed the option with some seriousness. The DUP leader knew that to raise the option of a unilateral declaration of independence (UDI) would split the party and the unionist bloc. Paisley's rhetoric chose to avoid painful choices: his most radical statements simply repeated the traditional loyalist cry in times of English perfidy: allegiance to parliament must be withdrawn but not loyalty to the Crown.[11] This rhetoric was treasonable, but was not a declaration of independence: rather it was a bargaining posture demanding the Union on the DUP's terms. Paisley increased the scope of his 'call to arms', and threatened the police who were called to evict his supporters from their occupation of Stormont, but he refused to lead a call for independence. In August 1986 his deputy leader felt compelled to give his followers work to do by leading a loyalist incursion into county Monaghan in the Republic of Ireland. He was arrested, and to the chagrin of his militant supporters, paid bail and eventually a fine: 'very revolutionary' as one official put it.

Since the DUP and UUP were not prepared to raise UDI as a serious alternative Thatcher and King were able to call their bluff, and eventually start prodding unionists after the 1987 Westminster elections to reconsider their outlook on a devolved government and negotiating within the framework of the AIA. Gradually the vigour of unionist opposition to the AIA became more muted: at first they refused to talk to the NIO at all while the AIA, the IGCs, and Maryfield were in being; then they began to show willingness to be prepared to talk if the AIA, the IGCs, and Maryfield were 'suspended'; and much much later they began to say they would consider discussions if there would be no IGC, and no servicing of the IGC by the Maryfield secretariat, while discussions took place.

During 1986–8 the failure of Molyneaux and Paisley to persuade the British government to abandon or suspend the AIA led to divisions and shifts of opinion amongst unionists. In 1986 a minority broke away from the UUP to campaign for complete electoral integration into Britain, arguing that Great British political parties should organize in Northern Ireland (Roberts, 1987; Aughey 1989). Most of these former unionists sought to organize Conservative party branches in the province, while others sought to persuade the British Labour party to organize in the region. Their overtures were rejected by the British Labour party and initially by British Conservative party chairman Peter Brooke. However, in October 1989 the Conservative party conference voted to recognize constituency associations in Northern Ireland, and four were officially formed in North Down, East Belfast, East Londonderry, and Lagan Valley in the following November.[12] Eventually fifteen Conservative candidates stood for Northern Ireland seats in the 1992 Westminster election (see Ch. 9: 321). Electoral integrationism became the preferred option amongst the unionist intelligentsia after the AIA (e.g. Aughey, 1989; Roberts, 1987; and Wilson,

1989), and a poll reported in April 1988 showed that 47 per cent of Protestants favoured complete integration with Great Britain as their first preference for the future of Northern Ireland (*Irish Political Studies*, 1989, 4: 159). Wishful thinking had become widespread amongst unionists.

By contrast the think-tank of the loyalist paramilitary organization, the UDA, published *Common Sense* in January 1987, in which they called for the establishment of a power-sharing devolved government ('co-determination'), subject to the abandonment of the AIA. In return for guaranteed power-sharing and minority vetoes more generous than those embedded in the Sunningdale agreement, the UDA pamphlet sought the ending of any Irish dimension: no intergovernmental conference and no AIA. In June 1987, after long consultations within the unionist community, the secondary leadership of the UUP and DUP produced the *Task Force Report*. They suggested that a power-sharing devolved government was no longer 'unthinkable', prompted in large part by Frank Millar of the UUP. In response Ian Paisley and James Molyneaux entered into 'talks about talks' with the NIO which lasted until May 1988, but their proposals 'lay on the table' until Peter Brooke replaced Tom King as Secretary of State in July 1989. Unionists still insisted that the AIA had to be suspended before broader talks with the SDLP or the Irish government could begin, a demand that remained unacceptable to both governments and the SDLP.

The posture of the unionist leaders and the lack of response from the NIO effectively shelved interest in the power-sharing option expressed in the *Task Force Report*, and their tactics until the summer of 1989 seemed to be based upon waiting for the AIA to collapse as a result of discord between the British and Irish governments, or as a result of some future 'hung parliament' at Westminster. On occasion unionist leaders hinted at their willingness to embrace direct negotiations with Dublin for a new agreement covering the 'totality of relationships' within the British Isles – but such suggestions were widely decoded as a stratagem to destroy the AIA. Although they remained agreed on their hostility to the AIA, the unionist political parties were in a state of internal ferment. The UUP was divided between a majority of integrationists and a vocal minority prepared to accept a power-sharing devolved government; and the DUP was divided over whether to embrace more extreme action against the AIA and over its united front with the UUP.

Table 7.2 Party performances in the unionist and nationalist blocs
before and after the Anglo-Irish Agreement
Source: O'Leary (1990).

Notes: All figures in per cent. The figures are rounded except that the 'net change' figures are to one decimal place. The figures for local government and European elections are percentages of all first-preference votes; for Westminster of the total vote.

unionist bloc

DUP

	before	after	net change
Westminster	1983: 20	1987: 12	− 8.3
Local Government	1985: 24	1989: 18	− 6.5
European	1984: 34	1989: 30	− 3.7

UUP

	before	after	net change
Westminster	1983: 34	1987: 38	+ 3.8
Local Government	1985: 30	1989: 31	+ 1.9
European	1984: 22	1989: 22	0

nationalist bloc

SDLP

	before	after	net change
Westminster	1983: 18	1987: 21	+ 3.2
Local Government	1985: 18	1989: 21	+ 3.3
European	1984: 22	1989: 26	+ 3.4

SF

	before	after	net change
Westminster	1983: 13	1987: 11	− 2.0
Local Government	1985: 12	1989: 11	− 0.5
European	1984: 13	1989: 9	− 4.1

Amongst the nationalist minority the initial widespread enthusiasm for the AIA, which fed into increased support for the SDLP in the 1986 by-elections, the 1987 Westminster elections, and the 1989 local government and European elections (see Tables 7.1 and 7.2), began to wane as the intergovernmental conference failed to deliver rapid, dramatic, and effective reforms of Northern Ireland. Indeed in one opinion poll reported in April 1988 only 16 per cent of Catholics believed the AIA had benefited the nationalist community (Wilson, 1988). The results of another poll, conducted in September 1988, showed that 28 per cent of Catholics agreed that the AIA had led to an improvement in the position of the nationalist community but 64 per cent disagreed; 29 per cent agreed that it had led to an improvement in the administration of justice but 58 per cent disagreed; and 36 per cent believed it had led to an improvement in the fair allocation of jobs but 54 per cent disagreed (*Irish Political Studies*, 1989, 4: 160).[13] The British government's early caution and immobility on reforms owed something to its desire to reassure unionists, but the predictable consequence was to reduce nationalist support. Sinn Féin sought to capitalize upon this vicious circle (Sinn Féin, 1989). However, because of the atrocities carried out by the IRA in the period after Hillsborough, as well as the resurgence of the SDLP, Sinn Féin had little success. Nevertheless much nationalist support for the AIA rested upon the negative fact that it was opposed by unionists.

The AIA was intended to shake up trends in party support: to stem and reverse the growth of Sinn Féin; to stabilize support for the SDLP; and to encourage productive attitudes towards devolution amongst unionists, by strengthening power-sharing devolutionists within the UUP at the expense of both extremists within the DUP and integrationists within the UUP. So what impact did the AIA have in these respects? Within the unionist bloc the DUP lost ground after Hillsborough. Table 7.2 demonstrates that in the three region-wide elections held after the signing of the AIA, including the European election of 1989, Paisley's party failed to match the share of the vote it obtained in the corresponding elections held before the Agreement. However, the DUP and UUP co-operated both politically and electorally after Hillsborough so these figures, alone, are misleading. Moreover, power-sharing devolutionists made little headway within the UUP.

The overall showing of the unionist bloc in the three region-wide elections held after the Agreement is significant. Its total share of the Northern Ireland vote (55 per cent in the Westminster election of June 1987, 49 per cent of the first-preference vote in the Local Government Districts elections of May 1989 and 51 per cent of the first-preference vote in the European elections of June 1989) fell below its level in each of the last corresponding elections; and the two 1989 elections produced the lowest and second lowest shares for the unionist bloc since 1969 (O'Leary, 1991d). Some unionists undoubtedly abstained, disillusioned with constitutional politics or with their 'natural parties'' campaign against the AIA, but the elections also suggested a fraying at the edges of their core support. However, although the AIA produced some electoral squeezing of loyalist extremists, it has not, as yet, produced a decisive accommodating response on power-sharing from within the UUP or the DUP; and for a while more Protestants favoured full integration of Northern Ireland into Britain (47 per cent) rather than devolved government with power-sharing (17 per cent) (Wilson, 1988). After the 1989 local government elections many UUP councillors engaged in cross-party co-operation with the SDLP and the APNI in the allocation of committee duties and elected posts in some district councils west of the Bann, suggesting some willingness to engage in local power-sharing.

The impact of the AIA on nationalist voting more clearly achieved the British and Irish governments' objectives. First, the AIA halted the growth of the Sinn Féin vote, and showed some signs of reversing it (see Tables 7.1 and 7.2). Sinn Féin's share of the vote fell in each of the elections, Westminster, local government, and European, held after Hillsborough, by comparison with the corresponding three elections before the AIA was signed. The SDLP's position within the nationalist bloc was decisively restored, as the sharp fall in Sinn Féin's share of the combined SDLP and Sinn Féin vote shows, and the SDLP's performance in the 1989 European poll was its highest ever share of a Northern Ireland election. Extremist nationalism was thus somewhat squeezed, although substantive reform of Northern Ireland would be required to reduce it further.

However, contrary to what most British architects of the AIA imagined, the SDLP appeared to lose interest in 'agreed devolution' after Hillsborough. One of the party's spokespersons declared that the SDLP had no 'ideological' attachment to devolution. The SDLP leadership, having learned the lessons of the mid-1970s, decided to be intransigent on the Irish dimension: unless unionists accepted that they were part of the island of Ireland then it was futile to discuss the internal arrangements for governing Northern Ireland. Instead three relationships had to be 'sorted out' by unionists: those between Great Britain and Ireland, those between Northern Ireland and the Republic of Ireland, and those within Northern Ireland. Hume's dismissal of the first 'feelers' which unionists made towards the SDLP revealed that he knew he could now bargain from strength.[14]

The most significant development within the nationalist bloc after the AIA was signed was unexpected talks between the SDLP and

Sinn Féin in the first eight months of 1988. The SDLP team tried to persuade Sinn Féin of the futility of the IRA's campaign, which they believed was not only morally wrong but also the major obstacle to Irish unity. Sinn Féin by contrast used the talks to try to legitimize itself within the nationalist community throughout Ireland. When the talks broke up both sides published their position papers and Hume later went on a renewed campaigning offensive against both Sinn Féin and the IRA, accusing them of being fascists who, far from 'defending' the Catholic minority, had killed more Catholics than any other organization since 1969. The talks succeeded in further isolating Sinn Féin from the broader nationalist community in Ireland but were condemned by the unionists as unprincipled. In their eyes the SDLP were sitting down with apologists for gunmen.[15]

Although the SDLP rejected unionist calls for negotiations on a political settlement which demanded either the abandonment or the suspension of the AIA or the Maryfield secretariat, informal discussions and talks between representatives of the constitutional parties continued after 1986, and occasionally came close to producing a formula for 'talks about talks' – as appeared after inter-party discussions under the auspices of a German mediator at Duisberg in February 1989. However, despite subterranean signs of political dialogue the internal politics of Northern Ireland seemed locked in a new stalemate, which did not begin to shift until the Brooke initiative gathered momentum in late 1989 (see below). Unionists were not prepared to negotiate under the AIA, the SDLP were not prepared to negotiate without it staying in place; and political leaders in both communities remained aware that compromise would be interpreted as surrender by their party colleagues and rivals in other parties. Talented, educated, and intelligent politicians like Frank Millar of the UUP, John Cushnahan of the APNI, and Austin Currie of the SDLP despaired of the prospect of an internal accommodation, and of finding a worthwhile political career, and chose to make their lives elsewhere.[16]

Social justice and legal justice

The British government eventually insisted against their Irish nationalist critics that major reforms were facilitated by the AIA (NIO,

1989). They pointed to: the repeal of the Flags and Emblems Act of 1954, which outlawed the display of Irish nationalist insignia; the Public Order (NI) Order of 1987 which strengthened the law on incitement to hatred and gave powers to the police to control marches likely to cause provocation; the establishment of an Independent Commission for Police Complaints; measures to promote police–community relations and monitor allegations of misconduct by the security forces; the modification of the Emergency Provisions Act, 1987, in a more liberal direction; the publication of a new code of conduct for RUC officers in 1988; legislation which now enables citizens of the Republic resident in Northern Ireland to vote in local-government elections (Elected Authorities (NI) Act, 1989); the Fair Employment Act, 1989, which strengthens the law against religious discrimination and promotes equality of opportunity in employment; and measures to facilitate the use of the Irish language. The British government also advertised the 'Making Belfast Work' project established in July 1988, and the extra expenditure directed to Northern Ireland under the 'International Fund for Ireland' (set up to accompany the AIA and receiving contributions from the USA, Canada, New Zealand, and the EC), as proof of the momentum for reform.

Why then has the commitment of the British government to social reform in Northern Ireland been questioned by nationalists? For one thing until the review of the intergovernmental conference the British government, to appease loyalists, maintained that none of the reforms was the by-product of pressure from the Irish government. They therefore left themselves, as one NIO official put it, 'in the strange position of being incapable of saying convincingly that the AIA had brought reforms which might not otherwise have occurred'. According to Irish officials many of the reforms in any case had the character of being 'too little, too late'; one maintained that what the British government had 'given with one hand it has taken back with the other' by accompanying reforms with repressive measures. Another maintained that the 'British present a mythical picture of making concessions and reforms, while the reality is of little substantive change' (non-attributable interviews). The two areas of prime concern for those interested in reforming Northern Ireland are social justice, especially fair employment, and legal justice, which we now consider.

Fair Employment

Ethnic inequalities in employment and unemployment in Northern Ireland are rooted in past and present discrimination (SACHR, 1987; Smith and Chambers, 1987a, 1987b, 1987c, 1991; Eversley, 1989). The SACHR report of 1987, and the MacBride campaign, suggested that injustices and inequalities in Northern Ireland's labour markets could no longer plausibly be held to be the responsibility of the former Stormont parliament since they had, with some exceptions, persisted under direct rule, and in some cases worsened.

However, most unionists denied that there is or *was* a problem of unfair employment. Poll-data confirm the persistence of widespread denial of the existence of discrimination against the minority by Ulster Protestants, and *a fortiori* by Ulster unionists. Thus in Rose's 1968 loyalty survey 74 per cent of Protestants denied that Catholics were treated unfairly in any part of Northern Ireland, exactly mirroring the percentage of Catholics who thought otherwise. In 1973–4 77 per cent of Protestants disagreed with the proposition that 'One of the main causes of the Troubles is the lack of job opportunities for Roman Catholics because Protestants are given preference' (R. Miller, 1978: 15), almost matching the number of Catholics who thought otherwise. In 1986 in response to the PSI survey 68 per cent of Protestants thought Catholics and Protestants had the same chance of obtaining a job, whereas 67 per cent of Catholics thought they did not. Whereas the overwhelming majority of Catholics who believed there was inequality in job-opportunities thought Protestants had better chances than Catholics, Protestants who believed there was inequality in opportunity were evenly divided between those who thought Catholics had better chances, those who thought Protestants had a better chance, and those who thought it depended on the area (Smith and Chambers, 1987c: Table 75). The objective evidence about Catholics' chances of obtaining jobs as opposed to Protestants, is completely at odds with most Protestants' perceptions.[17] The AIA has had no attitudinal impact upon Protestants' denial of past or present mistreatment of the minority. Indeed such denial has continued to be articulated by unionist politicians, and they draw for their support, in some cases, upon 'academic' arguments which sought to suggest that the differentials between Catholic and Protestant employment levels and employment status were rooted in cultural differences between the two communities rather than direct or indirect discrimination.[18]

Eight explanations which *apparently* do not rely on illegal discrimination or inequality of opportunity to account for the differences between Catholic and Protestant employment levels were identified and tested by the Policy Studies Institute in the mid-1980s on behalf of the SACHR (Smith and Chambers, 1991: 156–60 ff.):[19]

(i)   Fewer jobs are available in Catholic than in Protestant areas;

(ii)   Catholics tend to be concentrated in depressed industries to a greater extent than Protestants;

(iii) A higher proportion of Catholics than of Protestants belong to the lower socio-economic groups, which are far more likely to experience unemployment than the higher ones;

(iv) Protestants are more likely than Catholics to have the skills and qualifications required for the available jobs;

(v)   People with a low-earning potential and a large number of dependent children (disproportionately Catholic) are likely to choose not to work because they derive more from welfare benefits than from employment;

(vi) The number of economically active Catholics is growing while the number of Protestants is stable;

(vii) A higher proportion of Catholics than of Protestants belong to the younger age-cohorts which are subject to higher levels of unemployment; and

(viii) A growing population (Catholics) will have a higher rate of unemployment than a static one, even if members of the two groups have the same chance of getting a job (Compton, 1981).

However, as Smith and Chambers point out, many of these eight 'explanations' take the historic background of institutionalized discrimination for granted. Thus explanations (i), (ii), and (vi) rely on the assumption that Protestants and Catholics operate in separate labour markets which must have come from somewhere; whereas explanations (ii), (iii), (iv), and (v), if true, take for granted that Catholics are disproportionately concentrated amongst the poor and the educationally disadvantaged rather than asking why that is so. Thus even if many of these explanations were correct, which is questionable, they would still be entirely 'compatible with explanations based on discrimination or inequality of opportunity'

(1991: 160). Some of the explanations are just plain wrong: thus explanation (vii) faces the double difficulty that the contrast in unemployment rates amongst Catholic and Protestant men remains constant across age-cohorts, except among the youngest cohort (aged 16–24) in which Catholics do *relatively* better (1991: Table 5.6). Other explanations account for only a very small portion of the variation in employment opportunities: thus explanation (iv) faces the problem that the differences between Catholics and Protestants in academic qualifications cannot account for the scale of the variation in employment-opportunities, and that when academic and practical qualifications are held constant, very large differences remain between Protestant and Catholic unemployment-rates (1991: 170). Locational explanations of differential employment-opportunities are also effectively refuted by Smith and Chambers (1991: 171–5): throughout Northern Ireland there is a fairly uniform tendency for Catholics to have a higher chance of being unemployed than comparable Protestants (in age, gender, socio-economic group, skills, and qualifications). They accept, however, that there is some validity for explanation (v), but observe that the contrast between unemployment-rates between Catholic and Protestant males with the same number of children remains striking 'except that it is much reduced among those with four or more children'.[20] In Smith and Chambers's regression model, after socio-economic status, number of children, age, travel-to-work, and academic or practical qualifications are taken into consideration, the difference in rate of unemployment amongst Catholics and Protestants is reduced, compared with the actual rates, but 'for the typical group selected, the rate of unemployment predicted for Catholics is almost double the rate for Protestants in most travel-to-work areas' (1991: 183–4); and, as they remark, their model *understates* the scale of inequality of opportunity since present social policy discriminates against large families.

The PSI study from which we have quoted was subject to extended criticism to which its authors replied (see Smith and Chambers, 1991: 187 ff.). They accepted some minor criticisms, and re-ran some of their workings, but their conclusions remain robust and convincing. One point emphasized by the SACHR, and not by the PSI's first three reports, was important: differences in religious unemployment-rates could be partially explained by differential employment in security-related occupations. However, Smith and

Chambers (1991: 194) calculate that if we falsely assume that all of the 26,000 security-related jobs in 1984 were held by Protestant males, and work out what would have happened if all these jobs were re-allocated on a proportional basis then the Protestant male unemployment rate would be 18.8 per cent and the Catholic one would be 29.7 per cent, compared to the actual position in 1983–5 of 35.1 per cent for Catholics and 14.9 per cent for Protestants.[21]

The PSI study which formed the basis of the SACHR *Report on Fair Employment* argued that there were deep inequalities in standard of living between Catholics and Protestants for five clusters of reasons. A considerably higher proportion of Protestant than of Catholic men are in work, and Catholics are two-and-a-half times as likely to be unemployed as Protestants. A higher proportion of Protestant than of Catholic women are in work, so there are a higher proportion of Protestant than Catholic double-income families. The wealthier Protestant households on average support smaller families. Protestants (especially men) tend to have jobs higher up organizational hierarchies at all age-ranges. Finally, Protestants, especially those in lower-range occupations, are more likely than Catholics to work overtime. These inequalities obviously underpin the politics of antagonism.

The British government responded to the PSI and SACHR reports by promising a new act to remedy the defects of the old one. However, the Fair Employment Act of 1989, which sets out to remedy the weaknesses in the 1976 Act, was criticized on several grounds by anti-discrimination experts, especially because it fell short of the proposals contained in the SACHR report. The White Paper and first draft of the bill which preceded it were flawed (McCrudden, 1988, 1990, 1991), and provoked penetrating opposition from Labour's spokesperson on Northern Ireland, Kevin McNamara; and, despite some key concessions made by the Conservative government in the bill's passage through Westminster, critics believe the final legislation lacks the 'teeth' required to address the entrenched direct and indirect discrimination in Northern Ireland's labour markets with genuinely effective programmes of 'affirmative action'.

The new Act created a Fair Employment Commission (FEC) to replace the FEA. It also created a Fair Employment Tribunal (FET) to hear individual complaints and act as a first court of appeal for employers. The Act covers indirect as well as direct discrimination, on the same model as legislation against racial and sexual discrimination in Great Britain. Employers are required to register with the FEC, monitor the religious composition of their work-forces on pain of being guilty of a criminal offence, and review their employment-practices periodically. If the review demonstrates unfair employment-participation patterns the employer is expected to engage in affirmative action. The FEC has enforcement powers, more extensive than those enjoyed by the FEA; and contract-compliance has been put on a statutory basis so that employers failing to comply with the FEC's and the Fair Employment Act's minimum requirements will not receive government contracts.

However, the Act remains open to criticism. Affirmative action is restricted by the duty not to discriminate, directly or indirectly, and thus many affirmative actions programmes may fall foul of the Act. Affirmative action training programmes targeted at the minority are effectively prohibited – even though they are permitted under comparable Great British legislation. Small employers are not required to register with the newly created Fair Employment Commission. The monitoring provisions do not cover part-time work of less than 16 hours a week, i.e. frequently female employment. Moreover, the explicit exemption on 'national security grounds' available for some employers may well provide an extensive loophole. Finally, there are legal criticisms of the Act and of the way it is likely to be administered (McCrudden, 1988, 1990). The past record of British governments and Northern Irish courts does not inspire confidence.

The fair employment bill provides an insight into the new British and Irish co-operation brought about by the AIA. The Irish government's officials in the intergovernmental conference were briefed about the details of the bill 'before and better than the Westminster parliament' (non-attributable source). The Conservative government was primarily motivated by the need to respond to the 'MacBride principles' campaign in the USA, which sought to oblige US companies in Northern Ireland to practise fair employment in recruitment and promotion or be obliged to disinvest (Osborne and Cormack, 1989). The success of the supporters of the MacBride principles in passing relevant legislation in American states and in the US Congress prompted the Conservative government to engage in 'symbolic politics', to appear to be doing something about inequality,[22] and that obviously raised the bargaining power of lobbies operating through the Irish government. The Conservatives were worried that radical legislation facilitating extensive 'affirmative action' on religious discrimination in Northern Ireland might produce awkward demands for similar legislation to rectify ethnic and racial discrimination in England, Scotland, and Wales; and they were naturally disposed to consider the arguments of Northern Ireland's CBI that fair employment monitoring and procedural requirements would impose costly regulatory burdens on private enterprise. However, the MacBride campaign, and the existence of the intergovernmental conference did push the Conservative government into being more radical than it intended in the regulation of the Northern Ireland work-force.

Legal justice

Nationalist discontent with British reforming efforts since the signing of the AIA was most marked over legal justice. 'In national conflicts, law, order and justice are not just issues that happen to arise from other causes. National conflicts, once they are fully developed, revolve around these matters' (Wright, 1989: 153). Before the negotiation of the AIA legal justice matters were discussed, and although agreements in principle were reached, they were excluded from the Hillsborough communiqué (Moloney, 1986). They included agreements to remove powers of arrest from the UDR; to guarantee a numbering identification system for UDR soldiers to minimize the dangers of harassment; to make RUC constables pledge to defend the 'two traditions'; and to increase the representation of Catholic judges on the Belfast high court. The Hillsborough accord and communiqué publicly included commitments to ensure 'police accompaniment'[23] of the British Army and the UDR; to consider the reform of the controversial Diplock courts, either by creating 'mixed' (i.e. British and Irish judges on the bench) or three-judge courts; and to contemplate the establishment of a Bill of Rights.

On all these matters the Irish government and nationalists complain that the British government failed to deliver change in the first six years of the AIA, or that it did so half-heartedly. The courts have not been reformed, partly because of the resistance of Lord Hailsham, the Lord Chancellor, and Lord Lowry, the Lord Chief Justice of Northern Ireland. However, given that there is, to our knowledge, only one known *cause célèbre* which suggests that the Northern Irish courts have presided over a wrongful sentence for scheduled offences – and the case in question involves four former UDR soldiers[24] – there has been insufficient objective pressure for change. British officials claim that it would be difficult or redundant to create three-judge courts, which Irish officials deny and have numbers which prove them right. The controversy is symbolic, but symbolic issues matter in ethnic conflicts.

There has been no move to create a Bill of Rights, partly because it would be incompatible with most of the British government's 'counter-insurgency legislation', namely the Emergency Provisions Act and the Prevention of Terrorism Act. Officials point out that if the British government were to take the less radical step of incorporating the European Convention on Human Rights into Northern Ireland's domestic law they would either have to derogate from many of its provisions because of the emergency, or worse, not have to do so because the convention cedes too much power to state executives in assessing whether or not emergencies exist. The Irish government has not been enthusiastic about promoting an all-Ireland Bill of Rights, because, as its representatives testily point out in interviews, the Republic of Ireland already has entrenched in its constitution strong safeguards for its citizens against the abuse of executive power, but also because they might be required to extend the agenda of any such Bill of Rights to matters affecting divorce and abortion.

FitzGerald and Alan Dukes, former minister of justice under the coalition government and FitzGerald's successor as leader of Fine Gael, maintain that the British failed to deliver properly on 'police accompaniment'.[25] British officials maintain that the logistics of ensuring police accompaniment for all UDR patrols are impossible given existing resources. The UDR, some of whose soldiers continued to be involved in sectarian murders of Catholics and in overlapping membership of loyalist paramilitary organizations, remained a fundamental concern for the Irish government. An IIP investigation reported in Table 7.3 confirms that in the years 1985–9 members of the UDR were one-and-a-half times more likely to be convicted of scheduled (i.e. 'terrorist') offences than the adult civilians (aged 16–65) who they were supposed to be protecting.[26] The UDR's Catholic membership is now less than 3 per cent, and despite its low overall share of responsibility for the death-toll in Northern Ireland (until 1987 a mere 0.3 per cent of the total),[27] its Protestant nature continues to antagonize Catholics.[28] In August and September 1989 evidence that the files of IRA suspects had been given to loyalist paramilitaries who used them to carry out

Table 7.3

(a) Comparing the conviction rates for scheduled (i.e. conflict-related) offences of members of the security forces with the adult population (aged 16–65) in Northern Ireland

Source: IP (1990: 248–56)

Years	RUC	UDR	British Army excluding the UDR	All Security Forces	Adult Population (16–65) not in Security Forces
1985	2.3	3.1	2.2	2.5	6.5
1986	0.8	10.7	3.0	3.8	5.9
1987	0.8	11.0	0.0	2.8	7.3
1988	0.8	12.7	0.0	3.1	5.1
1989	0	7.9	3.1	2.8	4.4
1985–9	0.9	9.1	1.7	2.8	5.9

(b) Absolute numbers convicted of scheduled offences by population group

Year	RUC	UDR	British Army excluding UDR	Adult Population (16–65) not in Security Forces
1985	3 (12,767)	2 (6,478)	2 (9,014)	586 (895,955)
1986	1 (12,648)	7 (6,535)	3 (9,920)	536 (904,435)
1987	1 (12,880)	7 (6,364)	0 (9,645)	663 (912,756)
1988	1 (12,885)	8 (6,312)	0 (9,695)	471 (916,494)
1989	0 (n/a)	5 (6,342)	3 (9,658)	406 (n/a)
1985–9	6	25*	8	2,662

Notes:

(i) The figures in Table (a) are conviction-rates per 10,000 of the relevant population *not* absolute numbers convicted which are in Table (b).

(ii) The larger figures in Table (b) are absolute number of convictions in the relevant category and the figures in brackets are the relevant populations at year's end.

(iii) * The figure of 29 in the UDR column in Table (b) includes the 'Armagh Four', members of the UDR whose convictions may prove to have been concocted (Paisley, 1991).

murders raised questions about the partiality of both the UDR and the RUC. The UDR was accused of 'deficient' vetting procedures by the Deputy Chief Constable of Cambridge, John Stevens, who was appointed to investigate collusion between the security forces and loyalist paramilitaries. This collusion is apologized for by a minority of unionists who see it as necessary communal deterrence in the absence of appropriate powers being granted to the security forces; but these arguments simply reinforce nationalist perceptions of the UDR as the new B-specials, a partisan ethnic force. At a meeting of the intergovernmental conference in Dublin in the autumn of 1989, Peter Brooke, the new Northern Ireland Secretary, met the new Irish foreign minister, Gerry Collins. The longest ever session of the IGC broke up without any resolution of the issues raised by the UDR. The Irish government pressed for a renewed British commitment to reform the security forces, especially their recruitment policies, and to ensure police accompaniment. In the subsequent press conference Collins pointed to the extensive 'gap' between both governments which needed to be closed, and warned ominously: 'If we don't do that then the Anglo-Irish Agreement will be held up to question as to whether or not there is any reason for having it at all.' After four years the AIA had shown few signs of achieving minority confidence in the administration of justice and the security forces.

Violence and security

The IRA and Sinn Féin were desperate to ensure that the AIA would not produce minority confidence in British government of the region tempered by an Irish dimension. After November 1985 the IRA deliberately set out to raise the tempo of their 'long war' to break Britain's will, to prevent an internal political settlement within Northern Ireland and to encourage the British government into embarrassing repressive actions. In the summer of 1986 the IRA widened its definition of 'legitimate targets' to include civilians engaged in economic relations with the security forces, provoking a predictable response from the Ulster Freedom Fighters, the pseudonym for the militarily active section of the UDA, that it too would widen its definition of 'legitimate targets'. The rival paramilitaries had a shared interest in ensuring that the level of violence would rise after the AIA, so they could both say it was not

Table 7.4 Indicators of violence before and after the AIA, 1983–8
Source: RUC (1990)

Year	Deaths	Injuries	Shooting incidents	Explosions	Armed robberies
1983	77	528	299	266	622
1984	64	875	230	193	627
1985	54	939	196	148	459
----	--	---	---	---	---
1986	61	1462	285	172	724
1987	93	1146	489	236	858
1988	93	1053	358	253	653

before and after AIA comparison of totals

	Deaths	Injuries	Shooting incidents	Explosions	Armed robberies
1983–5	195	2342	716	607	1708
1986–8	247	3661	1132	661	2235
	---	----	----	---	----
absolute rise	52	1319	416	54	527
per cent rise	27	56	58	9	31

working. Table 7.4 shows that deaths, injuries, shooting incidents, explosions, and armed robberies indeed went up significantly in the three years after by comparison with the three years in the run up to Hillsborough. Injuries and shooting incidents went up over 50 per cent, armed robberies by 30 per cent, and deaths by just over 25 per cent. However, all these indicators fell again during 1989–90 and although the monthly death-toll rose in the years after the AIA, by comparison with the preceding three (O'Duffy and O'Leary, 1990), it fell again in 1989 and 1990. The annual death-rate still remained well below the levels of 1971–6 (see Ch. 1) and during 1986–8 it was inflated by internal feuds within paramilitary organizations which were not connected with the AIA. The IRA continually executed alleged informers; the Marxist paramilitaries of the INLA (who had killed Conservative spokesman Airey Neave in 1979) collapsed in an internal blood bath; and the UDA remained so prone to faction-fighting that some of its members colluded in helping the IRA kill their deputy leader John McMichael (co-author of *Common Sense*) in December 1987.

The IRA was fortified by renewed military supplies from Libya, following Mrs Thatcher's support for the American raid on Tripoli in April 1986. This helped it resupply its campaigns from 1987–8 onwards. It extended its campaign to England, and to attacks on

British security-force personnel on the European continent, the latter being more successful in killing members of the British armed forces and in generating publicity. However, the IRA suffered several notable reversals. In May 1987 it lost eight men in an attack on Loughall RUC police station which had been staked out by the SAS. It regularly made 'mistakes' which brought it almost universal condemnation, notably the murder of two Australian tourists travelling through the Benelux countries. The most notorious 'mistake' was the murder of 11 Protestant civilians and the injury of 63 others after a bomb at a Remembrance Day ceremony in Enniskillen in November 1987. In consequence Sinn Féin was unable to reap any electoral benefits from nationalist discontent over the pace of reform in Northern Ireland, and its leaders increased the number of times in which they criticized IRA actions, and circumscribed what they regarded as legitimate modes of armed struggle.

However, there is a long tradition of British policy-making in Ireland of ineffectively combining reform and repression (Townshend, 1983), even when nationalist paramilitaries are engaging in counter-productive actions. This tradition survived the AIA. New repressive measures against freedom of expression, introduced in the wake of Thatcher's anger when the IRA killed eight off-duty soldiers in August 1988, include the following: the Home Secretary's broadcasting ban on Sinn Féin, a legal political party (albeit in imitation of a similar ban by the Irish government); the requirement in the Elected Authorities Act, 1989, that all councillors in Northern Ireland take an oath repudiating the use of violence; and the removal of the right of the accused to have no inferences drawn from their silence by judges directing juries. The latter action was announced during the trial of three Irish people (the Winchester Three) exercising their common law 'right to silence' (see p. 274, n. 6). Making the Prevention of Terrorism Act permanent, despite its being in conflict with the judgements of the European Court of Human Rights, also did not help efforts to win minority confidence in the forces of order.

The AIA, at least in the public relations outputs of both governments, has led to some improvements in cross-border security operations, the sharing of intelligence between the two governments, the Irish government's signature of the European Convention on the Suppression of Terrorism, and, eventually, may lead to improved extradition arrangements, but there is no dramatic overall success story to report in these domains. The British authorities insisted on the legally less tractable device of extradition instead of making use of the Criminal Law Jurisdiction Act, which has a better track-record in the arrest, conviction, and jailing of paramilitary fugitives – presumably because of sovereignty-prerogatives, or their lack of faith in their Irish counterparts (a sentiment which is warmly reciprocated). The security policies of the British authorities appeared to be incapable of ending protracted paramilitary activity, and indeed in 1991 and early 1992 even the objective of containment appeared to be being less successfully met. In its public relations British security-policy after 1985 still seemed to merit the satirical description in Adrian Mitchell's poem, 'A Tourist Guide to England':

> 'No. Please understand.
> We understand the Irish.
> Because we've been sending soldiers to Ireland
> For hundreds and hundreds of years.'

British minsters equivocated between saying on the one hand that terrorism can be defeated, as a separate and discrete policy objective, and on the other that the IRA cannot be defeated militarily but only as part of a broader political settlement – as Peter Brooke suggested in the winter of 1989. However, it was evident to everybody else that until security and other public policies marched hand-in-hand the AIA could not deliver the framework for a long-term settlement.

Conclusion

In late 1989 and early 1990 there was evidence of disillusionment with the AIA amongst its supporters, both outside and inside Northern Ireland. The AIA, while entrenched, appeared to have become 'machinery for muddling through' (Thompson, 1989), or 'direct rule with a green tinge' (Bew and Patterson, 1991). Unionists remained adamant in their opposition to the AIA; nationalists remained disappointed at the pace and scale of reform. There were tempered hopes that the reforming momentum of the Agreement could be restored (Boyle and Hadden, 1989), and the Labour party promised to revitalize the AIA if it won the next British general election (McNamara *et al.*, 1988). Yet the emergent consensus of commentators was that the AIA had merely created a new stalemate; coercive consociationalism had run up against the limits of entrenched antagonisms. Northern Ireland's political élites lacked the autonomy, confidence, and capacity to negotiate a political accommodation which their communities would accept. However, against this unpromising background, the Northern Ireland Secretary, Peter Brooke, embarked upon a new labour of Sisyphus in what some predicted would be the last British-directed voluntary power-sharing initiative likely to occur in twentieth-century Ireland.

Notes

1. The unreferenced material in this chapter is based on the same materials cited in Ch. 6: Note 1.

2. At a micro-level the Maryfield secretariat has become a mechanism through which nationalist politicians can relay their constituents' grievances.

3. This decision led to a break-away faction being formed, Republican Sinn Féin, under the leadership of southern republicans who had been active in the 1956–62 'border campaign' and had been effectively displaced from senior positions in the republican movement by northern militants in 1975–6.

4. Interview with B. O'Leary 17 Oct. 1989.

5. When Lord Prior was asked whether Hailsham's hostility to reforms in Northern Ireland was based on his preoccupation with constitutional issues or upon unionist convictions he replied it was 'motivated mostly by his unionist connections . . . There's a statue to one of his ancestors in Northern Ireland quite close to Hillsborough . . . He was very much a Northern Irishman, and that at times came through' (interview with B. O'Leary, 14 Nov. 1990).

6. There was less sympathy for the Winchester Three, who were convicted of conspiracy to murder, having been found in grounds near to the home of Secretary of State Tom King. However, the Irish public, and British civil libertarians, were concerned by the fact that the three were tried in Winchester, a garrison town, and that after they had decided to invoke their common-law right to remain silent the government announced that it was going to remove this right in the case of suspected terrorists. The Winchester Three were later released by the Court of Appeal on the grounds that the fairness of their trial had been prejudiced by remarks made by both Tom King and Lord Denning.

7. Over two years later, in September 1988, 60 per cent of Protestants polled by *Fortnight* declared that they disagreed with 'protest action against the Agreement', while 37 per cent continued to favour such activities (*Irish Political Studies*, 1989, 4: 159).

8. The allusion was biblical: Gideon, an Old Testament paramilitary, reduced

the size of his army to its most valiant core and was more successful in war as a result.

9. Enoch Powell speaking at the Carlyle Club, Peterhouse College, Cambridge, 1989.

10. *Irish Times*, 21 Apr. 1986. Reverend Ivan Foster, DUP assembly member for Fermanagh, made his case with strained logic: if Gadaffi's haven for terrorism merited Reagan's raid on Tripoli, then surely a nuclear strike on the Irish Republic by Britain was in order. The Reverend may have been unaware that a nuclear strike on 'IRA bases' would have considerable fall-out upon his constituents.

11. *Irish Times*, 20 June 1986.

12. The new Conservatives badly damaged their credibility by foolish consistency. They called for the introduction of the 'poll tax' to Northern Ireland as a sign of the region's full integration within the UK. This gesture 'was magnificent, but it wasn't politics' to paraphrase what a French general said of the charge of the Light Brigade.

13. Protestant respondents shared these judgements, albeit for different reasons: a mere 3 per cent of them agreed that the AIA had led to an improvement in the position of the unionist community.

14. Harry West (former leader of the UUP, 1974–9), Austin Ardill (former deputy leader of VUP), and David McNarry proposed offering power-sharing to the SDLP in the wake of the AIA. However, Hume dismissed their informal talks with SDLP leaders because the unionists wanted the suspension of the IGC, and because the West group was no longer influential within the UUP (*Irish Times*, 6 Mar. 1986).

15. Of Catholics polled 57 per cent approved of the SDLP–Sinn Féin talks, while 32 per cent did not; of Protestants polled 8 per cent approved whereas 83 per cent did not (*Irish Political Studies*, 1989, 4: 160).

16. Millar became the *Irish Times*'s London editor; Currie was elected as a Fine Gael candidate for Dáil Éireann, and stood unsuccessfully for the Irish presidency in 1990; and Cushnahan joined Fine Gael and stood as one of its candidates for the European parliament in 1989.

17. See Ch. 3: 129–30 and Ch. 5: 206–8, and McGarry and O'Leary (forthcoming: Ch. 3).

18. Students will profit from comparing Thomas Boston's forensic examination of neo-conservative explanations of black disadvantage in the USA with David Smith's, Gerald Chambers's, Bob Cormack's and Bob Osborne's evaluation of unionist academics' explanations of Catholic disadvantage in Northern Ireland (Boston, 1988; Smith, 1987a, 1987b, 1987c; Smith and Chambers, 1991; Cormack and Osborne, 1991).

19. Smith and Chambers list nine: however, as they are aware, the first of these, namely the thesis that 'Protestants and Catholics belong to separate labour markets and the Catholic sector offers fewer opportunities than the

Protestant one in relation to the pool of labour belonging to it' (Miller and Osborne, 1983), is not an explanation independent of discrimination because it presupposes ethnic discrimination in labour markets.

20. They observe that there is a simple but expensive policy-solution: pay a constant amount of child-benefit regardless of whether the male member of the household is in or out of work.

21. There is a misprint in Smith and Chambers (1991: 194). The Catholic and Protestant figures are transposed.

22. Kevin McNamara, the Labour party spokesperson on Northern Ireland, pointed out that the UK spent even more lobbying in the USA to try to defeat the innocuous MacBride principles than in its efforts to stop the publication of *Spycatcher* (Doherty, 1988).

23. In other words police officers were to accompany soldiers everywhere, and take charge of apprehending and arresting suspects.

24. See the book by Ian Paisley jun. (1991).

25. Interviews with B. O'Leary 14 June 1989 and 19 Oct. 1989. FitzGerald complains that six years after the agreement one third of UDR patrols remain unaccompanied by the police (FitzGerald, 1991: 552).

26. The comparison is deliberately with those civilians who are eligible to serve in the UDR.

27. IIP Agenda data-base.

28. In the PSI survey 68 per cent of Catholics agreed with the proposition that 'the UDR treat Protestants better' *and* 27 per cent of Protestants also agreed with the proposition (Smith and Chambers, 1987c: 125).

8
Transcending Antagonism?
Resolving Northern Ireland in
the 1990s

*Is it not true that somebody outside Ireland will see more in
common between two Irishmen one of whom is a Unionist than
between two Unionists one of whom is an Irishman? . . . have
not you and I, Canon Elliott, got more in common than you
have with the Unionists in Great Britain?*
(Question posed by Deputy Peter Barry, Foreign Minister of
the Republic of Ireland).

*The trouble between me and you, between Northerners and
Southerners, is that we have things that divide us and things
that unite us, but . . . the animosity between those who are
totally separate is often less significant than between those who
are separate but have certain features of common identity*
(Answer given by Canon Eric Elliot, Church of Ireland minister
from Belfast at the New Ireland Forum, 1984, no 10: 18–19)

The last six chapters outlined the evolution of the politics of
antagonism in Northern Ireland. Historic Ulster was the site of
British settler colonialism and the greatest obstacle to British and
Irish nation-building in Ireland. The settlers' descendants blocked
nationalist movements to win autonomy or independence for Ireland in the nineteenth century; and were strong enough to resist
incorporation into independent Ireland after World War I. Unionists
won an ethically and politically contestable partition of the island,
and under the formal institutions of the Westminster model of
representative government built a system of hegemonic control over
the nationalist minority in Northern Ireland that persisted until the

late 1960s. Since then the region has been the site of the ethnic war described in Chapter 1. British efforts at arbitration and promoting a consociational settlement have failed to produce a durable solution; and so have the joint efforts of both the British and Irish governments since the Anglo-Irish Agreement. This historical track-record makes it tempting to conclude, as many do, that there can be no solution to the present conflict until one ethnic community triumphs at the expense of the other, or until they wear one another out and into compromise.

Any enduring, democratic, and legitimate settlement to the Northern Ireland imbroglio must address the interlinked causes of the present conflict:

- the national conflict between the two ethnic communities resident in the same political space who wish, in principle, to belong to two different nation-states;
- the ethnic divisions formed in colonial conquest and sustained through modernization by the sharp religious differentiation of the original communities;
- the patterns of state-development in Great Britain and the Republic of Ireland which adversely affect ethnic relations in Northern Ireland;
- the legacies of hatred, suspicion, and distrust which are daily reinforced by cycles of political violence and repression;
- the persistence of socio-economic inequalities between (and within) the two ethnic communities that inhibit a politics of accommodation.

The first of these interlinked causes of the conflict is fundamental. Even though it is true that not everybody within Northern Ireland falls into the unionist or nationalist camp (as survey data often show – e.g. Curtice and Gallagher, 1990), and that not everybody who does is uncompromisingly nationalist or unionist, the national conflict is nevertheless the primary one that needs to be addressed. Moreover, scepticism is in order about polling evidence which suggests that the two populations of Northern Ireland are more moderate in their respective forms of nationalist extremism than their voting and militaristic behaviour suggests. 'In Northern Ireland people try to sound more moderate than they really feel in replying to interviewers. I would suspect, then, that the proportion of Protestants who hanker after majority rule, and of Catholics who want a united Ireland, is higher than the survey evidence indicates, and that the proportion of Catholics who would accept integration with Britain, or of both communities who would settle for power-sharing, is lower than the data suggest' Whyte (1990: 82–3).

This chapter assesses solutions to the conflict canvassed by political parties and political actors, and how far they can remedy the causes of antagonism. We proceed by first evaluating the set of macro-constitutional solutions canvassed by the contending parties; second, by evaluating the merits of the rival decision-making rules that could be used to govern the region; and finally by assessing the grand public-policy objectives which government(s) might pursue to resolve the conflict. We argue that joint authority combined with maximum self-government for the peoples of Northern Ireland (preferably based on power-sharing) is the most feasible of the desirable solutions, and the most desirable of the feasible solutions.

Macro-constitutional solutions: which state and what form of government?

If the immediate likelihood of a European super-state is ruled out then there are five ways in which Northern Ireland's statehood could be arranged now, or in the future; and there are three territorial forms through which its statehood might be organized. The resulting options and sub-options are displayed in Table 8.1. Each option and sub-option is capable of much further sub-variation and permutation but Table 8.1 presents the major variants that have been canvassed by political parties, policy-makers, or academics. Our assessment first examines the vertical dimension of the matrix in Table 8.1 and later its horizontal counterpart.

(1) *An integral part of an Irish state.*

Northern Ireland could be incorporated into an all-Ireland state as Irish nationalist parties want, either now or in the long run. This option has considerable support within the British Isles. In the JRRT/Gallup polls conducted in Great Britain, the Republic of Ireland, and Northern Ireland in July 1991[1] a united Ireland was the most-favoured first-preference solution of the citizens of the

Table 8.1 Northern Ireland's macro-constitutional options

The state form of which NI forms part is	Northern Ireland is				
	(1) part of an all-Ireland state	(2) part of the UK state	(3) an independent state	(4) repartitioned into sub-regions of the UK and Ireland	(5) under the joint authority of the UK and Irish states
unitary	1.i. *centralized unitary state:* Sinn Féin (1986–) & Fianna Fáil (1983–) ii. *decentralized unitary state:* Fianna Fáil (1983–)	2.i. *direct rule:* O'Brien (1980) 2. ii. *centralized integration:* UUP 2. iii. *devolved integration:* DUP & within UUP 2. iv. *electoral integration:* Roberts (1987), Aughey (1989), Wilson (1989) 2. v. *devolved power-sharing:* APNI	3.i. *unitary state with power-sharing:* NUPRG (1979), de Paor (1990) 3.ii. *unitary state with majority rule:* some loyalist paramilitaries (1985–)	4.i. *four versions of British and Irish Ulster:* Kennedy (1990) 4. ii. *minor border adjustments:* various military figures (1972–)	5.i. *centralized dual direct rule:* (New Ireland Forum, 1984c). 5.ii. *joint authority with provisions for co-operative devolution:* Kilbrandon (1984), Dent (1988), Kenny (1991), and authors of this book (1992) NB. All forms of shared authority arguably would be con/federal, even if GB and the Republic remained unitary
federal	1. iii. *federal Irish state:* Fine Gael, SDLP, Sinn Féin (1972–86)	2. vi. *federal UK:* Smyth (1987)	3. iii. *Swiss model of 'cantonization + communization'?* partly suggested by Fennell (1989)	(–)	5. iii. *(joint authority with provisions for 'cantonization'?)*
con-federal	iv. *confederal Ireland:* Fine Gael (1979–), Palley (1990)	*(confederal UK within confederal Europe?)*	3. iv. *(independence within European confederation?)*	(–)	5. iv. *(joint authority within European confederation?):* hinted at by the SDLP 1980s –

Republic (41 per cent) and those of Great Britain (21 per cent).[2] However, the same poll showed that it was the third most-favoured first-preference solution in Northern Ireland – backed by just 14 per cent of respondents in the region (O'Leary, 1991b). Moreover, this option did not command majority first-preference support in any of the three jurisdictions, although no other option canvassed passed this test. Even though support for militant Irish nationalism amongst Catholics is underestimated in the JRRT/Gallup polls, as in all other polls (at least compared with their voting behaviour),[3] we can be confident that an all-Ireland state is vehemently opposed by a majority of Northern Ireland's electorate. Therefore this option cannot be implemented with the consent of a majority in the region. In a poll conducted in February 1988 a mere 2 per cent of Protestants chose membership of an Irish state as the best form of government for Northern Ireland. By contrast 32 per cent of Catholics chose this option as the best one, and a further 22 per cent considered it acceptable. In January 1990 60 per cent of Catholics polled considered either a federal Ireland or a unitary Irish state acceptable whereas 10 per cent of Protestants accepted a federal Ireland, and 3 per cent a unitary Ireland (*Irish Political Studies*, 1991, 6: 146). In the JRRT/Gallup polls 2 per cent of Protestants favoured the integration of Northern Ireland into the Republic of Ireland as their first preference, and a further 1 per cent chose it as their second preference.

Ulster Protestants believe that they are British, at least in political citizenship, and that as a local majority their preferences should be 'paramount' in determining the state in which the territory of Northern Ireland is located. They think they would be economically impoverished, politically dominated, and religiously oppressed in an all-Ireland state, and have regularly demonstrated their willingness to fight to prevent such an assimilation, in 1886, 1893, 1911–14, 1920–2, and most ferociously during 1971–6. Irish nationalists have failed to persuade Ulster Protestants that they are Irish, and that an all-Ireland state is a desirable proposition. All constitutional parties in the Republic of Ireland and the British Labour party (McNamara *et al.*, 1988) formally advocate achieving Irish unity by consent. However, short of demographic transformations it is difficult to see how even a simple majority for Irish unity by consent can be built in Northern Ireland by British and Irish parties.[4]

If widespread consent for Irish unity could be built then the national conflict, ethnic antagonisms, and political violence would diminish. There are also 'technocratic anti-partitionist' arguments (Lyne, 1990) which provide persuasive reasons why an all-Ireland polity might deliver widespread economic benefits. However, the enterprise begs so many questions. Irish unity by the consent of a bare majority of Northern Ireland's electorate would require 16 per cent of Northern Irish Protestants to be persuaded of its merits and the entirety of Northern Irish Catholics to be mobilized as Irish nationalists, an outcome unlikely to materialize in the next decade. But even if 'bare consent' materialized before the year 2,000, implementing Irish unification without substantial cross-community support might provoke more severe violence and a unilateral declaration of independence by Ulster loyalists. Even dramatic unilateral concessions by nationalists – such as a decision by the IRA to lay down their arms, by Sinn Féin to commit itself to peaceful constitutional change, and by all nationalist parties to give Northern Ireland dramatic autonomy within the new all-Ireland state – might not persuade more than a tiny fraction of Protestants to consider changing their national identity. The form of persuasion exercised by the IRA, and other nationalist paramilitaries, has been utterly counter-productive.

If an all-Ireland state cannot be accomplished by consent in the foreseeable future, could it be accomplished by coercion? Yes. In fact that is the only way in which it could be accomplished in the immediate future.[5] The British and Irish states could co-operate to coerce Northern Ireland into the Republic of Ireland. Two authors have set out a detailed scenario in which they show, to their satisfaction, how the British state could accomplish this endeavour by using its military prowess and its power to impose economic sanctions (Rowthorn and Wayne, 1988). However, there are two major problems with Irish 'unification' by coercion. It is not obvious that the treatment is ethically or politically better than the present maladies; and it is not clear why the British and Irish states should wish to embark upon such an enterprise. Forcing unionists into the Republic would be done against their will, and might provoke (a) a semi-genocidal reaction against Northern Ireland's more vulnerable nationalist communities, (b) rebellion by the RUC and UDR/RIR, and (c) mass-migration within the British Isles. The Republic's government and electorate would not welcome managing a recalcitrant minority, and even supposing that the new Ireland created by coercion came into existence the causes of antagonism would simply have been displaced rather than remedied. The national conflict would have been 'resolved' in favour of one community at the expense of the other. Short of the Irish government building a new system of hegemonic control over Ulster Protestants it is difficult to see how the new Irish state could generate stability, let alone legitimacy.

(2) *Northern Ireland as part of the UK state.*

In the 1990s Northern Ireland could remain within the UK as unionists insist it should, and as the British Conservative party suggests it wants. This option in some respects is the status quo, albeit qualified by the Anglo-Irish Agreement. The status quo is surely the problem, rather than the solution. The status quo is characterized by the levels of conflict documented in Chapter 1; and is the by-product of multiple historic injustices which it is in the self-interest of the British and Irish governments to rectify.

Some claim that because of the Anglo-Irish Agreement, and past British equivocation, the option of integrating Northern Ireland into the UK has never really been tried. We shall review these arguments presently. However, the option of integrating Northern Ireland into the UK was the first preference of a mere 13 per cent of respondents in Great Britain, and of 6 per cent of respondents in the Irish Republic in the JRRT/Gallup polls of July 1991; but it was the most-favoured first-preference of the citizens of Northern Ireland, with 39 per cent support (O'Leary, 1992). Although it was the first-preference of 61 per cent of Protestants only 8 per cent of Catholics felt the same way. Indeed the percentage of Catholics supporting British integration (as either their first or second preference) in the JRRT/Gallup polls marked a sharp fall from the more substantial levels of backing expressed in polls in 1989 and 1990 (*Irish Political Studies*, 1991, 6: 146–7).

Nationalists argue that the Irish people were denied their right to self-determination when the island of Ireland was partitioned, and unjustly and badly partitioned. Many of them believe that the Government of Ireland Act of 1920 and the Treaty between Britain and Ireland in 1921 were imposed by British might, and that the Irish state is right to claim sovereignty over Northern Ireland. The former Irish Taoiseach (1979–81, 1982, 1987–92) Charles Haughey, argued that Northern Ireland was 'a failed political entity' in which systematic political domination and economic discrimination has been endemic since its inception, a view which has considerable evidence to support it. British government has so far not 'solved' any of the major causes of conflict, indeed the claim that Northern Ireland is (exclusively) British is part of the problem. Ulster unionists have never been able to persuade more than a minority of Catholics that they or the UK state can treat them as full and equal citizens and administer the region justly or impartially; and as long as Northern Ireland remains an unqualified part of the UK there is no reason to suppose that the IRA's campaign will stop.

Retaining Northern Ireland is not a Great British priority: their governments stay primarily because the alternatives appear worse. The Great British, whether their governments, political parties, or their peoples do not regard Northern Ireland as truly or unequivocally British. In the JRRT/Gallup polls the Great British public gave most support to options which entail relinquishing British sovereignty over Northern Ireland or sharing it with the Republic (O'Leary, 1992). Despite Margaret Thatcher's assertion at the time of Sands's hunger strike that Northern Ireland 'is as British as Finchley', successive British governments, including her own, refused to integrate Northern Ireland fully into the UK. They have recognized since 1972 that there must be an Irish dimension for the government of Northern Ireland. Nevertheless some unionists argue that it has been the form of British government in Northern Ireland that has been the problem, not its presence, and we discuss these electoral integrationist arguments below.

(3)   *Northern Ireland as an independent state.*

The UDA's think-tank, the New Ulster Political Research Group (1979), the former British Prime Minister James Callaghan (Moore and Crimmins (1991), and the Dublin historian Liam de Paor (1990) are amongst those who have canvassed the independence option. As with the Scottish nationalists 'independence within the EC' is the only feasible mode in which independence for Northern Ireland would be advocated. However, independence is strongly opposed by the vast majority of the electorate within Northern Ireland. It was the first preference of 7 per cent of Protestants and 4 per cent of Catholics in a poll reported in April 1988, and acceptable to only a further 11 per cent of Protestants and 4 per cent of Catholics (Wilson, 1988). In the JRRT/Gallup polls of July 1991 independence was far more widely supported outside Northern Ireland than within it: 20 per cent of the Great British and 16 per cent of respondents in the Republic backed independence as their first-preference solution, compared with 10 per cent of the electorate in Northern Ireland (O'Leary, 1992). However, in this poll Catholics (12 per cent) favoured independence marginally more than Protestants (8 per cent), and, interestingly independence attracted a high level of second-preference support across both denominations (26 per cent of Protestants and Catholics).

Most unionists reject independence because it would mean they would no longer be British,[6] and leave them bereft of the material benefits of the British connection, whereas nationalists reject it both because they would not be part of the Irish Republic and because they would be a minority within the new state. The independence option appears just because it is like splitting the difference: both sides lose their most-preferred nation-state. However, the conditions for a stable political accommodation within an independent state would not be present: unionists would not be prepared to endorse widespread affirmative action in the new state; and both commu nities would differ radically over how law and order should be administered If the two communities, especially the unionists, could not share power under British sovereignty they are unlikely to do so under independence. One advocate of independence maintains that '60 per cent of the population could only oppress 40 per cent with British backing and consent' and that with external guarantees 'the unionists could not oppress the nationalists without bringing their province into chaos and ruin' (de Paor, 1990: 158). We are not so sanguine: some ethnic communities elsewhere in the world have shown themselves very willing to risk chaos and ruin in order to win perceived security and freedom from domination (*vide* what was 'Yugoslavia'). Moreover, since some republicans would see independence as a half-way house to Irish unity, the IRA would continue its campaign for a united Ireland after the Great British had gone.

British and Irish policy-makers reject independence for Northern Ireland as unthinkable, primarily because they do not believe such a state could be stable. Article 1 of the Anglo-Irish Agreement allows a majority in Northern Ireland to determine whether the territory is to belong to the UK or to the Republic, but it does not permit such a majority to choose independence. Independence is likely to materialize only in the aftermath of a precipitate British withdrawal, but in such a scenario the new state would not be founded upon principles of accommodation and is therefore not worth advocating. However, to rule out independence is not to rule out giving the population of Northern Ireland the maximum degree of self-government compatible with mutual political accommodation.

(4) *Northern Ireland is destroyed and its territory and people partitioned between the British and Irish states.*

A second, and presumably final, partition of Ulster could be contemplated by the British and Irish governments in the 1990s. Repartition might appear to be fair because it splits the difference between the rival communities. The creation of a smaller, more homogeneously unionist and Protestant, British region in north-eastern Ireland, and a larger Republic of Ireland which incorporated the majority of Northern Ireland's present nationalist and Catholic community might satisfy the first preferences of most members of each community. However, the JRRT/Gallup polls in July 1991 showed that repartition attracted a mere 1 per cent level of first-preference support within Northern Ireland; while 2 per cent of Protestants favoured it, 0 per cent of Catholics concurred (O'Leary, 1992). Repartition also had low levels of first-preference support in the Republic (5 per cent) and in Great Britain (4 per cent). Not surprisingly repartition proposals are not publicly favoured by any British, Irish, or Northern Irish political party. Repartition has been canvassed as a solution only by academics prepared to think the unthinkable (Compton, 1981; Kennedy, 1990), and the most intelligent, lucid, and detailed case for repartition is advanced in Liam Kennedy's *Two Ulsters: A case for repartition* (1986).

Organizing a just and stable repartition would, however, be problematic given the distribution of the relevant populations (see Figure 2.2, p. 59). In three out of Kennedy's four possible partitions of Northern Ireland, west Belfast (the heartland of the IRA), would remain in British Ulster; and his most extensive repartition would still leave substantial minorities on the 'wrong' side of the new borders, and make west Belfast Ireland's west Berlin but without the material prosperity. There would be major problems of consent and coercion in any major repartition. At which level of geographical or administrative unit would people be given the right to exercise self-determination? Would it be feasible to compensate those who would lose out in the new arrangements? The numerous lives lost in previous British-administered partitions of their former possessions (India, Palestine, and Ireland) cannot inspire confidence in the merits of any proposal to rectify Lloyd George's botched settlement of 1921. British policy-makers have toyed with the idea of minor repartitions on narrow security-grounds, and there has often been talk of transferring the village of Crossmaglen to the Republic of Ireland. Yet broader security reasons have usually counted against minor repartitions: 'To give an inch would give the IRA the feel that [just] one more push . . .' (Merlyn Rees, interview with B. O'Leary, 18 December 1990).

(5) *Northern Ireland is placed under the joint jurisdiction of the UK and Irish states.*

Finally, Northern Ireland could be made subject to the joint authority of the British and Irish states. This option involves the appealing idea of splitting the difference: both sides would gain because their national identity is respected by membership of their preferred nation-state, and by being governed by their preferred state; and both sides would lose because their national aspiration is accomplished at the expense of sharing the regional territory with another nation-state and another national community. However, given that the status quo is one of British sovereignty over Northern Ireland, tempered by the Anglo-Irish Agreement, it must be honestly acknowledged that Ulster unionists would experience an actual loss from joint authority, whereas nationalists face a speculative opportunity-cost from the creation of joint authority: the prospect of immediate or medium-term national reunification.[7]

Joint authority did not receive serious attention from policy-makers before the New Ireland Forum met in 1983–4,[8] where it emerged as the third-preference of the convened nationalist parties.[9] The Forum Report argued that joint authority would give 'equal validity to the two traditions in Northern Ireland and would reflect the current reality that the people of the North are divided in their allegiances' (New Ireland Forum, 1984c: §8.1). It admitted it would 'be an unprecedented approach to the unique realities that have evolved within Ireland and between Britain and Ireland' (ibid.: §8.2). Without much elaboration the report declared that joint authority would involve shared rule of Northern Ireland; directly in the first place, but with provision for the subsequent devolution of powers to a locally elected assembly and executive. The idea of joint authority in the Forum Report implied a permanent system of dual direct rule in Northern Ireland, with British and Irish ministers governing the region.[10] Joint direct rule, through legal, policing, and military organizations responsible to the appointees of both states would be tantamount to joint sovereignty.[11]

In response to the Forum a voluntary inquiry of UK-based academics, journalists, and politicians produced the Kilbrandon Report (1984). The majority on this inquiry advocated a different form of joint authority from that contained in the Forum Report: 'co-operative devolution' (Kenny, 1990). Under 'co-operative devolution' a five-person executive, consisting of one representative of the UK and Irish governments, and three (elected) representatives from Northern Ireland, would govern the region and resolve any disputes by majority rule. Co-operative devolution would provide direct representation for unionists and nationalists from Northern Ireland, thereby making the system of government non-colonial, and create incentives for such representatives to participate in the executive. The Kilbrandon Report made clear that in its preferred model the British government would be the dominant partner.

Joint authority is a comparatively novel idea for Northern Ireland, and until recently had been widely dismissed and won little public support. In a poll reported in April 1988 1 per cent of Protestants and 12 per cent of Catholics chose it as their first-preference solution, while an additional 4 per cent of Protestants and 17 of Catholics declared it would be 'acceptable' (*Irish Political Studies*, 1989, 4: 159). However, in the JRRT/Gallup polls of July 1991 respondents were given the opportunity to appraise the merits of Northern Ireland having 'a devolved government jointly guaranteed by and responsible to the British and Irish governments' (O'Leary, 1992). This more attractively worded 'democratized condominium' option attracted the first-preference support of 19 per cent of those interviewed in the Republic, 10 per cent of those in Great Britain, and 7 per cent of those in Northern Ireland; and the second-preference support of 26 per cent of those in Great Britain, 25 per cent of those in the Republic, and 11 per cent of those in Northern Ireland.

The JRRT/Gallup polls suggested a considerable convergence of public opinion in Great Britain and the Republic; respondents agreed that both British and Irish dimensions need recognition in Northern Ireland. Citizens of Great Britain are very willing to give the Irish government a major role in any new settlement (49 per cent), a considerable fraction is prepared to grant it a minor role (25 per cent), and only 11 per cent express the wish to exclude the Irish government from any new settlement. In the Republic there is widespread willingness to accept a 'British dimension' in any future settlement, with 40 per cent envisaging a minor role for the British government and 28 per cent a major role, compared with 24 per cent of die-hards who see no role for the British government (O'Leary, 1992: Table 5).[12] However, the same poll shows that a democratized condominium enjoys much greater support amongst Catholics than amongst Protestants within Northern Ireland.

Given unionists' dislike of the Anglo-Irish Agreement it is not surprising that they reject joint authority. Moreover, the few critics who have examined its merits have usually observed that most condominium-precedents have been colonial (e.g. Boyle and Hadden, 1985: 31). They have also maintained that joint authority would be undemocratic because it would have to be imposed against the wishes of a majority of Northern Ireland's citizens.

Proponents of joint authority and/or a democratized condominium can reply that there are mechanisms for making joint authority function democratically and accountably. The more detailed elaborations of joint authority (Dent, 1988; Kenny, 1991; and Kilbrandon, 1984) have often avoided the intricacies of how taxation, public expenditure, revenue-raising, economic management, international representation, and parliamentary representation of Northern Ireland in Westminster and Dáil Éireann would operate.[13] However, these difficulties could, in principle, be resolved in negotiations between the British and Irish governments, with some consultation with nationalists and unionists in Northern Ireland. When answering the undemocratic charge proponents of joint authority reply pragmatically that any macro-constitutional solution, apart from returning Northern Ireland to unionist majority control, has to be imposed against the first preferences of a majority in the region, including British direct rule; and they observe that the British and Irish governments have already imposed the AIA against the wishes of a majority of the region's electorate. In a principled rather

than pragmatic way proponents of joint authority can argue that
Northern Ireland cannot be a successful democracy if it is to be
purely British or purely Irish. Furthermore, they can maintain that
since both communities in Northern Ireland regularly democratically
express their wish to be governed by either the British or the Irish
states there is no good reason why they should not be (partly)
governed by both these states. Finally, since the governments and
electorates of both Great Britain and the Republic of Ireland have
direct stakes in Northern Ireland there is no argument in democratic
theory that can show why they should not create a form of shared
political responsibility in which the British, Irish, and Northern Irish
governments and peoples participate.

Comparing macro-options

The best way to assess the merit of joint authority properly is to
contrast it with the other macro-constitutional proposals. Tables
8.2 (a) and (b) present our judgements on the acceptability of
the five macro-constitutional options open to Northern Ireland's
nationalists and unionists, and the British and Irish electorates.
Table 8.2 (a) assumes that the British electorate – as opposed to
particular Conservative and Labour politicians – has weakly held
preferences: they would probably accept any solution which resulted
in peace. However, as the JRRT/Gallup polls data reveal, the British
electorate's combined first- and second-preference options strongly
favour either relinquishing British sovereignty over Northern Ireland
or sharing it with the Republic (O'Leary, 1991b). Table 8.2 (a)
assumes, also consistent with evidence from polls, that the Irish
electorate has more strongly held preferences than the British
electorate, strongly dislikes undiluted British rule in Northern
Ireland, and is prepared to accept all-Ireland or the joint authority
options, and perhaps the independence option. Table 8.2 (a) naturally
assumes that the preferences of the two political communities which
matter in Northern Ireland are very strongly held.

The preference-structures of the four communities can be crudely
expressed as follows:

- Irish nationalists in Northern Ireland prefer (a) united Ireland
  options to (e) joint authority; and they prefer joint authority

to (b) undiluted British rule in Northern Ireland or (c) independence or (d) a new partition. They are mostly indifferent between the latter three options, although the order in which we have presented them reflects our judgement of their most likely preference-ranking if they were obliged to choose.

- Ulster unionists prefer (b) undiluted British rule in Northern Ireland to (c) independence; independence to (d) a new partition or (e) joint authority; and any of the above to (a) any form of united Ireland.

- British voters are indifferent between (a) a united Ireland or (c) an independent Northern Ireland as their preferred options; and they prefer (e) joint authority to (b) undiluted British rule in Northern Ireland or (d) a new partition.

- Irish voters prefer (a) united Ireland options to (e) joint authority; and joint authority to (c) independence, which they prefer over either (b) undiluted British rule in Northern Ireland or (d) a new partition.

In simple terms the four political communities preference-structures can be expressed as follows (where > means 'is preferred to', and '=' means 'is indifferent between'):

Nationalists in Northern Ireland:	$a > e > b = c = d$
Unionists in Northern Ireland:	$b > c > d = e > a$
Great British public:	$a = c > e > b = d$
Irish Republic's citizens:	$a > e > c > b = d$.

If each community is given an equal weight in determining the future of Northern Ireland then a united Ireland, (a), would win easily as it is the first preference of three of the four communities. But a fair objection to this result would be that it does not reflect differential preference-intensities across the four communities. We may consider it fair to rule out a united Ireland because each community should be able to veto its most unacceptable option, and it is the most unacceptable solution for unionists. However, on the same decision-rule option (b), undiluted British rule in Northern Ireland, must be ruled out because this solution is the (or one of the) most unacceptable solution(s) to three of the four communities. Exactly the same reasoning excludes (d), a new partition, because it is considered an equally bad solution by three of the four communities.

Table 8.2 The acceptability and likely impact of macro-solutions for Northern Ireland

8.2 (a) Acceptability of the five macro-solutions

Macro-solution	to nationalists in Northern Ireland (preferences are very intense)	Is the macro-solution acceptable?		
		to unionists in Northern Ireland (preferences are very intense)	to the British electorate (preferences are mostly weakly held)	to the Irish electorate (preferences are mostly moderately held)
NI becomes part of an all-Ireland state	yes	no	very acceptable to 33%	very acceptable to 55%
NI stays part of the UK	no	yes	very acceptable to 5–10%	very acceptable to 5%
NI as an independent state	no	no	very acceptable to 25–33%	very acceptable to 35%
NI partitioned between Britain and Ireland	no	no	very acceptable to 5%	very acceptable to 5%
NI governed by British and Irish authority	yes	no	very acceptable to 25%	very acceptable to 45%

Note: The estimates of the levels of acceptability of the five options in Great Britain and the Republic of Ireland are based on poll-data tapping first and second preferences (O'Leary, 1991b) which is why the estimates across the five options do not add to 100.

8.2 (b) The likely impact of macro-solutions

What is the likely impact of the macro-solution in the medium term?

Macro-solution	on promoting political and legal reform and ethnic equality	on controlling political violence	on promoting political accommodation between the two communities	is the solution economically sustainable in worst-case scenarios?
NI becomes part of an all-Ireland state	unpredictable	poor prospects threatens more severe civil war	poor prospects	no
NI stays part of the UK	poor record to date	status quo, i.e. existing civil war	status quo	yes
NI as an independent state	poor prospects	poor prospects – threatens more severe civil war	poor prospects	no
NI partitioned between Britain and Ireland	irrelevant	potentially disastrous war(s) in the short-term, but then matters stabilize	irrelevant	yes
NI governed by British and Irish authority	positive prospects	not much worse than status quo in the short-term but good in the medium-term	no worse than the status quo	yes

On the premises of this argument, in which each community counts equally, and each can veto their worst alternative(s), the ultimate decision-choice must be between the difference-splitting solutions of independence or joint authority. How might this choice be resolved? On the premises of the above argument and evidence it cannot be resolved since both Irish nationalists in Northern Ireland and the Republic prefer joint authority to independence, while both Ulster unionists and the British electorate prefer independence to joint authority. But one further difference-splitting answer is to recommend a form of democratized condominium that maximizes the independence of the peoples of Northern Ireland within the framework of joint authority. Northern Ireland might be given a separate international legal personality, as an autonomous condominium. It might be enabled or encouraged to negotiate a special status within the European Community. Its internal government might consist of a power-sharing executive including representatives of the British and Irish governments (similar to that outlined in Kilbrandon's co-operative devolution proposals), checked and balanced by a locally elected assembly.

If weighting each community's preferences equally (albeit with veto-rights to rule out their worst option(s)) seems an unacceptable way of discussing the best options for Northern Ireland consider Table 8.2 (b), which presents our worst-case judgements of the impact of each of the five macro-constitutional solutions on medium-term prospects for reform, controlling violence, and long-run political accommodation between the rival communities. It also includes our worst-case assessment of the economic viability of each option.[14] The table suggests that each of the five logical ways in which Northern Ireland's statehood can be resolved entails obvious and profound costs, beyond those of violating some community's preferences, and much less obvious and more intangible benefits. However, it is vital to remember that the status quo has considerable, persistent, and predictable costs.

Durable joint authority that takes the form of a democratized condominium[15] (permitting the maximum feasible degree of self-government for the peoples of Northern Ireland) is the best of the five options in our judgement. It is more acceptable to more of the four communities than any other option (other than independence). Moreover, it survives the worst-case evaluations better than the other four options, including independence. It is a better option than repartition because it is more acceptable to more actors – admittedly more so to Irish nationalists and the Irish government than to unionists – and it is a better option than all the others in its potential for promoting the reform of Northern Ireland and controlling political violence.[16]

The presence of the Irish government in a system of joint authority would give a permanent impetus for fair employment and fair administration of justice. One reason why the UK state has not effectively reformed Northern Ireland is just because it is a *British* state. A fully equal Irish dimension (to match a British dimension) is indispensable to promote and implement substantive reforms which would benefit the Irish nationalist minority in Northern Ireland and ensure it genuine equal citizenship. The presence of the Irish government and its security forces, and a jointly supervised security apparatus will make the legitimate policing of nationalist paramilitary violence much easier to accomplish. One firm lesson of Irish history is that Irish nationalists are most successfully coerced by officials from a legitimate Irish state. Indeed hard-line law and order zealots should note that under any system of joint authority the opportunities for effectively administered and co-operative repression of paramilitaries are very good.

Joint authority, in the form of a democratized condominium, provided it was not presented and defended as a short-stay transit-lounge to Irish unification, could perform no worse than the other options in promoting the prospects for a long-term political accommodation. The outraged reaction of Ulster unionists to the AIA suggests that the prospects of promoting peaceful accommodation would at best be medium-term under joint authority, but it is nevertheless an option which we believe survives normative and predictive evaluation better than the others. Architects of a democratized condominium would have to ensure that there were very powerful incentives for unionists to participate within its institutions.[17]

Unitary, federal, and confederal formulae

Critics might argue that the above argument is superficial because 'the devil is in the detail', i.e. each of the options cannot be judged unless their substantive content is examined. Consider then the horizontal dimension of Table 8.1 which is based on the supposition that there are three modes of organizing liberal democratic states: in unitary, federal, or confederal forms. In their turn unitary states, federations, and confederations can be more or less centralized or decentralized, depending upon the structures of government, intergovernmental relations, and the allocation of powers and functions.

Irish unitary, federal, and confederal formulae

An Irish unitary state, advocated by Fianna Fáil in the Irish Republic, does not appeal to unionists (it was acceptable to a mere 3 per cent of Protestant respondents in a *Belfast Telegraph* poll of January 1990) even if it was accompanied by extensive devolution of authority to Northern Ireland. They find it unacceptable because it would vest sovereignty in the hands of the nationalist/Catholic majority in the island of Ireland. The fact that since 1982 it has also been the goal of Sinn Féin and the IRA to obtain a unitary Irish state does nothing to enhance its attractiveness to unionists.

An Irish federation or confederation, by contrast, would have to be either a two-unit federation or confederation, or built upon three or more freshly created political provinces throughout the island of Ireland. The problem with a two-unit entity is that the historical track-record of such political institutions in bi-ethnic societies is disastrous (Vile, 1982). They have proven consistently unstable elsewhere in the world. The problem with any more than two-unit entity is that it would entail a dramatic disruption of the institutional fabric of the Republic of Ireland, a price which neither its political élite nor its people seem prepared to pay.

An Irish confederation would be more acceptable than a federation to unionists both because a confederation is easier to secede from and because the constituent components enjoy greater self-government than in a federation. However, for the same reason it would be opposed by Irish nationalists as unstable and likely to give Ulster Protestants too much power within the confederal unit of Northern Ireland.

British unitary, federal, and confederal formulae

The UK is presently a unitary state. Since 1972 Northern Ireland has been centrally governed, under direct rule from Westminster and the Northern Ireland Office (tempered after November 1985 by the AIA). The centralization of government within the British unitary state has not proved much more legitimate than the Stormont arrangements it superseded, nor has it produced successful conflict-regulation or generated fundamental reform of Northern Ireland's political economy.

Northern Ireland used to have a devolved government within the UK: the Stormont parliament which presided over institutionalized discrimination against Catholics and nationalists. The DUP still contains activists who would like to see majority rule in a devolved government restored: a prospect rejected by nationalists within Northern Ireland, and by the British and Irish governments who insist that a devolved government must enjoy widespread consent across both communities.

All unilateral British attempts to establish an agreed form of devolved government within Northern Ireland have failed. So far bilateral British–Irish fostering of an agreed devolved government has also failed. Historically informed pessimists had good reasons to suppose that the Brooke initiative would go the way of its precursors.

Administrative and electoral integrationists within the unionist bloc maintain that if the UK government resolved that Northern Ireland was part of the Union for ever then the political uncertainty that bedevils the region would end, and the IRA would be demoralized and eventually defeated. This thinking is wishful. A sizeable body of opinion within the UUP favours administrative integration, treating Northern Ireland 'exactly like the rest of the UK'. It is rarely specified which sub-region of the UK they have in mind – Scotland, Wales, Yorkshire, London? The shortest and most elegant response to their contentions is that of Nicholas Scott, former Under-Secretary of State for Northern Ireland: 'Northern Ireland is different, so it must be governed differently.'[18] Moreover, despite the Westminster election results of 1992, there remains strong pressure for political and administrative devolution and differentiation within the UK which cuts across the aspirations of administrative integrationists.

Electoral integrationists contend that if 'real' British political parties, namely the Conservatives, Labour, and the Liberal Democrats, were to organize and compete in elections in Northern Ireland then its ethnic politics would be transformed, and 'normal' liberal democratic politics could develop (e.g. Aughey, 1989; Roberts, 1987; and Wilson, 1989). This argument rests on insecure foundations. It presupposes that parties matter more than cross-national evidence suggests in determining the nature of political conflicts: yet 'Spanish parties organize in the Basque country without preventing ethnic conflict there . . . Swiss parties organized in the Bernese Jura without preventing conflict and in Belgium the three main parties organized across the linguistic divide, but that did not stop tension between Fleming and Walloon from rising in the 1960s' (Whyte, 1990: 220).[19]

Moreover, the electoral integrationists suppose that Northern Irish residents will vote for British political parties in large numbers if given the opportunity. The evidence is not persuasive. The Conservatives, the solitary British political party to have organized in the region, lost their deposits in the European parliamentary election of May 1989 and the by-election in Upper Bann in May 1990, and have performed well in only one very unrepresentative local-government district, North Down. In the 1992 Westminster elections the Conservatives achieved a 5.7 per cent share of all votes cast in the region. Organizations seeking to persuade Labour to organize in the region have received derisory votes.

The electoral integrationist case also rests on the assumption that Northern Irish voters who will vote for British political parties will do so for non-ethnic reasons. Yet polling evidence confirms that the Conservatives appeal most to those in favour of the Union, i.e. Protestants; whereas the Labour party appeals most to those in favour of Irish unity, i.e. Catholics, because Labour favours achieving Irish unity by consent (*Irish Political Studies*, 1989, 4: 151). Far from transcending sectarian politics the organization of the major British political parties in the region, if it had any impact at all, would directly embroil them in its national/ethnic conflicts, and prevent them from playing the role of more disinterested arbiters.

Electoral integrationists erroneously assume that the major cause of conflict in Northern Ireland since 1920 was the absence of British party competition in the region:[20] an argument that presupposes that such parties would have been electorally successful and transcended historically-established antagonisms, and manages to forget that the Conservatives and the UUP were intimately and mutually beneficially linked.

The UK has never formally been a federation or a confederation. Even if it was to become more like a federation or a confederation, after the establishment of Scottish and Welsh devolution as well as powerful English regions by a reforming Labour government in the late 1990s, it is not clear what significance this transformation would have for the problems of Northern Ireland. Ulster unionists would seek a UK federation which gave them provincial control within Northern Ireland. Their preferred models of a UK federation or confederation completely deny Irish nationalists their aspiration for an Irish dimension (Smyth, 1987), and provoke fears that a UK federation would re-establish a new Stormont regime.

What about a federation or confederation of the British isles, or the archipelago of the Celtic Sea, or indeed 'the federation of Man'[21] as some utopians are wont to suggest? Such an institutional transformation might satisfy the dual national aspirations of the peoples in Northern Ireland, but the British and Irish states are unlikely to surrender sovereignty over all their territories to solve the Northern Irish question if they have found it so difficult to manage their conflicting sovereignty claims over the region. Moreover, Irish nationalists see any proposal for a federated or confederated British Isles as a Trojan horse for the reincorporation of Ireland into the UK.

European federal or confederal formulae

Federalists maintain that if the boundaries between the components of the federation match the boundaries between the relevant ethnic, religious, or linguistic communities, then federalism is an effective conflict-regulating device because it has the effect of making an ethnically heterogeneous society less heterogeneous through the creation of more homogeneous sub-units. However, of the seven genuine federations in long-term liberal democracies, only three achieve this effect, those of Belgium, Canada, and Switzerland (Lijphart, 1984: Table 10.3). In these three cases the success of federalism in conflict-regulation, such as it is, is based upon the lucky accident that the relevant ethnic communities are sharply geographically segregated, something that does not apply in Northern Ireland.

Perhaps Northern Ireland's problems could be transcended within the framework of an emergent European federation or confederation. Joint membership of the EC has aided the development of neighbourly relations between the London and Dublin governments but it is not obvious what impact spillovers from increasing European union will have on intra-communal relations within Northern Ireland. Issues such as dual-national identity, the administration of justice, militarized policing, paramilitary violence, discrimination, and the distribution of local political power are not likely to be resolved as by-products of 'post-1992 Europe'. The removal of tariff barriers and increased cross-border co-operation between the Republic of Ireland and Northern Ireland, if they materialize, will not resolve a conflict centred on national identity and ethnicity. Moreover, the border across Ireland is likely to remain one of the most heavily policed in the EC whatever the fate of '1992'. European co-operation is something desirable in its own right, not something to be favoured as a panacea for Northern Ireland (Lyne, 1990). However, that said, no future framework for resolving Northern Ireland can occur outside the EC.

Unitary, federal, or confederal formulae do not appear to advance the search for a solution any further than the arguments we surveyed in considering the macro-constitutional options. However, it might be maintained that one reason why these formulae are unhelpful is their imprecision about their implications for political decision-making.

What type of decision-making?

Whichever state Northern Ireland is to belong to, and whatever its constitutional nomenclature, *the* political question is straightforward: how should political power be organized over, across, and within the respective communities? There are four ideal typical ways in which this question can be answered: through arbitration, majority rule, cantonization/communization, and power-sharing, although each of these types can be permed in multiple ways.

Arbitration.

Arbitration was tried by the British government in Northern Ireland between 1972 and 1985. After the AIA arbitration has been exercised by the British government in consultation with the Irish government, providing 'direct rule with a green tinge'. In principle, as we have advocated, at some future conjuncture arbitration might be exercised by both Britain and Ireland in a system of joint authority. More fancifully arbitration might be exercised by personnel from the EC (or the UN), appointed by the British and Irish governments. While there is little support for UN involvement in Northern Ireland, in the British Isles the JRRT/Gallup polls data did suggest widespread agreement across nationalists and unionists that the EC should play 'a minor role' in the future government of Northern Ireland (O'Leary, 1991c).

The most fundamental problem with arbitration is that the arbitrated do not regard the most likely arbiters, namely Britain or the Republic, as sufficiently disinterested to be neutral. Irish nationalists regard direct British rule in Ireland as responsible for continuing economic discrimination, regular abuses of human rights by the security forces, and denial of their identity. Unionists, by contrast, find repulsive the mere idea of institutionalized consultation with the Irish Republic. Joint authority has the decided advantage that the two partisan-states would be forced to resolve their differences while adjudicating disputes between their respective nationals in the region.[22]

Majority-rule

Political power in Northern Ireland in principle might be exercised according to majority rule[G]. This norm of the Westminster model is, however, problematic in ethnically divided societies. Under the Stormont government there was one-party rule by the UUP for over fifty years, and no prospect of the nationalist opposition sharing power or achieving governmental authority through the alternation in power that characterizes functioning democracies. Majority-rule devolution provided a milieu for the systematic abuse of political power; and the application of majority-rule decision-making procedures in unitary, federal, or confederal formulae would create the same threat, whether Northern Ireland was Irish, British, or an independent state.

The question in any case is 'which majority?' Nationalists claim that Northern Ireland is illegitimate because its borders were drawn to create an artificial majority, and that they are the genuine majority in the island of Ireland; whereas most unionists claim that since they are a majority within Northern Ireland they should be allowed power commensurate with that status. Electoral integrationists, by contrast, argue that the true majority is in the entire UK. They favour majority rule through the operations of the UK two-party system throughout the state. They are as wildly idealist about the benefits of the Westminster model as Gaelic romantics are about Irish unification, and have no answer to the question of what could or should stop a UK majority from relinquishing British sovereignty over Northern Ireland. Political romanticism is not an exclusively Irish nationalist commodity.

Cantonization/communization

Northern Ireland could be cantonized, in a manner similar to the Swiss mode of government, or communized: the region could be subjected to a micro-partition in which political power would be devolved to new and very small political units – averaging about 20,000 people (Swiss cantons are much larger; it is Swiss communes which are small). Such political units could be designed *either* to create ethno-religiously homogeneous units where majority rule would be practically coterminous with the self-government of all the relevant community *or* to achieve a very local form of power-sharing government of Catholics and Protestants. Where intra-ethnic conflict is high then the partitioning of units to create homogeneity would be the operating administrative principle; and where such conflict was low local power-sharing might be encouraged through the design of balanced 'mixed' cantons/communes.

Cantonization/communization would decompose Northern Ireland into islands of nationalist, unionist, and power-sharing units, simultaneously combining majority rule, partitionist and power-sharing principles – and it could be carried out by a British arbiter or under joint authority. Some areas with high political violence would have to remain under direct rule, and a regional anti-terrorist force would obviously still be required. However, under 'rolling cantonization' policing and judicial powers could be gradually devolved to those areas where the population expressed a wish to exercise such powers, and where the British and Irish governments judged that the experiment had some prospects of success. Cantonization/communization is fraught with potential difficulties, notably the drawing and policing of appropriate units of government, winning consent for them, and the ever-present threat that the cantonization of policing and judicial powers might be used by paramilitary organizations to seize control of parts of Northern Ireland, and treat them as 'liberated zones'.[23] However, cantonization is at least as realistic as pushing traditional unionist or nationalist positions; it is more gradualist in its implications than drastic repartition because it permits both governments the freedom to reverse any experimental initiatives; and for these reasons it deserves to be debated more widely. But cantonization/communization could not be easily applied to the Greater Belfast area, where 49 per cent of Northern Ireland's population resides. As Figure 1.1 demonstrated Belfast experiences the highest levels of violence in Northern Ireland (p. 11). But there is no reason why all sub-regions of Northern Ireland should be governed and administered in a uniform way, so the exclusion of Greater Belfast from cantonization/communization does not necessitate the rest of the region being excluded from experimental cantonization.

Power-sharing

Finally, political relationships in Northern Ireland might be organized according to the power-sharing principles characteristic of some democratic and stable societies which survive despite being divided by ethnic cleavages. Consociational democracies usually have four features (see pp. 197–202): a grand coalition government incorporates the political parties representing the main segments of the divided society; full proportionality rules throughout the public sector; 'community autonomy' norms permitting each group self-government over those matters of most profound concern to them; and constitutional vetoes for minorities. However, the promotion of consociational arrangements for Northern Ireland, whether through voluntary or coercive means, has failed: even though public–opinion polls consistently find it an 'acceptable' solution to large numbers of both Catholics and Protestants.

Voluntary consociation cannot work effectively where the rival communities are fundamentally divided over their national as opposed to their linguistic or religious identities, and where they are divided over the legitimacy of the state. 'Northern Ireland is not Belgium' as one sage has put it. Nationality conflicts appear to have an irreducibly zero-sum character, a view daily reinforced by paramilitaries who kill for the proposition that 'one nation = one state'. The majority of constitutional unionists reject institutionalized power-sharing as 'un-British', i.e. foreign to the Westminster parliamentary tradition, and contend they cannot share power with people who want Northern Ireland to belong to a foreign country. The majority of constitutional nationalists reject any consociational proposals if they are not accompanied by an institutionalized linkage between Northern Ireland and the Republic. Political leaders of nationalist and unionist parties personally prepared to compromise fundamentally on a consociational settlement rapidly find themselves overthrown by revolts within their parties and their ethnic communities. Finally, since both the nationalist and unionist communities are internally divided into 'ultras' and 'moderates' the latter are insufficiently free to negotiate. The AIA was intended to break this stalemate, but it has not done so, so far.

Voluntary consociational solutions, while eminently desirable, seem destined to fall on stony ground. There are several ways in which the British and Irish governments might react if they recognize this increasingly palpable fact. They may simply opt, as they usually do, to engage in crisis-management. Alternatively they may agree to play a long-term strategy, reforming Northern Ireland's discriminatory economy and its administration of justice to win the political confidence of nationalists, isolating the IRA and Sinn Féin, whilst simultaneously gently coaxing unionists out of the cold. The logic of this strategy would be to accomplish all of the institutional features of consociationalism except grand coalition government, which would have to await a better tomorrow. The two governments could aim to ensure proportional representation in non-elected political institutions (including, eventually, the police), community autonomy, and a Bill of Rights guaranteeing equality of citizenship and entrenching some minority rights. Simultaneously they would have to ensure the fight against paramilitaries stayed within the rule of law.

The British and Irish governments might also take the more risky and drastic step of threatening a major new initiative, such as moving towards joint authority or repartition, to increase the pressure on unionists and nationalists to arrive at a power-sharing settlement. Arend Lijphart, the pioneering political scientist who developed the theory of consociational democracy, argues that partition is the most stable and least undesirable solution when consociationalism fails, and that threatening partition might sometimes bring the relevant actors to the negotiating table (Lijphart, 1977, and 1991). In *The Future of Northern Ireland* we sketched a similar argument (McGarry and O'Leary, 1991b: 294–300). However, we observed that threatening joint authority might be as beneficial as threatening partition (ibid.: 303, fn. 24) in encouraging a consociational settlement. We now firmly believe, for the reasons advanced at various points throughout this chapter, that threatening joint authority is a decidedly better option than threatening repartition, because if the internal parties 'call the bluff' of the British and Irish governments it is much easier and more desirable to implement the relevant threat: joint authority poses fewer threats of disaster than repartition.

To sum up on possible types of decision-making for Northern Ireland: British and Irish arbitration through joint authority would be more disinterested and productive in outcome than simply British or Irish arbitration; majority rule must provoke conflict unless it is kept to non-contentious issue-areas, or unless it takes place within a framework of joint authority; cantonization/communization outside the Greater Belfast area could be experimented with under joint authority or under the existing status quo of British direct rule tempered by the Anglo-Irish Agreement; and under joint authority both the British and Irish governments could continue to promote consociational solutions, with no worse prospects of success than under present circumstances, and with some medium-term prospects of creating more widely legitimate structures of government.

Joint authority 'responds to the analysis of the Northern Ireland problem as one of a clash of identities . . . is the logical goal towards which the Anglo-Irish Agreement of 1985 seems to be pointing, whether or not the signatories intended that fact . . . it is the point towards which various forces in the conflict appear to be converging – unionists' adamant refusal to be ruled by Dublin; nationalists' insistence on symbolic as well as practical equality in Northern Ireland; the declining interest of opinion in the south in outright unification; and possibly a British readiness for detachment from the problem without taking the risk of abandoning all say in how it should be handled' (Whyte, 1990: 241).

Grand public-policy objectives

Appraising the merit of macro-solutions, unitary, federal, and confederal formulae, and decision-making systems presupposes grand public-policy goals. In liberal democratic ethnic-conflict resolution inhumane, obnoxious, and indefensible objectives must be ruled out axiomatically: such as genocide, forced mass-migration, or allowing one ethnic group to establish hegemonic control over another. Liberal democratic policy-makers are faced with three fundamental choices in attempting to resolve policy-goals for resolving ethnic conflict:

- reinforcing ethnic separatism as a prelude to partition, repartition, federalization, confederalization, or cantonization; or
- pursuing the civic integration (and eventually the assimilation) of all members of the relevant communities into one (or a new transcendent) identity; or
- pursuing communal and individual equality, which we call ethnic and civic pluralism.

The first option has already been substantively discussed above so we can confine analysis to the second and third options.

From Integration to Assimilation.

Many people believe that the goal of public policy in Northern Ireland should be to reduce the differences between Catholics and Protestants (or nationalists and unionists) through civic integration, to enable ethnic assimilation to take place later. The advocates of integrated education (e.g. Fraser, 1973; and Heskin, 1980), and integrated housing policies share the supposition that the promotion of integration will accomplish eventual assimilation and is intrinsically desirable. The members of the Alliance party, predominantly composed of 'liberal' middle-class Protestants and Catholics, share these beliefs. It is not clear, however, whether they think public policy should be directed towards the dissolution of both ethnic identities, whether they be defined as Protestant and Catholic, or unionist and nationalist; or whether they favour the creation of a British middle-class semi-secularized identity, as their critics suggest.

There are two obvious questions about such civic 'integrationism'. Is it feasible and is it just? Compulsory educational and housing integration produce considerable ethnic violence, as the US experience of 'bussing' confirms. Using state-incentives to encourage educational integration would have to work at the expense of the voluntary, i.e. the predominantly Catholic sector, which would signal a clear message that integration is taking place at the differential expense of one identity. As one British minister taxed with the task of investigating integrated education in Northern Ireland in 1974–5 put it: 'I became persuaded that integrated education meant Protestant education.'[24]

The key problem is that too many parties to the conflict are integrationists, but on their terms. Unionists wish to integrate Northern Ireland into the UK, administratively, electorally, or culturally, by ignoring or diminishing the importance of their minority's Irish national identity, while nationalists, north and south, have sought an all-Ireland state while ignoring or diminishing the importance of their minority's British and religious identity. Each national integrationist project is majoritarian. Christians in both communities are either opposed to co-operative interaction or they are concerned that any ecumenical developments do not take place at the expense of their theological commitments. There are also secular integrationists who are equally exclusivist: some (usually originally Protestant) socialists and liberals maintain that integration into the UK party-system will advance a secular socialist and liberal agenda in Northern Ireland, whereas some (usually originally Catholic) socialists and liberals maintain that the integration of Northern Ireland into the Republic will advance the causes of social democracy, pluralism, and secularism in all of Ireland. All such integrationists, national, Christian, socialist, and liberal engage in varying degrees of wishful thinking. Creating civic homogeneity out of intense ethnic divisions may seem desirable, although that is debatable, but it is hardly practical.

Ethnic and civic pluralism.

The alternative public-policy objective is to secure the rights, identities, freedoms, and opportunities of both national-ethnic communities, and to create political and other social institutions that enable both to enjoy the benefits of equality without forced assimilation. This policy goal would not entail any efforts by governments to force people to be schooled or housed together. However, it does require full equality of public provision for each community, and an end to the unjustified underfunding of Catholic schools and Catholic housing estates identified by recent and careful research (Cormack, Gallagher, and Osborne, 1991: 144–6; Smith and Chambers, 1991: 330–67). Ethnic pluralism does imply a commitment to proportionality and equality in political, legal, and economic work-organizations since here ethnic differences are likely to produce violence, instability, and perpetuation of conflict. One might see the British government's decision, announced in 1991, to merge the (overwhelmingly Protestant) UDR with the Royal Irish Rangers (which recruits some Catholics from all of Ireland as well as Protestants) as consistent with this objective.[25] Ethnic pluralism requires Bills of Rights, fair employment, institutional respect for the two traditions, proportionality in policing, judging, and military pacification, and mutual vetoes on matters of communal and national autonomy. Ethnic pluralism, which we favour, would be best advanced through a form of joint authority that maximized the self-government and autonomy of the communities of Northern Ireland. It is also compatible with ensuring that secular, bi-confessional or non-christian individuals and families, and people who are neither British nor Irish in their national or ethnic origins, enjoy the full benefits of a liberal democratic civil society.

Notes

1. The full data-set was made available to O'Leary (1991b, 1991c, and 1992) by the Joseph Rowntree Reform Trust.

2. Thus if a referendum was held in all three jurisdictions a united Ireland would be the plurality-rule winner. Alternatively if each jurisdiction was given one vote and the future of Northern Ireland was decided by a majority vote then a united Ireland would defeat Northern Ireland being integrated into Great Britain by two votes to one.

3. Catholics understate their Irish nationalist militancy, *inter alia*, because of fear of being identified as subversive, suspicion of pollsters, and on the sour grapes' principle that 'if a united Ireland cannot be had it's not worth supporting'.

4. If Northern Ireland's economy were reformed through affirmative action

then presumably the differential between Catholic and Protestant emigration-rates would be reduced and the Catholic/nationalist electorate of Northern Ireland would expand. However, such a transformation would take time and might reconcile Catholics to Northern Ireland's status as a part of the UK.

5. We share the mainstream belief that a British governmental and military withdrawal from the island of Ireland would be more likely to provoke unionists to create an independent, albeit smaller, Northern Ireland, rather than encourage them to negotiate their place in a new Ireland.

6. The lower level of first-preference support for independence amongst Protestants in the JRRT/Gallup polls compared with Catholics may reflect the fact that the question made it emphatically clear that this option would make Northern Ireland completely independent of the UK as well as of the Republic.

7. The New Ireland Forum sub-committee noted that under joint authority there would be a case for the British staying in Northern Ireland even if a simple majority emerged for a united Ireland: 'it could be argued that if Joint Authority is justified where there is a nationalist minority of 35–40 %, it would be equally justified when there was a substantial Unionist minority in the North' (Kilbrandon, 1984: 70). We agree.

8. The deliberations of the Forum sub-committee were leaked and published in the Kilbrandon Report (1984: 61 ff.)

9. The idea of joint authority was first put on the agenda in 1971 by a nationalist intellectual (Fennell, 1985: 156 ff.). It was briefly taken up by the SDLP in a policy document published in 1972: its condominium proposal entailed a self-governing Northern Ireland under the joint control and supervision of the London and Dublin governments (SDLP, 1972), but as the precursor to a united Ireland established by an all-Ireland referendum. Joint authority was also aired in a pamphlet by the British-based intellectual T. J. Pickvance (1975), and by political scientist Bernard Crick (1982). See also Dent (1988), Kenny (1991), and Wright (1989). The subtle and intelligent arguments of Ruane and Todd (1991) provide the best normative underpinning for a democratized condominium, whether or not that is the explicit intention of the authors.

10. The Forum sub-committee envisaged a vaguely specified Joint Authority Commission, one British and one Irish person (in effect dual prefects), who might appoint 'Deputy Commissioners'; and, an alternative model under which the Joint Authority Commission supervised a local executive 'supported by' a locally elected assembly (Kilbrandon, 1984: 62).

11. The term 'joint sovereignty' was avoided by the proponents of joint authority because of Thatcher's acetose distaste for losing one iota of sovereignty, and because of the ideological debates about sovereignty.

12. The Irish dimension is so strongly entrenched in the minds of the Great British public that more of them (49 per cent) think the Irish government should

have a major role in the affairs of Northern Ireland than think the same should apply to their own government (32 per cent).

13. We explore these issues in McGarry and O'Leary (forthcoming).

14. Here we have not elaborated the empirical bases for our judgements. We leave it to readers to assess how far our recommendation of joint authority is vulnerable to the challenge that our judgements are not robust. We defend our judgements in depth in McGarry and O'Leary (forthcoming).

15. Transitional joint authority as a prelude to a British withdrawal would be destabilizing while permanent joint authority would entail constitutional inhibitions upon future widely agreed changes to a more acceptable form of self-government. Therefore we prefer the expression durable joint authority, which should be operationalized as meaning not less than twenty years. To ensure that durable joint authority is not seen as 'creeping Irish unification' it would have to be accompanied by changes in Articles 2 and 3 of the Irish Constitution, as well as a new constitution of Northern Ireland which specified that (after the twenty-year period) a very high level of consent (over 75 per cent) would be required for Northern Ireland to become (exclusively) part of the Republic or (again) exclusively part of the UK.

Incentives for a powerful local input into the system of joint authority could include an executive structured like the Kilbrandon model, with special provisions for the appointment of functional ministers from a locally elected assembly, and for agreed appointments to senior bureaucratic, judicial, and security posts.

16. In the JRRT/Gallup polls joint authority (26 per cent) came third behind full integration with the Republic (38 per cent) and an independent Northern Ireland (33 per cent) as the cumulated first and second preferences of the public in Great Britain. In the Republic, joint authority (44 per cent) came second to full integration with the Republic (55 per cent) and ahead of an independent Northern Ireland (35 per cent).

17. See Note 15 above.

18. Interview with B. O'Leary, 3 Jan. 1991.

19. State-wide party-organization and competition have not stopped ethnic conflict or prevented the development of powerful local ethnic parties in democratic states as large and as diverse as India and Canada; and the nation-building ambitions of successive Nigerian constitutional designers who have emphasized electoral integration have not been realized.

20. Roberts (1987: 335) claims that the British party 'boycott' of the region is '*the fundamental reason* for the continuing conflict' (our emphasis). We wonder whether Indian party-organization in Sri Lanka, Indian party-organization in Kashmir, Serbian party-organization in the disintegrating Yugoslav republics, Israeli party-organization in the west Bank and Gaza strip, or Greek (or Turkish) party-organization in Cyprus would remove the *fundamental reasons* for conflict in these territories.

21. One intellectual has proposed a Federation of Man; and later followed it up with a proposed Confederation of Man, comprising only Scotland, Wales, and Ireland, with its confederal institutions in an independent island of Man (Fennell, 1985: 179). He did not discuss whether the federation or confederation should be tax-havens.

22. Joint authority like the Kilbrandon model of co-operative devolution would combine the benefits of arbitration and majority rule.

23. All of these problems were manifest in the EC's ill-fated and ill-conceived cantonization plans for Bosnia Herzegovina during 1991–2.

24. Roland Moyle (interview with B. O'Leary, 3 Jan. 1991).

25. It transpired in late 1991, however, that the British Army had greatly overestimated the Catholic and southern proportion of the Irish Rangers which is to be merged with the UDR to create the RIR. The Catholic/Irish membership of the Rangers is a mere 6 per cent, not 30 per cent as first suggested. This predictable failure at integration confirms that only joint authority can produce ethnically balanced security forces in Northern Ireland.

9
Epilogue: the Brooke initiative and after, 1990–

The trouble with Ireland may well be that you get this slow burning fire all the time which never solves anything either by constitutional negotiation or by the sort of traumatic experience that everybody wants to shy away from.
(Roland Moyle, interview with B. O'Leary, 3 January 1991)

The future is not what it used to be.
(Anonymous)

When Peter Brooke was appointed Secretary of State for Northern Ireland in July 1989 he 'dusted off' papers submitted by unionists in 1987–8 and began a series of interventions to create an atmosphere conducive to talks between the constitutional political parties in Northern Ireland and the Irish government. Sinn Féin was to be excluded until it renounced support for political violence. Initially it was unclear whether Brooke's style was 'oracular or simply inept' (Pyle, 1989).[1] However, before long, he had managed to impress nationalists, unionists, and the Irish government that it would not be in their interests to oppose his initiative which he announced formally in January 1990. Throughout 1990 and early 1991 doubts persisted over whether the internal political parties would agree on an agenda for talks, let alone conduct the discussions. The NIO team nevertheless persisted in its ambitions, even though Brooke's diplomatic manœuvring sowed, possibly deliberately, considerable confusion.

In August 1990 one leading nationalist MP's political adviser posed a riddle:[2]

'Question: What do you get when you cross Peter Brooke with the

Mafia? Answer: An offer you cannot understand, but cannot refuse.

At least two inferences could be drawn from this joke. The leaders of Northern Ireland's constitutional political parties felt obliged to demonstrate their willingness to talk, and endeavoured to avoid responsibility for the breakdown of any prospective talks, but none of them believed that a new British–Irish agreement could be constructed to command widespread assent.

Yet Brooke's 'talks about talks' eventually delivered an agreement to hold discussions starting on 30 April 1991, with a 'gap' of ten weeks assured before the meeting of the next intergovernmental conference due on 16 July, and on the understanding that the Maryfield secretariat that services the conference would be run down during the talks.[3] Brooke's officials sold unionists the merits of working with John Hume's agenda, which declared that three relationships – between unionists and nationalists in Northern Ireland, between unionists and the Republic of Ireland, and between Ireland and Great Britain – needed to be negotiated and resolved. All parties to the prospective round of talks – the two governments and the four constitutional parties in Northern Ireland (the UUP, the DUP, the APNI, and the SDLP) agreed to the formula announced by Brooke in the House of Commons in March 1991.

Driving into the strands

The agreed formula consisted of three strands of talks. The first was to involve cross-party talks in Northern Ireland about internal structures of government for the region. The second was to consist of all-Ireland discussions, and the third was to settle British–Irish relations. The second and third strands were to be launched 'within weeks' of the first. However, after 30 April the talks were delayed by wrangling for seven weeks over the proposed agenda and standing orders, the venue for the proposed second strand of the negotiations, and finally over the choice of a chair for the second strand. The debate over the agenda and procedures focused on the subjects of the various proposed strands of discussion, and the order and location in which they would be processed. The debate over the venue(s) at one stage produced the remarkable outcome that the British and Irish governments, the SDLP, and the APNI were agreed that the second phase of the talks should take place in Northern Ireland while the UUP and DUP were holding out for a venue on the European continent. It was eventually accepted that the talks would centre in Belfast, but would also take place in London and Dublin. Since the UUP and the DUP were not prepared to hold talks with the Republic's government in Dublin under the chairmanship of the Irish Foreign Minister, Brooke and Collins proposed that an independent chairman be appointed to preside over such talks.[4] However, their first proposal for the post, Lord Peter Carrington, produced an outraged response from the DUP and the UUP who felt that Carrington was anti-unionist, and complained bitterly that as British Foreign Secretary he had sold out Rhodesia in 1980.[5] An alternative chair for the second phase of the talks, in the person of the former Governor-General of Australia, Sir Ninian Stephen, was finally agreed by all parties, and proper discussions began on 17 June 1991 about the possible replacement of the Anglo-Irish Agreement.

Had the talks produced a British–Irish Agreement then 'History' would have been made. However, prognoses that the latest consociational initiative would not succeed proved correct. The cherished assumptions of inexperienced journalists that Charles Haughey, James Molyneaux, and Ian Paisley wanted to establish more benign reputations with twenty-first century historians, that 'public opinion' was pushing the rival leaders to a political accommodation, and that 'young unionist turks' of moderated dispositions were thrusting into view, all proved false, at least for the time being.

The procedure for managing the discussions, had they taken place for any length of time, was open to criticism. It was impossible to disentangle the separate strands so perhaps one set of talks should have been organized. Some maintained that there are four not three relationships at stake:

• within Northern Ireland,
• across all of Ireland,
• between Great Britain and Northern Ireland, and
• between the Republic of Ireland and Great Britain.

Others maintained that the European dimension should not be overlooked in any full-scale talks.

In the prematurely terminated first strand of talks all the internal parties set out their wares as predicted. The UUP held out for greater integration with the UK and weak 'administrative devolution'; the DUP wanted strong devolved government but did not declare themselves committed to executive power-sharing; the APNI wanted an internal settlement and some Irish dimension; and the SDLP declared that the 'abiding reality' recognized by the Anglo-Irish Agreement 'is the right of the Irish Government to involvement in the affairs of Northern Ireland'.[6] The participating parties did not agree to sign provisional 'heads of agreement' before strands two and three could begin. Everything was to be left 'undecided' until all strands of discussion were completed, to prevent any side from breaking the negotiations at a favourable juncture for them.[7]

Substantive issues did arise. One was whether an 'internal settlement' – involving an agreed devolved government for Northern Ireland – could be part of the overall settlement. But it was clear that any 'internal settlement' was impossible to detach from any prospective 'external settlement'. The thorny external issues were:

- the relationships between any Northern Ireland government and the institutions of the Anglo Irish Agreement (or its successor) and Westminster and Whitehall;
- the constitutional status of Northern Ireland; and
- the stability of any devolved government without 'external guarantees' from the British and Irish governments.

Unsurprisingly there was little evidence by the end of June that an internal agreement was likely to be negotiated by the parties, and even if it were, that it would prove stable.

A joint UUP–DUP document on 'Administrative and legislative devolution' (first composed in 1987) formed the basis of their negotiating posture during the Brooke talks.[8] It envisaged an executiveless assembly based upon strong committees, in which the elected parties would be proportionally represented according to the d'Hondt rule, and it also foresaw an assembly large enough to ensure that there would be no danger that Unionists lacked a permanent majority on every committee! 'Proportionality, yes; power-sharing no' was this document's code.

Unionists wanted any internal settlement tied to a fundamental modification or scrapping of the Anglo-Irish Agreement. Molyneaux and others in the UUP also wanted to marry a very weak form of devolution (little more than local government) to 'integrationist' measures at Westminster, like the ending of Orders in Council and a beefed-up parliamentary committee for Northern Ireland. The SDLP was not enthusiastic about these proposals. The SDLP refused to respond with detailed proposals for devolved government because it believed – correctly – that the UUP and the DUP were about to pull out of the talks. The SDLP saw the Anglo-Irish Agreement as a minimum and irreversible base-line from which to negotiate. Unionists insisted on the clarification of the status of Northern Ireland's position within the UK, whereas the SDLP wanted it to be compatible with future membership of an all-Ireland entity. The SDLP (and to an extent the APNI) wanted to tie down any new internal arrangement with 'external guarantees'. The furthest the SDLP was prepared to go in negotiations was to accept the Anglo-Irish Agreement as a default-option, which would come back into full force in the event of a collapse of a negotiated devolved government.

There is no evidence that unionists were prepared to consider the SDLP's minimal requirement to stabilize an internal settlement, i.e. accept something like the Anglo-Irish Agreement. The Unionists participated in the talks knowing that if they produced nothing then the default-option would be a return to the Anglo-Irish Agreement. However, accepting under protest the Anglo-Irish Agreement as a default for talks was very different, for them, from building in the entire Agreement as an agreed default-option for a settlement which Unionists would sign. Since such a deal would lock them into power-sharing with the SDLP – without being able to threaten their resignation from a devolved government at an acceptable price – they considered such a default-option unacceptable.

This division could not be glossed over by diplomacy, but was not highlighted as the talks broke over another issue: the refusal of Unionists to continue discussions given the fact that the British and Irish governments had committed themselves to going ahead with their scheduled Intergovernmental Conference on 16 July 1991. Paisley called for 'injury time' on the grounds that the seven weeks of delay after 30 April had prevented substantive talks. His critics pointed out that most of that delay was because of Paisley and Molyneaux's behaviour, and suspected that the DUP and the UUP wanted to 'wear down' the institutions of the Anglo-Irish Agreement rather than engage in constructive negotiations.[9] The

SDLP offered the possibility of another 'gap' between meetings of the Intergovernmental Conference as the basis for further discussions, but Unionists considered it unacceptable to negotiate with the threat of continuous Inter-Governmental Conferences. Brooke therefore brought the talks to an end on 3 July, which led to widespread criticisms of the unionists. By 12 July Paisley was renewing rhetorical war, describing Charles Haughey as the Saddam Hussein of Ireland.[10]

Resuscitating the Brooke initiative

After the summer parliamentary recess the unionist leadership sought to repair some of the damage done to the unionist position in Great Britain.[11] In September 1991 Molyneaux and Paisley met Brooke at Westminster. Paisley demanded that Collins, the Irish Foreign Minister retract a remark he had made earlier in the month to the effect that the Republic would be as flexible as possible in future talks, 'consistent of course with our commitment to the Anglo-Irish Agreement'. The unionist leaders demanded also that any future talks to replace the AIA with a new British–Irish Agreement should (initially) be conducted only at Westminster and only amongst MPs from Northern Ireland (a device to exclude the APNI from participation in any talks). These demands were non-starters for the SDLP and the Irish government, but later in a conciliatory response on RTE radio Haughey stated that Collins had been misinterpreted, and had not meant that new talks could only take place under the auspices of AIA (interview 22 September 1991). On 1 October Brooke and Collins met, and the latter confirmed that the Irish government wanted the previously agreed procedures for talks to be maintained.

During the next three months both loyalist and republican paramilitary violence reached levels unseen for over a decade and increased the pressure on the parties to renew dialogue. The press in Great Britain and the Republic, and in Northern Ireland, called for a revival of talks and were particularly vigorous in their condemnation of unionist intransigence.[12] Polls continued to show that Great British public opinion favoured the withdrawal of British troops from Northern Ireland.[13] On 21 November 1991 Brooke met Paisley and Molyneaux for further 'talks about talks', but at the DUP's party conference, just over a week later, Paisley called for the talks to be at Westminster, while demanding that the Republic immediately rescind the territorial claim in Articles 2 and 3 of its constitution, suggesting there was little room for progress. In early December the British Prime Minister John Major, who had succeeded Margaret Thatcher the previous year, met Charles Haughey in Dublin, in the first formal visit by a British Prime Minister to the Irish capital since 1980. The two Prime Ministers agreed that there would in future be a summit between them twice a year, and Major pointedly declared that he saw no reason for 'time-wasting', and believed that talks could restart before the next British general election, due in 1992.

On 19 December 1991 Brooke met the Northern Irish party leaders to present a new formula for renewed talks. It was to consist of the previous formula (three strands, a gap between IGCs, and the running-down of the Maryfield secretariat) with a series of amendments, all of which appeared to have been put forward by Molyneaux and Paisley. Strand one talks would take place in London, although later stages of the talks could take place elsewhere. Second, the number of people on each party's negotiating team would be reduced from ten to three. Third, the talks would take place during a gap between meetings of the Intergovernmental Conference, commencing on 20 January 1991 and continuing until the British general election campaign, whenever that took place. However, Molyneaux and Paisley would guarantee to continue the talks if and only if a Conservative government was returned to power in the forthcoming Westminster election. There were also rumours that Paisley was insisting that Sir Ninian Stephen be dropped as the prospective chair of the second strand of talks.

The first amendment in principle was acceptable to the Irish government and the SDLP, provided it did not mean the exclusion of the APNI, and provided the north–south talks would not take place in London.[14] The second amendment was capable of resolution, neither the number ten nor three had any sacred status with the respective parties. The third amendment, that talks should continue until the next British general election, was apparently acceptable to a sceptical Irish government and the SDLP, even though it might conceivably mean that the 'gap' between IGCs could be even shorter than the ten weeks agreed the last time.

However, the idea that the continuation of the talks should be made conditional upon the re-election of a Conservative government was completely unacceptable to the SDLP and the Irish government (which would then have been interfering in the British electoral process). Kevin McNamara, Labour's shadow Secretary of State publicly indicated to Brooke that a new Labour government would be happy to pick up any talks where they were left by an outgoing Conservative government, and the SDLP insisted that any new agreement to hold talks would have to be on the basis that they would continue irrespective of who formed the next government at Westminster. The SDLP, Labour's sister-party in the Socialist International, did not look kindly on a proposal to exclude a prospective Labour government, which favoured Irish unity by consent, from the terms of a new set of talks.

Brooke therefore had some diplomatic finessing to do if there was to be a further round of talks before the general election. He also had to allay the suspicion that he was keeping the unionists sweet in order for the Conservative party to have at least one party it could do business with in the event of a hung parliament in Westminster, which was then being predicted by nearly all public opinion polls. However, Brooke had lost his diplomatic touch. On 17 January the IRA killed 8 Protestant workers at Teebane Cross, on the grounds that they were collaborators with the security forces. On the following night Brooke was seen singing a song live on Irish television in Dublin, which prompted calls for his resignation. Brooke did offer to resign, and although Major promptly rejected the offer, his political position had been decisively weakened.

Just when the prospects for a renewal of talks looked extremely bleak the Irish Prime Minister, Charles Haughey, whose government had been dogged by scandal, resigned. He was replaced by Albert Reynolds on 6 February. Reynolds had the decisive advantage of not being Haughey, i.e. of not having a reputation as a hard-line republican, and promptly declared his willingness to meet unionist politicians, anywhere, at any time. He also replaced Collins as Irish foreign minister with David Andrews, who also declared that everything would be on the table in any new cross-party and intergovernmental talks. Under prompting from various Irish nationalists, north and south, both Reynolds and Andrews subsequently amplified their position to argue that the Government of Ireland Act of 1920, along with Articles 2 and 3 of the Irish constitution, must be on the agenda for discussion,[15] which was not well received by unionists.

However, the impetus for talks had been restored by a fresh-faced

Irish government. By 28 February agreement had been reached by the two governments that talks to create a new British–Irish Agreement should resume after the IGC planned for 6 March. At that meeting it was decided not to reconvene the IGC until after the British general election, but to allow for the relaunch of the talks, under the terms originally agreed by Brooke with the relevant parties in March 1991, saving only that this time there would be a three-month 'gap' between meetings of the IGC. One entire year had passed to achieve an agreement to start talks again on almost exactly the same basis as had been agreed before. By coincidence the talks would eventually restart on 30 April 1992, again exactly one year after their last ill-fated start.

The Westminster election of April 1992 and its aftermath

During the Westminster general election campaign there was much speculation about what role Northern Ireland's MPs might play in the event of a hung parliament. It was clear, especially from Brooke's conduct, that the Conservatives were prepared to enter into arrangements with the UUP's MPs, and that the SDLP would take the Labour whip. Nevertheless all three British party leaders declared during the campaign that the Anglo-Irish Agreement, an international and bilateral treaty, could not be negotiated away in the event of a hung parliament. In any case the speculation proved idle as, against expectations, the Conservatives were returned to office, albeit with a much reduced majority, on 9 April 1992.

However, the outcome of the election in Northern Ireland was beneficial for the voices of moderation in both communities (see Table 9.1). Within the nationalist bloc the SDLP recorded its highest ever share of the vote in a Westminster election, 23.5 per cent, while Sinn Féin fell back to 10 per cent, and Gerry Adams lost his West Belfast seat to the SDLP's Dr Joe Hendron.[16] Within the unionist bloc the UUP's share of the vote fell to 34.5 per cent, and the DUP's rose only very slightly to 13.1 per cent, despite the fact that the party was running more candidates than in 1987.[17]

The election delivered a stable British government, and had shown the long-term party-political benefits of the AIA. The SDLP had continued to gain at the expense of Sinn Féin, and unionist 'ultras' lacked electoral momentum. The election had also come after a

Table 9.1 Party performances in Westminster elections, 1983–92
(votes in per cent, seats in absolute numbers)

Party/bloc performance	1983		1987		1992		net gain, 83–92	
	votes	seats	votes	seats	votes	seats	votes	seats
unionist bloc	54	14	49.5	12	47.6	12	–6.4	–2
UUP	34	11	37.8	9	34.5	9	0.5	–2
DUP	20	3	11.7	3	13.1	3	–6.9	0
nationalist bloc	31.3	2	32.5	4	33.5	4	2.3	2
SDLP	17.9	1	21.1	3	23.5	4	5.6	3
SF	13.4	1	11.4	1	10	0	–3.4	–1
non-ethnic								
APNI	8	0	10	0	8.7	0	0.7	0
WP	1.9	0	2.6	0	0.6	0	–1.3	0
Conservatives	-	-	-	-	5.7	0	5.7	0

Notes: (i) To include the Conservatives within the unionist bloc or to define them as non-ethnic is a matter of taste. Their support is overwhelmingly Protestant.

(ii) We do not treat the non-ethnic parties as a bloc.

(iii) Support for the unionist bloc is underestimated as one seat has been held by James Kilfedodder of the Ulster Popular Unionist Party.

(iv) Since 1983 the Westminster constituencies boundaries have remained the same.

major transition in Irish politics, which in fifteen months had seen the election of a new Irish prime minister and of a new Irish president, Mary Robinson, not associated with traditional irredentism. If British–Irish–Northern Irish talks were ever to succeed in delivering widespread agreement then the Spring of 1992 seemed an auspicious time

An IRA bomb which exploded in the City of London the day after the British election, leaving three people dead, reminded all optimists of the scale of the task facing peacemakers. Major had appointed Sir Patrick Mayhew to replace Brooke as the Secretary of State for Northern Ireland,[18] and by 30 April 1992 talks were scheduled to restart at Stormont Castle, on the understanding that the IGC would be suspended for three months (long enough for unionists to have time to negotiate, and short enough to prevent the Anglo-Irish Agreement being damaged by filibustering). As the parties prepared for serious discussions in the first week of May it remained to be seen whether the talks would prove more productive than their predecessors'.

What if?

Let us imagine, for the sake of argument, and superseding all precedents, that there could be a provisional agreement about a devolved power-sharing internal settlement during strand one of the new round of talks (or subsequent talks), and that the parties could shuffle towards Dublin or between Dublin and Belfast to develop strands two and three. What might happen then?

The fault-lines are predictable. Unionists (in return for whatever concessions they are prepared to consider on the constitution of a devolved government, the administration of justice, and fair employment) will want the teeth of Articles 2 and 3 of the Irish constitution to be drawn. Indeed at several stages during 1990–2 they declared they would enter talks only if the Irish government made a public commitment to alter Articles 2 and 3. However, it is not apparent whether Unionists are content to have Articles 2 and 3 minimally altered (so that they are compatible both in letter and spirit with the Anglo-Irish Agreement), or whether they hold the maximalist position of agreeing to settle only if Articles 2 and 3 are deleted from the Irish Constitution, and the aspiration to Irish unity left without any constitutional expression in *Bunreacht na hÉireann*.

Since the Irish government (unlike the British government) cannot alter its Constitution simply with a bare parliamentary majority, changing Articles 2 and 3 requires the DUP and the UUP to give Irish nationalists something which could be sold by both the Irish government and the SDLP in the referendum which would have to be held to endorse the settlement. The minimum price the UUP and the DUP would have to pay the Irish government and the SDLP would be two Irish dimensions. Unionists *might* be prepared to concede the first: a constitutional provision for Northern Ireland, like that in the Anglo-Irish Agreement, which permits Irish unity at some future juncture if a majority in the region were to vote for it in a referendum, or if a devolved government were to agree to negotiate Irish unity. But the second and more important Irish dimension would stick in their throats: a constitutionally entrenched Intergovernmental Conference with a policy-advisory and possibly policy-making role in Northern Ireland. The IGC could consist of the Great British, Irish, and the (devolved) Northern Irish governments; of the Northern Irish and Irish governments; or, of the Irish and Great British governments, as at present. The agenda of the IGC could be security, economic development and EC co-operation, and other matters of high politics, but whatever its intergovernmental character and agenda one of the governments involved would have to be that of the Republic of Ireland. The SDLP and the Fianna Fáil/Progressive Democrats government have to be offered something as good as, if not better, than the Anglo-Irish Agreement in return for modifying/terminating Articles 2 and 3. In the Spring of 1992 no leading Unionists appear to want to make such an offer, but even if some of them do it is doubtful whether their inter-party and intra-party strains could survive such a bargaining posture. Unionist supporters will say they have not come all this way to sign up to something they disagree with.

Let us star-gaze one light-year further. Imagine that strands one and two have brought into public view the outlines of a feasible agreed settlement – a power-sharing devolved government, transformation of Articles 2 and 3 into aspirational articles, and two Irish dimensions, one being an Intergovernmental Conference which includes the Irish government, and the other being a mechanism to permit Irish unity by consent. What would then remain to be done, apart from putting the package to the peoples of Ireland in two referenda, and hoping thereby to delegitimize paramilitary violence through an all-Ireland vote which would show that Sinn Féin and the IRA and loyalist paramilitaries are completely isolated? The answer is that the relations between Great Britain and Ireland would remain to be 'sorted out' in strand three. What would be at stake? Apart from the possible issue of Irish re entry into the British Commonwealth we cannot think of anything likely to cause a major hiatus in this strand.

Standing back from this optimistic scenario questions must arise. If the two governments could outline the parameters of what they would regard as a reasonable settlement – like that outlined above – would it not be much easier to see whether or not Northern Ireland's parties could agree to them? Why are they going through the process of taking people over hurdles they show no particular enthusiasm to jump in order to bring them to consider the elements of a settlement broadly agreeable to the British and Irish governments?

Are not the external governments (the exogenous actors) once more leaving the (endogenous) parties in Northern Ireland to show the world that they cannot agree, by leaving them the widest possible agendas to consider ? One response to this line of criticism might be that if the British and Irish governments frame the basis for an agreed settlement then Unionists will not be prepared to sign it. We would reply that, as with the Anglo-Irish Agreement, it would be a matter of time before Unionists came to negotiate its terms. This assessment is consistent with our case for the construction of a system of joint authority which maximizes the self-government of the peoples of Northern Ireland, a solution which grapples with both the exogenous and endogenous sources of conflict and instability.

Conclusion

The experience of voluntary consociational initiatives in Northern Ireland is so far consistent in its message. From Whitelaw in 1972 to Brooke during 1991–2 they have not worked. The collapse of talks in July 1991 portended a renewal of deadlock, and though the talks have subsequently been resuscitated there is no cause for undue optimism.

Failures in constitutional politics have encouraged the two sets of paramilitaries to renew their campaigns. Loyalist paramilitaries, reinvigorated by a purge of their more corrupt leaders, and of police-informants within their ranks, have been killing Catholics on a scale not seen since 1976, and successfully targeting republican activists in a way which suggests informed access to supposedly confidential security sources. They are motivated by frustration that Unionist politicians have failed to negotiate the Anglo-Irish Agreement away, and by the fear that the British government's decision to merge the UDR with the Royal Irish Rangers to create the Royal Irish Regiment might be the first step in 'disarming Protestants'.[19] Republican paramilitaries are also displaying a new recklessness: seasoned observers speak of a 'third generation' taking the place of their predecessors. The 'ballot box' component of the 'armalite and ballot box' strategy is blocked. Sinn Féin almost certainly cannot grow much in the foreseeable future, and may be beginning a permanent decline, but if so the IRA may increasingly act in a purely militaristic fashion.

There are always stirrings in the undergrowth to which one can point if one wishes to be optimistic about Northern Ireland: such as renewed peace marches, vigorous north–south exchanges, a developing civil society of non-aligned people, the prompting of voluntary, academic, and media organizations, and, not least, sheer exhaustion with the present conflict. However, we believe that there are also reasons for supposing that ethnic antagonisms are presently being reforged rather than resolved. The widespread despair that the cruel conflict will continue, apparently with no end in sight, has solid empirical foundations. Two centuries after the United Irishmen promised to 'abolish the memory of all past dissension', the statecraft required to break the manacles of the past has not yet materialised.[20]

Notes

1. In August 1989 when Brooke invoked a non-existent phrase in Article 29 of the Review of the Intergovernmental Conference to suggest the possibility that the two governments had agreed that the AIA could be transcended he was interpreted as either shrewd or stupid; and in November 1989 when he declared that he could 'never' say that he or his successors would 'never' talk with Sinn Féin his comments gave rise to similarly polarised interpretations.

2. Non-attributable interview with B. O'Leary in Derry/Londonderry, August 1990.

3. Unionists wanted the secretariat suspended. Instead, it was agreed that it would not service the Intergovernmental Conference when the Conference was suspended (a negotiating victory for the Irish government).

4. The Irish government understandably was not prepared to discuss altering Articles 2 and 3 of its constitution under the chairmanship of a British minister.

5. They had ample evidence of unsympathetic statements by Carrington about Unionist leaders, especially Paisley. The NIO were apparently not aware of the reaction that proposing Carrington would have on unionist politicians. The Unionists' complaint that Carrington had 'sold out' Rhodesia was not publicly analysed even though it suggested that Unionists empathized with a 'settler minority' 'betrayed' by the British metropolis.

6. From 'The SDLP Analysis of the Nature of the Problem', written in May 1991, and submitted to the plenary session of the talks.

7. Otherwise the DUP and the UUP could choose to break over the Irish dimension or the SDLP could choose to break over power-sharing (i.e. over

326 The Politics of Antagonism

issues where they could expect to receive a sympathetic hearing in Great Britain or the Republic).

8. It was leaked to former UUP politician Frank Millar, now the London editor of the *Irish Times* (*Irish Times*, 3 July 1991).

9. Interview with Irish public official, London, July 1991.

10. *Guardian*, 13 July 1991.

11. The JRRT/Gallup polls showed that unionist politicians were held most responsible for the breakdown of talks in Great Britain, the Republic, *and* in Northern Ireland (O'Leary, 1992).

12. The most memorable criticism maintained that the UUP leadership was 'as set in its views as a mammoth preserved in Siberian ice' (*Irish Independent*, 29 Oct. 1991).

13. A MORI poll for the Channel 4 documentary *Pack up Your Troubles* found that 61 per cent of respondents in Great Britain favoured the withdrawal of British troops (24 October 1991) and in November 1991 the British Social Attitudes survey found that 60 per cent of respondents favoured their withdrawal, and 56 per cent favoured Irish unification, very marginally higher support (+1 per cent) for these policies than had been recorded the previous year (Gallagher, 1991: 61).

14. The UUP and DUP were determined to sideline the APNI as an unwelcome distraction, who made them appear unreasonable to the world's media, which is why Molyneaux proposed in the Autumn of 1991 that Northern Ireland's MPs (who included no APNI representatives) should have discussions at Westminster on relatively low-level issues, an idea rejected by the SDLP.

15. Their argument was echoed by the SDLP's Dennis Haughey (no relation of Charles) who argued that the British as well as the Irish constitution had to be on the table in any discussion of the future of Ireland.

16. Sinn Féin's total vote held steady in West Belfast. Hendron's victory owed something to higher turn-out and the collapse of the Workers' Party, but it also owed something to unprecedented tactical voting by a couple of thousand working-class Protestants in West Belfast, who voted for a moderate nationalist to defeat the ultra-nationalist.

17. The squeeze on the unionist bloc was partly caused by Conservative candidates taking 5.7 per cent of the regional vote (although they also undoubtedly won Protestant voters from the APNI).

18. The same man had, as Attorney General, caused grave offence to the Irish government and Irish nationalists. See Ch. 7: 247.

19. See however Ch. 8: 311, n. 25.

20. In *Explaining Northern Ireland: Broken Images* we examine in greater depth what we believe such statecraft requires, building upon the arguments advanced here (McGarry and O'Leary, forthcoming).

Glossary

AIA	Anglo-Irish Agreement.
AOH	Ancient Order of Hibernians.
APNI	Alliance Party of Northern Ireland.
CEC	Campaign for Equal Citizenship.
Confederation	States unified by treaty for certain functions, but which retain their sovereignty and international identity.
Consociation	Political system used in some ethnically divided societies to share governmental power proportionally between the relevant communities – in the executive, the legislature, and public employment. Each community enjoys cultural autonomy and public expenditure may be allocated on a proportional basis.
CSJ	Campaign for Social Justice (part of NICRA).
Devolution	Sub-central government with executive and legislative powers inside a unitary state.
DL	Democratic Left (party formed in 1992 from split in Workers' Party).
DUP	Democratic Unionist Party.
EOC	Equal Opportunities Commission.
EPA	Emergency Provisions Act.
FEA	Fair Employment Agency.
FEC	Fair Employment Commission.
FET	Fair Employment Tribunal.
Federation	State in which executive and legislative powers are shared and divided between central and sub-central governments, and intergovernmental relations are constitutionally regulated.
GAA	Gaelic Athletic Association.

Hegemonic control	A system of ethnic domination, in which the power-holders make revolt by the controlled ethnic group(s) unworkable.
IGC	Intergovernmental conference of the AIA.
IIP	Irish Information Partnership.
IIP	Irish Independence Party.
INLA	Irish National Liberation Army.
Integration	Unifying a territory or culture under one set of norms. In Northern Ireland two main types of integration are advocated: into the UK and into Ireland. British integrationists argue that Northern Ireland should be fully integrated into the UK's administrative system (England's, Scotland's, or Wales's?), into its party political system, and some maintain that educational integration (socializing Protestants and Catholics within the same institutions) should be an imperative of social policy. Irish integrationists suggest, by contrast, that Northern Ireland should be administratively and electorally integrated into the Irish Republic.
IRA	Irish Republican Army – see (P)IRA and (O)IRA.
IRB	Irish Republican Brotherhood.
Joint authority	The sharing of ultimate governmental authority over a territory by two or more states (a *condominium*).
JRRT	Joseph Rowntree Reform Trust.
Majority rule	Simple majority or plurality-rule is a decision-making norm used in many democracies – especially in electoral, constitutional, government-formation and policy-making systems. It usually means rule by those with the most votes rather than absolute majority rule, and is less pleasantly described as the 'minimum winning coalition' norm, or the 'tyranny of the majority'.
NICRA	Northern Ireland Civil Rights Association.
NILP	Northern Ireland Labour Party.
NIO	Northern Ireland Office.
NUPRG	New Ulster Political Research Group.
(O)IRA	Official IRA.
OUP	Official Unionist Party (see UUP).

Partition	The division of a territory with a view to creating ethnically or culturally homogeneous political units.
(P)IRA	Provisional IRA.
Power-sharing	See consociation.
PR	Proportional Representation.
PSF	Provisional Sinn Féin.
PTA	Prevention of Terrorism Act.
RIR	Royal Irish Regiment (regiment of British Army presently being created from the merger of the UDR with the Royal Irish Rangers).
RUC	Royal Ulster Constabulary.
SACHR	Standing Advisory Commission on Human Rights.
SDLP	Social Democratic and Labour Party.
SF	Sinn Féin.
STV	Single Transferable Vote.
UDA	Ulster Defence Association.
UDR	Ulster Defence Regiment (soon to be merged into the RIR).
UFF	Ulster Freedom Fighters.
UUC	Ulster Unionist Council.
UULCC	United Ulster Loyalist Central Coordinating Committee.
Unitary state	State in which sub-central governments enjoy no autonomous sovereign power.
UUP	Ulster Unionist Party (also known as the Official Unionist Party (OUP)).
UUUC	United Ulster Unionist Council.
UVF	Ulster Volunteer Force.
UWC	Ulster Workers' Council.
VUP	Vanguard Unionist Party.
Westminster model	A 'majoritarian' political system, characterized by the concentration of executive power in one-party and bare-majority governments, the fusion of executive and legislative powers under Cabinet dominance, and the plurality-rule (first-past-the-post) election system.
WP	Workers' Party.

Bibliography

(London is place of publication of books unless otherwise stated; more than one date in parentheses indicates different editions)

Adams, G. (1986), *The politics of Irish freedom*, Dingle.

Allison, G. (1971), *Essence of decision: explaining the Cuban missile crisis*, Boston.

Amnesty International (1978), *Report of an Amnesty International mission to Northern Ireland 1977*.

Anderson, B. (1983), *Imagined communities: reflections on the origin and spread of nationalism*.

Arthur, P. (1974), *The People's Democracy, 1968–73*, Belfast.

Arthur, P. (1977), 'Devolution as administrative convenience: a case study of Northern Ireland', *Parliamentary Affairs*, 30: 97–106.

Arthur, P. (1980, 1984), *The government and politics of Northern Ireland*.

Arthur, P. (1985), 'Anglo-Irish relations and the Northern Ireland problem', *Irish Studies in International Affairs*, 2 (1): 37–50.

Arthur, P. and Jeffery, K. (1988), *Northern Ireland since 1968*, Oxford.

Aughey, A. (1989), *Under siege: Ulster unionism and the Anglo-Irish Agreement*.

Aunger, E. A. (1975), 'Religion and occupational class in Northern Ireland', *Economic and Social Review*, 7 (1): 1–17.

Aunger, E. A. (1981), *In search of political stability: a comparative study of New Brunswick and Northern Ireland*, Montreal.

Barnard, T. C. (1973), 'Planters and policies in Cromwellian Ireland', *Past and Present*, 61: 31–69.

Barnard, T. C. (1975), *Cromwellian Ireland: English government and reform in Ireland, 1649–60*, Oxford.

Barrington, T. J. (1972), 'Council of Ireland in the constitutional context', *Administration*, 20: 28–49.

Barritt, D. P. and Carter, C. (1962, 1972), *The Northern Ireland problem*, Oxford.

Barton, B. (1988), *Brookeborough: the making of a prime minister*, Belfast.

Beckett, J. C. (1966), *The making of modern Ireland, 1603–1923.*

Beckett, J. C. (1976), *The Anglo-Irish tradition*, Belfast.

Beckett, J. C. (1986), *A short history of Ireland.*

Bell, G. (1976), *The Protestants of Ulster.*

Bennett Report (1979), *Report of the committee of inquiry into police interrogation procedures in Northern Ireland*, Cmnd. 7397.

Beresford, D. (1987), *Ten men dead: the story of the 1981 Irish hunger strike.*

Beresford Ellis, P. (1988), *Hell or Connaught: the Cromwellian colonisation of Ireland, 1652–60*, Belfast.

Bew, P. (1978), *Land and the national question in Ireland, 1858–82*, Dublin.

Bew, P. (1987), *Conflict and conciliation in Ireland, 1890–1910: Parnellites and radical agrarians*, Oxford.

Bew, P. and Patterson, H. (1985), *The British state and the Ulster crisis.*

Bew, P. and Patterson, H. (1987), 'Unionism and the Anglo-Irish Agreement: the new stalemate', in Teague, P. (ed.), *Beyond the rhetoric: politics, the economy and social policy in Northern Ireland.*

Bew, P. and Paterson, H. (1991), 'Scenarios for progress in Northern Ireland', in McGarry, J. and O'Leary, B. (eds), *The future of Northern Ireland*, Oxford, pp. 206–18.

Bew, P., Gibbon, P., and Patterson, H. (1979), *The state in Northern Ireland, 1921–72: political forces and social classes*, Manchester.

Binder, L. *et al.* (eds) (1971), *Crises and sequences in political development*, Princeton.

Birrell, D. and Murie, A. (1980), *Policy and government in Northern Ireland: lessons of devolution*, Dublin.

Bishop, P. and Mallie, E. (1987), *The Provisional IRA.*

Bogdanor, V. (1979), *Devolution*, Oxford.

Boland, K (1988), *Under contract with the enemy*, Cork.

Boston, T. (1988), *Race, class and conservatism.*

Boulton, D. (1973), *The UVF, 1966–73: an anatomy of loyalist rebellion*, Dublin.

Bowen, K. (1983), *Protestants in a Catholic state: Ireland's privileged minority*, Montreal.

Bowman, J. (1982, 1989), *De Valera and the Ulster question, 1917–73*, Oxford.

Bowyer Bell, J. (1979), *The secret army: the IRA, 1916–79*, Dublin.

Boyce, D. G. (1988), *The Irish question and British politics, 1868–1986.*

Boyle, K. and Hadden, T. (1985), *Ireland: a positive proposal*, Harmondsworth.

Boyle, K. and Hadden, T. (1989), 'Breathing new life into the accord', *Fortnight*, 272: 11–12.

Bradshaw, B. (1979), *The Irish constitutional revolution of the sixteenth century*, Cambridge.

Brady, C. (1974), *Guardians of the peace*, Dublin.

Brady, V. and Gillespie, R. (eds) (1986), *Natives and newcomers: the making of Irish colonial society, 1534–1641*, Dublin.

Bruce, S. (1986), *God save Ulster! The religion and politics of Paisleyism*, Oxford.

Buchanan, R. H. (1982), 'The Planter and the Gael: cultural dimensions of the Northern Ireland problem', in Boal, F. W. and Douglas, J. N. H. (eds), *Integration and division: geographical perspectives on the Northern Ireland problem*, pp. 49–74.

Buckland, P. (1972), *The Anglo-Irish and the New Ireland*, Dublin.

Buckland, P. (1979), *The factory of grievances: devolved government in Northern Ireland, 1921–39*, Dublin.

Buckland, P. (1981), *A history of Northern Ireland*, New York.

Budge, I. and O'Leary, C. (1973), *Belfast: approach to crisis. A study of Belfast politics, 1613–1970*.

Bulpitt, J. (1982), *Territory and power in the United Kingdom*, Manchester.

Burke, W. (1969), *The Irish priests in penal times (1660–1760*, Shannon.

Callaghan, J. (1973), *A house divided*.

Calvert, H. (1968), *Constitutional law in Northern Ireland*, New York.

[Cameron] (1969), *Disturbances in Northern Ireland: report of the commission appointed by the Governor of Northern Ireland* (the Cameron Report), Belfast.

Campaign for Social Justice (CSJ) (1964, 1969), *Northern Ireland: the plain truth*, Dungannon.

Cathcart, R. (1984), *The most contrary region: the BBC in Northern Ireland 1924–1984*, Belfast.

Chief Constable's Annual Report [RUC] (1989), Belfast.

Chief Constable's Annual Report [RUC] (1990), Belfast.

Clarke, A. (1966), 'The colonisation of Ulster and the rebellion of 1641', in Moody, T. W. and Martin, F. X., *The course of Irish history*, Dublin, pp. 189–203.

Compton (1971), *Report of the inquiry into allegations against the security forces of physical brutality in Northern Ireland arising out of events on 9th August 1971* (Compton Report), Cmnd 4823.

Compton, P. A. (1981), 'The demographic background', in Watt, D. (ed.), *The Constitution of Northern Ireland*, pp. 74–92.

Compton, P. A. (1985), 'An evaluation of the changing religious composition of the population of Northern Ireland', mimeo.

Connolly, M. and Loughlin, J. (1986), 'Reflections on the Anglo-Irish Agreement', *Government and Opposition*, 21 (2): 146–60.

Coogan, T. P. (1970, 1980, 1987), *The IRA*, Glasgow.

Corish, P. (1976), 'The Cromwellian regime, 1650–1660', in Moody, T. W. *et al.* (eds) *A new history of Ireland, vol. III*, Oxford.

Cormack, R. J. and Osborne, R. D. (eds) (1991), *Discrimination and public policy in Northern Ireland*, Oxford.

Cormack, R. J., Gallagher, A. M., and Osborne, R. D. (1991), 'Religious affiliation and educational attainment in Northern Ireland: the financing of schools in Northern Ireland', *Sixteenth Report of the Standing Advisory Committee on Human Rights*, Annexe E, pp. 118–212.

Coughlan, A. (1986), *Fooled again? The Anglo-Irish Agreement and after*, Cork.

Coughlan, A. (1991), 'A unitary Irish state', in McGarry, J. and O'Leary, B. (eds), *The future of Northern Ireland*, Oxford, pp. 48–68.

Cox, W. H. (1987), 'Managing Northern Ireland intergovernmentally: an appraisal of the Anglo-Irish Agreement', *Parliamentary Affairs*, 40 (1): 80–97.

Crick, B. (1982), 'The sovereignty of parliament and the Irish question', in Rea, D. (ed.), *Political co-operation in divided societies*, Dublin, pp. 229–54.

Cronin, S. and Roche, R. (eds) (1973), *Freedom the Wolfe Tone way*, Tralee.

Crossman, R. (1977), *The diaries of a cabinet minister: vol iii.*

Cullen, L. M. (1981), *The emergence of modern Ireland, 1600–1900.*

Curtice, J. and Gallagher, T. (1990), The Northern Irish dimension', in *British social attitudes: the 7th report*, Aldershot, pp. 183–216.

Curtis, Jun L. P. (1980), 'Incumbered wealth· landed indebtedness in post-Famine Ireland', *American Historical Review*, lxxxv: 332–67.

Darby, J. (1976), *Conflict in Northern Ireland: the development of a polarised community*, Dublin.

Darby, J. (ed.) (1983), *Northern Ireland: the background to the conflict*, Belfast.

Darby, J. (1986), *Intimidation and the control of conflict in Northern Ireland*, Dublin.

Darby, J. and Morris, G. (1974), *Intimidation in housing*, Belfast.

Darby, J. and Williamson, A. (eds) (1978), *Violence and the social services in Northern Ireland.*

de Paor, L. (1971), *Divided Ulster*, Harmondsworth.

de Paor, L. (1990), *Unfinished business: Ireland today and tomorrow.*

Dent, M. (1988), 'The feasibility of shared sovereignty (and shared authority)', in Townshend, C. (ed.), *Consensus in Ireland*, Oxford, pp. 128–156.

Dillon, M. (1989), *The Shankill butchers: a case study of mass murder.*

Dillon, M. and Lehane, D. (1973), *Political murder in Northern Ireland*, Harmondsworth.

Diplock Report (1972), *Report of the commission to consider legal procedures to deal with terrorist activities in Northern Ireland*, Cmnd 5185.

Doherty, J. E. and Hickey, D. J. (1989), *A chronology of Irish history since 1500*, Dublin.

Doherty, P. (1988), 'MacBride effort: US map keeps on getting darker', *Fortnight*, 264: 11–12.

Donnison, D. (1973), 'The Northern Ireland civil service', *New Society*, 5 July: 8–10.

Dudley Edwards, R. (1977), *Patrick Pearse: the triumph of failure.*

Dudley Edwards, R. (1981), *An atlas of Irish history.*

Elliott, M. (1982), *Partners in revolution: the United Irishmen and France*, London and New Haven.

Elliott, S. (1973), *Northern Ireland parliamentary election results, 1921–1972*, Chichester.

Elster, J. and Slagstad, R. (1988), *Constitutionalism and democracy*, Cambridge.

Esman, M. (1987), 'Ethnic politics and economic power', *Comparative Politics*, 19 (4): 395–418.

Eversley, D. (1989), *Religion and employment in Northern Ireland.*

Farrell, B. (1971), *Chairman or Chief? The role of Taoiseach in Irish government*, Dublin.

Farrell, M. (1976, 1980), *Northern Ireland: the Orange state.*

Farrell, M. (1983), *Arming the Protestants.*

Faulkner, B. (1978), *Memoirs of a statesman.*

FEA (1983), *Report of the investigation by the Fair Employment Agency for Northern Ireland into the non-industrial Northern Ireland civil service*, Belfast.

Fennell, D. (1985), *Beyond nationalism: the struggle against provinciality in the modern world*, Swords, Co. Dublin.

Fisk, R. (1975), *The point of no return. The strike which broke the British in Ulster.*

Fisk, R. (1983), *In time of war: Ireland, Ulster and the price of neutrality, 1939–45.*

FitzGerald, G. (1991), *All in a life.*

Fitzpatrick, B. (1988), *Seventeenth-century Ireland: the war of religions*, Dublin.

Fitzpatrick, B. (1989), 'Ireland since 1870', in Foster, R. F. (ed.), *The Oxford illustrated history of Ireland*, Oxford, pp. 213–74.

Flackes, W. D. and Elliott, S. (1989), *Northern Ireland: a political directory, 1968–1988*, Belfast.

Foot, P. (1989), *Who framed Colin Wallace?*

Foster, R. F. (1988), *Modern Ireland, 1600–1972.*

Foster, R. F. (ed.) (1989), *The Oxford illustrated history of Ireland*, Oxford.

Frame, R. (1990), *The political development of the British isles, 1100–1400*, Oxford.

Fraser, M. (1973), *Children in conflict*, Harmondsworth.

Gallagher, F. (1957), *The indivisible island.*

Gallagher, T. (1991), 'Justice and the law in Northern Ireland', in Jowell, R., Brook, L., and Taylor, B. (eds), *British social attitudes: the 8th report*, Aldershot, pp. 59–86.

Garvin, T. (1981), *The evolution of Irish nationalist politics*, Dublin.

Gellner, E. (1983), *Nations and nationalism*, Oxford.

Gellner, E. (1989), *Plough, sword and book: the structure of human history*.

Goldstrom, J. M. (1981), 'Irish agriculture and the Great Famine', in Goldstrom, J. M. and Clarkson, L. A. (eds), *Irish population, economy and society: essays in honour of the late K. H. Connell*, Oxford, pp. 155–71.

Government of Northern Ireland (1979), *A working paper for a conference*, Cmnd 7763, November.

Green, E. R. R. (1966), 'The Great Famine (1845–50)', in Moody, T. W. and Martin, F. X. (eds), *The course of Irish history*, Dublin, pp. 263–274.

Greer, S. (1986), 'Supergrasses and the legal system in Britain and Northern Ireland', *Law Quarterly Review*, 102: 198–249.

Greer, S. (1978), 'The rise and fall of the Northern Ireland supergrass sytem', *Criminal Law Review*: 663–70.

Guelke, A. (1988), *Northern Ireland: the international perspective*, Dublin.

Gwynn, D. (1950), *The history of partition, 1912–25*, Dublin.

Haagerup Report (1983–4), *Report drawn up on behalf of the political affairs committee on the situation in Northern Ireland* (rapporteur: N. Haagerup, European Parliament working documents, 1983 4: 1 1526/83).

Hadden, T. and Boyle, K. (1989), *The Anglo-Irish Agreement, commentary, text and official review*.

Hadfield, B. (1989), *The constitution of Northern Ireland*, Belfast.

Hamill, D. (1985), *Pig in the middle: the British army in Northern Ireland*.

Harbinson, J. (1973), *The Ulster Unionist Party, 1882–1973: its development and organization*, Belfast.

Harkness, D. (1977), 'The difficulties of devolution: the post-war debate at Stormont', *The Irish Jurist*, xii: 176-86.

Harkness, D. (1983), *Northern Ireland since 1920*, Dublin.

Haslet, E. (1987), *The Anglo-Irish Agreement: Northern Ireland perspectives*, Belfast.

Hechter, M. (1975), *Internal colonialism: the Celtic fringe in British national development, 1536–1966*.

Helsinki Watch (1991), *Human rights in Northern Ireland*, New York.

Hepburn, A. C. (1983), 'Work, class and religion in Belfast, 1871–1911', *Irish Economic and Social History*, 10: 33–50.

Hepburn, A. C. and Collins, B. (1983), 'Industrial society: the structure of Belfast, 1901', in Roebuck, P. (ed.), *Plantation to partition*, Belfast.

Heskin, K. (1980), *Northern Ireland: a psychological analysis*, Dublin.

Heskin, K. (1985), 'Societal disintegration in Northern Ireland: a five year update', *Economic and Social Review*, 16 (3): 187–99.

Hewitt, C. (1981), 'Catholic grievances, Catholic nationalism and violence in Northern Ireland during the civil rights period: a reconsideration', *British Journal of Sociology*, 32 (3): 362–80.

Hickey, D. J. and Doherty, J. E. (1980), *A dictionary of Irish history*, Dublin.

Hillyard, P. (1988), 'Political and social dimensions of emergency law in Northern Ireland', in Jennings, A. (ed.), *Justice under fire: the abuse of civil liberties in Northern Ireland*.

Hobsbawm, E. (1990), *Nations and nationalism since 1870*, Cambridge.

Hogan, G. and Walker, C. (1989), *Political violence and the law in Ireland*, Manchester.

Holland, J. (1987), *The American connection: US guns, money and influence in Northern Ireland*, Swords, Co. Dublin.

Hopkinson, M. (1988), *Green against Green: the Irish civil war*, Dublin.

Hoppen, K. T. (1989), *Ireland since 1800: conflicts and conformity*.

Hunt Report (1969), *Report of the Advisory Committee on Police in Northern Ireland*, Cmd. 535, Belfast.

Huntington, S. P. (1971), 'The change to change: modernization, development and politics', *Comparative Politics*, 3 (3): 283–322.

Hutchinson, J. (1987), *The dynamics of cultural nationalism: the Gaelic revival and the creation of the Irish nation state*.

Inglis, B. (1987), *Moral monopoly: the Catholic Church in modern Irish society*, Dublin.

Irish Information Partnership (1986a), *Irish information agenda: volume A, update, 1985*.

Irish Information Partnership (1986b), *Irish information agenda: volume B, update, 1985*.

Irish Information Partnership (1989), *Information service on Northern Ireland: conflict and Anglo-Irish affairs*, 11 August 11 1989.

Irish Information Partnership (1990), *Irish information agenda: update, 1987–9*.

Jennings, A. (ed.) (1988), *Justice under fire: the abuse of civil liberties in Northern Ireland*.

Kearney, H. (1989), *The British Isles: a history of four nations*, Cambridge.

Kedourie, E. (1960), *Nationalism*.

Kelley, K. J. (1982, 1988), *The longest war: Northern Ireland and the IRA*.

Kelly, J. (1971), *Orders for the Captain*, Dublin.

Kennedy, D. (1988), *The widening gulf: Northern attitudes to the independent Irish state, 1919–49*, Belfast.

Kennedy, K., Giblin, T., and McHugh, D. (1988), *The economic development of Ireland in the twentieth century*.

Kennedy, L. (1986), *Two Ulsters: a case for repartition*, Belfast.

Kennedy, L. (1991), 'Repartition', in McGarry, J. and O'Leary, B. (eds), *The future of Northern Ireland*, Oxford, pp. 137–61.

Kenny, A. (1986), *The road to Hillsborough*, Oxford.

Kenny, A. (1991), 'Joint Authority', in McGarry, J. and O'Leary, B. (eds), *The future of Northern Ireland*, Oxford, pp. 219–41.

Kilbrandon Commission (1973), *Report of the royal commission on the constitution, 1969–1973*, Cmnd 5460, Vol. 1.

Kilbrandon Report (1984), *Northern Ireland: report of an independent inquiry*.

Kitson, F. (1971), *Low intensity operations: subversion, insurgency and counter-insurgency*.

Laffan, M. (1983), *The partition of Ireland, 1911–1925*, Dublin.

Lawrence, R. (1965), *The government of Northern Ireland*, Oxford.

Lee, J. (1973), *The modernisation of Irish society, 1848–1918*, Dublin.

Lee, J. (1989), *Ireland, 1912–1985: politics and society*, Cambridge.

Lehmbruch, G. (1975), 'Consociational democracy in the international system', *European Journal of Political Research*, 3 (4): 377–91.

Lemarchand, R. (1991), 'Burundi in comparative perspective: dimensions of ethnic strife', mimeo.

Lijphart, A. (1968), *The politics of accommodation*, Berkeley, California.

Lijphart, A. (1975), 'The Northern Ireland problem: cases, theories and solutions', *British Journal of Political Science*, v (1): 83–106.

Lijphart, A. (1977), *Democracy in plural societies*, New Haven.

Lijphart, A. (1984), *Democracies*, New Haven.

Lijphart, A. (1991), 'Foreword', in McGarry, J. and O'Leary, D. (eds), *The future of Northern Ireland*, Oxford, pp. vi–viii.

Lustick, I. (1979), 'Stability in deeply divided societies: consociationalism versus control', *World Politics*, 31: 325–44.

Lustick, I. (1985), *State-building failure in British Ireland and French Algeria*, Berkeley, California.

Lustick, I. (1987), 'Israeli state-building in the West Bank and Gaza Strip: theory and practice', *International Organization*, 41 (1): 151–71.

Lustick, I. (1990), 'Becoming problematic: breakdown of a hegemonic conception of Ireland in nineteenth-century Britain', *Politics and Society*, 18 (1): 39–73.

Lyne, T. (1990), 'Ireland, Northern Ireland and 1992: the barriers to technocratic anti-partitionism', *Public Administration*, 68 (4): 417–33.

Lyons, F. S. L. (1973), *Ireland since the famine*, Glasgow.

McArdle, D. (1951), *The Irish Republic*, Dublin.

MacDonagh, O. (1989), *The emancipationist: Daniel O'Connell, 1830–1847*.

MacDonald, M. (1986), *Children of wrath: political violence in Northern Ireland*, Oxford.

Machin, G. I. T. (1987), *Politics and the churches in Great Britain, 1869–1921*, Oxford.

MacIntyre, T. (1971), *Through the Bridewell gate: a diary of the Dublin arms trial*.

Mair, P. (1987), 'Breaking the nationalist mould: the Irish republic and the Anglo-Irish Agreement', in Teague, P. (ed.), *Beyond the rhetoric: politics, the economy and social policy in Northern Ireland*, pp. 81–110.

Mandel, M. (1989), *The Charter of Rights and the legalization of politics in Canada*, Toronto.

Mansergh, N. (1936), *The government of Northern Ireland, a study in devolution*.

Mansergh, N. (1965), *The Irish question, 1840–1921*.

McAllister, I. (1975), 'Political opposition in Northern Ireland: the National Democratic Party', *Economic and Social Review*, 6 (3): 353–66.

McAllister, I. (1977), *The Social Democratic and Labour Party of Northern Ireland*.

McCaffrey, L. J. (1979), *Ireland: from colony to nation state*, Englewood Cliffs, N.J.

McCloskey, C. (1989), *Up off their knees: a commentary on the civil rights movement in Northern Ireland*, Galway.

McCormack, V. and O'Hara, J. (1990), *Enduring inequality: religious discrimination in employment in Northern Ireland*.

McCormick, D. N. (1970), 'Delegated legislation and civil liberty', *Law Quarterly Review*, 86: 171–80.

McCrudden, C. (1982), *A report to the Fair Employment Agency*, unpublished.

McCudden, C. (1988), 'The Northern Ireland Fair Employment White Paper: a critical assessment', *Industrial Law Journal*, 17 (3): 162–81.

McCrudden, C. (1989), 'Northern Ireland and the British constitution', in Jowell, J. and Oliver, D. (eds), *The changing constitution* (2nd edn), Oxford.

McCrudden, C. (1990), 'The evolution of the Fair Employment (Northern Ireland) Act 1989 in Parliament', in Hayes, J. and O'Higgins, P. (eds), *Lessons from Northern Ireland*, pp. 57–79.

McCrudden, C. (1990), 'The evolution of the Fair Employment (Northern Ireland) Act in Parliament', in Cormac, R. J. and Osborne, R. D. (eds), *Discrimination and public policy in Northern Ireland*, Oxford, pp. 244–64.

McDowell, R. B. (1964), *The Irish administration, 1864–1914*.

McGarry, J. (1988), 'The Anglo-Irish Agreement and the prospects for power-sharing in Northern Ireland', *Political Quarterly*, 59 (2): 236–50.

McGarry, J. (1990), 'A consociational settlement for Northern Ireland?', *Plural Societies*, xx (1): 1–21.

McGarry, J. and O'Leary, B. (1991a), 'Conclusion. Northern Ireland's options; a framework and analysis', in McGarry, J. and O'Leary, B. (eds), *The future of Northern Ireland*, Oxford, pp. 268–303.

McGarry, J. and O'Leary, B. (eds) (1991b), *The future of Northern Ireland*, Oxford.

McGarry, J. and O'Leary, B. (forthcoming), *Explaining Northern Ireland: Broken images*, Oxford.

McKeown, C. (1984), *The passion of peace*, Belfast.

McKeown, M. (1985), *De Mortuis*, Gondregnies, Belgium.

McKeown, M. (1986), *The greening of a nationalist*, Lucan, Co. Dublin.

McKittrick, D. (1989a), *Despatches from Belfast*, Belfast.

McKittrick, D. (1989b), 'FitzGerald attacks "inept" Britain', *The Independent*, 7 June.

McKittrick, D. (1991), 'Cost of security is triple UK average', *The Independent*, 29 May.

McNamara, K. *et al.* (1988), *Towards a united Ireland Reform and harmonisation: a dual strategy for Irish unification*, Westminster.

Miller, D. (1978), *Queen's rebels: Ulster loyalism in historical perspective*, Dublin.

Miller, R. (1978), *Attitudes to Work in Northern Ireland*, Research Paper 2, Belfast.

Miller, R. and Osborne, R. D. (1983), 'Religion and unemployment: evidence from a cohort survey', in Cormack, R. J. and Osborne, R. D. (eds), *Religion, education and employment*, Belfast.

Mitchell, J. K. (1979), 'Social violence in Northern Ireland', *Geographical Review*, April, 179–200.

Mokyr, J. (1985), *Why Ireland starved: a quantitative and analytical history of the Irish economy, 1800–1950*.

Moloney, E. (1986), 'A good deal for Unionists', *Fortnight*, 231: 6–7.

Moloney, E. and Pollack, A. (1986), *Paisley*, Swords, Co. Dublin.

Moody, T. W. (196), 'Fenianism, Home Rule and the Land War (1850–91)', in Moody, T. W. and Martin, F. X. (eds), *The course of Irish history*, Dublin, pp. 275–93.

Moody, T. W., Martin, F. X., and Byrne, F. J. (eds) (1976–1986), *A new history of Ireland, volumes I–IX*, Oxford.

Moore, M. and Crimmins, J. (1991), 'The case for negotiated independence', in McGarry, J. and O'Leary, B. (eds), *The future of Northern Ireland*, Oxford, pp. 242–67.

Murphy, R. (1986), 'Walter Long and the making of the Government of Ireland Act, 1919–20', *Irish Historical Studies*, 25: 82–96.

Murray, R. (1982), 'Political violence in Northern Ireland 1969–1977', in Boal, F. W. and Douglas, J. N. H. (eds), *Integration and division: geographical perspectives on the Northern Ireland problem*, pp. 309–22.

NEC (1981), *Northern Ireland: statement by the National Executive Committee to the 1981 conference.*

Nelson, S. (1984), *Ulster's uncertain defenders*, Belfast.

New Ireland Forum (1984a), *The cost of violence arising from the Northern Ireland crisis since 1969*, Dublin.

New Ireland Forum (1984b), *The legal systems, north and south*, Dublin.
New Ireland Forum (1984c), *Report*, Dublin.
New Ireland Forum (1984d), *Sectoral studies: an analysis of agricultural developments in the north and south of Ireland and of the effects of integrated policy and planning*, Dublin.
New Ireland Forum (1984e), *Sectoral studies: integrated policy and planning for transport in a new Ireland*, Dublin.
New Ireland Forum (1984f), *Sectoral studies: opportunities for north/south co-operation and integration in energy*, Dublin.
New Ireland Forum (1984g), *The macroeconomic consequences of integrated economic policy, planning and co-ordination in Ireland*, Dublin.
New Ireland Forum Public Sessions (1983–4), *Report of Proceedings, Nos 1–12*, Dublin.
New Ulster Political Research Group (1979), *Beyond the religious divide*, Belfast.
Newark, F. H. (1955), 'The Law and the Constitution', in Wilson, T. (ed.), *Ulster under home rule*, Oxford.
NIO (1974), *Northern Ireland, finance and economy: discussion paper*.
NIO (1989), *Developments since the signing of the Anglo-Irish Agreement*, Belfast and London.
Northern Ireland Census (1981), Belfast.
O'Brien, C. C. (1974), *States of Ireland*.
O'Brien, C. C. (1980), *Neighbours*.
O'Brien, C. C. (ed.) (1988), 'Introduction', in Arnold, M. (ed.), *Edmund Burke's Irish Affairs*.
O'Brien, M. and O'Brien, C. C. (1985), *A concise history of Ireland*.
O'Dowd, L., Rolston, B., and Tomlinson, M. (1980), *Northern Ireland: between civil rights and civil war*.
O'Duffy, B. and O'Leary, B. (1990), 'Political violence in Northern Ireland, 1969–June 1989', in McGarry, J. and O'Leary, B. (eds), *The future of Northern Ireland*, Oxford, pp. 318–41.
O'Ferrall, F. (1981), *Daniel O'Connell*, Dublin.
O'Ferrall, F. (1985), *Catholic emancipation: Daniel O'Connell and the birth of Irish democracy, 1820–1830*, Dublin.
O'Halloran, C. (1985), *Partition and the limits of Irish nationalism*, Dublin.
O'Leary, B. (1987a), 'The Anglo-Irish Agreement: statecraft or folly?', *West European Politics*, 10 (1): 5–32.
O'Leary, B. (1987b), 'Towards Europeanization and modernization? The Irish general election of February 1987', *West European Politics*, 10 (3): 455–65.
O'Leary, B. (1989), 'The limits to coercive consociationalism in Northern Ireland', *Political Studies*, xxxvii (4): 562–88.
O'Leary, B. (1990), 'Northern Ireland and the Anglo-Irish Agreement', in

Dunleavy, P., Gamble, A., and Peele, G. (eds), *Developments in British Politics 3*, pp. 269–90.

O'Leary, B. (1991a), '*An Taoiseach*: The Irish prime minister', *West European Politics*, 13 (2): 133–62.

O'Leary, B. (1991b), 'Then talk some more', *Fortnight*, 298: 18–19.

O'Leary, B. (1991c), 'Reform agenda proves popular', *Fortnight*, 299: 16–17.

O'Leary, B. (1991d), 'Party support in Northern Ireland, 1969–1989', in McGarry, J. and O'Leary, B. (eds), *The future of Northern Ireland*, Oxford, pp. 342–57.

O'Leary, B. (1992), 'Public opinion and Northern Irish futures', *Political Quarterly*, 63 (2): 143–70.

O'Leary, B. and Peterson, J. (1990), 'Further Europeanization: the Irish general election of July 1989', *West European Politics*, 13 (1): 124–36.

O'Leary, C., Elliott, S., and Wilford, R. A. (1988), *The Northern Ireland assembly, 1982–6: a constitutional experiment*.

O'Malley, P. (1983), *The uncivil wars: Ireland today*, Belfast.

O'Malley, P. (1990a), *Biting at the grave: the Irish hunger strikes and the politics of despair*, Belfast.

O'Malley, P. (1990b), *Northern Ireland: questions of nuance*, Belfast.

Osborne, R. D. (1979), 'The Northern Ireland parliamentary electoral system: the 1929 reapportionment', *Irish Geography*, 12: 42–56.

Osborne, R. D. (1982), 'Voting behaviour in Northern Ireland 1921–1977', in Boal, F. W. and Douglas, J. N. H. (eds), *Integration and division: geographical perspectives on the Northern Ireland problem*, pp. 137–66.

Osborne, R. D. and Cormack, R. J. (1986), 'Unemployment and religion in Northern Ireland', *Economic and Social Review*, 17 (3): 215–23.

Osborne, R. D. and Cormack, R. J. (1989), 'Employment equity in Northern Ireland and Canada', *Administration*, 37 (2): 13–51.

Paisley, I. jun. (1991), *The case of the UDR Four*, Dublin.

Palley, C. (1972), 'The evolution, disintegration and possible reconstruction of the Northern Ireland constitution', *Anglo-American Law Review*, 1: 368–476.

Palley, C. (1986), 'When an iron hand beckons a federal union', *Guardian*, 20 Jan.

Pearce, E. (1991), 'One long piece of perplexity', *Fortnight*, 296: 15.

Pickrill, D. A. (1981), *Ministers of the Crown*.

Pickvance, T. J. (1975), *Peace through equity: proposals for a permanent settlement of the Northern Ireland conflict*, Birmingham.

Poole, M. (1983), 'The demography of violence', in Darby, J. (ed.), *Northern Ireland: the background to the conflict*, Belfast.

Powell, E. (1986), 'Dirty tricks that link Dublin and Westland', *Guardian*, 20 Jan.

Pringle, D. G. (1980), 'Electoral systems and political manipulation: a case study of Northern Ireland in the 1920s', *Economic and Social Review*, 11 (3): 187–205.

Prior, J. (1986), *A balance of power*.

Purdie, B. (1988), 'Was the civil rights movement a republican/communist conspiracy?', *Irish Political Studies*, 3: 33–41.

Purdie, B. (1990), *Politics in the streets: the origins of the civil rights movement in Northern Ireland*, Belfast.

Pyle, F. (1989), 'Chiselling away at unionist tablets', *Irish Times*, 23 Dec.

Rea, D. (ed.) (1982), *Political co-operation in divided societies: a series of papers relevant to the conflict in Northern Ireland*, Dublin.

Rees, M. (1985), *Northern Ireland: a personal perspective*.

Republic of Ireland Statistical Abstract (1981), Dublin.

Robbins, K. (1988), *Nineteenth-century Britain. England, Scotland, Wales. The making of a nation*, Oxford.

Roberts, H. (1987), '"Sound stupidity": The British party system and the Northern Ireland question', *Government and Opposition*, 22 (3): 315–35, also in McGarry, J. and O'Leary, B. (eds) (1991b), pp. 100–36.

Robinson, P. (1982), 'Plantation and colonisation: the historical background', in Boal, F. W. and Douglas, J. N. H. (eds), *Integration and division: geographical perspectives on the Northern Ireland problem*, pp. 19–38.

Rokkan, S. (1975), 'Dimensions of state-formation and nation-building: a possible paradigm for research on variations within Europe', in Tilly, C. (ed.), *The formation of national states in Western Europe*, Princeton.

Rose, R. (1971), *Governing without consensus: an Irish perspective*.

Rose, R. (1975), *Northern Ireland: a time of choice*.

Rose, R. (1976), 'On the priorities of citizenship in the Deep South and Northern Ireland', *Journal of Politics*, 38 (2): 247–91.

Rose, R. (1989), 'Northern Ireland: the irreducible conflict', in Montville, J. V. (ed.), *Conflict and peacemaking in multiethnic societies*, Lexington, Mass. and Toronto, pp. 133–50.

Rowthorn, B. and Wayne, N. (1988), *Northern Ireland: the political economy of conflict*, Oxford and Cambridge.

Royal Ulster Constabulary (1990), *Statistical information* (to 30 Nov. 1990, updated to 31 Dec. by telephone), Belfast.

Ruane, J. and Todd, J. (1991), '"Why can't we get along with each other?" Culture, structure and the Northern Ireland conflict', in Hughes, E. (ed.), *Culture and politics in Northern Ireland*, Buckingham, pp. 27–44.

(SACHR) Standing Advisory Commission on Human Rights (1977), *The protection of human rights in Northern Ireland*, Cmnd 7009.

(SACHR) Standing Advisory Commission on Human Rights (1987), *Religious and political discrimination and equality of opportunity in Northern Ireland: report on fair employment*, Cmnd. 237.

Schellenberg, J. A. (1977), 'Area variations of violence in Northern Ireland', *Sociological Focus*, 10: 69–78.

SDLP (1972), *Towards a new Ireland*, Belfast.

Simms, J. G. (1966), 'The restoration and the Jacobite war (1660–91)', in Moody, T. W. and Martin, F. X. (eds), *The course of Irish history*, Dublin, pp. 204–16.

Simms, K. (1989), 'The Norman invasion and Gaelic recovery', in Foster, R. F. (ed.), *The Oxford illustrated history of Ireland*, Oxford, pp. 53–103.

Sinn Féin (1989), *Hillsborough. The balance sheet, 1985–88. A failure*, Dublin.

Smith, A. (1986), *The ethnic origins of nations*, Oxford.

Smith, D. and Chambers, G. (1987a), *Equality and inequality in Northern Ireland, pt. 1: employment and unemployment*.

Smith, D. and Chambers, G. (1987b), *Equality and inequality in Northern Ireland, pt. 2*.

Smith, D. and Chambers, G. (1987c), *Equality and inequality in Northern Ireland, pt. 3: perceptions and views*.

Smith, D. and Chambers, G. (1989), *Equality and inequality in Northern Ireland, pt. 4: public housing*.

Smith, D. and Chambers, G. (1991), *Inequality in Northern Ireland*, Oxford.

Smith, M. L. R. (1991), 'The role of the military instrument in Irish republican strategic thinking: an evolutionary analysis', Ph.D. thesis, University of London.

Smith, P. (1986), *Why unionists say 'no'*, Belfast.

Smoolha, S. (1980), 'Control of minorities in Israel and Northern Ireland', *Comparative Studies of Society and History*, Oct.: 256–80.

Smyth, C. (1983), 'The Ulster Democratic Unionist Party: a case study in political and religious convergence', Ph.D. thesis, Queen's University, Belfast.

Smyth, M. (1987), *A federated people*, Belfast.

Squires, M. and Cowling, M. (1991), 'Normal British misconduct: an alternative view of discrimination in Northern Ireland', *Politics*, 11 (1): 3–7.

Stalker, J. (1988), *Stalker*.

Stewart, A. T. Q. (1967), *The Ulster crisis*.

Stewart, A. T. Q. (1986), *The narrow ground: patterns of Ulster history*, Belfast.

Taagepera, R. and Shugart, M. S. (1989), *Seats and votes: the effects and determinants of electoral systems*.

Taylor, C. L. and Jodice, D. A. (1983), *World handbook of political and social indicators, Volume III: 1948–77*, Ann Arbor.

Taylor, P. (1980), *Beating the terrorists?*, Harmondsworth.

Teague, P. (ed.) (1987), *Beyond the rhetoric: politics, the economy and social policy in Northern Ireland*.

Thompson, B. (1989), 'The Anglo-Irish Agreement, 1985, machinery for muddling through', paper presented to the Annual Conference of the Political Studies Association, Warwick.

Todd, J. (1987), 'Two traditions in unionist political culture', *Irish Political Studies*, 2: 1–26.

Townshend, C. (1983, 1984), *Political violence in Ireland: government and resistance since 1848*, Oxford.

Townshend, C. (1986), *Britain's civil wars*.

Townshend, C. (ed.) (1988), *Consensus in Ireland: approaches and recessions*, Oxford.

Van Dijk, J., Mayhew, P., and Killias, M., (1990), *Experience of crime across the world: key findings of the 1989 international crime survey*, Cambridge, Massachusetts.

Vile, M. (1982), 'Federation and confederation: the experience of the United States and the British commonwealth', in Rea, D. (ed.), *Political co-operation in divided societies*, Dublin, pp. 216–28.

Walker, B. (ed.) (1978), *Parliamentary election results in Ireland, 1801–1922*, in Moody, T. W., Martin, F. X. , and Byrne, F. J. (eds), *A new history of Ireland: ancillary publications IV*, Dublin.

Wall, M. (1989), *Catholic Ireland in the eighteenth century: the collected essays of Maureen Wall*, ed. G. O'Brien, Dublin.

Walsh, D. (1983), *The use and abuse of emergency legislation in Northern Ireland*.

Watt, D. (ed.) (1981), *The constitution of Northern Ireland: problems and prospects*.

Weitzer, R. (1990), *Transforming settler states: communal conflict and internal security in Northern Ireland and Zimbabwe*, Berkeley, California.

Wheare, K. (1963), *Federal government*, Oxford.

White, B. (1978), 'Public Services', in Darby, J. and Williamson, A. (eds), *Violence and the social services in Northern Ireland*.

Whyte, J. H. (1966), 'The Age of Daniel O'Connell (1800–47)', in Moody, T. W. and Martin, F. X. (eds), *The course of Irish history*, Dublin, pp. 248–62.

Whyte, J. H. (1978), 'Interpretations of the Northern Ireland problem: an appraisal', *Economic and Social Review*, 9 (4): 257–82.

Whyte, J. H. (1983), 'How much discrimination was there under the unionist regime, 1921–68', in Gallagher, T. and O'Connell, J. (eds), *Contemporary Irish Studies*, Manchester.

Whyte, J. H. (1988), 'Interpretations of the Northern Ireland Problem', in Townshend, C. (ed.), *Consensus in Ireland: approaches and recessions*, Oxford, p. 24–46.

Whyte, J. H. (1990), *Interpreting Northern Ireland*, Oxford.

Williams, T. D. (ed.) (1966), *The Irish struggle, 1916–26*.

Wilson, H. (1971), *The Labour government, 1964–70*, Harmondsworth.

Wilson, R. (1988), 'Poll shock for Accord', *Fortnight*, 261: 6–8.
Wilson, T. (1989), *Ulster: Conflict and Consent*, Oxford.
Woodham-Smith, C. (1962), *The great hunger: Ireland, 1845–9.*
Wright, F. (1973), 'Protestant ideology and politics in Ulster', *European Journal of Sociology*, 14: 213–80.
Wright, F. (1987), *Northern Ireland: a comparative analysis*, Dublin.
Wright, F. (1989), 'Northern Ireland and the British–Irish relationship', *Studies*, 78: 151–62.
Wright, P. (1987), *Spycatcher*, New York.
Younger, C. (1972), *A state of disunion*, Glasgow.
Zimmermann, E. (1989), 'Political unrest in Western Europe', *West European Politics*, 12: 179–96.
Zimring, F. E. (1987), *The citizen's guide to gun control*, New York.

Subject Index

348   *The Politics of Antagonism*

148; Westminster, (1918), 97–99, (1955), 160, 178, (1959), 160, 178, (1974), 199, (1983), 212–3, (1986 by-elections), 250–2, (1987) 244–5, (1992) 320–2

Fair Employment Act, (1976), 206–8, (1989), 261, 265–7
Fair Employment Agency (FEA), 206
Fair Employment Commission (FEC), 265–66
Fair Employment Tribunal (FET), 265–66
fair employment (see discrimination)
federalism, 295–300
Fenians, 85–6
Fianna Fáil, 136, 146, 155, 222, 228, 236, 243–4, 246, 280
Fine Gael, 146, 222, 225, 228, 231, 238, 240, 243–4, 246, 268, 275, 280
Flag and Emblems Act, 116–7, 128, 134, 261
Forum Report, 213, 215, 238
French Revolution, 71–2
Friends of the Union, 253

Gaelic Athletic Association (GAA), 82–3, 92
Gaelic revival, 82–3
Gardiner Report, 202
gerrymandering, 120–1, 165
Glorious Revolution, 68–9
glossary, 5, 328–9
Government of Ireland Act, 98, 100, 101, 110, 112–9, 136, 139, 142, 177, 194, 319
Great Famine, 76–8,
Guildford Four, 19, 49, 249

hegemonic control, 2, 133–5, 108–52 *passim* , 153–80 *passim*, 159, 161, 165, 171, 172, 176, 177; coercive control, 125–7; constitutional

control, 112–9; economic control 129–32; electoral control, 119–25; exercising control, 108–52; external environment 142–7; in Israel and South Africa, 158; legal control 127–8; losing control, 153–80; motives for, 135–41

Home Rule, 74, 138; first bill, 87–8; second bill, 88–90; third bill, 91–6 *passim,*
hunger strikers, 205–6, 214, 216
Hunt Report, 173–4

incarcerations, 40–4, 44–5
independence, 284–6
Independent Commissioner for Police Complaints, 261
injuries, 40–4, 40–1
integration, integrationism, 142–5, 173, 189, 209, 210, 255–6, 283–4, 297–9, 306–7
Intergovernmental Conference (IGC), 221, 226, 231, 234–5, 243, 245–6, 249, 253, 254, 270
internment, 31–2, 175–6, 196–7, 197
intimidation, 40–4, 42–4
Ireland, Act, 145, 153, 155
Ireland, Constitution (Bunreacht na Éireann), 136, 153, 225, 318, 319, 322–3; Articles 2 and 3, 136, 200, 225, 318, 319, 322–3
Ireland, history; Act of Union, 72–4; after 1958, 155, 236; American war of independence, 71; Anglo–Irish War 21, 98ff; Battle of the Boyne, 69; civil war, 21, 146; compared with Scotland and Wales, 83; Cromwellian conquest, 67–8; Easter Rising, 96; economic divergence from Great Britain 75–6; fateful triangle 65; French Revolution 71–2; Gaelic League, 82–3; Glorious Revolution, 68–9;

Names Index

354   *The Politics of Antagonism*